ASPECTS OF DALES' LIFE THROUGH PEACE AND WAR

BAKEWELL · GREAT LONGSTONE · LITTLE LONGSTONE
HASSOP · WARDLOW · ROWLAND · OVER HADDON
ASHFORD IN THE WATER · SHELDON

KEITH TAYLOR

ASHRIDGE PRESS / COUNTRY BOOKS

Published by Ashridge Press/Country Books
Courtyard Cottage, Little Longstone, Bakewell, Derbyshire DE45 1NN
Tel: 01629 640670
e-mail: dickrichardson@country-books.co.uk

ISBN 978 1 901214 89 5

British Library Cataloguing in Publication Data.
A catalogue record for this book is available from the British Library.

By the same author:
DARLEY DALE REMEMBERED:
THROUGH 50 YEARS OF WAR AND PEACE

WENSLEYDALE REMEMBERED: THE SACRIFICE MADE
BY THE FAMILIES OF A NORTHERN DALE 1914-1918 AND 1939-1945

SWALEDALE AND WHARFEDALE REMEMBERED
ASPECTS OF DALES' LIFE THROUGH PEACE AND WAR

TANSLEY REMEMBERED:
ASPECTS OF VILLAGE LIFE THROUGH PEACE AND WAR

THE HISTORY OF A DERBYSHIRE MINING FAMILY

By the same author in conjunction with Trevor Brown:
A DERBYSHIRE PARISH AT WAR:
SOUTH DARLEY AND THE GREAT WAR 1914 – 1919

A DERBYSHIRE PARISH AT PEACE AND WAR
SOUTH DARLEY 1925 – 1955

Printed and bound by HSW Print

CONTENTS

ACKNOWLEDGEMENTS

Duncan Rhodes for help with computer work.

Curators of a number of Regimental Army Museums, and in particular, Cliff Houseley, former curator of the Sherwood Foresters Regimental Museum.

The Longstone Local History Group (especially Hilary Clarke, Sheila Hurst and Michael Stuart)

Staff of the Local Studies Library at Matlock for their help and patience.

Derbyshire Records Office, Matlock.

Local Studies Libraries in other areas of the country.

The Old House Museum, Bakewell (Anita Spencer)

Editors of various church and parish magazines for Bakewell, Great Longstone and Ashford.

Lady Manners School Library (Nicky Hetherington and staff).

Special thanks for their time, information, memories and loan of photographs goes to the following people (please accept our apology if we have left out any name by mistake). Molly Andrews, Margaret Bagshaw, Mrs Bendell, Jean Blackwell, Harry Blagden, Graham Bond, Eric Bradbrook, Ian Bright, Ken Brocklehurst, Tom and Jean Brocklehurst, Barbara Brooke-Taylor, Trevor Brown, M Bunting, John Buss, Chatsworth Settlement Trustees, Hilary Clarke, John Clark, Ian Cox, Margery Critchlow, Frank Dickins, John Douglas, Dowager Duchess of Devonshire, J Duncan, Stanley and David Fearn, Pam Fletcher, John Frost, Peter Gilbert, Mary Glover, Ian Green, Noel Green, Gillian Hall, Nigel Hare, Mark Hargreaves, Pauline Harrison, G M Heathcote, Nicky Hetherington, Geoffrey Hewson, Tony Hill, Sandra Holland, John Hollingworth, Tony Holmes, A Hoskins, Joe Hoskins, Sally Hudson, John Hudson, Sheila and Frank Hurst, Harry Hutchinson, Ken Ibbotson, Peter Johnson, Dorothy and Albert Keir, Mrs Kidd, Lawrence Knighton, D Lane, Pat Lewis, Andrew Lomas, Mary Longsdon, Ralph Lord, E. McMillan, Kathryn Maltby, Mr Marsden, Sylvia Marsden, Alice Marshal, Olive Mead, Ian Morgan, Peter and Pat Moorby, Fred Morton, John Morton, Leri Morton, P Mosley, Margaret Mountney, David Neal, John Nelson, Joe Oldfield, Carolyn Pearce, Joan Pennington, John Pennington, Ethel Plumtree, R Richmond, Frank Robinson, Stephen Rose, M. Rowland, Brian Sheldon, David Sherwin, K Skidmore, Alastair Slack, Margaret Slin, Henry Stephenson, M Stewart, Michael Stuart, Bill Sudbury, Sandra Taylor, Peter Thornhill, Joe Twigg, Mary Upton, Jim Webster, Bessie Whitworth, Bill and Barbara Wild, John Wilson, Sandra Wood

BIBLIOGRAPHY AND SOURCES

Squadron Histories by Peter Lewis, Putnam and Company.

Fighter Squadrons of the RAF by John Rawlins, Macdonald and Janes.

Bomber Squadrons of the RAF by John Rawlins, Macdonald and Janes.

Bomber Losses of the Second World War.

Battalion war diaries and regimental histories.

Pen and Sword publications on various battles.

The Face of Battle by John Keegan, Jonathan Cape.

History of the First World War by Liddell Hart.

The Grenadier Guards in the Great War by Sir Frederick Ponsonby Macmillan and Company.

The Second World War – Winston Churchill.

Information from the 1871, 1881, 1891 and 1901 Census.

Newspapers, including 'The High Peak News' and 'Derbyshire Times'

Information on the Commonwealth War Graves Commission website.

CD Rom of 'The Soldiers died in the Great War'.

Thornhill Papers at the Records Office.

Articles published by members of the Longstone Local History Group (especially Hilary Clarke and Sheila Hurst, with contributions on Little Longstone by Michael Stuart).

50th Royal Tank Regiment by Stephen Hamilton. (Lutterworth Press).

The Diaries of Maria Gyte of Sheldon, Derbyshire at the Derbyshire Records Office, Matlock.

Through Limestone Hills by Bill Hudson – Oxford Publishing Company.

'The Diaries of Maria Gyte of Sheldon, Derbyshire (edited by G. Phizackerley) Scarthin Books.

Articles on farming by Frederick Brocklehurst (Tom Brocklehurst, his son).

The most valuable sources of information and many accompanying photographs have been generously provided by people connected to the area being studied.

FOREWORD

A little over a year ago, when I was working on his family history, *The History of a Derbyshire Mining Family*, I mentioned to Keith Taylor that I was thinking about researching the men from the village war memorial. The Longstones being small, I thought it better to widen the scope to include Bakewell and district, and Keith offered to help. He had already researched and written similar books on Wensleydale, Swaledale and Wharfedale (Yorkshire) and Darley Dale (Derbyshire). Two books on South Darley were written in conjunction with Trevor Brown.

Pressure of work on me resulted in Keith doing all the work, and I could not have hoped for a better researcher/author to undertake the task, for his books are about real people and the impact of world wars on the community. Numerous volumes have been published on Bakewell, usually 'picture books' and even the history books have relied heavily on printed sources – here, at last, is a book thoroughly researched including oral sources, with many photographs which have never appeared in print before.

We owe a great deal of gratitude to Keith for his unstinting work in this tribute to the fallen of two world wars, for there is no finer writer on this subject than him in the country. There have been many books published on the conflicts – battles, regiments and the generals, but he sings the praises of the common man – the man in the firing line. I commend this book to you in the sincere hope that it is not his 'last'.

Dick Richardson
Publisher
October 2007

INTRODUCTION

War memorials are sited in virtually every parish in the United Kingdom, but who now remembers the "Pals" of 1914 – 1918 and those who fought for democracy and against fascism during the Second World War? The First World War is passing from human memory into history and those who fought during 1939 – 1945 are getting fewer in number. This book celebrates the lives of the servicemen of those "lost" generations and honours these men whose story is part of a wider shared sense of history that has shaped our age.

On the following pages I have attempted therefore to rekindle memories of the servicemen whose names are inscribed on the war memorials in Bakewell, Over Haddon, Great Longstone, Wardlow, Ashford and Sheldon, by finding out, wherever possible, about their lives and deaths.

My aim has been to set these men back into the market town, villages and landscape that they would have been so familiar with, either before the Great War or during the inter-war years of the 1920's and 1930's.

Through words and photographs, a picture emerges of life in the relative backwater of Bakewell, Over Haddon, Great and Little Longstone, Hassop, Wardlow, Rowland, Sheldon and Ashford in the Water before events on the world scene were to rudely intervene and take these young men away from their families and to their deaths during the two world-wide conflicts of the 20th century.

120 men from these areas gave their lives for "King and Country" between 1914 and 1919, whilst the supreme sacrifice was again asked of 35 men during the years 1939 - 1945.

Who were these men, born towards the end of the Victorian Age and destined, during the Great War, to lie in "some corner of a foreign field that is for ever England"? The vast majority worked locally, on nearby farms, hewing for chert (stone) in local quarries, on the Midland Railway, at the DP Battery Works, or in local shops and businesses.

Their lives revolved around the daily grind of hard physical labour, social events involving church activities, the Church Lads' Brigade and Oddfellows Clubs, training with the local units of the Territorial Army and Derbyshire Yeomanry and playing in or following the fortunes of the local football and cricket teams.

The arrival of the Midland Railway in the 1850's and 1860's had linked up the Bakewell district to the outside world, with easy access north and south, but most people living in the area worked, played, married and brought up families within the narrow confines of the market town and its surrounding villages. The onset of the Great War in August 1914 resulted in many young men being despatched far afield, to France, Flanders, Gallipoli, Egypt, Salonika and Mesopotamia. Sadly, 120 men from the area would eventually be listed on the town and village war memorials. This is their story.

It is the aim of "Aspects of Dales' Life Through Peace and War" to celebrate the lives of these lost generations (and their colleagues who were fortunate to survive these conflicts). In doing so, I have felt privileged to be delving into their histories, and hope that it will help others to appreciate their supreme sacrifice.

Keith Taylor
October 2007

COVER PICTURES

From left to right:

FRONT TOP ROW: *The Pullen family; carters at Thornbridge Hall.*

FRONT SECOND ROW: *Bakewell War Memorial and Square; John Timm, carter, Little Longstone.*

BACK TOP ROW: *Soldiers at Hassop Station; Sheldon Church tea party.*

BACK SECOND ROW: *Monsal Head in the 1920's; Hay cart on a Sheldon farm.*

CHAPTER ONE

SETTING THE SCENE

A VIEW OF BAKEWELL AND THE SURROUNDING VILLAGES

Many of the men whose names are carved on the war memorials, though by no means all, came from families long associated with Bakewell and the surrounding district. Those who came from elsewhere to live and work would still have been familiar with the landscape and history of this beautiful area.

BAKEWELL

Well before the arrival of the Midland Railway at Bakewell in the early 1860's, the settlement had already developed as a focus of regional traffic in the southern Pennines (a market charter appears in 1254, plus a 15 day fair, whilst a bridge was constructed around 1300 AD).

In 1697 a bath house was built by the Duke of Rutland in an attempt to promote Bakewell as a spa town, whilst various mills were built along the River Wye and marble and chert were extracted, establishing the town as a market and commercial centre.

Henry Watson (1714 – 1786), of Ashford and Bakewell, established the marble industry in both settlements. He purchased the marble workshops at Ashford and set up a small factory near the Wye, using water power to operate machinery to cut, saw and polish marble, as well as to turn columns and vases. He introduced his operations to Bakewell and in 1806 John Lomas took over at new works near Bakewell Bridge, employing 12 men by 1833.

Also, by 1772, Josiah Wedgewood had realised the importance of the siliceous rock chert in the process of making pottery. Between then and the 20th century, over a dozen chert quarries and mines were developed in Bakewell, with especial importance attached to Holme Bank Quarry, behind Holme Hall. Mills near Leek, in Staffordshire, received the chert to grind flint, which was then sent for use in the Potteries.

Sir Richard Arkwright had erected a cotton spinning mill on the River Wye at Lumford in 1778, together with housing for his workers in New Street and Arkwright Square. Quarries in the Bakewell area, such as Ball Cross and Wicksop

Continued on page 12

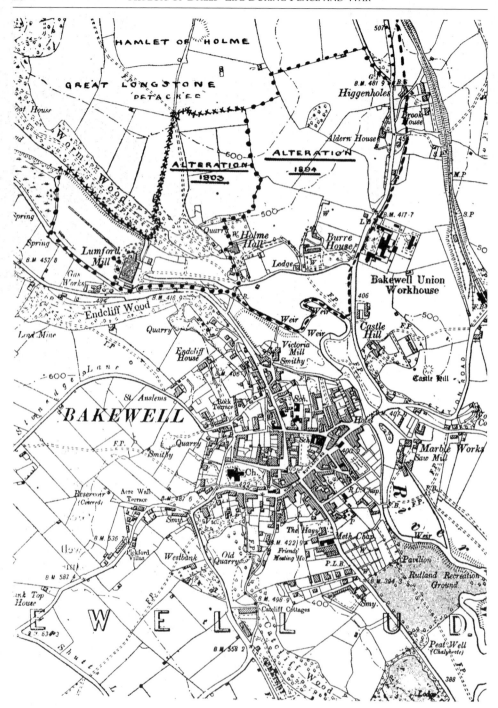

Map of Bakewell c1900.
Longstone Records

A view of All Saints Church, Bakewell, from Yeld Road, c1900. The Normans took down the former Anglo-Saxon church, erecting their own more imposing structure. In 1825 the spire was removed and in 1830 the octagon, with bells and clock, was dismantled, because of the danger of collapse. By 1841, however, the foundations for a new tower and spire were begun.

A view of Bakewell c1905, taken from the golf course side of town.
Tony Holmes

A view of Bakewell in the early 1920's.
Tony Holmes

Wood, also developed as better quality stone was needed during the Georgian Period, as town building increased.

Turnpike roads helped the improvement of transport and communications, thereby helping the development of new industries and the reorganisation of the town itself. The first turnpike road was built in 1759 from Matlock to Bakewell, promoted by the Duke of Rutland, who we have seen, saw the merit of Bakewell as a spa and coaching centre.

The old White Horse Inn, owned by the Duke of Rutland, was demolished in 1804, as the Duke planned a new town centre. A new coaching inn, the Rutland Arms, was completed in 1805, together with fine coaching stables across the square. William Greaves and his wife Ann were the proprietors and Bakewell began to rival Buxton as the main coaching town of the High Peak. Coaches to London, Birmingham, Buxton, Manchester, Nottingham and Sheffield all passed through Bakewell, making use of the coaching stables as they carried numerous passengers, as well as the Royal Mail (in the summer months the number of tourists arriving in Bakewell just before the First World War meant that the Rutland Arms stables were

Continued on page 17 ☞

The Rutland Arms Hotel, a Regency coaching inn, formed an important part of the new town centre created by the Duke of Rutland 1804-1805. The cast iron gas lamp in the centre of the square was erected to celebrate Queen Victoria's Diamond Jubilee of 1897 (the War Memorial is now situated in its place). A men's charabanc trip waits to depart, pre-1914.

R. Richmond

The Rutland Arms possessed a fine coaching stables and yard. In the background can be seen a motor vehicle and the new garage to cater for the evolving horseless carriage. It was here that the horses commandeered for the cavalry and artillery were brought to be inspected in August and September, 1914.

D. Lane

Carriage tours to either Monsal Dale, Matlock Bath, Chatsworth House or Haddon Hall are about to depart from outside the Rutland Arms Hotel c1905. To the right are the Rutland Arms Stables.

Tony Holmes

The Rutland Arms and North Church Street c1910.

Tony Holmes

Ernest Wood ran the Rutland Arms Hotel, Bakewell, between 1911 and 1938.
Tony Holmes

*The Square, Bakewell, c1908. In 1805 the White Horse Inn was replaced by the present
Rutland Arms and was the start of a reorganisation of the town's centre.*
Ian Cox

Rutland Arms Hotel and Square c1925.
Tony Holmes

Bakewell Square 1920's.
Tony Holmes

The Castle and Commercial Hotel (nowadays the Castle Hotel) c1910.
It was here that the Bakewell Horse Fair was held in the years before the First World War.
The horses were washed in the river and trotted through Bath Street.
J. Duncan

not sufficient to cater for them and cabbies were allowed to park and wait at the bottom of North Church Street). Before 1895, Bakewell Post Office was at the Rutland Arms Hotel, with proprietor William Greaves the postmaster (it was Ann Greaves who helped to bring the renowned Bakewell Pudding to the town).

The centre of Bakewell was provided with a Georgian style facade by the Duke of Rutland. Mill Street (now Buxton Road) received a fine Regency row of houses in Rutland Terrace, other fine houses rose on Bridge Street and Castle Street, while Horsecroft Lane (now Matlock Street) had shops and houses erected along its length. The smelly livestock markets were removed from the streets in 1826, whilst in 1828 Bakewell Bridge was widened. As the new professionals were attracted to the town (bankers, doctors, chemists etc.) they demanded finer town houses.

Few of the streets were metalled and some shops and business premises were approached by causeways. Dust in the Square and in the streets was kept under control in the summer by use of a water cart. The Square could be messy at the time of the fair and thick layers of straw were scattered over the surface to absorb the mud.

The arrival of the railway to Bakewell was a boost to its industries, farming interests and tourist trade. Shortly after the station was built in 1863, three coal

Continued on page 29 🖙

Bakewell Horse Fair at the Castle and Commercial Hotel c1910.
J. Duncan

The Red Lion Inn and Post Office, Bakewell, c1910.
Ian Cox

Market Square. The ornamental lamp standard in Rutland Square was erected in 1897 to honour Queen Victoria's Diamond Jubilee. The Red Lion stands to the middle right and the Post Office faces the oncoming traffic.
Tony Holmes

Looking from the Square towards the new Bakewell Post Office, in the centre of the photograph, was erected in 1894. The building on the left, nowadays the Royal Bank of Scotland, was originally the Rotherham and Sheffield Bank, built in 1838.
Tony Holmes

A view from Anchor Square, Bakewell, c1885. The buildings with the sign 'Bradbury's' above them were demolished and replaced by the new town hall in 1890.

D. Lane

Bridge Street, Bakewell.

Tony Holmes

King Street and South Church Street, Bakewell. At the bottom right hand corner is St. John's Hospital, six stone slated almshouses. First erected in 1602 and given the name 'hospital', the cost was met by the Manners family. These premises were demolished in 1709 and the houses rebuilt, resulting in six houses, each with two tiny rooms, one up and one down. Toilets, water supply or kitchens were not provided, with cooking taking place on the open fire. The aim of the charity was to address the problem of affordable housing, by helping to shelter destitute locals (in 2007, the Bakewell Almshouse Trustees and the District Council have turned the buildings into three residential units). It is believed that the thatched cottage, also shown, was the site of the first grammar school, founded by Lady Grace Manners in 1637.

R. Richmond

The left side of Bakewell Square, facing towards the Rutland Arms.
'The Clothing Store' (drapery and clothing business) in its Jacobean building, had been in existance since 1747 but the structure was sadly demolished in 1936-1938 and a new building erected to house R. Orme and Co. Critchlow's butchers shop and Fred Allen's drapery and haberdashery later became the site of John Sinclairs.

Tony Holmes

The Almshouses on South Church Street c1910.
Tony Holmes

Crossing Bakewell Bridge during a more leisurely era, c1905.
Tony Holmes

Bridge Street and Market Place c1910. The old Market Hall in the centre is an early 17th century stone building that easily betrays its original purpose, the open space and arches revealing it to be spacious for commerce. It has mullioned windows and an oriel window bears a plaque of the Manners family. It has been used as a wash-house, chip shop and library, and now serves as a Tourist Information Centre for the Peak District National Park.

Tony Holmes

Bridge Street from Bakewell Bridge. A bull and cattle being led through the streets c1910.

Tony Holmes

King Street, Bakewell, looking down towards the Square c1910. The shop on the left is Thompson's the chemist and druggist. Hubert Thompson died in the Great War and his name is commemorated on Bakewell War Memorial. Established in 1780, the shop sold a wonderfully bizarre selection of goods, such as glucose dip, oil paints, Guiness and stout and wines and spirits. The property had been purchased from Alfred Coates by John Thompson, who left it in his will of October 19th 1891 to his eldest son, John Roberts Thompson.

Tony Holmes

The Square and War Memorial c1928. The memorial was unveiled and dedicated on Friday August 6th 1920, in honour of the Bakewell men who lost their lives whilst serving in the Great War.

Tony Holmes

The War Memorial in The Square, Bakewell, c1923. It was built in 1920 and took the place of the ornamental lamp standard that had been erected in 1897 in honour of Queen Victoria's Jubilee.
Tony Holmes

The old iron footbridge at Bakewell, leading to Smith's timberyard on Coombs Road.
Mary Upton

The Square, Bakewell, c1948.
Mary Upton

Burgon's Stores stands at the junction of Bridge Street and Water Lane.
The horse drawn van delivered goods to the door.
D. Lane

The well-known Bakewell grocery firm of R. Orme and Company became motorised in its delivery service during the late 1920's, delivering to outlying villages.

D. Lane

Michael Skidmore stands at the entrance to the family shop on Matlock Street, Bakewell, in the 1950's.

Michael Skidmore / Julie Bunting

Timber for Bakewell Parish Church roof restoration leaving Bakewell Station 1906
after being unloaded from rail wagons.
Fred Morton

Unloading timber for the parish church roof restoration, Bakewell Railway Station 1906.
Fred Morton

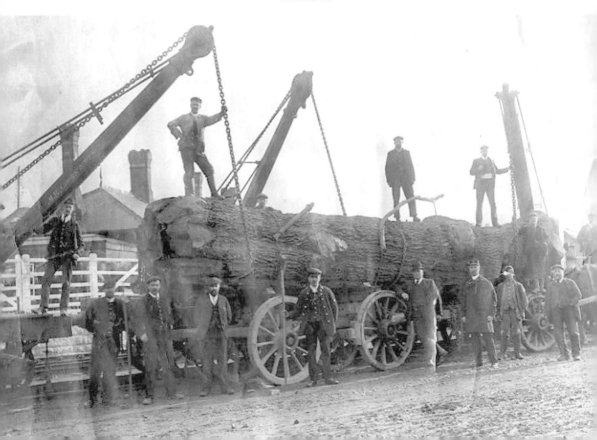

Bakewell Railway Station 1906. In that year Bakewell Parish Church was having its nave roof restored. The large oak logs have been unloaded onto six-wheeled drays to be taken down Station Road to Smith's Sawmills on Coombs Road to be cut into joists and beams for the roof.
Fred Morton

offices were erected and a small stone wharf. By the early 1900's the staff comprised a station master, five parcel and seven goods porters, two booking clerks, three goods clerks, a goods checker, draymen and signalmen.

For those passengers requiring to leave for distant destinations, Bakewell Station served Ashford, Baslow, Hassop, Over Haddon, Pilsley and Youlgreave and was the fifth busiest station between Ambergate and Chinley. Annual passenger bookings passed the 50,000 mark in 1900 and reached a peak of 70,126 in 1920. The freight traffic was varied, with livestock traffic being heavy, especially related to the weekly cattle market.

Large amounts of coal were brought in to supply Bakewell Gas Light Company, whose works were set up adjacent to the cotton mill, on the Buxton Road. Up until 1881 the Magpie Lead Mine at nearby Sheldon also required a great deal of coal and it had to be brought by horse and cart up the steep slope from Bakewell to Sheldon (650 feet above the town). The long, steep climb meant that chain horses were used all the way. The need for coal at Magpie Mine lasted until 1919.

With general merchandise to be delivered to the fifty shops and businesses in the market town, over 11,000 tons of goods passed through Bakewell Station Yard annually up to 1920, resulting in 12 to 14 wagons being unloaded each day.

The 2-20pm train from Manchester Central Station to London passing through Bakewell Station one day in 1934. The young lad is the elder son of railway enthusiast E.R. Morton.
John Morton

Traffic was also substantial for the DP Battery Works, which set up in business in Arkwright's former cotton spinning mill at Lumford, Bakewell. The Duke of Devonshire sold the Lumford cotton mill site in 1898 to the DP Battery Works of Charlton, makers of stationary batteries for railway stations and country houses since 1888. Batteries from this works also powered the first radio stations, telephone exchanges and electric vehicles. The initials DP were those of two French inventors, Dujardin and Planté, who invented a new method of battery plate construction at the end of the 19th century. Until the 1920's the Midland Railway delivered lead and acid to the works. When the firm took over the site in 1898, it continued to use the old water wheels of the cotton spinning mill. The large wheel, made in 1827, measured 25 feet in diameter and was 18 feet wide. The smaller wheel, made in 1852, measured 21 feet and was 7 feet wide.

Continued on page 33 ☛

A view inside the DP Battery works c1905, showing battery plates being stacked on the trolley. The initials DP were those of two French inventors at the end of the 19th century. The compnay became the main employer in the town, closing in 1970.

D. Lane

The staff of the DP Battery Company in front of the old mill waterwheels at Lumford, Bakewell, in 1902. The main employer within Bakewell, a considerable number of employees were killed whilst serving in the forces during the First World War.

J. Duncan

Submarine batteries about to leave Bakewell Station in April 1940.
The DP Battery Company was producing them for the war effort.
Lawrence Knighton

The old waterwheels from Richard Arkwright's cotton mill were used by the DP Battery
Company Ltd., until 1955. The large wheel was built in 1827 and the small wheel in 1852.
Sally Hudson

During the First World War, the production line was changed over to the making of submarine batteries for the war effort and this work continued throughout the inter-war years and especially during the Second World War (between 1939 and 1945, Furniss and Hassell, Bakewell's largest firm of builders had the task of producing wooden boxes to contain the finished items, to enable them to be despatched to ports such as Barrow-in-Furness). The Battery Works became the largest employer of labour in the town (300 employees) until its closure at the end of 1970. The last submarine battery cell was despatched on June 26th 1970.

We have seen that chert, a hard flint-like material found in limestone outcrops, was used as a whitening agent in pottery manufacture in the Staffordshire Potteries. Fine examples were extracted from Holme Bank Quarry, across the river from Lumford Mill and from Pretoria Quarry, on the Monyash road. The blocks of stone were taken to the station yard by horse and wagon to be inspected by buyers and loaded into rail wagons.

The marble works at Ashford opened in 1748 and as we have already discovered, it cut and polished marble by water power, producing table tops, statues and vases. These items were sent out by rail from Bakewell Station and although the Ashford works closed in 1905, the Wye Marble Works, near Bakewell Bridge, begun in the 1850's, continued in business for awhile. Large quantities of foreign marble was also imported and large blocks arrived at the station in low sided wagons.

The latter years of the Victorian period saw a fresh impetus of town building in Bakewell. The corner stone of the new Town Hall was laid with full masonic honours on August 21st 1889 and the Duke of Rutland opened the building in 1890.

Holme Bank Chert Quarry workers, Bakewell, just after the First World War. Quite a number of the men who lost their lives during the war had worked in the various chert quarries and mines.

P. Mosley

Quarry workers at the Chert mine, Holme Bank Quarry, Bakewell c 1941.
LEFT TO RIGHT: *X, foreman Mr. Davey, Charles Carroll (quarry blacksmith), X, Mark Critchlow.*
Marjery Critchlow

Its architect, George Statham, had also helped to build John Smedley's Hydro at Matlock (now the County Hall).

A much needed new post office was also erected in 1894 (the old premises were beside the Rutland Arms Hotel). In 1893, Critchlow's footwear shop was demolished and Bakewell builder, Thomas Allsop, erected the post office on the site. It had been planned to build the post office next to the new Town Hall, around the corner on Bath Street. Instead, when the outbuildings and rundown cottages were demolished on Bath Street, a new Lady Manners School was built on the site, being opened by the Duchess and Duke of Rutland in September 1896. However, even these new premises were inadequate from the start and we shall see later that eventually, work began on a new Lady Manners site on Shutts Lane, in 1936 and the present school was opened in 1938.

The new town centre and square witnessed interesting scenes during Queen Victoria's Golden Jubilee in 1887 and Diamond Jubilee in 1897. For the Diamond Jubilee, a large tent was erected in the Market Place and a roast beef dinner was provided to men and boys over 14 years old. The women and girls over 14 years old were served a meat tea. A commemoration mug was presented to each child. The entertainment ended with the letting off of fireworks in the evening. The 1887 celebrations had been remembered with the planting of an oak tree on the

Charles Critchlow's Shoe Shop was demolished in 1893 and Bakewell's post office
was built on the site in 1894.
R. Richmond

Recreation Ground, whilst in 1897, a cast-iron gas lamp was erected in Rutland Square (we shall see that this was taken down in 1920 and its position in the square became the site of the town's war memorial. It is interesting to think that some of the men whose names are on the memorial would have been involved in one way or another in the 1897 Jubilee celebrations).

Newholme Workhouse had been opened in 1841, after a four acre piece of land at Newholme, on the Bakewell to Sheffield Turnpike was purchased for £415 from the Earl of Carlisle. Plans for the new building, which was to accommodate 200 inmates, were inspected and the design finally accepted was by Mr. Johnson of Sheffield. The bricks for the building were made locally from cast clay. A water supply for the Workhouse was provided by the digging of a large pond which could hold 120,000 gallons of spring water. The main Workhouse block was a Jacobean-style two-storey building. It was embellished with a turret clock and bell costing £80. In 1841, the ground floor of the main building's north wing was converted into use as a hospital. However, in 1848 work began on a separate infirmary block. A larger infirmary block was added further to the east in 1899-1900, as well as a mortuary. The Workhouse later became known as Bakewell Public Assistance Institution and then under the National Health Service as Newholme Hospital (we shall see that at the start of the Great War, in 1914, the infirmary block was taken over as a Red Cross Convalescent Hospital).

Bakewell's new post office nears completion 1893/1894. Fred Clark, stone mason and carver stands in bowler hat and apron, fourth from the right on high scaffolding platform (his son, Cecil, was killed in the Great War). Thomas Allsop, the builder, stands on the street, in bowler hat in the centre, whilst Sam Welch holds the horse's head next to him.
R. Richmond

Bath Street c1890. The Old Bath House, built by the Duke of Rutland over the ancient bath or spring in 1697, can be seen behind the group of women. The barns in the foreground were demolished in 1895 to make way for the premises of the new Lady Manners School, which came here from its former site at the Old Town Hall. The foundation stone was laid on May 16th 1895 and the school was opened by the Duke of Rutland on September 22nd 1896, with 50 pupils on its roll, (by 1900 there were 65 boys and 56 girls). Lady Grace Manners had originally founded the school in 1637 at a time when there was no provision for education in Bakewell.

Mr. R.A. Harvey, in his book 'The Story of the School of Grace, Lady Manners, Bakewell', records that "before the First World War, despite the existence of boarding accommodation, many pupils had considerable daily journeys to school, some from as far as Belper in the south and Buxton in the north. The railway provided the only means of public transport, and it must have been very exhausting for those whose homes were remote from the nearest station. Those travelling from Belper left at 7-30am on the milk train which stopped at every station. Pupils from Crich, Bonsall, Tansley and Two Dales had long walks before boarding the train. Reserved carriages were provided on the train, with prefects in charge. Lighting was provided by oil lamps suspended from the roof, and the only heating was by hot water foot warmers. No school meals were provided, those unable to go home for lunch ate sandwiches in the cookery rooms, where a week's supply of tickets for cocoa could be bought for 2$\frac{1}{2}$d. At the end of the afternoon school, pupils went into South Train Prep., to do home - work until it was time to leave for the 5-25pm train. This arrived at Belper at 6-25pm – an eleven hour day." The establishment of the Herbert Strutt School at Belper in 1909 reduced the catchment area to the far south.
R. Richmond

Charabanc trip from the Rutland Arms c1910.
Tony Holmes

*A Derbyshire Imperial Yeomanry soldier poses with 'Old Paul' after it had been shot.
It weighed four tons. After it was buried at Bakewell tip, it is reported that 'trophy hunters' raided
the site and made off with the four feet, which were made into umbrella stands.*
Lawrence Knighton and Tony Hill

*Lord Sanger's Circus was in Bakewell on May 25ᵗʰ 1905, when a performing bull elephant called
'Old Paul' went amok. The Derbyshire Yeomanry and soldiers from the Company of Sherwood
Foresters (Territorials) arrived from their camp on Coombs Road and it was shot.
Children from the town pose with the dead animal. Harry Hurst and his brother William from
Ashford (later Great Longstone), were employees of Smith's timberyard on Coombs Road, and were
sent with a hoist, horses and drug to remove the carcass. It was carried away to be buried at the tip
on Buxton Road.*

J. Duncan

*'D' Company of the Derbyshire Imperial Yeomanry are on parade in Bakewell Square 1902, on the
occasion of Edward VII's coronation. The Yeomanry, an irregular force, was raised in 1899 as
mounted infantry and served in the Boer War. By 1900 a Territorial Company of the Sherwood
Foresters was also based in Bakewell, stationed at a camp along Coombs Road. Chatsworth Hall and
Hardwick Hall were used as summer training camps for the Derbyshire Yeomanry.*

R. Richmond

Many of the Bakewell lads who were killed whilst serving their country during the First World War were former members of the Church Lads' Brigade. The group is posing during the Boer War, in 1901, in uniforms representing the forces of the British Empire. Sadly, some of those in the photograph would be killed between 1914 and 1918.
The Church Lads's Brigade was formed in Bakewell in 1898, with its own brigade hall and gymnasium behind the Boy's School on Bath Street, erected by Messrs. Cox-Wilson of Ashford. They used military drill and discipline to instill religious and moral improvement in the lads. 'Sure and Steadfast' was the motto they used and the anchor was their badge. Although it was a religious organisation, it provided a steady stream of recruits for the army during the First World War.
R. Richmond

Holme Hall, Bakewell, home of the Hoyle family during the Great War. This Jacobean residence was built for the Gloucestershire lead merchant, Bernard Wells in 1626, whose co-heiress married Henry Bradshaw, of Marple, and Robert Eyre, of Highlow.
Mary Upton

Burton Closes, built between 1845 and 1848 for the wealthy Quaker banker and stockbroker,
William Allcard of Manchester, and later Smith Taylor-Whitehead. Designed by
Augustus Welby Pugin, the gothic revivalist, and extended by T.D. Barry,
the gardens were laid out by Edward Milner, a pupil of Sir Joseph Paxton at Chatsworth.

D. Lane

The Vicarage at Bakewell, home to the Reverend Abraham and his sons. Built on the site of an
earlier one by Archdeacon Balston in 1869, the architect was Alfred Waterhouse, who had designed
Manchester Town Hall. In 1919 it became the School House (boarding house) for Lady Manners
School pupils until 1939. Later still, it became a home for the elderly.

D. Lane

The Bakewell Carnival of 1934 in Rutland Square. Behind the Carnival Queen and attendants is Bakewell fire engine. The old Clothing Hall shop, next to Burgons is already closed and awaiting demolition, ready for a new building and facade, to house R. Orme and Co.

J. Duncan

A significant number of Bakewell men were employed in the local chert quarries (a siliceous rock). Holme Bank Quarry, behind Holme Hall, provided the best beds of chert. Here, the quarry is advertising its product on Bakewell Carnival Day during the 1920's.

R. Richmond

Bakewell Carnival during the 1930's.
Tony Holmes

Bakewell Carnival during the 1930's.
Mary Upton

Members of the Derbyshire County Council Barber Green team
laying tarmac onto the gravel surface of a country road near Bakewell c1948.
Hector Mansfield of Bakewell is driving the steam roller.
Sylvia Marsden

The sheep pens at the old Bakewell Market c1950's.
Derbyshire County Council, Libraries and Heritage

SHELDON

In the mid 1850's the population of Sheldon was 197, with its inhabitants mainly involved in farming activities and work at the nearby Magpie Lead Mine. Fifteen lead miners were of Cornish descent, having brought their skills to Derbyshire from the South West peninsula. By 1910, however, the population of the village had declined to 128, partly due to a decrease in the profitability of the lead mining industry.

At an altitude of 1000 feet above sea-level, conditions for hill farming were not easy, due to its exposed position to the vagaries of the weather, but cattle, sheep, hens and pigs were tended and wheat, potatoes, hay and turnips cultivated. The siting of Woodbine Farm, Devonshire View Farm, Top Farm, Home Farm, Rose Farm, Manor Farm, Johnson Lane Farm and Anthony Gyte's farm at the Devonshire Arms shows the importance of work on the land in such a small settlement as Sheldon.

The work was hard and varied, following the passing of the seasons. Always there was the milking of the cattle and transportation of milk churns by horse and float to Longstone Station, two and a half miles away, to catch the 8-40a.m. milk train or the night train at Bakewell in hot weather so that the milk did not go sour.

Ploughing and sowing was difficult on the limestone uplands, whilst harvesting of the hay and corn depended on the kindness of the weather. Stacking and thatching followed the harvest, whilst lambing and calving times meant that the farming folk often stayed up with the animals all night. Sheldon sheep were taken to be washed at Ashford in the Water sheep wash, by the bridge, whilst the Sheldon farmers took their sheep to be dipped at the Devonshire Arms farm of Anthony Gyte.

The Diaries of Maria Gyte 1913-1920 written by Anthony's wife, provide a flavour of late Autumn work on the Gyte farm:

> *October 18th 1913: Finished corn on moor. Finished Bole Piece. Brought that home, about 350 thrave (a thrave consisted of a dozen sheaves).*
> *October 21st 1913: Dull but fine. Tom thatching on moor. Anthony and Tony thatching corn stacks in stack yard.*
> *October 24th 1913: Very frosty and cold. Our men and Jack Naylor are getting potatoes on moor.*
> *November 3rd 1913: Tom Gyte and William Gould went to Sterndale for lime. Brought 38 cwt. for £1 7s 10d, to be used for repairing meres. Tony and Wilf Goodwin began turnip cutting (account from diaries in Derbyshire Records Office).*

Cheese making occurred, especially when there was surplus milk. Fred Brocklehurst, a cousin of three of the Sheldon men to be killed during the Great War, described how the cheese was made in his youth. The milk was carried across the

Continued on page 50 ☛

View of Sheldon c1910. In the foreground is Woodbine Farm, home of Thomas William Brocklehurst and family. His son, George Brocklehurst, is thatching the hay stack.
Tom Brocklehurst

View of Woodbine Farm and Sheldon.
Ralph Lord

Clarice Brocklehurst with triplet calves, at Woodbine Farm, the Sheldon farm belonging to her father,
Thomas William Brocklehurst. She was the sister of Fred and cousin of John and 'Tant' Brocklehurst,
both brothers killed during the Great War.

Ken Brocklehurst

John Brocklehurst of Sheldon, mowing with his horse. His two sons were killed
in the First World War.

Tom Brocklehurst

Thomas William Brocklehurst of Woodbine Farm, Sheldon, broadcasting the oats in the time-honoured manner.
Tom Brocklehurst

Dinner time on Sheldon Moor. The two men in the middle are Thomas William Brocklehurst and his son George.
Tom Brocklehurst

Arthur Bramwell, farm worker, leading the horse into the yard of Woodbine Farm, c1930's.
Ken Brocklehurst

The Sheldon farmers brought all their sheep to be dipped at the Devonshire Arms farm
of the Gyte family.
LEFT TO RIGHT: *Alfred Brocklehurst, Thomas William Brocklehurst, John Brocklehurst.*
Ken Brocklehurst

Sheldon farmers washing their sheep in the River Wye at Ashford sheep wash n the 1920's.
John Brocklehurst stands on the extreme right.
Tom Brocklehurst

Stacking the hay from the harvest at Sheldon. The men are Arthur Bramwell,
Thomas William Brocklehurst and George Brocklehurst.
Ken Brocklehurst

During the inter-war years, Herbert Frost of Manor House Farm, Sheldon, took a great interest
in the breeding of Highland cattle. He would travel to Scotland, from where they were brought
by rail to Longstone Station and driven along the roads to Sheldon. Here, the cattle
are being driven through the lower end of Sheldon.
Ken Brocklehurst

fields in cans strung from a shoulder yoke, to the farm dairy, where part of it was heated on the fire and rennet (part of a cow's stomach) was added. The milk eventually curdled and it was broken down, with the whey (liquid) separated from the curd. This curd was then pressed to the bottom of the pan, where it was cut up, placed under a cloth and into a press, to release the last of the whey. In a pansion, the curd was worked with the hands and salt added and mixed. Placed into a cheese vat, a weight was added and acted as a cheese press, and finally the cheese was stored in a drying room.

In the Autumn a fattened sow, fed on maize meal and bran, was killed by the village slaughter man. Helpers held the pig down whilst the pig killer, Matthew Hodgkinson or Ben Naylor, stuck the animal, with some of the resulting blood collected and made into black pudding.

Bristles would be removed with boiling water and the liver, kidneys, heart and cuts of pork would be taken as the pig was hung up. The rest of the carcass was placed in salt, with brown sugar and salt petre added. It was a communal affair, with relatives or friends receiving cuts of meat and returning the favour when their pig was slaughtered.

Continued on page 54 ☛

Main Street, Sheldon c1905. The people are outside the house and workshop
of Sheldon joiner, Edwin Brocklehurst.

Tom Brocklehurst

Sheldon School c1919
BACK ROW: *Miss Whitehead, Frank Goodwin, Jim Bramwell, X, X, Arthur Bramwell, X.*
FOURTH ROW: *X, Dorothy Brocklehurst, X, X, John David Frost, Herbert Frost.* THIRD ROW: *X, X,*
Elsie Brocklehurst, X, X, Mabel Hallows, Mary Roberts Second row: *X, X, X, X, X, X.*
FRONT ROW: *Arthur John Sherwin, X*

David Sherwin

Sheldon School 1916/1917
BACK ROW: *Winnie Brocklehurst, Addie Hallows, Amy Brocklehurst, Vera Carson, Connie Goodwin.*
THIRD ROW: *John Frost, Leslie Carson, Clarice Goodwin, Ethel Brocklehurst, Jessie Goodwin,*
Dorothy Roberts, Kathleen Rowland, Charlie Brocklehurst, Herbert Frost, Henry Frost.
SECOND ROW: *Ben Sheldon, Dick Rowland, Jean Brennan, X, Betty Sherwin, Nancy Brennan,*
Jim Rowland, Frank Goodwin. FRONT ROW: *Clarice Bramwell, Arthur Bramwell, Jim Bramwell,*
Mabel Hallows, X, Ida Ward, Elsie Brocklehurst, X.
Ken Brocklehurst

Sheldon School c1919
STANDING BACK ROW: *X, Pupil Teacher, X, John David Frost, Herbert Frost, Dorothy Roberts,*
Elsie Goodwin, X CENTRE ROW: *Mary R oberts, Frank Goodwin, Jim Bramwell, Betty Sherwin, X,*
Leslie Carson FRONT ROW: *Arthur Bramwell, X, X, X, Charles Brocklehurst*
Ethel Plumtree

Sheldon School c1919/1920
BACK ROW: X, Henry Frost, John Frost, Herbert Frost, X THIRD ROW: X, Ben Sheldon, X,
Charlie Brocklehurst, X, Jim Bramwell, Teacher (Miss Louise Broadhurst) SECOND ROW: X,
Betty Sherwin, Winnie Brocklehurst, Dorothy Roberts, Vera Carson, Ethel Brocklehurst, Mary Roberts,
X, X FRONT ROW: Arthur Bramwell, X, X, X, X, X.
*The school closed in 1933 and Sheldon children then travelled to Ashford School. It became the Village
Hall until, after the Second World War, it was renamed the Hartington Memorial Hall, in memory of
the Marquis of Hartington who was killed in action during the war*
Ken Brocklehurst

Sheldon School mid 1920's
BACK ROW: *A. Brocklehurst, Jim Bramwell, ? Sherwin, Frank Goodwin, Arthur Bramwell*
THIRD ROW: *Elsie Broomhead, Mabel Hallows, Mary Roberts, Kathleen Rowland, Clarice Bramwell,
Ida Ward, Phyllis Green* SECOND ROW: *Douglas Rowland, Bessie Eaton, Margery Brocklehurst,
Millie Brocklehurst, Lucy Eaton, Elsie Brocklehurst, Fred (Sonny) Carson*
FRONT: *George Green, Stanley Rowland*
Ethel Plumtree

Sheldon School mid 1920's
BACK ROW: *Bessie Eaton, Elsie Brocklehurst, Elsie Broomhead, Margery Brocklehurst, Lucy Eaton,*
Miss Whitehead CENTRE ROW: *Bert Mather (standing), Alice Eaton, Ivy Hurn, Joe Andrews,*
Betty Hurn, Ada Eaton, Arthur Mather FRONT ROW: *George Eaton, Mabel Goodwin,*
Thelma Goodwin, ? Mather, ? Mather, ? Mather (two Mathers were Kathleen and Mary).
Ethel Plumtree

Sheldon Village School, built in 1878 (and closed in 1933), was situated near the top end of the Main Street (the building is nowadays called Hartington Memorial Hall, named to honour William Cavendish, Marquis of Hartington, who was killed whilst serving in the Second World War). It could house 40 pupils, taught by one school mistress. However, the building was used for many purposes and was the focus of social events in the village, including evening classes, confirmation classes, weddings, socials and dances. Maria Gyte reports in her diaries that on November 20th 1913 a social was held at the school room. Mr. Skidmore and son brought a gramophone and a most enjoyable evening was spent. There was singing, dancing and recitations.

St. Michael and All Angels Church was built in the Gothic style in 1865, the land having been provided by the Duke of Devonshire and consecrated as a burial ground in 1853. It replaced an even smaller church, sited on the village street and built during the 1400's, and some of its stone was used to build the new church.

Though rivalries existed, the villages of Sheldon and Ashford were closely connected, with the vicar of Ashford being also the incumbent of Sheldon (during the Great War, the vicar was the Reverend Harry Ernest Sherlock, who remained as incumbent until his retirement in 1940).

Continued on page 56 ☛

St. Michael and All Angels Church tea party at Sheldon c1905.
Tom Brocklehurst

St. Michael and All Angels Church, Sheldon, June 2007.
Keith Taylor

Sheldon Primitive Methodist Chapel c1905, situated near to the entrance to Church Lane. By the early 1920's it was no longer taking services and for many years afterwards was used as a workshop for Sam Bramwell. Employed at the DP Battery Works, he also had a smallholding in the village. The Chapel was demolished in 1967.

Margaret Slin

A Primitive Methodist Chapel, built in 1848, formerly stood at the bottom of Church Lane. During the years of the Great War, its Society Steward and preacher was David Frost, who lived at Town Head Farm and was a brother of Herbert Frost of Manor Farm. By the early 1920's it was no longer taking services and for many years afterwards was used as a workshop by Sam Bramwell. The chapel was demolished in 1967.

The Gyte family ran the other focal point of village social life, the Devonshire Arms public house. By the time of the Great War they had been inn keepers there for over 100 years (and continued to run it until December 31st 1972, when it closed). The barn next door was used as a dance hall for the inn and was especially busy during Wakes Week and on other important occasions. The public house also functioned as a working farmhouse. The ale was always fetched from the barrels in pint and quart jugs, even into the early 1970's, for there were never any beer pumps installed (the dance hall barn has now been converted into a new public house, called "The Cock and Pullet").

Close to the village lie the remains of Magpie Lead Mine, which once provided work for local men (the mine is actually sited in Ashford Parish). Its recorded history goes back to the 1740's, with its most fruitful period of production during the 19th century, although the life of the mine only ended in 1958.

During the 1740's it was worked only spasmodically but production rose

Sheldon village June 2007. In the foreground is the 'Cock and Pullet Inn', constructed from the barn belonging to the old 'Devonshire Arms'. The old pub, belonging to the Gyte family, is the house in the middle dsitance. The loft of the old barn was the dance hall for the original pub.
Keith Taylor

significantly by 1800 when there began a ten year search for ore. At the end of that decade a main vein was discovered near the present main shaft (the shaft is 729 feet deep). It helped to pay off the debts that had accumulated over the years.

Between 1811 and 1820 there were considerable dividends to the shareholders. Drainage was simply by means of a horse-gin, but by 1824, steam power was required and a Newcomen Cornish beam engine was brought to the site and placed in a newly built engine-house. The cost helped towards closing the mine in the mid-1830's.

The mine re-opened in the 1840's with the installation of another engine, then closed and re-opened in 1869. The engine pumped water all the way to the surface, but the high cost of coal led the miners to drive a sough (drainage tunnel) so that the engine only had to pump water from the levels below the sough. Magpie Sough was driven between 1873 and 1881, the last major sough in Derbyshire, with its tail in the River Wye, at Shacklow Wood, near Ashford, just one and a quarter miles from the mine.

Profitability declined with the cost of driving the sough and productivity declined through the 20th century, with a last rise in profitability 1953 - 1958, with the Korean War boom.

Continued on page 60 ☞

Magpie Lead Mine ruins, June 2007 (near Sheldon)
LEFT TO RIGHT: *1. corner of the Agent's house, 2. corrugated shed from 1950's housing a converted trawler winch, 3. steel headgear from 1950's, 4. ruins of stone engine house that contained Newcomen steam engine, 5. circular flue chimney.*
Keith Taylor

Magpie Lead Mine ruins, June 2007 (near Sheldon)
The steel headgear from the 1950's stands next to the main shaft, 729 feet (222metres) deep.
The stone engine house contained a Cornish Newcomen beam engine from 1869 to drain the mine.
The cylindrical flue chimney took the fumes away.
Keith Taylor

Magpie Lead Mine ruins, June 2007 (near Sheldon)
Replica of a horse gin. Such a piece of equipment would have been used to haul up lead ore
and associated materials in much earlier times.
Keith Taylor

Magpie lead miners in the 1890's. On the extreme right is William Harry Brocklehurst, son of the
engine driver, 'Wingy One Arm' Brocklehurst, standing next to Fred Buxton.
Tom Brocklehurst

The Magpie Lead Mine, near Sheldon. Thomas Brocklehurst, known as 'Wingy One Arm', was the driver of the Newcomen beam engine in the 19th century. He originated from Foolow, where he had lost one of his arms in a wheel at a lead mine.

Ken Brocklehurst

There were several mines originally on the site. Magpie miners worked the North Bole Vein whilst the Maypitt miners worked the neighbouring Great Redsoil Vein. The Magpie miners eventually broke through into the Great Redsoil Vein where the two veins met and arguments broke out in meetings of the Barmote Court over who had the rightful title to work the mine. Both sides of underground miners lit fires of straw and tar to smoke out their opponents, resulting in three Maypitt miners being killed in 1833 by the sulphurous fumes created by the Magpie men. At Derby Assizes in 1834, the Magpie miners were acquitted.

During the years of the Great War there were only two shops in Sheldon. One was run by two young sisters, Kate and Ruth Brocklehurst, in between their work as Red Cross VAD nurses at the Red Cross Convalescent Hospital at Newholme. The shop was to be found in one of the rooms of their father's house (nowadays called "Orme Cottage", on Main Street), their father being Edward Brocklehurst, the village joiner. The second shop was run by Benjamin Sheldon and his family.

Water was always a problem for the inhabitants of Sheldon, living as they did high up on the limestone plateau. Because of the shortage of water, especially in the

Continued on page 63 ☛

Sheldon men at the Sheldon Waterworks ('Pot Boil'), on the bank of the River Wye. They are in the process of building the engine house, to be used in pumping water up to Sheldon.
LEFT TO RIGHT: *Tom Gyte, Billy Carson, Jack Naylor, Stanley Brocklehurst, X, John Brocklehurst, Anthony Gyte, Thomas William Brocklehurst.*
Margaret Slin

The water tank belonging to the Sheldon Waterworks. Water was brought by pipe from a spring called the 'Pot Boil' on the bank of the River Wye, for Sheldon village. It closed in 1956.
John Frost

Mr Boam was the driver of the water tanker that brought water to Sheldon when the Waterworks broke down or 'dried up' in summer. He filled the farmers' milk churns c1950.

Ken Brocklehurst

The ruins of the Bobbin Mill and waterwheel by the River Wye.

Ethel Plumtree

summer months, the villagers helped establish the Sheldon Water Works, in the years before 1900.

Close to where the tail of the Magpie Lead Mine Sough entered the River Wye, an engine house was built on the bank of the river, operated at first by a water wheel. A pipe was laid to the village up the steep slope beneath Shacklow Wood and water was pumped up through the pipe from a spring, known as the "Pot Boil".

A large iron water tank was raised high above the ground on a stone base in a field close to Manor House Farm, Sheldon, and was kept filled with water from the "Pot Boil", one and a quarter miles away (at the time of writing, just the ruined walls of the base remain standing). Pipes were laid to Manor Farm and to houses on Main Street.

The iron panels for the water tank, made in Chesterfield, were brought to Hassop Station, and were then transported, four at a time, up the steep hill to Sheldon in a horse and dray belonging to Herbert William Frost of Manor Farm. A chain horse was required to help drag the heavy load to the village and then the panels were riveted together (the tank was 6 panels long by five panels wide).

The Duke of Devonshire had provided stone and other materials for the engine house and the tank but it was the men of Sheldon who actually provided the labour to construct the building. We have already seen that Herbert Frost provided transport.

During periods of prolonged dry weather during summer time or when break downs and damage to the pipes occurred, the supply occasionally "dried up" and villagers had to make do with the wells and pumps to be found in the yards or gardens of many Sheldon cottages (this water was usually used for washing clothes etc. and so when it was occasionally required for drinking purposes, it needed to be boiled). During the 1950's, a lorry driven by Mr. Boam would bring in extra water if the Sheldon Water Works "dried up", and farmers would store it in milk churns.

Sheldon Water Works became redundant in 1956, when the village was brought onto the mains supply, and the metal tank was removed.

Adjacent to the Sheldon Water Works engine house was the "Bobbin Mill", producing many items made from wood, including wheel barrows and cart wheels. It had been operated by James Frost of Yew Tree House, Sheldon, until he died around 1898. In 1900, Herbert William Frost took Manor Farm, Sheldon, together with his brother John from Home Farm and it was they who continued to work the Bobbin Mill for a few years after James's death, until it was taken over by Mr. Morton, who used it to grind animal bones to produce bone meal fertiliser. The water wheel in the Bobbin Mill was operated by water flowing in a leat from the River Wye.

WARDLOW

The village of Wardlow (the name meaning "watch hill and slope") and Wardlow Mires derives its name from Wardlow Hay Cop, a lookout hill at the western end of Longstone Moor, rising to over 1100 feet above sea level. Until 1875 Wardlow was divided between the parishes of Hope and Longstone. The Hope side of Wardlow became part of the new parish of Bradwell.

Lead mining was the initial attraction for the villagers, but the largest venture, Water Grove Lead Mine, near Wardlow Mires, closed in 1853 after years of battling with the problem of flooding (across the road from the mine was an isolation hospital, made from corrugated iron, surrounded by railings, to which people with infectious diseases such as smallpox were sent. During the 1930's and 40's the care-taker was Reuban Robinson of Wardlow, but the building was demolished around 1945/1946).

Even after the decline of lead mining, its underground workings still affected the area. Just before the First World War, the road running alongside Wardlow church and school opened up due to former underground lead mining activity, when the heavy weight of a Bailey's Mill corn wagon and horses passed over. The wagon had to be pulled clear and much of the grain disappeared into the hole.

Continued on page 66 ☛

Wardlow village main street c1905, looking from the Bakewell side. The Bull's Head Inn stands on the right and Elm Cottage on the left.

Margaret Bagshaw

Joseph and Margaret Simpson at Hall Farm, Wardlow, before the Great War.
Margaret Bagshaw

The Church of the Good Shepherd, Wardlow, was built in 1872.
Ian Morgan

A Sunday School had been built at Wardlow in 1835, which was also used as a day school. However, the village did not possess a church. Indeed, in the eyes of the church authorities, Wardlow was regarded as a "lost place". An oft repeated saying said that Wardlow women scarcely **could** trudge the long Derbyshire miles to either Hope or Longstone churches and the men seldom **did**.

However, in 1871, the vicar of nearby Tideswell, the Reverend Samuel Andrew, put forward the case of the need for practical schools and small churches in hamlets remote from their parish church. It was due to his resolute efforts that a small wayside church called The Church of the Good Shepherd was built onto the newly enlarged Church of England National School at Wardlow.

It was opened during the village wakes on Friday September 20th 1872. The newspaper account of the event tells how the villagers provided 200 teas, served in relays in the two small rooms, with families contributing bread, butter and cream. The work was not completed and building work was proceeding as funds allowed.

Continued on page 70 ☛

Wardlow School c1916.
BACK ROW: *Teacher Helen Robinson, Lily Harrison, Charlie Turner, Arnold Turner, Sam Gillott, George Haslam, Horace Turner, X, Helen Cooper, Teacher Annie Robinson.* THIRD ROW: *Headteacher Mrs Robinson (Hey Farm), Gladys Turner, Martha Haslam, X, X, X, X, Edith Cooper, Betsy Gillott.* SECOND ROW: *Maggie Turner, Jessie Turner, X, Evelyn Simpson, X, X.* FRONT ROW: *Ellis Armitt, George Lomas, Norman Howe, X, Tom Armitt, X.*
Margaret Bagshaw

Wardlow School 1921.
BACK ROW: *Horace Turner, Sam Gillott, Hilda Turner, Nora Cooper, Essie Simpson, Edith Cooper, Gladys Turner, Dolly Turner, Martha Haslam, Bessy Gillott.* CENTRE ROW: *Gladys Higginbottom, Edith Turner, Harriet Gillott, Evelyn Simpson, Tom Furness, Fred Furness, Maggie Turner, Mary Howe, Hector Haslam, Lily Harrison, Helen Cooper and sister.* FRONT ROW: *Charlie Turner, Tom Turner, Frank Turner, Arnold Turner, Norman Howe, Ellis Armitt, Sam Turner, Tom Armitt.*
Margaret Bagshaw

Wardlow School c1920.
BACK ROW: *Tom Armitt, Ellis Armitt, Charlie Turner, X, Tom Turner, X, Teacher Helen Robinson.* CENTRE ROW: *Nora Cooper, Edith Cooper, Martha Haslam, Betsy Gillott, Marjorie Turner, Hilda Turner, Edith Turner, Dolly Turner, Gladys Higginbottom.* FRONT ROW: *Arnold Turner, Frank Turner, Maggie Turner, Jessie Turner, Fred Furness, Tom Furness, X, Sam Turner, Hector Haslam, Bessie Simpson, Evelyn Simpson, Mary Howe, Norman Howe, Mabel Turner.*
Margaret Bagshaw

A Sunday School had been built at Wardlow in 1835, which was also used as a day school. The Church of the Good Shepherd was built onto the school in 1872 and was dedicated in 1873.

Keith Taylor

Group of schoool children outside Wardlow School c1905.

Margaret Bagshaw

Wardlow School 1928 with Butts Farm in the background.
BACK ROW: *Bob Bramwell, Frank Turner, Fred Furness, George Lomas, Frank Harrison, Hector Haslam, Walter Herrington, Tom Furness.* CENTRE ROW: *Sam Turner, Jessie Turner, Bessie Simpson, Mabel Turner, Mary Howe, Evelyn Simpson, Mabel Armitt, Marjorie Rurner, Joe Furness, Teacher Helen Robinson.* FRONT ROW: *Gladys Berresford, Maria Turner, Gertrude Simpson, Jim Bramwell, Joe Hall, Patsie Bramwell, Lily Berresford, Bessie Turner, Violet Haslam, Daisy Turner, Rene Haslam, Graham Haslam, Frank Gregory.*
Margaret Bagshaw

Wardlow School Concert c1930.
BACK ROW: *Emily Bramwell, Fred Furness, Joe Furness, Joe Hall, Graham Haslam, Marjorie Turner, Jim Bramwell, Gertrude Simpson, Frank Gregory, Bessie Simpson, Alfred Turner, Mabel Turner, Sam Turner, Bertha Jackson.* FRONT ROW: *Violet Haslam, Pat Bramwell, Connie Simpson, Tom Darbyshire, Rene Haslam, Daisy Turner, Connie Haslam X, Ethel Darbyshire.*
We shall find that Pat Bramwell was engaged to Leslie Blears, who lost his life in the sinking of HMS 'Barham', in the Second World War. I believe that Alfred Turner could well be the person who lost his life in Burma during the Second World War.
Margaret Bagshaw

The day's collection of over £50 would be used to pay for the rest of the church to be roofed before the onset of winter.

The single aisle church, with 100 sittings, was built in Perpendicular Gothic style and the completed Church was dedicated to the Good Shepherd in June 1873. A doorway in the side chapel opened into the nave, whilst folding doors in another wall could be used to shut off the schoolroom, when necessary.

At Wardlow School, in 1908, Mrs Frances Bramwell was the schoolmistress, but during the Great War, Mrs. Robinson, from Hey Farm, Wardlow, became the head teacher, with her daughter Helen acting as the infant teacher (another daughter, Anne Robinson, eventually became the infant mistress at Bath Street School, Bakewell). Mrs. Robinson was also the Sunday School superintendent and her day pupils were expected to attend on Sundays without fail. When the school closed around 1948/1949 there were only five pupils in attendance. The old school building now acts as the village hall.

With the decline in lead mining, agriculture was now of first importance. The farms were strung out along the village street as in pre-enclosure times, with their crofts and fields extending behind them in a medieval pattern. Even in the 1950's and 60's there were ten milk producers in the village.

Before the Great War and during the 1920's, the Wardlow farmers took their milk in churns, by horse and cart, to Monsal Dale Station, from where it was then taken by rail to Manchester Dairy. Later, by the 1930's, it was being transported in 10

Reuban Robinson, a farmer from Butts Farm, Wardlow, wanders home along the Main Street with his dog, Sambo, in 1930. Elm Cottage is on the right and the Bull's Head public house is on the left. Reuban's wife, Rhoda, was the headteacher at Great Hucklow School.

Frank Robinson

gallon churns by lorries owned by Pheaseys of Ashford in the Water to Express Dairy at Sheffield.

For Wardlow villagers who did not work on the land, work could be found at Cressbrook Cotton Mill, in Monsal Dale. The mill workers normally walked to their place of work through Ravensdale, or "Bury-Me-Wick", as it was known to the locals. Other Wardlow residents found work in the shoe factories at either Stoney Middleton or Eyam.

During the late 1920's and 1930's Wardlow people could obtain their weekly necessities from the many shops in nearby Tideswell. Travelling tradesmen also arrived on a regular basis, including Mr. Shimwell on his horse and dray from Ormes of Bakewell, delivering groceries, Caudwells of Rowsley delivering animal feed to the farmers and flour for home baking, whilst Henry Cook, an Over Haddon man, brought yeast in his pony and trap.

The Three Stags Head at Wardlow Mires. Standing almost in a time-warp, with its stone-flagged floors, beer drawn mainly from the barrel (from Abbeydale Brewery, Sheffield), and large range, the servicemen of Wardlow returning home on leave during the First World War would still recognise the interior of the pub.

Ian Morgan

The Furness family who kept the Three Stags public house, Wardlow Mires, taken around 1895.
LEFT TO RIGHT: *Tom Furness, Tom Furness (senior), Margaret Furness (sister), Sarah Furness (wife), Ann Furness.*
By the 1920's and 1930's the Furness brothers ran the public house and farm, together with a garage with petrol pump, across the road from the pub.
Margaret Bagshaw

Thomas Furness, landlord and farmer at the Three Stags Head, Wardlow Mires, with his bull-nose Morris, late 1920's.
Margaret Bagshaw

The Furness family who kept the Bull's Head, Wardlow, c1905.
BACK ROW, STANDING: *Frank Furness, Peter John Furness, Charlie Furness*
FRONT ROW: *Edgar Furness, Peter John Furness (senior), Herbert Bramwell Furness,*
Hannah Furness (nee Bramwell), John Henry Furness (on knee).
Margaret Bagshaw

Wardlow did not receive mains water until 1937. The village pump was the main source.
In periods of drought, the upland village suffered from a shortage of water.
Around 1933 was such a time and here, the villagers receive their daily water rations,
provided by horse and cart, by the Bakewell Rural Council.
LEFT TO RIGHT: *Tom Furness (senior), Jack Turner, Tom Hall, Pattie Bramwell, Bob Bramwell.*
Margaret Bagshaw

The winter of 1947 at Wardlow. Norah Jackson holds her son George's hand, whilst the girl in front of her is her daughter Christine (who married Raymond Salt).

Margaret Bagshaw

GREAT AND LITTLE LONGSTONE

Lead mining and farming were the two occupations that formed the mainstay of the villagers' lives, but by the 1850's, lead mining had declined.

The resulting poverty and loss of jobs was softened a great deal by the arrival of the Midland Railway line from Derby to Manchester by 1862. Rowsley had been reached from Derby by June 4th 1849 but it would take another 13 years before the railway reached Great Longstone.

In the early 1860's, some of the villagers were able to help with the construction of the line, whilst others later worked for the railway company. Other jobs became available in the large houses and mansions built during the period for Manchester business men, who were now able to commute to the city each day.

By 1861 a third of the population of Little Longstone were railway navvies (60 out of 180), whilst in Great Longstone, a fifth of the inhabitants were working on the construction of the railway. Many navvies lodged with local families. Others lived in specially constructed huts with walls of timber planking and corrugated iron

Continued on page 77 ☛

Village cross, Great Longstone, c1900. Situated on the green, it is of great antiquity.
The village stocks were fixed in the most public spot near the foot of the steps to the cross.
However, around 1860, the stocks were removed from this site. Twice a year, cattle sales took place
near the cross and travelling hawkers were allowed to sell their wares.
Wright: Longstone Records

A view of the interior of Great Longstone Church before restoration 1872.
Wright: Longstone Records

A view of St Giles Church, Great Longstone from the north-east in 1873.
Wright: Longstone Records

Interior of Great Longstone Church in 1872, before restoration of 1873, when a vestry and organ chamber were added, and an organ introduced. The whole project cost £2,800.
Wright: Longstone Records

Great Longstone Church from the south-east in 1873.
Wright: Longstone Records

roofs such as the one at Monsal Head that today forms part of the cafe (in recent times the walls of timber planks have been altered). Another hut was to be found besides the viaduct in the dale, Irish navvies lived in three huts in Broad Roods on Ashford Lane, whilst in fields between the Croft and Barley Lees Farm, Great Longstone, were four huts housing other navvies.

Although lead mining had declined by 1850, it is interesting to find that by 1861 a few lead miners were to be found in Great Longstone. Some had been employed as tunnelers by the Midland Railway but it is also known that during the railway work being carried out, a vein of lead was discovered west of Great Longstone and the lead miners worked it.

Accounts in local newspapers show that the first train had arrived at Hassop Station on June 14th 1862 and the first passenger train, consisting of five carriages carrying 30 passengers, left Hassop Station for Great Longstone on August 1st 1862, with very little ceremony. In September 1862 the first special train arrived at Hassop from Matlock, conveying 180 Sunday School scholars on a church treat, bound for Monsal Head, where games were played and refreshments provided.

The line finally reached Buxton on May 30th 1863 and the line was opened. We find that on this occasion Great Longstone Station was splendidly decorated with bunting and greenery, whilst at Cressbrook Mill and in Monsal Dale large crowds gathered to welcome the directors' train with loud cheers.

Longstone Station was built in 1863, in a Tudor style, and included

Continued on page 81 ☛

Monsal Head c1920. The building on the right, nowadays Ray Lamb's café and craft centre, was originally built to house the navvies who helped construct the Midland railway line and viaduct. One can see that in 1920 the walls were still constructed from the original timber planks.

Ray Lamb's café and craft centre, Monsal Head, in 2007.
The timber panels have been faced with stone.
Keith Taylor

Monsal Dale in 1860, with the River Wye in full spate. At this stage, the viaduct, which was to drive the writer Ruskin to despair, had not been constructed. The stepping stones across the river were replaced by a footbridge in 1870.

The station staff await the arrival of a train at Longstone Station (for Ashford) c1905. By 1908, the stationmaster was Bernard Wilson.

J Duncan

*Railway accident at Great Longstone Hole Bridge,
involving a Midland Railway Company coal train, c1910.*
Lawrence Knighton

*Monsal Dale footbridge c1900. It was paid for by public subscription to allow those people living in
the dale to cross the river to get to Monsal Dale Station. Stepping stones had been used before.
It was built in 1870.*
Alastair Slack

accommodation for the Station Master. It was not until 1881 that the steps were built up to the road to provide safe access to the platform. The name of the station was changed to Great Longstone in 1913 and included the wording "For Ashford". The station served a catchment population of about 1300 from Ashford, the Longstones, scattered farms and nearby Thornbridge Hall. Monsal Dale Station was opened in 1866 and for those people living in the dale, the only way to it across the river was by stepping stones, difficult and dangerous in winter. The Midland Railway ignored the pleas for a bridge and so a footbridge was provided by public subscription in 1870 (Monsal Head Hotel, which goes back to before 1783, when it was called the Bull's Head, was rebuilt in 1887).

During the late 18th century and early years of the 19th century, the cotton industry played a small part in the life of Great Longstone. The cottages in Main Street and Victoria Terrace had been formerly warehouses and weaving shops and Longstone Lodge (sometimes known as "Mount Pleasant", "The Mount" or "The College") on Station Road (formerly Mill Lane), had been a carding mill. There is evidence of a horse capstan in the basement for powering the mill's machinery, since it was difficult to use water in this area of the limestone uplands.

The mill's creator was James Longsdon, a prosperous Great Longstone farmer, born in 1745, who, by the 1780's was on good terms with Sir Richard Arkwright, who had established nearby Cressbrook Mill.

In 1783, John Morewood of nearby Thornbridge Hall, went into partnership with James, who was involved in various textile ventures in Manchester and Russia. The Longstone Mill was built and included nine spinning jennies, with a total of 550 spindles driven by horse power, whilst there were 24 weaving looms, housed almost certainly in what is now a row of cottages on Victoria Terrace.

The Morewoods gave notice to quit the partnership in 1787, seeing its limitations.

The whole operation also included the outworkers in the Longstones and surrounding villages, together with a Manchester warehouse, exporting raw cotton and selling finished goods. By 1808 the business was struggling, though, and had ended sometime in the late 1820's.

The residence of the Longsdon family for nearly 800 years has been the Manor House, Little Longstone. It had been rebuilt, though on a small scale, by Thomas Longsdon in 1700 and was enlarged during the time of James, the cotton mill entrepreneur. When his business failed, it seemed that the house and estate would have to be sold but his son, William, arrived back from his prosperous business activities in America and the estate was saved for the family.

Longstone Hall, the seat of the Wright family, was an ancient mansion, one wing of which, dating from the 15th century, contains a room panelled in oak, with the arms of Wright carved in high relief over the mantlepiece (Walter Herbert Wright was in residence during the Great War).

Longstone School, between the White Lion Inn and the village cross, was erected

Continued on page 91 ☛

The grade two listed Manor House, Little Longstone, home of the Longsdon family for nearly 800 years. The house was substantially rebuilt on a smaller scale following a fire c1700. A large stone carving of the famly coat of arms forms an overmantel in one of the bedrooms.
Wright: Longstone Records

The brick built Great Longstone Hall, c1900, showing remnant of the medieval stone hall on the left.
Wright: Longstone Records

The Hall, Great Longstone, from the south-east c1900,
when George Thomas Wright was in residence.
Wright: Longstone Records

The Hall, Great Longstone c1900, at the time of George Thomas Wright.
Wright: Longstone Records

The Hall, Great Longstone from the west, c1900.
Wright: Longstone Records

Old barn at The Hall, Great Longstone c1900. The building has since been converted to dwellings.
Wright: Longstone Records

Longstone School 1888.
BACK ROW: *A. Lomas, H. Hancock. Arthur Ward, Fred Slack, Willie Eyre, Fred Nuttall, Teacher Mrs Parkin.* CENTRE ROW: *Polly Carrington, Alma Morton, Annie Hambleton, Mary Hamilton, Pamela Mullins.* FRONT ROW: *Nelly Blackwell, Florrie Lewis, Mary Blackwell, Lizzie Orr, Harriett Blagdon, Gertrude Morton.* SEATED: *William Lomas, William Hancock, Fred Morton, William Carrington.*
Sadly, Arthur Ward, Fred Slack and Fred Morton would all be killed during the Great War.
Wright: Longstone Records

Longstone School 1888
BACK ROW: *Tom Brightmore, Jem Parkin, George Wall, George Carson, J.T. Oldfield, Willie Orr, Headmaster Henry Arthur Spanton.* CENTRE ROW: *Goerge Lomas, T.G. Orr, Matthew Carson, Tom Morton, John H. Lomas.* FRONT ROW: *M.J. Hewitt, Fanny Hill, Mary Ann Carson, S.I. Timm, Sarah Wall, Ethel Hewitt, E. Morton, Alice Jupp, Pattie Timm.* SEATED: *Sam Morton, Matthew Morton, Arthur Eyre, William Jupp, Charles Brightmore, Henry Timm, Jem Morton.*
Wright: Longstone Records

Longstone School 1888.
BACK ROW: *Miss Hill, Percy Daubney, William Nadin, Harry Carrington, George Hill,*
Arthur Sellars, George Blackwell, Headmaster Henry Arthur Spanton. CENTRE ROW: *Charles Booth,*
Arthur Drabble, Tom Blackwell, Charles Hancock, Agnes Lewis, Clara Hewitt.
Front row: Lizzie Ward, Sarah Hancock, Ada Daubney, Ada Furniss, Annie Booth, Nora Eeley,
Amelia Doddemeade. SEATED: *Albert Blackham, Christopher Ward, H. Mullins, Tom Mullins.*
Wright: Longstone Records

Great Longstone cross and old cottages, prior to the rebuilding of the infant school in 1877.
The School was erected around 1787, rebuilt in 1832 and again in 1862, when a new school was
built on the site of the former and extended. An infant section was completed in 1877.
Thornhill: Further Longstone Records

Longstone School Cricket Club 1893.
BACK ROW: *Willie Orr, Sam Morton, C. Booth, Mr. Spanton, W. Maltby, Ben Hambleton,*
Albert Wager, G. Blackwell, T. Blackwell. FRONT ROW: *Fred Slack, Willie Nadin,*
Charles Brightmore, George Hill, Christopher Ward.
Wright: Longstone Records

Longstone School, with headmaster Mr. Spanton, at the village cross, August 1894.
Wright: Longstone Records

Longstone School at the village cross on Empire Day 1904. It was a British imperial celebration held annually on May 24th, the anniversary of Queen Victoria's birthday. The schoolchildren had special lessons on the Empire, sang patriotic songs and marched through Little Longstone to Monsal Head and back. We can see that the cross is entwined with garlands. In 1900, during the Boer War, the school - children marched to the village cross where they sang patriotic songs and gave three cheers for the generals at the front, when news was received of the relief of Ladysmith. Headmaster, Henry Arthur Spanton, is to the left of the flag, whilst Miss Ella Southgate, in the hat, is to the right of the photograph.
Wright: Longstone Records

Great Longstone School, 1930's.
BACK ROW: *Gerald Hurst, Charles Oldfield, James Shimwell, Derek Tompkins, Eric Bacon, Eric Robinson.* CENTRE ROW: *X, Katherine Blagden, Elsie Waring, Alice Johnson, Edna Unsworth, Alice Knight, Molly Gregory, Frank Garrett.* FRONT ROW: *Pat Waring, Mary Wallwyn, Cathy Sales, Betty Shimwell, Mabel Smith, Betty Sims, Noel Green.*
Noel Green

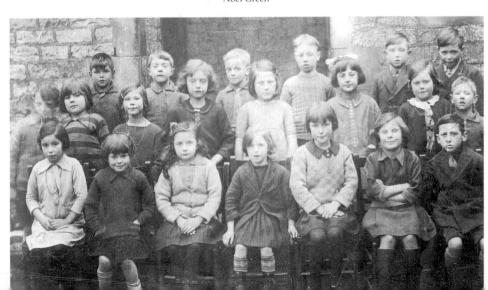

Great Longstone School 1933.
BACK ROW: *Frank Ward, Eddy Bennett, Tom Rangley, George Parker, Richard Gregory, Eddy Roberts,
George Salisbury.* THIRD ROW: *Ernest Hamilton, Eileen Smith, Betty Upton, Primrose Attewell,
Molly Gregory, Dorothy Herrington, Ellis Turner.* SECOND ROW: *Alice Knight, Edna Unsworth,
Pat Waring, Betty Sims, Elsie Waring, Mabel Smith, Alice Bacon, Kathleen Blagden.*
FRONT ROW: *Philip Horne, Ben Shimwell, Derek Tompkins, Ray Croft, Gerald Hurst,
Ernest Hambleton.* TEACHERS: *Headmaster Percy Buggins, Miss Charlesworth, Miss Bramwell.
Ernest Hamilton would be killed whilst flying with Bomber-Command during the Second World War.*
Longstone Local History Group, courtesy of Derbyshire Records Office

Great Longstone School 1938.
BACK ROW: *Adeline Hurst, Roy Finney, Arnold Turner, Harry Johnson, George Jones,
Gerald Brassington, Annie Holmes.* FRONT ROW: *Mary Furness, Muriel Thorpe, Stella Mary Knight,
Maureen Sales, Joan Gilbert, Audrey Unsworth.*
Olive Mead

Great Longstone School September/October 1939.
BACK ROW: *Martin Oliver, Geoffrey Adams, Leonard Berrisford, Bill Bennett, X, X (could be two evacuees?)* CENTRE ROW: *Sheila Hurst, Audrey Turner.* FRONT ROW: *Joan Barnes, Margaret Gilbert, Kathleen Blower, Mary Johnson, Margaret Furniss, Betty Udale, Mollie Skidmore.*
Peter Johnson

Members of the Inkerman Lodge, Oddfellows Friendly Society, outside the White Lion Inn, Great Longstone c1900. On Hospital Sunday they paraded around the parish behind the hired band, rais-ing money. Six members of the Lodge were killed during the Great War.
Longstone Local History Group, courtesy of Derbyshire Records Office

around 1787, was rebuilt in 1832 and in 1862 a new and larger school was built on the site of the former, with an infant section completed in 1877. The school also catered for the needs of Little Longstone pupils. Meanwhile, at the hamlet of Rowland, in Great Longstone parish, a Public Elementary School had been built by subscription in 1862 at a cost of £450, and was enlarged in 1876. The teachers during the Great War were Mrs. Lily Coath, headmistress, Miss. Florence Henshaw, assistant mistress and Miss. Winifred Beavon, the infant mistress.

There were many ale houses and public inns in Great Longstone in earlier times. One of these inns was the White Lion and it was there that the Inkerman Lodge of the Oddfellows Society met. The Oddfellows raised funds for local hospitals, to provide money to members who were injured or ill and so out of work, to provide money to pay for visits by the doctor and to pay for stays in hospital.

The Inkerman Lodge was founded in the village on November 10th 1855 by 28 men. It was named after the military victory at Inkerman, in the Crimean War, on November 5th 1855. Its first Secretary was Charles Morton. Thirteen men from the village would eventually be named on the war memorial for the Great War and six of them would be members of the Inkerman Lodge, including Fred and Arthur Morton, relations of the Lodge's first Secretary.

A Great Longstone serviceman who thankfully survived the horrors of the Great War was able to return home to the village and develop his earlier passion in breeding poultry, resulting in the building of a business that provided many jobs for locals and outsiders for many years to come.

JOHN THORNHILL AND SONS,
POULTRY FARM, EGG PACKING STATION AND POULTRY MEAT DISTRIBUTORS

The Thornhills were a farming family based at Beech House, Great Longstone, and John Thornhill took an early interest in the breeding of poultry. By 1912, poultry was a mainstay of the farm, but John had to take a break from this work when he went off to fight in the Great War 1914-1918, as a member of the Royal Field Artillery.

On his return to Beech House in 1919 the poultry business gradually developed under his guidance. A major turning point came in 1929 when the Ministry of Agriculture granted John Thornhill a licence for eggs to be packed under the new National Mark Egg Scheme and the farm became the first Derbyshire Egg Grading and Packing Station in a barn attached to Beech House.

Millions of eggs a year were collected, graded, packed and marketed. Every egg was examined by an expert "candler", using a light to grade for quality. By 1936 the Egg Station was providing 15 or 30-dozen size, lidded egg boxes, delivered each week by the Thornhill's motor van to each farm, which were collected fully laden seven days later (at the start of the Second World War the National Mark came to an end when the newly formed British Egg Marketing Board introduced the little "Lion" symbol, to be stamped on each egg).

John Thornhill kept over 10,000 hens himself (mainly Rhode Island Reds) in

John Thornhill in the orchard of Beech House, Great Longstone, c1918. Showing a great interest in poultry breeding from childhood, he became the founder of J. Thornhill's poultry business in the village.
Peter Thornhill

John Thornhill, founder of the poultry farm, egg packing station and slaughterhouse at Great Longstone.
Peter Thornhill

poultry houses and runs, to produce their own eggs, whilst pedigree hens were produced for selling to other breeders. Eggs were collected from farms all over Derbyshire, as far afield as south of Ashbourne. Competition came from R. Orme and Co's own egg packing station in Bakewell and from another station in Chesterfield.

Other developments took place in the 1920's and 30's with the selling of both grit and live chicks. Fine quality grit, which was sold to other poultry farmers, came from Longcliffe Quarry, near Brassington. It was rich in calcium and helped to produce a hard egg shell.

Day old chicks were produced in

incubators at Beech House and sold on to poultry farmers and breeders. The incubator, heated by means of a boiler, had a capacity of 12,000 eggs (chicks). Second World War production dropped a little because of a shortage in chicken feed, although land on the farm was ploughed up to grow their own corn.

The end of the war saw an increase in the size of the transport fleet, with the purchase of a number of army-surplus lorries.

In 1952, a new purpose-built egg packing station was built on Beech House land. However, throughout the 1950's, the production of eggs began to decline in importance and by the mid 1950's the firm developed the production of birds for the table. A slaughterhouse was built onto the factory to process the birds.

Live old laying hens, which were of no use to local farmers, were first brought in from outlying farms, but then broilers, bred specially for the table, were brought from specialist broiler sites from Shropshire and elsewhere. Egg production ceased and these workers joined the workforce employed in the processing of poultry meat.

By the late 1970's, approximately 450 workers were employed on the site near Beech House and many had to be brought to work in a small fleet of buses belonging to the firm, from as far afield as Chesterfield, Buxton and the Matlock district. The birds produced for the table were sold in many places across the country, including on John Thornhill and Sons own stalls on Smithfield Market, London and elsewhere.

The Company, which had come into the ownership of the Vestey empire in the early 1980's, eventually closed around 1986.

Continued on page 100 ☞

Chicken houses on John Thornhill's poultry farm 1922. They had been built by Bakewell joiner and undertaker Messrs. J.W. and J. Mettam for the farm.
Peter Thornhill

Chicken houses on the poultry farm belonging to John Thornhill of Great Longstone 1922.
Peter Thornhill

*Free range hens on John Thornhill's poultry farm, Great Longstone, produced eggs
for his 'National Mark' egg packing station.*
Peter Thornhill

Another development at John Thornhill's poultry farm, Great Longstone, was the selling of day-old chicks to poultry farmers and breeders.

Peter Thornhill

The selling of grit to poultry farmers developed as another branch of John Thornhill's poultry business during the late 1920's.

Peter Thornhill

Longcliffe Quarry, near Brassington c1932. John Thornhill came here to buy the grit which he sold to poultry farmers. The grit was of a very high calcium content and when fed to the birds, helped them to produce a hard shell.

Peter Thornhill

The first Derbyshire Egg Grading and Packing Station, under the National Mark Egg Scheme, was opened at John Thornhill's poultry farm, Great Longstone, in 1929. Bill Bowers drove the first vehicle used for transportation of the eggs.
Peter Thornhill

Baskets of birds from John Thornhill's poultry farm waiting to be despatched by rail from Great Longstone Station for display at poultry shows, 1930's.
Peter Thornhill

Workers Bill Bowers (driving) and Arthur Slater delivering eggs in March 1940.
Notice the covered headlamps, due to the 'blackout' during the war.
Peter Thornhill

'Candling', grading for weight and packing at the 'National Mark' egg packing station
of John Thornhill, Great Longstone, in December 1931.
Peter Thornhill

Candling, grading for weight and packing at John Thornhill's egg packing factory, Great Longstone, December 1951. Candling (placing the egg under the glare of the light helped the workers pick out blood spots, rotten eggs and fertilised eggs.
LEFT TO RIGHT: *Annie Garratt, Iris Casey, Margaret Mansfield, Gertrude Simpson, Mary Ward.*
Peter Thornhill

John Thornhill and Sons egg packing factory at Great Longstone.
Peter Thornhill

J. Thornhill and Sons transportation fleet at their egg packing factory, Great Longstone,
June 6th 1950. A nmber of the lorries were former Second World War army vehicles.
Peter Thornhill

J. Thornhill and Sons transportation fleet, Great Longstone, 1980's.
These vehicles were used to bring live birds to the slaughterhouse.
Peter Thornhill

Another section of the transport fleet belonging to J. Thornhill and Sons, Great Longstone, 1980's.
These vehicles distributed the meat and poultry products nationwide. With a workforce of 450,
the company also had a small fleet of buses to bring in the workers from outlying areas such as
Chesterfield, etc.
Peter Thornhill

In the late 1930's, another Longstone entrepreneur, though on a smaller scale, was Herbert Charles Gilbert, who founded the ice cream "factory" of **Peak Ices** at Little Longstone.

During the inter-war years of the 1920's and 30's there were quite a few shops in Great Longstone, including that of Edward Lewis Birkhead (known as "Neddy" to

Herbert C. Gilbert of Peak Ices, Little Longstone.
Noel Green

many Longstone inhabitants). Situated on the left side entrance to Station Road, the shopkeeper also sold fish and chips on certain evenings, cooked in an out-building. He also made and sold ice cream. Neddy Birkhead pushed a hand trolley, filled with ice cream, along the road to Monsal Head and stood with it under a veranda of the Monsal Head Hotel, selling it to parties of people who arrived at the beauty spot on charabanc trips.

In 1938 he gave this business up and Herbert Charles Gilbert took over, with the help of his wife, Beatrice. They lived at Little Longstone in a small cottage called Ivydene and Herbert had worked previously on the Midland Railway as a plate layer.

They had their ice cream "factory" in an

outbuilding at the back of their cottage and set up in business as "Peak Ices". They rented sites at Monsal Head, Bakewell Market and Recreation Ground and delivered to Baslow and Rowsley. They even delivered ice cream to Leek Cinema.

During the war years, 1939-1945, they delivered ice cream around the Bakewell district by horse and cart because of a lack of petrol due to rationing.

Herbert Gilbert died in 1958 and his wife Beatrice carried on the business with the help of her daughter, Joan Pennington, and her son-in-law, Ron Pennington, until 1984. For the next two years, Joan and Ron ran the business until selling it to Mr. Mantle in 1986.

Herbert Charles Gilbert and his wife Beatrice of Little Longstone, with their ice-cream van at Monsal Head in 1939. Herbert was the founder of Peak Ices of Little Longstone.
John and Joan Pennington

Herbert C. Gilbert, owner of Peak Ices of Little Longstone on the back of his ice cream cart in wartime Bakewell, Boxing Day 1944. Petrol rationing was still operating.
John and Joan Pennington

Ron Pennington and his mother in the early 1980's.
John and Joan Pennington

Little Longstone club and reading room. The Institute is the second building from the left (now an open space), between Parva and Christmas Cottages. Note the ice cream vans belonging to Peak Ices, one in the piufold and another in front of the factory, lower far right.
Michael Stuart

The village cross, Great Longstone, c1900, looking towards Station Road. The shop on the left was originally an ale house known as the 'Miners' Arms' in the days of the lead miners (at one time, the village had numerous pubs and ale houses). In the 1930's the shopkeeper was Edward Lewis Birkhead, who, amongst other items, sold home-made ice cream and fish and chips.
Wright: Longstone Records

Village children at 'The Mires', at the entrance to Great Longstone, c1900. The house on the extreme left is The Willows.
Wright: Longstone Records

Village green and main street, Great Longstone, c1900.
Wright: Longstone Records

Village green and cross in Great Longstone, c1900.
Wright: Longstone Records

Village green and cross in Great Longstone, c1905.
Ian Cox

Village cross in foreground, with the war memorial in the middle distance, Great Longstone, c1925.
Ian Cox

Joshua Oliver, the Longstone butcher, stands with his wife Alice and daughter Laura
(later Laura Johnson) outside the butcher's shop, Great Longstone in 1908.
The shop was erected in 1906/1907. He had been born in Great Longstone, was apprenticed to a
Levenshulme butcher, and returned to the village.
Fred Mellor

The Great Longstone butcher, Joshua Oliver, stands in the doorway of his shop c1909.
Fred Mellor

Mr. A.W.J. Eyre, on the extreme left, with Mrs. Eyre and their two children, together with the groom, Joseph Hamilton. They stand in front of their house, The Elms, Great Longstone (the avenue of elms was cut down in 1973 due to disease and replaced with chestnut trees). The Elms is nowadays called Church Lady House (the abode of Roy Hattersley).
Mr. Eyre was a local builder and Chairman of the Parish Council in 1914. He gave £100 in Government Bonds c1922, for the upkeep of the village war memorial (today this provides £3.60 annually towards its upkeep).
Fred Mellor

The village blacksmith, Great Longstone, c1900. The Forge House was lived in and the smithy worked by Joseph and Isaac Bennett. Note the thatched roof. The cottage, later demolished, was formerly the residence of the family of Miss Furness of The Croft.
Wright: Longstone Records

Main Street, Great Longstone, c1948. The milk churns await collection for their journey to the dairy. The shop on the right was the grocery shop of Mr. Mansfield, who was also the choir master at Ashford and Great Longstone Churches.

Alastair Slack

The service bus belonging to North Western Bus Company arrives on Main Street, Great Longstone. c1948. Mr. Mansfield's grocery shop is on the left, next to the two people walking along the pavement. In earlier days McKay's bus, driven by Ted Jordan, passed through the village and later, Ted drove for North Western.

Alastair Slack

In April 1923 Constable Thomas Dennis of Great Longstone retired after 28 years in the service of Derbyshire Constabulary, eight of these years spent on the beat in Longstone.
During the Great War, we are told in Maria Gyte's diaries that he helped in Ashford and Sheldon when their policeman joined the army.

Mrs. Goodwin's Choir (ladies section) Great Longstone 1949/1950.
BACK ROW: Maureen Sales, Joan Smith, Mary Johnson, Mary Ward, Nellie Herrington, Betty Cox, Sylvia Frankland, Janet Frankland, Olive Knight. CENTRE ROW: Joclynn Wall, Vera Bingham, Muriel Nicholson, Mrs. Bramwell, May Nicholson, Nancy Frankland, Madge Griffith, Sally (Sarah) Ward, X. FRONT ROW: Mrs. G. Sims, Margaret Thorpe, Ethel Berresford, Mrs. Goodwin, Miss Walton, Elsie Wood, Mrs. H. Shaw.
Peter Johnson

Two cottages at Bullfinch Square, Great Longstone, c1930, just before they were demolished.
Laura Johnson (nee Oliver) holds her daughter, Mary.
Peter Johnson

The Packhorse Inn, Little Longstone, c1900.
Michael Stuart

The Outrake, Little Longstone, in the early 20th century. The Outrake was owned and occupied by the Longsdon family as a 'dower house', for older members of the family when younger ones took over at the Manor House. It was also used by friends, such as the Morewoods and relatives, the Shaw family, who purchased it in 1870.

Michael Stuart

The village stocks still remained in Little Longstone in 1906 and can still be seen today. The house in the background was known as Fynney Cottage in Victorian times but is nowadays called The Stocks, and is the oldest house in the village.

Wright: Longstone Records

Cressbrook Mill in Monsal Dale, just over the parish boundary from Little Longstone. During the 1780's Richard Arkwright built a mill with a dam across the Cress Brook to allow for water power. A dam was built to provide a lake in Water-Cum-Jolly and then in 1814 the 'big mill', with its bell tower was built by William Newton, allowing water from the River Wye to be used. Cottages had been built in Ravensdale to accommodate the workers. McConnel and Company of Manchester bought the mill in 1835, building Cressbrook Hall and many homes in the village, and a school was provided in 1878. Cressbrook's sister mill at Litton, a mile upstream, became notorious for the ill-treatment of its young apprentices, but Cressbrook Mill's reputation was somewhat better.
John Douglas

Cressbrook Mill today. By the year 2007, the facade has been restored and the inside of the mill converted into apartments.
Keith Taylor

Little Longstone Congregational Chapel. When the Reverend Malkin Mills, the popular vicar at St. Giles, Great Longstone, moved on, his successor was extremely unpopular. His leanings towards the Oxford Movemnet resulted in some of the congregation, who did not want to 'go over to Rome', becoming Congregationalists. Initially they used the Baptist Chapel on Ashford Lane, but in June 1844 the foundation stone of the Little Longstone Congregational Chapel was laid by James Longsdon.The two war memorial plaques are found inside the entrance porch.

Keith Taylor

Castle Cliffe Guest House, Monsal Head c1930's.

Peter Johnson

Cliffe House (now named Ruskin's), near Monsal Head, during the inter-war years.
Andrew Lomas

One of the old industries of Little Longstone was basket making. Henry Nuttall, the late Dorothy Adamson's father, had a workshop behind Sunnyside. He was a basket maker for a number of cotton mills, including Cressbrook, Litton and Belper. He gave up the work because his customers did not pay their bills on time!
Michael Stuart

HASSOP

By 1914, Hassop Hall was the seat of Charles Stephen Leslie, D.L., J.P. The mansion was begun in the reign of Henry VIII and completed in that of Queen Elizabeth. The property had been confiscated by Oliver Cromwell, at the end of the Civil War, because it had been garrisoned for Charles I by Colonel Anthony Eyre in December 1643. It was, however, subsequently restored to the Eyre family.

The present stone front (south) was built, together with various other alterations, by Thomas Eyre, during the period 1827-1833. Before the start of the Second World War, Lieutenant Colonel Sir Henry Kenyon Stephenson was lord of the manor.

Near the entrance to the Hall is a Catholic church, dedicated to All Saints in the Grecian style, built between 1816 and 1818 by Anthony James, 4th Earl of Newburgh. The Roman Catholic architect was Joseph Ireland and was built as a private chapel for the Eyre family. The building is a Classical Revival temple with an impressive pillared portico in the Etruscan style and a barrel vaulted interior with a covered coffered ceiling. In the back gallery is a gem of a chamber organ by H.C. Lincoln dating from the 1820's. Above the altar is a valuable painting of the "Crucifixion" attributed to Luigi Caracci. The church was thoroughly restored in 1886 and by 1914 the priest in charge was the Reverend Patrick Quilter.

Hassop Hall in the 1960's, before it became a hotel/restaurant. The present stone front (south) was built 1827-1833.

A Catholic Public Elementary School at Hassop was erected in 1859 for 100 children, the average attendance in 1918 being 24, taught by the mistress, Miss Emily Dykes. In the past the children had been taught by the nuns of the Sisterhood of Peace.

During the war years, 1914-1918, the sub-postmaster and shop keeper at the Dower House, Hassop, was George Kilpin, whilst at nearby Hassop Station, the Station Master was Frederick Bent, who was replaced by William Horace Hough by 1918.

The station was built at the insistence of the Duke of Devonshire and opened to passenger traffic in August 1862 (Monsal Head Viaduct had been built in limestone in 1862. The 100 yard structure began to show signs of movement that required its southernmost arch to be rebuilt in 1893, with further superficial repairs dealt with in 1908.

Hassop Station never had great success in its passenger traffic but fared much better in terms of freight traffic, serving Baslow, Calver, Ashford, Hassop, as well as Great and Little Longstone.

Livestock traffic, as well as mineral traffic was plentiful, with coal also being brought in for the Baslow Gas Light and Coke Company, opened in 1870. Raw cotton also came in for Calver Mill, which continued spinning cotton until the 1920's. The Ashford firm of Frank Cox-Wilson and Son, timber merchants and builders, also brought in materials by rail (a number of this firm's employees were killed during the Great War), whilst large quantities of spar and other minerals arrived from Longstone Edge.

The Chatsworth Hotel at Edensor (now the Edensor Institute) became a convalescent hospital during the Great War 1914-1918. Hassop Station was used as a transfer point by the Royal Army Medical Corps. Photographs show RAMC personnel preparing to leave the station for Edensor, with their horses and equipment, after arriving by special train.

The Roman Catholic Church of All Saints, at Hassop, built in the Grecian style 1816-1818.
Keith Taylor

All Saints Roman Catholic School, Hassop, c1917. Mrs. M.P. Kirwan (nee Kennedy) is first on left, second row. Philip Kennedy is second on left in front row. The group includes three sisters, Cissie, Alice and Bela Widdowson. The boy in the front row, third from the left, is Billy Bromley.
Derbyshire County Council, Libraries and Heritage

The Dower House, Hassop in 2007. In the past, the bay on the right served as Hassop Post Office.
Keith Taylor

A Midland Railway passenger locomotive passes over the viaduct at Monsal Dale, c1905.
Ian Cox

OVER HADDON

The village is located on a ledge, high above the beautiful Lathkill Dale. Rising in a cave near the top of the dale, the river, containing some of the purest water in the country, disappears underground in its upper reaches before displaying its full beauty as it widens out below Over Haddon.

It was not its beautiful setting, however, that resulted in the settlement becoming established, but the presence of lead. There is evidence that the Romans found lead in Lathkill Dale and one of the earliest recorded lead mines in Derbyshire was Mandale Mine. Large quantities of lead was produced and it is interesting to recall that a former public house on the site of the present Lathkill Hotel was called the Miner's Arms. Lathkilldale Lead Mine opened in 1763 and was worked until 1842. The water wheel used in this mine was the second largest in the country.

However, as the lead mining industry declined, together with the population of the village, its inhabitants came to rely mainly on farming for a living. Hopes were raised and then dashed in 1854 when a mini-gold rush began when gold was discovered in one of the lead mines. Over Haddon was besieged with bounty hunters and hundreds of people invested money in a company that was set up. Unfortunately, the company collapsed with the news that the gold was in small quantities and buried deep, resulting in the investors losing all their money.

St. Anne's Church, a chapel of ease, had been erected in 1880, whilst a Wesleyan Reform Chapel had been built in 1861. One year earlier, in 1860, the Public

Elementary School had opened for Over Haddon pupils and was enlarged in 1894 to hold 45 children, with the average attendance in 1908 being 28.

Earl Cowper had a reservoir erected on the New Close Farm, which was supplied with water pumped by machinery from the River Lathkill, to supply the inhabitants of this upland area, who in times of drought, suffered badly. The overflow from the reservoir was conducted by pipes to supply the village.

Street scene at Over Haddon in the late 1920's. The tea van makes a delivery.
Tony Holmes

Main Street, Over Haddon.
Carolyn Pearce

Main Street, Over Haddon.
Carolyn Pearce

The Post Office, Over Haddon.
Carolyn Pearce

Jack Blackwell near Lathkill Farm, Over Haddon, c1930's.
Carolyn Pearce

Manor Farm, Over Haddon, c1920's. Part of it dates back to around 1550. It was originally the farm for the actual Manor House, which was eventually demolished.
Carolyn Pearce

An aerial view of Manor Farm, Over Haddon, and surrounding area, taken c1950.
Carolyn Pearce

New Close Farm, Over Haddon, was built c1848, of stone that came from the demolished Manor House. The farm was run by the Wildgoose family until the 1920's, by the Lytle family until 1940, and then the Pearce family.
Carolyn Pearce

Horse ploughing, Over Haddon.
Carolyn Pearce

Over Haddon School, c1928.
BACK ROW: *Teacher Alice Calladine, Doug Glossop, George Nuttall, Frank Marsden, Reg Cowley, Tom Holmes, X, X, George Richardson, Headmistress Mrs. Hill.* THIRD ROW: *X, Joffre Nuttall, Bill Hayto, Graham Moss, Ernest Wright, Bill Holmes, George Coates, Ivan Marsden.*
SECOND ROW: *X, Flo Cawley, Marjorie Holmes, Doris Wildgoose, Margaret Oldfield.*
FRONT ROW: *Ken Prime, Joe Oldfield, Renée Oldfield, Mary Holmes, Sylvia Tomlinson, Amy Holmes, Sadie Oldfield, Freddie Hambleton, Hilda Armitt.*
Carolyn Pearce

St. Anne's Day parade through Lathkill Dale, Over Haddon. It was the Patronal Festival, the feast day of the saint to whom the church was dedicated.
Carolyn Pearce

ASHFORD IN THE WATER

Situated on the River Wye, the majority of Ashford's cottages and houses are of 18th century origin and owe a great deal to the period when the village prospered from its association with lead mining, Ashford being a centre up until the mid 19th century (its population in 1795 was 545, whilst by 1850 it was 950).

It was with another mineral, however, that Ashford's name is remembered. Ashford black marble is an impure form of limestone naturally impregnated with a bitumen. When polished, it changed its colour from grey to a glossy black and became popular as a decorative material. In 1580, Bess of Hardwick used Ashford marble for the chimney piece of the Great High Presence Chamber at the Hall, whilst in the mid 1830's the 6th Duke of Devonshire came to Ashford when he required massive marble doorways for his new wing at Chatsworth.

In 1748, Henry Watson set up a marble mill on the Wye near Ashford (a memorial to him in Ashford marble can be seen in the church near the main door). By the mid 19th century the massive wooden machinery in the mill was being driven by powerful waterwheels, whilst just across the river, beside the road to Sheldon, was Arrock Quarry, the main source of black marble. The blocks of stone were removed across the river to be sawn to size, ground and polished in the mill complex.

The Ashford Marble Works, just outside the village, on the road towards Taddington.
Black Ashford marble was mined from nearby Kirk Dale and Rookery Wood.
Tony Holmes

Inlay work was introduced and demand soared, for the glowing geometric and floral designs proved to be highly successful, especially after they had been shown at the Great Exhibition of 1851. Inlay work was mainly carried out by homeworkers in Ashford. Coloured minerals were used in the process from different localities close to Ashford. Rosewood marble came from Nettler Dale at Sheldon and Bird's Eye from Wetton and Sheldon.

By 1900, Ashford Marble Mill had replaced its water wheels with turbines but the industry had peaked, resulting in the mill closing in 1905, although inlay work was carried on for a few more years until the reserves of marble were used up.

In earlier times, another industry that existed in the village was that of candle making. The "Candle House" in Greaves Lane, stands on the site of the candle factory (greaves was the name given to dregs of melted tallow). Derived mainly from beef and mutton suet, the fat was "rendered" or separated by steaming under pressure in large vats. The top layer was drawn off and allowed to solidify. The smell emanating from this establishment would have been most unpleasant. Anything left over was often fed to the local pigs. The twisted, spun cotton wicks were hung from metre long horizontal rods and dipped into the tanks of mutton tallow for a few seconds and then lifted out. Solidification could then take place, the whole process being repeated many times to get the correct thickness of candle.

Continued on page 129 ☛

The shop on Church Street, Ashford in the Water, c1902 (nowadays Ibbotson's and affectionately known as 'Harrods of Ashford'). The house on the extreme right was the village forge and the one to its left had been a candle factory.

Ken Ibbotson

Holy Trinity Church, Ashford, is only one of a few to retain maiden's funeral garlands. They were carried before the coffins of young unmarried girls by a girl of a similar age as the deceased. Also known as crowns or crants, they were made of white paper cut to form rosettes and fixed to a wooden frame. A glove or handkerchief was hung from the centre.

The sheepwash, Ashford. The thatched cottages of Fennel Street are in the background.
The Peak of Derbyshire: Its Scenery & Antiquities by John Leyland 1891

The sheepwash bridge, Ashford. This was originally a packhorse bridge. In earlier days, when sheep were brought from Ashford, Sheldon and Longstone farms to be washed before shearing, it was known for lambs to be placed in a walled pen and for the ewes on the other side to swim across.

The sheepwash, Ashford. The Middleton's cottage on the left was demolished for the new A6 road.
Jean Blackwell

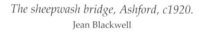

The sheepwash bridge, Ashford, c1920.
Jean Blackwell

George Daybell driving his cart over the sheepwash bridge, Ashford.
Jean Blackwell

Part of the tower of the Church of Holy Trinity dates back to the 13th century, whilst the north arcade is from the 14th century, but most of the church is in the Decorated Style, after its restoration between 1867 and 1870. At the time of the Great War, the Curfew Bell was still rung, as well as the pancake bell, rung at 11a.m. on Shrove Tuesday.

Ashford's close connection to farming is illustrated by the siting of the sheep wash bridge over the River Wye. It was originally a packhorse bridge, but eventually sheep were washed here prior to shearing. It catered for the needs of farmers from other parishes, besides those from Ashford. Sheldon farmers always drove their sheep from their uplands farms. Often, the lambs were penned within the stone-walled pen on one side of the river, whilst the mothers were put in the river on the other side, resulting in them receiving a soaking as they swam across to their young.

Fine large houses are to be found within the parish. Ashford Hall was built in 1785 to a design by Joseph Pickford, Churchdale Hall was founded in 1336, whilst The Rookery, set in splendid grounds through which the River Wye flows in a loop, has its origins in the 16th century. Some distance away, but still within the parish is Thornbridge Hall.

Thornbridge Hall in its original style was built in 1790 as part of the Longsdon Estate and was for a time the home of the Morewood family, who were in partnership with James Longsdon in his cotton enterprise. However, alterations began just after 1871, and especially between 1897 and 1918, under its owner, George Jobson

The Rookery, Ashford, in June 2007.
Keith Taylor

Marples, son of a Sheffield businessman.

He was a director of the Midland Railway and built "Woodlands" in 1903-1904, behind the down platform at Longstone Station, with waiting rooms on the ground floor and a huge recreation room for domestic staff and estate workers on the first floor.

Marples lost a great deal of his money in the First World War and immediately afterwards because he had a large shareholding in Krupps of Essen, the armaments and steel works in Germany, and was forced to turn "Woodlands" into flats, renting them out to help run the Thornbridge Estate.

G.J. Marples died a bachelor in 1929, bequeathing his estate to his mistress, Miss Dorothy Green, on condition that she change her name to Marples and never married. She quickly sold the estate to Charles Boot, and retired to Eastbourne.

Charles Boot, a Sheffield builder, won many demolition contracts. In doing so he gained valuable items for his new home. He bought panelling from Derwent Hall when the Derwent Dams were being constructed. Marble columns and fireplaces came out of Clumber Park, as well as balustrades and statuary from the gardens. The buffet fountain was bought from Chatsworth for £15 (in 1946 Sheffield City Council purchased the buildings and developed them as a teacher training college, but at the time of writing, the premises are once again being used as a private residence).

A view of Thornbridge Hall in 1871. From the 12th to the late 18th century, it was a seat of the Longsdon family. The Morewood family who lived there between 1790 and 1859, enlarged the house. In 1859 Frederick Craven rebuilt the house in Jacobean style and installed the William Morris/Burne-Jones window in the Great Hall. In 1896, George Marples (Sheffield business man and lawyer), enlarged the house to nearly its present form, built lodges and cottages, landscaped the park and gardens, added his own private railway station, and acquired the Watson buffet fountain from Chatsworth. Charles Boot (Sheffield entrepreneur), bought the Hall in 1929, added items from Clumber Park and panelling from Derwent Hall.
Alastair Slack

Thornbridge Hall, after rebuilding by Frederick Craven in the Jacobean style.
Alastair Slack

The stables at Thornbridge Hall.
Alastair Slack

Charles Boot with his mother and wife in the grounds of Thornbridge Hall, c1930's.
Alastair Slack

Charles Boot and wife with one of the brass bands he was so fond of,
in the grounds of Thornbridge Hall, 1930's.
Alastair Slack

The staircase, Thornbridge Hall, during the time of Marples.
Alastair Slack

The outer hall, Thornbridge Hall, during the time of Marples.
Alastair Slack

The central hall, Thornbridge Hall, during the time of Marples.
Alastair Slack

The billiards room, Thornbridge Hall, during the time of Marples.
Alastair Slack

The morning room, Thornbridge Hall, during the time of Marples.
Alastair Slack

The Winter Garden, Thornbridge Hall, during the time of Marples.
Alastair Slack

The Gardener's cottage, Thornbridge Hall, during the time of Marples.
Alastair Slack

Carters employed at Thornbridge Hall whilst putting in a new boiler for Mr. Marples, c1890's.
Alastair Slack

The gardeners at Thornbridge Hall in the 1930's.
STANDING LEFT TO RIGHT: *John Morrison (head gardener), Percy Barker (second in charge), Dick Hurst, George Croft, Bob Spalding, Ted King, Mr. Childs.* SEATED: *Charlie Elliott, Herny Ward ('Whiffty'), Billy Elliott (estate office).*
Sadly, Dick Hurst would be killed whilst fighting for his country in Normandy, 1944.
Noel Green

Hill Cross, Ashford. Returning to his home in Hill Cross after visiting the pump in Greaves Lane. Note the barrels placed to collect rain water, which would be used for washing purposes.
Derbyshire County Council, Local Studies Library

Ashford. The parish pump and the Top Pump are to be found at opposite ends of Fennel Street. The pumps have been removed and a shelter was erected over both wells in 1881.
Ian Cox

The pump, Bridge House, and the sheepwash bridge, Ashford, c1920's.
Jean Blackwell

*The old Ashford Post Office c1900, still with it's thatched roof.
The building was dramatically altered in the 1920's.*
Caryl Heath

A coach party outside the new Ashford Post Office, adjacent to the Devonshire Arms (now the Ashford Arms) c1925. They are dressed up for some special occasion. The old thatched post office had been converted into the building shown here. The Ashford Arms was an important coaching inn with Royal Mail, Lord Nelson and Peveril of the Peak coaches stopping to change horses. Originally called the Stag's Head, it changed its name to the Devonshire Arms before reverting back to the Ashford Arms.

Tony Holmes

A church feast day procession files past the Top Pump in Ashford, c1905.

Tony Holmes

Ashford School c1930.
BACK ROW: *Jack Halewood, Eric Dalton, Ronnie Bright, Fred James, Gordon Mosely,*
Colin Sharman, Walter Hallows. THIRD ROW: *Eileen Pickering, Ada Bond, Betty Upton,*
Betty Carter, Dorothy Thorpe, Ivy Noton, Frank ? SECOND ROW: *Fred Garrett, Nellie Goldstraw,*
Evelyn Sheldon, Hilda Barnes, Nancy Johnson, Peggy Raper, Ethel Hawley.
FRONT ROW: *Norman Garrett, Jasper Johnson, Sam Foxlow, Philip Doxey, Tom Carter.*
Mrs. Bendell

Scene on a farm in the Ashford/Longstone area c1920's.
Peter Johnson

Stacking stooks in the fields on a farm in the Ashford/Longstone area, c1920's.
Peter Johnson

*Thatched hay ricks to the left and hay stacks to the right at Ashford's Long Roods Farm,
near Monsal Head, c1910.*
David Neal

Isaac Shimwell of Long Roods Farm, Ashford (near Monsal Head), stands with his Blue Albion cow, c1905. A native breed to Derbyshire, in 2002 there were only 115 beasts on the rare breeds list.
David Neal

The construction of the new A6 road at Ashford, 1931.
Jean Blackwell

The construction of the new A6 road at Ashford, 1931.
Jean Blackwell

Widening Greaves Lane, Ashford, 1930's? Greaves is the old name given to the bits of melted tallow left during candle making.
Jean Blackwell

Neville Old Hall, Ashford, demolished in 1937. It was divided into tenements occupied by John and Edith Bond, Dick and Muriel Needham and Miss Firth.
Jean Blackwell

The comb mill, operated by Rowland Holmes, made combs from tortoise-shell (the horny plates of the hawksbill turtle), for much of the second half of the 19th century. The mill used water from the same leat as the marble works to turn a water wheel. Ashford, c1900.
Jean Blackwell

Looking towards the Ashford Arms, Ashford, c1920.
The thatched cottages on the right have been demolished.
Jean Blackwell

The Rookery, Ashford c1920. In 1941 it was the first home of the Marquis of Hartington (the late Duke), and his wife when they were married.
Jean Blackwell

The Middleton family outside Bridge House, Ashford, where they moved after their cottage was demolished in 1931 when the new A6 road was constructed.

Jean Blackwell

Cox Wilson, who built many of the cottages in Ashford.
Jean Blackwell

The men whose lives are told within the following pages of this book were connected in one way or another to the market town of Bakewell or the villages and landscapes portrayed by words and photographs in Chapter One. As the momentous events of July and early August 1914 unfolded in Europe, leading to war, the lives of many of the men from this area would be lost and those of their families shattered.

CHAPTER TWO

1914 'IT WILL BE ALL OVER BY CHRISTMAS'

The weekend of June 27th/28th 1914 was sunny and warm across Derbyshire, and in Great Longstone, as in many villages across the Derbyshire Dales, happy events were taking place. Through the generosity of Mr and Mrs Eyre of 'The Mount' (nowadays called 'The Lodge') the whole of the children of Little and Great Longstone were entertained to an annual tea on Saturday 27th June. An excellent tea was provided in the Social Institute, kindly lent by its members. 130 children sat down, attended to by local ladies and gentlemen and afterwards an adjournment was made to a field lent by the Tennis Club. Two cricket matches were arranged for the boys and other games for the girls. At the close, each child received a bun and a pack of sweets.

In *The Diaries of Maria Gyte of Sheldon, Derbyshire 1913 – 1920* (Scarthin Books), Maria reports that Saturday June 27th was "A very lovely day. There was a cricket match between Sheldon and Monyash played at Sheldon. The scores were Sheldon 40 Monyash 20. Tom Gyte bowled 5 for 8 runs and William Henry Brocklehurst 5 for 10 runs. Sheldon have played 6 matches this year and won them all. June 28th – a lovely day today. Anthony (her husband) – and Mr Sneap went on moor and brought off a cow. Archduke Franz Ferdinand assassinated at Sarajevo by Gavrilo Princip."

On the Friday there had been the 16th Annual Sports of Lady Manners School, held on Bakewell Recreation Ground in ideal weather and the following Tuesday (30th June) was the hottest day recorded since August 9th 1911, 120° having been recorded. Considerable progress had been made in the hayfields, as a large number of Irish labourers had arrived in the district. There seemed no justifiable reason why these idyllic scenes of Edwardian life should not continue through the remainder of the summer months.

However, the day after the Great Longstone tea party, on the gloriously sunny morning of Sunday June 28th 1914, two pistols shots rang out on a street in the far away provincial Serbian town of Sarajevo, shots which would irretrievably affect the lives of families living in Bakewell, Over Haddon, Ashford-in-the-Water, Sheldon, Hassop, Little Longstone, Great Longstone, Rowland and Wardlow.

The shots were fired from the gun of a Bosnian/Serbian student nationalist, Gavrilo Princip, and his assassination of the heir to the Austro-Hungarian Empire, Archduke Franz Ferdinand and his wife, the Duchess of Hohenberg, would result in a dramatic change to the lives of the inhabitants of these Derbyshire settlements as Britain and the European Powers become entangled in a diplomatic power struggle that would lead to open conflict on Tuesday August 4th. 120 men from the Derbyshire market town and the surrounding villagers and hamlets would perish as a result of the ensuing conflict and the lives of many others be blighted and saddened (nine men died shortly after the war ended, but their names are not on any memorial). France, Belgium, Italy, Gallipoli, Egypt, Salonika or Mesopotamia became the destination for these men of the Derbyshire Dales, many of whom had never been further from home than Derby, Buxton or Chesterfield, and sadly, some would perish in these foreign lands, their names to be inscribed later on the parish war memorial back home.

Enthusiasm for war was high amongst the populations of the belligerent nations as the march towards hostilities began throughout the long hot days of July. Vast crowds swept onto the streets of the European capitals, each supporting vociferously their country's hostile stance.

Austria presented Serbia with impossible conditions to avoid annexation; Russia immediately mobilised in support of her fellow Slavs, Germany responded at once and France followed suit.

As the German and French armies moved inexorably towards each other on Tuesday August 4th, hopes that Great Britain could somehow stay out of the conflict were dashed when, following the long prepared Schlieffen Plan, German forces entered neutral Belgium, en route to Northern France.

August 1st/2nd was Bank Holiday weekend and at Great Longstone, Sunday 2nd August witnessed the march of the Loyal Inkerman Lodge of Oddfellows (Manchester Unity) as they held their annual demonstration to raise money in aid of the local hospitals. They met at the Club House and, preceded by the Darley Dale Brass Band, hired for the day, walked to Headstones Head and afterwards divine service was conducted in the parish church by the vicar, the Reverend Giles Andrew. In Bakewell, a similar fund raising march was being undertaken by members of the local lodge.

Monday August 3rd was a Bank Holiday in Britain, with the weather beautiful, ideal for a visit to the seaside. As thousands flocked to the railway stations to catch special trains bound for the coast, they discovered their exertions had been in vain, for the British Fleet has been mobilised and all excursions trains had been commandeered for use by naval reservists returning to their ships.

The market town of Bakewell always attracted crowds of visitors on August Bank Holiday Monday, but owing to the shadow of war, the town was unusually quiet and the day was uneventful. There were fewer visitors than usual owing to the fact that certain railway facilities had been curtailed. However, many locals settled down around the Recreation Ground cricket pitch to watch Bakewell Cricket Club defeat Boothstown. The visitors scored 62 in reply to Bakewell's 110 for four wickets. Thoughts for the forthcoming 66th Bakewell Show on Wednesday August 5th were also to the forefront of the minds of show officials and Bakewell inhabitants. As the international tension rose to breaking point, little did they realise that four and a half years of deadly conflict lay ahead, a conflict that would claim many lives in the locality.

At 4 pm on August 5th (the day of the Bakewell Show) the British Army was mobilised. Britain demanded that the German Army be withdrawn from Belgium by midnight 5th August or a state of war would exist between the British Empire and Germany. The ultimatum was ignored and war was declared at 11pm. The Great War had begun.

The news was announced to Bakewell folk at a large gathering in Rutland Square, Bakewell, on Wednesday 5th August. That same day the Bakewell Show went ahead, despite the war clouds. Most people were talking about the war and the entries of cattle were affected when the Midland Railway Company wired to the effect that they were unable to convey cattle to the show owing to the uncertainty of the train service. Several special excursion trains had also been stopped (there would be no further Bakewell Shows until 1920).

In 1914 Britain was essentially a maritime power, with only a small, if highly trained and professional army. Only 120,000 men would initially make up the British Expeditionary Force (BEF) that embarked for France, compared with some four million Frenchmen and four and half million Germans.

Lord Kitchener shocked a meeting of the War Council on August 6th by predicting a long war; countering the popular cry of, "it will be all over by Christmas." On August 7th Kitchener publicly called for 100,000 volunteers. By September 12th an amazing total of 480,000 men had enlisted as volunteers.

For some years prior to the Great War, Bakewell had fostered strong relations with the military. The old 'Volunteers' had been around since Napoleonic times. The Derbyshire Imperial Yeomanry, an irregular mounted force, was raised in 1899 and served in South Africa during the Boer War. Chatsworth House and Hardwick Hall estates were used as summer training camps for the Yeomanry, whilst by 1900 a Territorial Company of the 6th Battalion Sherwood Foresters was also based in Bakewell, stationed in a camp on Coombs Road. Many Bakewell and District men were part time soldiers with either the 'Volunteers', Territorials or Yeomanry and were to be called up once war broke out.

The local Territorials returned to Bakewell Station from their annual camp at Hunmanby, three miles from Filey, early on Tuesday August 4th, having left the N.E. coast on Monday night at 10 pm. Tuesday night also saw the King's proclamation posted in Buxton, Bakewell and Tideswell. In Buxton the Territorials of 'C' Company 6th Battalion Sherwood Foresters and the Derbyshire Yeomanry prepared themselves.

All day long on Wednesday, Buxton was alive with excitement and from a very early hour khaki-clad figures were out and about town and the drill-hall was the

Summer camp pf the Derbyshire Yeomanry c1910 at Hardwick Hall. The camps were held each year after the harvest (traditionally, a number of the soldiers were farm labourers) and were usually hosted by a local landowner. A church service is taking place in the grounds of Hardwick Hall. A number of local lads were serving in the Derbyshire Yeomanry, a cavalry unit, when the Great War began.

Derby Museum and Art Gallery

Kit inspection of the Derbyshire Yeomanry at summer camp, Hardwick Hall, c1910.

Derby Museum and Art Gallery

Inspection of the Derbyshire Yeomanry at their summer camp at Chatsworth House, c1910.
Derby Museum and Art Gallery

centre of attention. By 10am Territorials were present and the drill hall lined with many rifles and the men's kits. As the morning wore on the Yeomanry became more numerous and the Midland Station proved a scene of much excitement. Baggage and saddles were piled on the platform under the guard of members of the force, but one of the most touching scenes was the departure of the Reserves, men, who had, before today, fought for the Homeland. They were destined for the Front and many an eye was dimmed as the 10-45 am train moved slowly out of the station.

Then came the hour for the departure of the Yeomanry. As 11-25 am drew nigh, farewells were once more said. As the train got on the move, khaki-clad heads were thrust from the windows of the crowded carriages, hats and handkerchiefs were raised and they left to the strains of 'Rule Britannia'. They were on their journey to Bakewell, from which district they would draw their supply of horses.

'C' Company of the 6th Battalion Territorials travelled by road. 50 men formed into column, with the band playing, and were cheered loudly by a large crowd who accompanied them along High Street. The men camped at Ashford on Wednesday and at an early hour were again moving in the direction of Chesterfield.

Amidst the good wishes of hundreds of townsfolk, the High Peak Squadron of the Derbyshire Imperial Yeomanry left Bakewell on Monday August 10th at 9-30 am, going by road. Major Gretton was in command. They had been billeted in the town for a few days and only awaited the arrival of suitable horses prior to setting forth on active service. They numbered about 70. Twenty others, who could not be

Bakewell inhabitants and members of the Territorial Army Company gather in the Square to hear the declaration of war, in the first week of August 1914 by the Reverend Abraham, Bishop of Derby and vicar of Bakewell. The Bath Gardens railings are in the foreground and happier times come to mind with the banner advertising the 66th Bakewell Show on Wednesday August 5th.

R. Richmond

supplied with mounts, left Bakewell by train about an hour later. The scene on the Recreation Ground, where the Yeomanry assembled, was animated and enthusiastic in the extreme. Amongst those present were the Duchess of Rutland, Lady Diana Manners, Lady Maud Cavendish and Lord Vernon. Reveille was sounded at 4.30 am, there was a parade at 5 am and breakfast was served at 8 am.

Further impressive and heart-rending scenes were witnessed in Bakewell when the local Territorials (6th Battalion Sherwood Foresters), who had mobilised on Wednesday 12th August, left on Thursday morning, 13th August, in full marching order. Sherwood Foresters and Yeomanry also arrived at the town from the various districts and Bakewell presented quite a military appearance.

Small posters were placed around the town announcing that there would be an open-air service on Rutland Square at 8.30 am on Thursday as a send-off for the men.

The day dawned beautifully fine and bright. One of the biggest crowds seen in the Square for a long time past, assembled. A horse-less landau had been drawn up facing the Rutland Square and from here the Bishop of Derby, Dr Abraham (also vicar of Bakewell) conducted an eloquent yet stirring service. Colonel Herbert Brooke-Taylor, one of the most prominent of the Old Guard (Volunteer Force) was present, together with others like Captain Thomas Swann, who had rendered yeoman service in the cause of the Old Volunteers in the days of long ago. (One of Colonel Brooke-Taylor's sons would be killed at Gallipoli, whilst Captain Thomas Swann would die at home in Bakewell).

Prior to the service, the Bakewell Brass Band, under the conductorship of B.W. Duckmanton, paraded the streets with the Territorials and a large number of the Boy Scouts took up a position near the improvised platform. The Territorials, who were under the command of Captain H.C. Brooke-Taylor and Lieutenant E. Brooke-Taylor, numbered about 100 men. The National Anthem having been sung with great fervour, the Bishop of Derby gave his address:-

During the past few days the call had come for them to be prepared for active service in the present war, and they had all responded most nobly. They must not, he said, make any mistake about the position in which dear old England stood today. They were face to face with a strain which would test the manhood and endurance of their country such as they of that generation and many before had never known. At that very moment the nations on the Continent were engaging in a war the end of which it was impossible to foresee.

They in that district had been called to help and they had responded well. Nobody, surely, a fortnight ago, would hardly have dreamt of such a terrible thing as war being possible, yet it had broken out so suddenly that they could hardly yet realise it. It was all very dreadful, but they must meet eventualities with a good heart. Their friends across the Channel had been assailed and it was for England and her allies to thwart the doings of Germany.

He, as a Minister of the Gospel, would not have been present that morning if he did not feel to the very uttermost that this was a cruel war which had been begun by Germany. He most sincerely believed that the cause, which England had taken up in the defence of her friends, was a right and just one, and that in the end, right would prevail. God would be on their side. They had been called upon to fight for their King, country and their homes, and he was sure that in this dark hour they would not fail.

Let them all, therefore, go forward with a good heart and unfaltering step. They had within the past week or so done all they could to preserve the peace amongst the nations, but that had failed, and the only course open was to resort to war.

They believed in the justice of the cause upon which they had embarked. It was for the liberty and justice of our people. Let them as Territorials do their duty bravely as Englishmen had ever done in the past and all would be for the best. Let them stand firmly side to side and remember the most noble traditions of the race from which they sprang. (*It is worth noting here that Reverend Abraham's four sons would fight in the war, with one being killed in action in Palestine in 1917 and another son taken as a prisoner of war by the Germans).

Prayers were offered by the Bishop on behalf of the troops. Three cheers were next given for the Territorials, on the call of Mr. Woodiwiss. The troops filed up, and headed by the Brass Band and the Scouts with their drum and bugle band, set out on their long march to Chesterfield, proceeding over Bakewell Bridge and along Baslow Road. A large number of people followed to the outskirts of the town. The Band, which had played loyal and patriotic airs, dropped out at Castle Hill, but the Scouts proceeded a good deal further, (by the end of the war 517 men from Bakewell Parish would have served their country).

In the week preceding their departure, considerable interest was manifested by local people in the commandeering of horses likely for the purpose of Yeomanry Service. A large number of farmers also brought in horses, many of which were accepted. The work of sorting out the horses and testing their responsibilities, which was carried out in the Rutland Arms stable yard, was entrusted to Ernest Wood, proprietor of the Rutland Arms Hotel and Edward Marrison, the chief vet, of Bakewell.

In one or two instances, the authorities commandeered horses attached to vehicles and the owners had to get home the best way they could. Little grumblings on their part were of no avail. At the 66th Bakewell Show, on August 5th, some of the horses entered for competition could not be shown, having been required by the War Authorities for other purposes. In the same week that the Territorials departed Bakewell, Ernest Wood received an intimation from the War Authorities at Sheffield that 85 more horses would be required for the cavalry and 35 for artillery purposes. (Maria Gyte, in her diaries, reports on August 6th that men were examining horses in Longstone Station Yard).

Several men who were employed on the outdoor staff of Bakewell Post Office had left for active service in the early weeks of the war and the day to day work of the post office had been somewhat upset. Efforts were being made by the postmaster, A.T. Thompson, and his staff to keep the department going as regularly as possible.

The Bakewell and District police force was also affected in a similar way, for policemen who were ex-soldiers of the Regular Army had proceeded to join their various regiments for active service (Police Constable Mellon from Bakewell, who would die during the war, P.C. Young from Ashford, P.C. Johnson from Monyash and P.C. Gough from Tideswell).

Great excitement was caused on Saturday August 8th when it became known that the local police had arrested three German nationals who had been working at Rowsley, installing new machinery at Caudwell's Mill.

Maria Gyte reports that at Sheldon Church on Sunday, August 9th, special hymns were sung on account of the war and the National Anthem sung at the close. At the Devonshire Arms, Sheldon, on Saturday August 15th, there was a full house and Billy Naylor, after consuming a number of drinks, made a speech to the men about defending their country and also promised, if they were short of money to give a sovereign.

Meanwhile, great efforts were being made by the local gentry in Bakewell and the surrounding villages, to encourage local men to answer Kitchener's call to 'join up'. On Monday evening, August 17th 1914, a Recruitment Meeting was held in Ashford Schoolroom, with Mr F. Lees, J.P., of Ashford Hall, presiding and the objects of the meeting fully explained by Sergeant S. Allcock of Bakewell, who referred to the desirability of likely young men enlisting in the Territorials. Mr Frank Cox-Wilson, builder, saw mill owner and under-taker, of Ashford, also made a vigorous appeal.

In early September, a Recruit-ment Meeting was held in the Village Institute at Great Longstone, with A.W.J. Eyre, Chairman of the Parish Council, presiding and efforts were made to get as many recruits as possible. Three suitable young men from the village gave in their names. Three Longstone Territorials had already left for the war. Mr Allcock, headmaster of Bakewell Boys School, enlisted many volunteers for the Sherwood Foresters and in October 1914 he set off with them, marching to Buxton, to become part of the $2^{nd}/6^{th}$ Battalion.

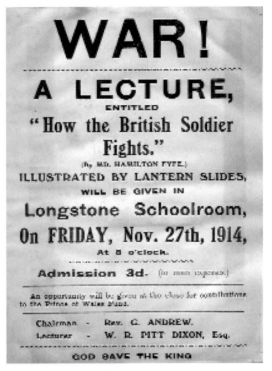

A poster advertising a series of lectures on the war, to be held in the Great Longstone Schoolroom November 1914.

Thornhill Papers, Derbyshire Records Office

The *Daily Mail* newspaper organised a series of lectures on the war throughout the towns and villages of England. Lecturers could hire a series of lecture notes and 80 lantern slides for 10s 6d. The money collected at each lecture would go towards the Prince of Wales' Relief Fund. Beginning in November 1914, Mr W.R. Pitt-Dixon of Great Longstone delivered the lectures in Longstone School and also at Ashford (1, 'Fire and Sword in Belgium: How Germany makes war' 2, How British pluck won through in France' 3,'How the British Soldier Fights' 4, 'The Kaiser's Blow at Britain!)

Meanwhile, the professional and Territorial units of the British Expeditionary Force (BEF) had crossed the English Channel on declaration of war and moved into Belgium. Near the town of Mons the British were struck by the full weight of the German First Army Group. Outnumbered, the British fought back stoutly, their rifle fire discipline taking heavy toll of the close German formations, but they were forced back onto a long retreat during August. In the days between Mons and the Battle of the Marne, the BEF, smallest of the Allied armies, played a vital role, for it found itself at the outset right across the axis of advance of General Kluck's army, the most powerful of all the German armies, 320,000 strong.

An important holding action by the BEF took place at the Battle of Le Cateau, August 26th, whilst at the Battle of the Marne, September 5th to the 10th, the German advance was brought to a halt, and then turned back, with the BEF, severely mauled but showing great powers of recuperation, playing a vital role. Now came the "Race to the Sea", between September 15th and November 24th, as each side tried to out-flank the other in a bid to take the Channel ports.

The final action of the "Race to the Sea" was the bloody "First Battle of Ypres", October 30th to November 24th, in which the BEF was nearly wiped out in a successful, gallant defence against a heavily reinforced German drive that was expected by them to capture the Channel ports.

Men from Bakewell and the surrounding villages participated in the desperate fighting of 1914, both as regulars and territorials, and although some were wounded during the battlefield action, fortunately no soldier from these parts was killed.

It was during the ferocious actions of September, November 1914, when thousands of battlefield casualties were returning to England to receive medical attention and recuperation, that Bakewell Red Cross Hospital was established at the Workhouse Infirmary on Baslow Road (Newholme) and the first wounded soldiers (8 British and 6 Belgian) arrived in mid November. The Bakewell Stretcher Bearer Company, which was formed on the outbreak of war, and now numbered about 35 members, had been officially recognised by the military authorities and was now included as a Men's Voluntary Aid Detachment under the British Red Cross Society. In the Territorial Drill Hall on Castle Street, there were good attendances. On a Thursday evening, Mr Cecil Armitage of Great Longstone, the director of Voluntary Aid Detachments for the County, made an inspection of the men and expressed satisfaction at the progress they had made. He said that the Detachment was only for those men who were unable, for physical and other reasons, to enlist in the Army. The Honory Commandant was Mr E.L. Hoyle of Holme Hall.

The Red Cross Hospital was staffed by VAD nurses who had been in training since before the war. Maria Gyte of Sheldon reports in her diaries on Wednesday September 2nd that her daughter Evelyn and Kate Brocklehurst went to Holme Hall to practice for Red Cross Work. Thursday October 29th saw Evelyn and Ethel Gyte and Kate and Ruth Brocklehurst walking to the Workhouse Infirmary to prepare for the wounded soldiers, who arrived on November 14th. By March 12th 1915 there were 33 wounded soldiers.

Throughout the war the work was hard. The girls often rose at 5.30am and started from Sheldon at 7 am to be on duty at Bakewell by 8 am. They remained on duty until 9 pm, with an hour or two off in the middle of the day (during 1913 Ethel, Evelyn and Mary Gyte had attended nursing lessons at Castle Hill, Ashford and at Ashford Hall).

A Royal Naval Convalescent Hospital was also set up in the Edensor Hotel (nowadays the Edensor Institute) at Chatsworth, with Medical Corps Staff and wounded arriving at Hassop Station. 72 recovering sailors were under the command of J.P Cockerell, estate agent on the Estate, with Mrs Cockerell acting as Quartermaster.

Continued on page 160 ☛

A contingent of Voluntary Aid Detachment Nurses (VAD) from the Hassop,
Ashford and Longstone areas in the early days of the Great War.

Peter Thornhill

The Red Cross Hospital at Bakewell Workhouse Infirmary (nowadys part of Newholme) 1915, which
tended the wounds of Belgian and British soldiers. Evelyn Gyte is the VAD nurse on the extreme left,
whilst the Duchess of Devonshire stands by the bed, in the middle.

Margaret Slin

Members of the Voluntary Aid Detachment (VAD) Red Cross nurses 1914. The VAD nurses worked at the wartime Red Cross Hospital for wounded Belgian and British soldiers in the Bakewell Workhouse Infirmary (Newholme) 1914-1918.
BACK ROW: Evelyn Gyte, Ethel Gyte, Mary Gyte
FRONT ROW: Ruth Brocklehurst, Kate Brocklehurst

Margaret Slin

Royal Army Medical Corps soldiers arrive at Hassop Station. They are about to set off by road to Chatsworth, where the Edensor Hotel (now the Institute and Estate Office) had been taken over as a Naval hospital and a place for the recuperation of naval personnel.

Peter Thornhill

Royal Army Medical Corps men form up after arriving at Hassop Station by special train.
They wre to be used in the hospital, set up at the Edensor Hotel, Chatsworth.
Peter Thornhill

In November 1914 the Chatsworth Estate also provided a winter training ground for the Derbyshire Imperial Yeomanry Reserve (340 men in total). Some were billeted at the hotels in Baslow, whilst a number of others found excellent quarters near the Chatsworth stables. These men would find themselves embarking for action in the Gallipoli Campaign the following year, and by 1916 would find themselves fighting the Bulgarians in Salonika. When the Derbyshire Yeomanry finally helped defeat the Bulgarians in September 1918, they brought one of the white flags used by the Bulgars to surrender, back to Bakewell as a trophy and it now can be found at the Old House Museum.

1914, however, was not without its first casualty from Bakewell and District, though the death of the serviceman, Malcolm Tomlinson, came about as the result of natural causes and occurred whilst in training in England, during December 1914.

GUNNER MALCOLM ELIAS TOMLINSON No 21754
285TH BATTERY ROYAL FIELD ARTILLERY
DIED DECEMBER 20TH 1914 AGED 34

The first Bakewell casualty of the war was Malcolm Tomlinson, the fourth of five children of Elias and Mary Tomlinson of Matlock Street, Bakewell. Elias, born at Ashford-in-the-Water, married Mary, a London girl and they raised their family in Bakewell, where Elias was a watchmaker and jeweller.

By the time of the 1901 Census, Malcolm, aged 20 years, is not to be found at the family home. It is almost certain that he was out of the country, for we know that he spent a number of years in West Africa as a trader. A few years before the war began, he returned home and when war broke out he enlisted in the Royal Field Artillery and spent much of his training in the Aldershot area. A few weeks before his death he was in Bakewell for a weekend and appeared to be well and strong.

However, in late December 1914 Elias and Mary received news on the Monday morning that their son had died rather suddenly in hospital in Aldershot. He was 34 years of age. Only on the previous Friday he had written stating that he was about to have a few days sick leave and was coming home. He had had a severe cold and pneumonia supervened. Malcolm Tomlinson was buried in Deepcut Military Cemetery, Surrey.

In France and Belgium, throughout December 1914, an Allied offensive beat unsuccessfully for ten bloody days against the rapidly growing German system of field fortifications. The era of stabilised trench warfare from the North Sea to the Swiss border had begun.

The enormity of the conflict became apparent to everyone as casualty lists were posted. By this time, operations on the Western Front had already cost the Allies nearly one million casualties, with German losses almost as great. The Germans had not won a quick victory and now the Western Front would settle down to four years of bloody attrition. Sadly, Bakewell and District would not continue to be spared its share of the nation's heartache.

*** As a footnote to the conclusion of the year 1914 in Bakewell we read in the *High Peak News*, as Christmas approached, that there was scarcely a plum pudding to be had for love or money in the town. Everyone, it seems, was responding to the appeal made by Lord Charles Beresford for a supply of plum puddings for the men of the Royal Naval Fleet. By mid December, 120 had already been received in Bakewell.

CHAPTER THREE

1915 THE CASUALTIES MOUNT

The vast casualties resulting from the early campaigns and the widening of the conflict to new theatres of war had brought home to the British public the increasing toll they would have to pay. All thoughts of an early end to the conflict had been dispelled. Nevertheless, the feeling persisted that once Kitchener's 'New Army' of volunteers was ready in 1915, the combined efforts of the Allies would then soon defeat the enemy.

We have already seen that Bakewell had strong connections with the military, with the 'Volunteers' being companies of militias dating from the Napoleonic Wars as a defence force, in case of invasion. A rifle club had been established by a volunteer rifle corps, that had originated in 1860, with a firing range near Coombs viaduct. It is not surprising therefore that when the Government proposed the setting up of Rifle Clubs during the Great War and the formation of Home Guard contingents in towns and villages throughout the land, that Bakewell was to the forefront in such schemes. Shooting competitions were organised against other rifle clubs and the Home Guard practiced route marches, drilling and went on 'manoeuvres'.

In early 1915 a public meeting had been held in Longstone Schoolroom, convened by the Chairman of Great Longstone Parish Council, Mr A.W.J. Eyre, with a view to forming a section of the Home Guard for the village. Amongst those present were Captain Hubert Pitt-Dixon and Lieutenant Shaw (both would be killed in the war). The object was for men outside the fighting years of 19 to 39 to find a proper scope for their energies and natural desire to serve their country. 13 men from the village promised to join the new section.

During the early part of 1915, several Belgian refugee families arrived in the district and fund raising events for the 'Belgian Appeal' were held to provide relief. A number of Belgian families arrived in Bakewell and 'London House' on Matlock Street provided accommodation for them during the war years until it was closed in March 1919. Four Belgian boys attended Lady Manners School. The church parish magazine for March 1915, at Great Longstone, reported that Mr Wright had kindly offered the use of a house rent free. A committee was formed to find support for the maintenance of a small family of Belgians (Mr W.I. Eyre to act as Secretary and Mr Harvey Wood as Treasurer).

Derbyshire Volunteer Regiment of Home Guard at Haddon Hall, June 1915, ready to be inspected by the Duke of Rutland, who was staying at Rowsley. This was part of their second route march. At Haddon Hall they were to meet the Rowsley detachment. The 70 strong Bakewell detachment marched from the Drill Hall in Bakewell. Each man wore a red armband with the letters GR (King George V) on his left arm.

In May, at the invitation of the Longstone Belgian Family Relief Committee, Mr W.C. Mallison of Cressbrook Hall, kindly gave a lecture on his experience in Belgium during the earlier part of the war and recounted the severity of the suffering endured by the people of that country. Mr G.H. Wood, on behalf of the Committee, said any contributions would be acceptable for providing a home in the parish. The sum of £1 17s $1^1/2$ d was collected.

By June 1915 a house for a Belgian family had been well supplied by furniture and articles kindly given and was now occupied by two married women and a little boy. Their husbands were still on active service.

However by September 1916 Madame Varlaet and her son, together with Madame Senepart, had left Longstone, suitable employment having been found for their husbands in England. By this stage £91 12s had been contributed to the Belgian Relief Fund at Longstone.

All communities within the area, especially the women, were also eager to play their part in the war effort by forming Comfort Funds for local servicemen. Money was raised and knitting circles made clothes so that gift parcels could be sent to servicemen fighting in the war or to those who had been wounded, in order to maintain their morale. A National Egg Collection Scheme was organised, aiming to collect eggs for distribution to the hospitals and convalescent homes tending to the needs of the wounded servicemen. In the Bakewell district the scheme was organised by the Red Cross and local schools were often used as collecting points. Weekly or monthly lists appeared in the local newspapers highlighting the number of eggs collected by each town or village.

Many of the men who volunteered for service in 1914 or early 1915 were destined for service overseas and 1915 saw continued British involvement on the Western Front and in other theatres of war. Turkey's entrance into the war on Germany's side in October 1914 had changed the war's complexion. Russia, already shaken by the reverses of 1914, was now virtually cut-off from Franco-British war supplies. In an

Lady Manners School, Bath Street, Bakewell, in 1917.
Headmaster, Mr, Trevor Dennis, stands in front of the school orchestra and choir, in preparation
for a concert to raise funds for the Red Cross and the war effort.
Lady Manners School

A motor smashes through the parapet of the old Baslow Bridge leading to Bubnell, on May 10th 1915.
The soldiers came from the detachment stationed at Chatsworth.
Tom Slin

attempt to help Russia, a naval expedition was mounted to clear the Dardanelles for Russian ships in the Black Sea. When this venture stalled, an attack was planned on a little known peninsula called Gallipoli.

On the Western Front during 1915 the BEF extended its front southwards across the wet levels of the River Lys into the dreary coalfields east of Lille, where, during 1915, it fought a series of murderous trench to trench battles (Neuve Chapelle in March, Festubert May to June, and Givenchy) and also mounted one major, mis-carried offensive at Loos in September to October.

British casualties mounted as these attacks were launched during 1915 and increased again when the Germans launched their own major assault at the Second Battle of Ypres (April to May), this latter assault seeing poison gas being used by the Germans for the first time in the west.

Increase of lethal fire-power had given the advantage to the defence, for a continuous battle line prevented classical offensive manoeuvres. The Germans had adopted an elastic defence, in two or more lines, highly organised with entrench-ments and barbed wire heavy in machine guns and supported by artillery. Assaulting troops broke through the first line only to be decimated by the fire from the succeeding lines. As a consequence of these facts we find that the number of Bakewell and District men who died on the fields of battle or succumbed to their wounds throughout 1915 rose dramatically to ten.

The first of these casualties was a regular army officer from Great Longstone.

CAPTAIN HUBERT BRADSAW PITT-DIXON
1ST BATTALION SHERWOOD FORESTERS
DIED MARCH 12TH 1915 AGED 36

Hubert was the youngest son of William Pitt-Dixon and Martha Dixon of Thornbridge Cottage (next to Longstone Station) Great Longstone. His father, born at Halifax was the proprietor of lime works and quarries and had married Martha, a girl from Liverpool. Hubert was born at Didsbury, Manchester, but by 1891 he was a 12 year old boarder at Packhurst School, Fairfield, Buxton, before he furthered his education at Repton and Christ Church, Oxford.

Hubert was a member of the Derbyshire Volunteers and the Militia and decided to make the army his career. In 1900 he was gazetted a 2nd Lieutenant in the 2nd Battalion Sherwood Foresters and was promoted Captain in 1908. He served in the South African War, receiving the Queen's Medal with 5 clasps and was five years in Nigeria, where he did a great deal of big game shooting (many reminders of this were to be found on

Hubert Bradshaw Dixon
of Great Longstone.

the walls of his Great Longstone home). Whilst in Derbyshire, Hubert was an influential freemason, being a prominent member of the Dorothy Vernon Lodge at Bakewell.

Hubert was serving in India with the Sherwood Foresters when the First World War began but did not return to England with the 2nd Battalion immediately because he was on a course at the Quetta Military Staff College (he was a good linguist and could converse in Baluchi and Hindustani). He arrived in England in October 1914 and went to France early in November 1914, where he was attached to the 1st Battalion Sherwood Foresters.

By this time, his father had died and in January 1915 he was home on 4 days leave at Great Longstone and arrived just one and a half hours before the death of his mother, Martha. At the front he acted as Brigade Major to General Davies, during the temporary absence of the major through illness. He had had some 'narrow shaves' (a bullet through his hat and another grazed his thigh) and was mentioned in dispatches for bravery.

On March 10th 1915 the British forces, including 1st Battalion Sherwood Foresters, attacked the German lines, their objective being the village of Neuve Chapelle. Hubert was killed during this battle.

March 12th dawned very misty and the Germans opened severe shell fire and they attacked in a dense mass, sweeping over the right wing of the Foresters. A fighting mass of British and Germans, intermingled, at last reached the support trenches.

The Rookery, Ashford in the Water. This was the home of Walter C. Tinsley, Master of the High Peak Harriers (Hunt), and his son, Alan Deane Tinsley. The house dates from the 16th century.
Keith Taylor

It was at this stage that Hubert found himself in a difficult situation in the trenches, holding an exposed corner, with a few of his men, and although he was wounded, they managed to cut their way out of a very dangerous corner. He was then informed that there was an awkward situation elsewhere and he volunteered to help. He and his men again set out to render assistance, but they had only proceeded a few yards when he fell, being mortally wounded by a bullet through the head.

Hubert Bradshaw Pitt-Dixon's body was not recovered and his name is commemorated on Panel 26 and 27 Le Touret Memorial, on the south side of the Bethune-Armentieres road.

News of his death was announced to the residents of Great Longstone by the tolling of the parish church bells.

Two months later, a man from the neighbouring village of Ashford, who had emigrated to Canada prior to the war, and was wounded and taken prisoner at the Battle of Neuve Chapelle, died in a German military hospital in Belgium.

PRIVATE ALAN DEANE TINSLEY NO 1638
8ᵀᴴ BATTALION 90ᵀᴴ WINNIPEG RIFLES, MANITOBA REGIMENT
DIED MAY 13ᵀᴴ 1915 AGED 27

Alan's father, Walter Chapman Tinsley, came with his wife and family to the 'Rookery', Ashford, in 1910, and succeeded Colonel Robertson Aikman as Master of the High Peak Harriers, bringing with him his own pack of hounds from the Dove Valley (he resigned as Master in 1920).

Alan Deane Tinsley had been ranching in Manitoba, Canada, and when war broke out he joined the Canadian Expeditionary Force, with the 8th Battalion 90th Winnipeg Rifles, Manitoba Regiment. During the winter of 1914/1915 he had paid a visit to his parents in Ashford and also had a day with the High Peak Harriers (the Harriers hunted hares over the limestone uplands).

He embarked for France in early 1915 and his Battalion took part in the ill-fated Battle of Neuve Chapelle which began on March 10th. After an intense bombardment of 35 minutes duration, the artillery lengthened their range and dropped a curtain of fire to prevent reinforcements reaching the enemy's battered trenches, which were rapidly overrun by British and Canadian infantry. In the second phase of the battle, however, artillery support proved inadequate and a delay of five hours allowed the Germans time to organise fresh resistance. Too late, Haig ordered the attack to be pressed 'regardless of loss'. And loss was the only result, with casualties being severe.

One casualty was Alan Tinsley. His parents received information that he had been seriously wounded and taken prisoner by the Germans. He went into a German hospital behind the lines in Belgium, but on May 13th 1915, he died. He was buried

The Marquis of Hartington makes a presentation to Mr. Walter C. Tinsley, late Master of the High Peak Hunt, at Bull-i'-Th'-Thorn, early 1920's. Walter had lost his son during the Great War.

High Peak Hunt (Harriers) Point to Point meeting at Flagg 1927. Members race.
Left to right: Walter Chapman Tinsley, Mr. Clark (groom), Sir Francis Stephenson (winner).
Henry Stephenson

in grave III.A.1 Roeselare Communal Cemetery (Roulers), 20 kilometers N.E. of Ypres. Many POW's are buried there since it was occupied by the Germans throughout the war.

It was an extremely sad time for Mrs. Tinsley (nee Deane) because thirteen days before the death of her son, her brother, Major John Deane, a regular soldier in the 2nd Battalion Hampshire Regiment was killed at the Dardanelles.

A fortnight after Alan's death, a Bakewell soldier was killed by a German sniper whilst undertaking routine day to day duties in the front line trenches.

Private Hubert Holmes Fewkes No 2242
'C' Company 6th Battalion Sherwood Foresters
died May 27th 1915 aged 24

Hubert Holmes Fewkes of Bakewell.

Hubert was born in 1890 at Bakewell, the second eldest of the five children of Alfred Payne Fewkes and Fanny Fewkes. Alfred had been born at Oakham in Rutland and it was in Rutland, at South Luffenham, that his father, Alfred, senior, was the Station Master. The family eventually arrived at Bakewell around 1878, where Alfred Fewkes senior became station master. His son, Alfred Payne Fewkes, became the clerk at the station. Sadly Alfred, senior had died by 1881.

Alfred Payne Fewkes married Fanny, a Bakewell girl, and they began married life on Rutland Terrace, raising five children, including Hubert. In later life Alfred Fewkes played the piano in the little orchestra that played during silent films at the 'Picture Pavilion', Bakewell's first cinema, that opened in 1912 near the Railway Station. Mr Fewkes also played and sang in the local public houses.

After leaving school, Hubert became a clerk in the office of Alfred Hawes, Clerk to Bakewell Board of Guardians and Rural Council. In his spare time he belonged to the Bakewell Football Club, playing at full back in the first eleven. He was also a member of Bakewell Brass Band. He was known in footballing circles in West Derbyshire as 'Cloggy'.

By the time war was declared, the family was living on Buxton Road and Hubert's father was a pianoforte tuner, not a railway clerk. Hubert was a Territorial soldier and was one of those who gathered in Bakewell in the week that war was announced, joining the 6th Battalion Sherwood Foresters. By Easter 1915 they were stationed in the Ypres Salient, South of Ypres. In a letter sent home to a pal, in 1915, Hubert wrote, "We have been in and out of trenches since Easter Monday – we don't mind the bullets, it's the shells that make us jump. We have had no Bakewell lads hurt so far and I hope our good luck will continue. There isn't much chance of sleep when you are out, but in the daytime, when we return to our billets (an old barn), we get a bit in. Some days we are without a wash or a shave and we begin to look like blacks. I used to think we got some samples through the Bakewell Workhouse but they look respectable compared with us. The Germans have some good snipers. You have only got to show your head and off goes the top of it".

The latter point was to prove prophetic. News came to Bakewell in late May 1915 that Hubert had been shot through the head by a German sniper. Whilst in the trenches he had raised his head and fell back with a bullet wound. Word came the next day that he had been killed and buried nearby, with Private Joseph Marsden, a Bakewell man from Monyash Road, helping with proceedings.

Hubert is buried in grave E.25 Kemmel Chateau Military Cemetery, 8 km south of Ypres.

Sadly we shall find that his uncle, Walter Fewkes, another Bakewell man, would be killed in action in August 1917, almost at the same spot.

A memorial service for Hubert was held at the Parish church, with 60 members of Bakewell Home Guard marching to the church. Next came 20 convalescent soldiers from the Bakewell Red Cross Hospital (nowadays Newholme).

Just over a week later, in a different and distant theatre of war, two more Bakewell soldiers lost their lives on the same day. Gallipoli was about to claim another two lives.

LIEUTENANT ARTHUR CUTHBERT BROOKE-TAYLOR
6TH BATTALION MANCHESTER REGIMENT
DIED JUNE 4TH 1915 AGED 27

Arthur Cuthbert Brooke-Taylor of Bakewell.
Barbara Brooke-Taylor

Cuthbert was the second son of Bakewell solicitor Colonel Herbert Brooke-Taylor of 'The Close', Bakewell. Born on March 15th 1888, he was educated at Cheltenham College from 1899 and Manchester University, becoming a member of the engineering firm of Messrs. Sanders and Taylor Ltd of Manchester (he had spent the year 1898 at Lady Manners School). He joined the Second Volunteer Battalion, Sherwood Foresters and became a Second Lieutenant in the 6th Battalion. Early in 1914, finding it difficult to perform his duties in the Sherwood Foresters, due to Manchester work commitments, he transferred into the 6th Battalion Manchester Regiment. When this Battalion was part of the East Lancashire Division, he went out with them to Egypt early in the Autumn of 1914. He had already been appointed to command a machine gun section and was an instructor of musketry to his

Battalion when he was killed.

Germany had built up a close relationship with Enver Pasha, the new Turkish leader, and encouraged a declaration of war by Turkey against Russia and Britain on October 29th 1914.

In January 1915, approval was given for a naval expedition to be mounted to clear the Dardanelles for Russian ships in the Black Sea. When this venture stalled, an amphibious operation led by General Ian Hamilton was planned on a little known peninsula called Gallipoli.

The plan provided for two daylight assaults on April 25th, one at Cape Helles on the tip of the Peninsula, the other by the Anzacs (Australian and New Zealand Army Corps) on the western side. Both assaults failed

Geoffrey Brooke-Taylor of Bakewell, brother of Cuthbert,

to capture the hill masses towering above the beaches and without these critical heights the landings were doomed to failure. The Allied forces found themselves pinned down on their tiny beach heads, involved in the same kind of trench warfare experienced on the Western Front.

It was during this period of trench warfare, with heavy Turkish shelling of the Allied lines, combined with sniper fire, that Cuthbert was killed in action on June 4th 1915. His parents received the telegram after returning from Church. It came a few days after the funeral of Colonel Herbert Brooke-Taylor's eldest brother, Francis James Taylor. (The retired Colonel was the County Recruiting Committee Secretary and Secretary and organiser of Derbyshire Home Guards Movement).

Colonel Herbert Brooke-Taylor, father of Cuthbert.
Barbara Brooke-Taylor

PRIVATE ALBERT EDWARD VICTOR MITCHELL No 9988
2ND BATTALION HAMPSHIRE REGIMENT
DIED JUNE 4TH 1915 AGED 17

Victor, as he was known, was the youngest of three sons of Charles and Sarah Mitchell. Charles and Sarah were Hampshire born and bred, from an area just east of Southampton. Charles had served in the Hampshire Regiment, seeing fighting in India and serving through the Burma campaign 1885-1890.

By 1901 Charles was a bricklayer's labourer and was living with Sarah and his three sons in the village of Swanmore, east of Southampton, where Victor had been born in 1898. By the start of the Great War, however, the family was to be found on

The three Mitchell brothers of Bakewell. Leonard, Victor and Archibald.

Church Lane, Bakewell, where Charles Mitchell was verger of the parish church. All three sons were already in the army by the end of December 1914. Seventeen year old Victor had enlisted at Derby with his brothers and joined the Hampshire Regiment in which their father had served, Victor and his brother Archibald joining the 2nd Battalion whilst brother Leonard joined the 1st Battalion. Although only 17 years of age, Victor was 6 feet tall and was accepted for service, with he and Archibald becoming drummers (his two brothers were even taller).

The 2nd Battalion served in the Dardanelles and it was at Gallipoli that Victor Mitchell was killed. His parents in Bakewell received a letter from Archibald (Archie) from his hospital bed at St Andrews Hospital, Malta, stating, 'Dear Dad, I am sorry to have to let you know that poor 'little' Victor was killed in action on June 4th. It was in that terrible charge when he got a bullet through his head. Poor lad, he did not feel much of it, as he died immediately. Dear dad, do take this as well as ever you can for mine and Len's sake. I am going back as soon as I can and will have revenge. I am far from well and am making myself worse through thinking about this sad affair, so must close and remain your loving son, Archie'.

Archie had served with his brother Victor at the Dardanelle's and had been wounded, but thankfully recovered. Their brother Leonard, a Lance Corporal in the 1st Battalion Hampshire Regiment, had fallen victim to frost bite in France, during November 1914, but recovered and both brothers survived the war, unlike Victor. Victor Mitchell's name is commemorated on the Helles

Memorial, in the Dardanelles.

The main action for the Allies in 1915 still remained the Western Front and a further two Bakewellians sacrificed their lives, both in the dreaded Ypres Salient. The Germans had the advantage of commanding the higher ground and could unleash a deadly hail of shell fire and sniper fire. The first of these casualties resulted from being hit whilst on routine trench duty, simply being in the wrong place, at the wrong time, whilst the second man was killed during a raid on the enemy trenches.

2ND LIEUTENANT BERNARD GIBBS, MILITARY CROSS, 6TH BATTALION (ATTACHED TO 1ST BATTALION) RIFLE BRIGADE DIED JULY 6TH 1915 AGED 22

The Gibbs family was living in the St Pancras area of London in 1901. Bernard is shown to be 8 years of age and was born in Madeira, Portugal, as were his two older siblings. Their father, George Rutterford Gibbs, was an electrical engineer working with submarines, and had married, Elizabeth, a girl from Ashbourne, Derbyshire.

Bernard's grandparents were George Rutterford Gibbs, senior, and Caroline Gibbs. Their daughter (Bernard's aunty) was married to Mr F. Lees of Ashford Hall and they often stayed at the Hall with their daughter and son-in-law or at Grange Cottage, Ashford. It is quite clear, therefore, that young Bernard Gibbs and his family would also visit Ashford on frequent occasions and stay with their relatives (George Rutterford Gibbs senior and his wife Caroline spent a great deal of the year at their home in Portugal, with their periods in England spent mainly in Ashford. This also explains why their grandchildren, including Bernard, were born in Portugal. By 1910, Caroline Gibbs was a widow and lived at Grange Cottage and the Hall for the last seven years of her life, until her death in October 1917).

Another possible link between Bernard and Ashford is that his father, George Rutterford Gibbs junior's work was in connection with submarines. During the First World War, the DP Battery Works in Bakewell played an important part in the war effort, when the production line changed over to the making of submarine batteries. Bernard's father could have been involved in supervising this transition.

Bernard Gibbs was educated at Exmouth, Macclesfield Grammar School, Shrewsbury and Pembroke College, Cambridge. He volunteered at the start of the war and gained his commission as Second Lieutenant in the 6th Battalion Rifle Brigade. By June 1915 he was attached to the 1st Battalion and stationed in the Ypres Salient. Routine Service in the front line trenches of the Salient was always dangerous, with shelling by the Germans, as well as sniper fire, taking a daily toll on the quietest of days, due to the enemy commanding the high ground.

On July 6th 1915, one such quiet day, 2nd Lieutenant Bernard Gibbs was killed. He was buried in grave 1.D.8. Talana Farm Cemetery, near Ypres.

LIEUTENANT GEOFFREY MORGAN HOYLE
3ᴿᴰ BATTALION (ATTACHED TO 2ᴺᴰ BATTALION) SHERWOOD FORESTERS
DIED AUGUST 9ᵀᴴ 1915 AGED 21

Geoffrey Morgan Hoyle
of Bakewell
Cliff Housley

Geoffrey was the second son of Edward Lascelles Hoyle and Margaret Hoyle of Holme Hall, Bakewell. Edward Hoyle was born in Salford, whilst his wife was American, and he earned his money as a cotton spinner and manufacturer in Lancashire. In 1901 the family was living at the Hall in Pott Shrigley, north of Macclesfield, but eventually arrived in Bakewell before the start of the Great War. Edward was on the Commission of the Peace for Cheshire and attended the Macclesfield Courts as J.P.

Geoffrey, born in 1895 at Knutsford, was educated at Rugby, where he was in the School Officer Training Corps. On leaving Rugby in 1913 he went to Germany to study languages and returned at the very end of July 1914, only a few days before the outbreak of war. He immediately applied for a commission in the 3rd (Special Reserve) Battalion Sherwood Foresters and was gazetted 2ⁿᵈ Lieutenant on August 15ᵗʰ. On March 31ˢᵗ 1915 he went to the front, attached to the 2ⁿᵈ Battalion and was promoted Lieutenant in July 1915.

His two brothers were also serving in the forces, John Baldwin Hoyle in the 7ᵗʰ Battalion South Lancashire Regiment and Lieutenant E.B. Hoyle on H.M.S. Albemarle. Their father had taken a keen and generous interest in the Bakewell Home Guard movement (providing rifles) and was one of its best marksmen. Sadly, we shall find that not only would Geoffrey be killed in the war, but also his brother John.

Geoffrey was killed on August 9ᵗʰ 1915 at the Battle of Hooge, in the Ypres Salient.

On July 30ᵗʰ the Germans had forced the British out of the village of Hooge and a plan was made to recapture it, involving the 2ⁿᵈ Battalion Sherwood Foresters, who were stationed in the vicinity of Sanctuary Wood. At 3.30 am on August 9ᵗʰ the advance commenced. By 5 am the German artillery was in full blast and the trenches occupied by the Foresters were being blown in all directions. At midday the men were holding onto the trenches, but a hail of shells was falling and at 9-30 pm the Battalion was relieved. Nine officers and 105 men were killed or died of wounds. Geoffrey Hoyle was one of the officers killed, his body never being recovered, and his name is commemorated on Panel 39 and 41 of the Menin Gate.

Meanwhile, the last fatality from Bakewell and District to occur in the Dardanelles, was a member of the Derbyshire Yeomanry, who lost his life in August 1915.

LANCE CORPORAL ALEXANDER BOWMAN JONES No 1468
DERBYSHIRE IMPERIAL YEOMANRY
DIED AUGUST 21ˢᵀ 1915 AGED 24

Alexander (Alec) was born in 1890 at Chorlton cum Medlock, Manchester, the son of Alexander and Fanny Jones. Alexander, senior, was a 'lurryman', the driver of a horse-drawn cart, and he had married Fanny, a girl from Over Haddon, near Bakewell, when she had been in service in the Manchester area. However, by 1901, Fanny Jones was a widow and living with her two young sons, Alec and William, at Monyash, where she earned a living as a dressmaker.

Eventually, the family moved to live on Butts Road, Bakewell, and Alec became apprenticed to the joinery trade at Mr Robert Smith's works on Coombs Road, but for the few years before the start of the war he was employed at the DP Battery Works. In his leisure time he belonged to Bakewell Church Lads' Brigade and was Assistant Scoutmaster of Bakewell Troop of Boy-Scouts.

Alec Jones enlisted at Bakewell, early in the war, for he had been a Territorial soldier in the Derbyshire Yeomanry, and become a Lance Corporal and Signaller. His brother Frank was serving in the Kings Royal Rifles.

The Derbyshire Yeomanry took part in the actions at Suvla Bay, Dardanelles, in August 1915. At Mudros Bay they boarded an Irish packet boat and sailed for Suvla Bay. Just before dawn on the 18ᵗʰ August they landed under shell fire and dug in. On August 21ˢᵗ the Derbyshire Yeomanry provided 300 men for a frontal attack on the Turks. Covered by a heavy bombardment from naval vessels they advanced towards 'Chocolate' Hill. The hills were not gained and the men lay exposed to shells and heavy rifle and machine gun fire. The thick scrub of the Salt Lake Plain caught alight and blazed furiously, but the attack continued in the darkness that night, each man carrying a pick or shovel in one hand and rifle and fixed bayonet in the other. Casualties quickly mounted under the withering machine gun fire at close quarters and the men had to retire.

One of eight men from his platoon killed and lost on the hillside that day was Alexander Jones. His name is commemorated on Panel 17 of the Helles Memorial.

The actions at Gallipoli throughout 1915 had proved to be a failure. When the peninsula was finally evacuated on January 19ᵗʰ 1916, the eight and a half month campaign had lost the Allies some 215,000 men, of whom 145,000 were due to sickness, 50,000 from dysentary.

The final two casualties for 1915 were both Bakewell residents, one a member of the DP Battery Works staff, and the second a chemist at a shop on Matlock Street. The Ypres Salient became the resting place of the first, whilst the Battle of Loos claimed the life of the Bakewell chemist.

PRIVATE THOMAS D'ARCY NO 2276
6TH BATTALION SHERWOOD FORESTERS
DIED SEPTEMBER 30TH 1915 AGED 25 YEARS

Thomas, who had been born in Kilkenny, Ireland, in 1890, came of a good Irish family, but was orphaned, his nearest relation being a Mrs Edmunds of Twyford, Berkshire. He had travelled extensively and had served with the Army in Egypt (he was a Territorial soldier) but eighteen months before war started he arrived in Bakewell. Thomas lodged with Mrs. Hawksworth in Mill Street and was employed at the DP Battery Works. Being a good linguist he had been offered a post at the DP as foreign correspondent, but this he modestly declined.

Thomas D'Arcy enlisted at Bakewell, joining the 6th Battalion of the Sherwood Foresters, and during early August 1915 they were involved in severe fighting in the Ypres Salient, which Thomas survived. Except for occasional heavy shelling, the tours of the Battalion were uneventful in late August until the final night of 30th September/October 1st, when the relief of the Battalion occurred. About 7-15 pm on the 30th, a mine was exploded by the Germans under a trench on the Bluff held by 2nd Lieutenant Dickenson and No 9 Platoon. The officer and most of the men were buried, only one of whom was dug out alive. The Germans attacked but were frustrated and there was heavy shell fire.

Thomas D'Arcy was one of those killed by the explosion of the mine and his body is buried in grave I.B.2 Chester Farm Cemetery, 5 km south of Ypres.

Eight days later, another Bakewell resident was killed over the border, in France, at the Battle of Loos, in which Kitchener's New Armies and Territorials were set to play a prominent role. The ground in this coal mining region was unfavourable, swept by machine gun fire from the numerous fortified villages behind the lines.

The Battle of Loos opened with an artillery bombardment and the release of chlorine gas from over 5000 cylinders, but some gas drifted back and poisoned British soldiers. Those who were able to advance were soon stopped and slaughtered by German machine gunners. When gaps did appear in the German defences, the British reserves were held too far back and could not exploit the opportunity. The Battle petered out on October 14th with the minor gains made being out of proportion to the casualties suffered (100,000 French, 60,000 British and 65,000 Germans).

PRIVATE (GUARDSMAN) LEONARD NEEDHAM NO 21084
3RD BATTALION GRENADIER GUARDS
DIED OCTOBER 8TH 1915 AGED 31

Leonard was the son of Richard Needham, J.P. a wholesale chemist of Ashdale, Stalybridge. His ancestors originally sprang from Flagg and Buxton. He was also the nephew of C.T. Needham, M.P. for Salford.

Leonard was educated at a college on the Isle of Man, although by 1901, at the age of 16 years, he was a pupil (boarder) at Dalton Hall in Stalybridge. He studied to become a chemist and became a member of the Pharmaceutical Society, was a keen naturalist and was well versed in engineering work.

Two years before war began, he arrived in Bakewell to take up the position of manager of the chemist shop belonging to Edward Carrington on Matlock Street, Bakewell. By the time of his death in 1915 he was married, with his wife and 3 year old son Richard ('Dickie') living in the market town.

On March 18th 1912, twenty eight year old Leonard married seventeen year old Emma Scott at Holy Trinity Church, Gee Cross, on the outskirts of Hyde, Cheshire. She lived at 8 Harrison Street, where her father, Frederick, was a publican. In that same month they moved to Bakewell, where Leonard took up his new position as chemist, and in December of that same year, their son, Richard (Dickie) was born in the market town.

When war was declared he enlisted at Buxton in December 1914 and was offered a good position in the Royal Army Medical Corps but he preferred to join the Grenadier Guards. His last visit to Bakewell before his death had been on Easter Monday 1915. He went to the front in July 1915. On September 25th 1915 the British planned an assault on German positions near the village of Loos, in the bleak coal mining region between Bethune and Lens. Many of those taking part on the British side were untried members of Kitchener's New Army, with inadequate heavy artillery backing and shells. The omens were not good.

The 3rd Battalion had embarked for France, near the end of July 1915, on the steamboat Queen Alexandra and on August 18th took part in a review held on the aviation ground at St. Omer, when they paraded in front of Lord Kitchener and Sir John French.

The following two months were spent in training in preparation for the forth-coming Battle of Loos, that began on September 25th. The 3rd Battalion entered the Battle the following day, and when they were relieved on September 30th they had suffered 229 causalities. Thankfully, Leonard survived the action.

The 3rd Battalion remained in billets until October 4th, when it took over a line of trenches resting against the German strongpoint, known as the Hohenzollern Redoubt and there it remained until October 10th. Life proved very unpleasant for the Grenadiers with the Germans being so close.

On October 8th the enemy made a determined attack on this line and surprised the 3rd Battalion bombers, killing most of them. The bombs, with which the guardsman were armed, proved useless, as they had got very damp and refused to detonate. Bombs and shells rained down upon them, but after an initial retirement, the Battalion held on. Sadly, 137 men were listed as killed, wounded or missing during the assault.

It was on this day that Leonard Needham lost his life. His body was found lying between the trenches, killed in the bombing attack. On him was found a photograph of little 'Dickie' his son. However, in the confusion of battle his body was not recovered and Leonard's name is commemorated on Panel 5 to 7 of the Loos Memorial.

As 1915 came to its sad conclusion, appalling losses had been suffered by both sides on the Western Front throughout the year. 612,000 Germans, 1,292,000 French and 279,000 British became casualties. The year ended with no appreciable shift in the hostile battle lines scarring the land from the North Sea to the Swiss Alps. In 1916 it would prove to be the Germans who profited more heavily from the offensive and defensive lessons learned during 1915. Ten men from Bakewell and district had lost their lives during 1915 but the sacrifice made in 1916 would prove even greater, with the loss of twenty men.

CHAPTER 4

1916 – THE YEAR OF THE SOMME

1916 was to witness a terrible escalation in the number of casualties for both the Allies and the Germans on the Western Front as a result of two major battles waged that year; the German offensive against the French at the Siege of Verdun (February to December 1916) and the British and French offensive against the German forces, in the Battle of the Somme (July to November). They resulted in the cost to the British and the French of upwards of one million casualties for very little gain, especially on the Somme.

The Germans attacked Verdun in order to 'bleed France white', in the certain knowledge that the French would defend the city to the last man. By June 1916 the French situation was desperate and the French asked the British Commander–in-Chief, General Haig, to hasten a relieving action on the Somme.

The Somme area was chosen simply because here the British and French armies met, and even though the Allies knew the German defences were very strong, the offensive was set for July 1st. From that date, no fresh German divisions would be sent to the Verdun front; the German attack slowly stalled, then failed. The Somme battles therefore contributed to save Verdun but at a terrible cost to Britain's citizen army. The optimistic view by most people in 1915 on the outcome of the war was shattered by the unfolding events of 1916. Twenty service men from the Bakewell district died in 1916 and thirteen of these lost their lives on the Somme.

Voluntary enlistment was now no longer an option for Britain and even before the Somme, casualties on the Western Front and elsewhere demanded replacements that could only be filled by conscription. In January 1916, by the Military Service Act, the voluntary system was abandoned and compulsory enlistment came into being.

When conscription was introduced and more men went off to fight, many women throughout Britain took their places in the factories and on the transport systems. We find a good example of this in Bakewell, where, after 1916, Bakewell women helped in munitions works at the DP Batteries factory on Buxton Road, making submarine battery cells for the Royal Navy.

Despite the overwhelming significance of the Somme battles for 1916, we find that casualties from the Bakewell area were occurring in the months leading up to July

1st. The first of these lost his life in the Ypres Salient after a German raid into the British trench system near the Canal, in February.

PRIVATE GEORGE THOMAS HAYTO NO 17446
'C' COMPANY 10TH BATTALION SHERWOOD FORESTERS
DIED FEBRUARY 14TH 1916 AGED 23

The hamlet of Over Haddon was the home of George Hayto in 1901. He was eight years of age and living with his parents George and Elizabeth Ann Hayto, together with his two older siblings and three younger ones. George senior had been born at Derby, his father William being a gas manager, and George was employed as a gas worker at Bakewell for the Bakewell Gas Light Company on Buxton Road. His wife was a Hathersage girl and the family of six children was raised in Bakewell and Over Haddon.

After leaving school, George Hayto junior became a quarry worker, employed by R.W. Allsop of Bakewell. He served four years in the Territorial Army, leaving 12 months prior to the outbreak of war. He re-enlisted in September 1914 at Buxton, joining the 10th Battalion Sherwood Foresters and was at the Front since April

George Hayto of Over Haddon and Bakewell.

1915. his older brother Herbert was serving in the Royal Engineers.

The Battalion was stationed in the Ypres Salient during December 1915. They were relieved on January 6th 1916 and went by train and route march into rest camps west of St Omer, where they stayed till February 8th, resting and training.

On February 8th they moved into reserve in the Ypres Salient and on the night of 13th/14th February 1916 they relieved the 7th Lincolnshire Regiment who were holding the Bluff and trenches immediately north of the Ypres – Comines Canal. The relief was a quiet one, but on the morning of the 14th the enemy bombarded the lines with all available artillery, trench mortars and rifle grenades.

At about 2-30 pm the bombardment assumed tremendous intensity, continuing for two hours. At 5-40 pm a mine was exploded under trenches occupied by 'C' Company, causing many casualties, followed by an enemy attack that was repulsed by means of a counter-attack. 16 officers and 334 men of the Battalion became casualties and one of those who was reported missing in the carnage was George Thomas Hayto.

He has no known grave and his name is commemorated on the Menin Gate at Ypres.

It was not until a year later, in January 1917, that his widowed mother was notified that he was officially registered as having been killed. In 1920, at Over Haddon, there took place the funeral of George's brother, 30 years old Herbert. He had served in the Royal Engineers and then the Leicestershire Regiment during the war and was a POW of the Germans for some months, and suffered badly. His health was never the same. He lived at Littleborough, near Rochdale and was a police constable there. He was married to Lilian with a 6 month old baby called William. It surprises us that Herbert Hayto is not on the Over Haddon Memorial.

PRIVATE H. O'NEAL (O'NEIL)
MANCHESTER REGIMENT DIED FEBRUARY 1916

These details, printed above, are to be found on the roll of honour in Bakewell Parish Church and the soldier's name is also on the war memorial in Rutland Square. Sadly, we have been unable to find any further details, either about his background or service record, but his name is recorded with honour in the pages of this book, along with all the other men from the town who died.

RAF casualties from Bakewell and district appear quite frequently on the Second World War memorials, but during the First World War the vast majority of men from the district who were killed, served in the Army. One of the few exceptions to this was a Bakewell motor mechanic who joined the Royal Flying Corps and was shot down on the Western Front.

AIRMAN FIRST CLASS JOHN WILLIAM NEWTON No 3098
15 SQUADRON ROYAL FLYING CORPS
DIED MARCH 14TH 1916 AGED 19

John was the third and youngest son of George Henry Newton and Sarah Ann Newton of Buxton Road, Bakewell. His father, born at Over Haddon, married Sarah Ann, a Lincolnshire girl, and began married life at Over Haddon, before shortly moving to Bakewell, where George Henry set up in business as a cab proprietor, whilst also working as a chimney sweep.

John William Newton was born in Bakewell in 1897 and was employed before the war as a mechanic at Mr B. Needham's motor garage, Bakewell. Known to friends as 'Billie', he enlisted early in 1915, joining the Royal Flying Corps ground crew as an Air Mechanic (this was a generic term, much like 'Private' in the Army. He could have been a mechanic, but equally could have been a rigger, fitter, driver etc.)

John William Newton
of Bakewell

One can tell from his letters he sent back to Bakewell that he was enjoying his work. In September 1915 he wrote to his old Sunday School teacher, Mr Tiplady, saying that he had had three nasty smashes whilst flying, through no fault of his own, and escaped with just a severe shaking. He received promotion to Airman First Class on September 1st 1915 and wrote that, 'I have got my ambition in life'.

He was based with 15 Squadron Royal Flying Corps, which had been formed at South Farnborough on March 1st 1915. From Hounslow, the Squadron moved to Dover but because of training commitments it was December 1915 before Billie and the squadron embarked for France and began operations from the airfield at Droglandt, before moving on March 8th to the airfield at Vert Galand. Six days after arriving at Vert Galand, Billie Newton was killed in action.

In March 1916 the main aircraft used by 15 Squadron was the B.E.2C, their primary role being reconnaissance – spotting for artillery or photographing enemy positions. As an air mechanic First Class, Billie's time spent in the air could vary. It was not unusual for any stray ground staff to be used as ad-hoc observers/gunners when the need arose, and some would be used regularly. Billie described in a letter home a flight over German lines lasting two hours, during which time the machine was struck by pieces of shrapnel. Other journeys were also made.

His luck ran out on him, however, on March 14th 1916. John William Newton was killed in a B.E.2C flown by Lieutenant J.W. Cunningham while escorting a reconnaissance aircraft. They were shot down in flames by a Fokker aircraft flown by Lieutenant G. Leffers at about 11 am on March 14th. They crashed near Achiet Le Grand, 19 km south of Arras. Cunningham was killed outright and Billie Newton later died of wounds.

His parents suffered many anxious months, not knowing whether he was dead or a Prisoner of War. After a long delay they were sent official notice of his death. John William Newton's body is buried in grave III.K.21/22 Achiet-Le-Grand Communal Cemetery Extension, side by side with his pilot.

During April 1916 there were no large scale operations on the British sector of the Western Front. However, daily casualties always resulted from day to day shelling of the front and back lines or from small raids made by both sides to test the enemy's strength and seek information. In one such enemy incursion, a Bakewell Territorial was killed.

PRIVATE BERTIE BIRLEY NO 240392 'C' COMPANY
6TH BATTALION SHERWOOD FORESTERS
DIED APRIL 23RD 1916 AGED 20

In 1901 Bertie Birley, aged 4 years, was the youngest of three children of George and Mahala Birley, of North Church Street, Bakewell. Parents and children were all natives of Bakewell, with George Birley working as a chert miner in a local quarry.

When the war began in August 1914, 18 year old Bertie, who was already a member of the Territorial Company of the Sherwood Foresters, joined immediately. He was invalided to a hospital in England after being wounded and after recovery, spent ten days with his family in Bakewell, before returning to the Foresters.

In January 1916 the 6th Battalion moved by rail to the French Mediterranean port of Marseilles, ready for embarkation to Egypt, but by the end of January the move was cancelled and they entrained for the North of France again. Shrove Tuesday was spent at the village of Ivergny, where the Ashbourne men of No.9 Platoon organised their famous football match as played in Ashbourne (the special 'ball' had been sent out from the Derbyshire town).

Soon afterwards they marched into the trenches near Mont St. Eloi. They were relieved from front line action on April 3rd but in late April (April 23rd) 1916, whilst back in the front line, a German mine was exploded and in the fighting that followed an officer and 3 men were killed and 14 wounded.

Bertie Birley of Bakewell.

One of those killed was Bertie Birley. As a result of the explosion, his body was never recovered and his name is honoured on Bay 7 of the Arras Memorial, France.

Shelling of the enemy lines was a daily occurrence, even on the quietest day. The batteries of the Royal Field Artillery and Royal Garrison Artillery were always active, but they were also on the receiving end of enemy artillery retaliation. A Gunner in the RFA, who was a former printer from Bakewell, became the next victim during a short but savage enemy bombardment.

GUNNER FREDERICK WILLIAM BARNETT NO 26853
'C' BATTERY 83RD BRIGADE ROYAL FIELD ARTILLERY
DIED MAY 5TH 1916 AGED 25

Frederick Barnett's parents were both born at Staunton, SW of Tewkesbury, in Gloucestershire. His father, William, was a railway signalman and by 1901 his job had brought him to Bakewell where he and his wife Mary resided on Station Road, where they lived with their three sons, all born in Bakewell. Frederick was the eldest son (the others being John and Charles).

By 1914 Frederick Barnett was employed at Mr Gratton's printers on Matlock Street and the family home was now on Oddfellows Terrace, Bakewell. The family attended Bakewell Congregational Church, where Frederick was a junior deacon.

All three brothers eventually enlisted, with

Frederick William Barnett of Bakewell.

Frederick becoming a gunner in the Royal Field Artillery. Another brother joined the Royal Army Medical Corps, whilst the third was also in the Royal Field Artillery.

On May 5th 1916 Frederick was serving his gun during a sharp and sudden bombardment by the enemy, to which his battery was replying, when, at 2-30 am they were hit by a 6 inch shell. Only one of the four men at the gun escaped with his life and Frederick was killed instantly. He had been in that section of the battery since October 1914 and had been only recently promoted from gunner to bombardier.

Frederick William Barnett's body is buried in grave F.26 Suzanne Communal Cemetery Extension on the Somme.

One of the deadliest sectors of the Western Front was to be found in the Ypres Salient, where even the 'quietest' days of routine trench duty resulted in casualties. It was here that a Bakewell man who had started a fresh life for himself in Canada, returned home and lost his life on Belgian soil.

TROOPER ERNEST MOSLEY TAYLOR NO 108573
CANADIAN MOUNTED RIFLES, SASKATCHEWAN REGIMENT
DIED MAY 7TH 1916 AGED 30

In 1891, five year old Ernest was living on King Street, Bakewell, with his father, James Taylor, a retired banker, born in Bakewell, his mother Ellen, born at Liverpool and eight siblings, all born at Bakewell.

Ernest's grandfather, James Taylor senior, had been born at Retford in 1788, the son of a book seller. James came to Bakewell as a mercer (dealer in silks and other costly materials), built a large house on King Street and opened the first banking office in Bakewell, alongside the Rutland Arms Hotel. Ernest's father continued the banking business during the mid and late 1800's. By 1890, Ernest's father, James Taylor, had sold his business in King Street and moved to new premises in Water Lane (now the National Westminster Bank).

By 1901, however, 15 year old Ernest was not with his family on King Street. After attending Lady Manners School, on Bath Street, from 1897 to 1899, he became a boarder at Newick House, a school in Cheltenham. We do not know what profession or occupation Ernest chose when he left school, but before the start of the First World War he had begun a new life for himself by emigrating to Canada and was living in the province of Saskatchewan.

On the outbreak of war, Ernest Taylor enlisted and joined the Canadian Mounted Rifles, Saskatchewan Regiment. When Britain declared war on Germany, the Dominions, including Canada, responded quickly and volunteers flocked to the Colours to go overseas and fight for the 'Motherland'. With very little training behind them, the first Canadian contingent, 30,000 strong, reached Plymouth on October 14th 1914 and found themselves on Salisbury Plain, involved in intensive training. The Canadian First Division embarked for France on February 7th 1915 and

The Taylor family relaxing at their house on King Street, Bakewell, in the early 1890's.
Ernest Mosley Taylor's father, James, the Bakewell banker, sits on the grass on the extreme right.
By the year 2006, the house had been converted into an antique centre.

J. Duncan

by April 17th were in the Ypres Salient, Belgium. Five days later the Germans launched their offensive (Second Battle of Ypres) with a gas attack and the Canadians were heavily involved in the fighting, receiving 5,500 casualties.

There was very little respite for the Canadians, because in early May they were sucked into the British attacks to the south, in the Battle of Festubert, where again their casualties were severe.

A year later, in May 1916, the Canadian Mounted Rifles were back in the Ypres Salient, in the vicinity of the Menin Road. With their advantage of occupying the high ground, the Germans could observe the movements of the Allied forces in the front and back lines in the Ypres Salient. The accuracy of their artillery and snipers was enhanced by this advantage and the daily casualty rate in the Allied lines was high on even the quietest day.

Ernest Mosley Taylor was killed by shell fire on May 7th 1916 and his body was buried in grave I.M.15 Menin Road South Military Cemetery.

It was a further four weeks before word arrived back in the market town that another one of its townsfolk had died in France, this time from natural causes, although the harsh conditions experienced by the men in the trenches, day after day, would undoubtedly have contributed to his death.

PRIVATE PETER BOND NO 240065
6TH BATTALION SHERWOOD FORESTERS
DIED JUNE 6TH 1916 AGED 27

In 1901 the Bond family was living at 7 Rock Terrace, Bakewell. Peter, aged 11, was the second eldest of five children of Abraham and Martha Bond. Both parents had been born in Bakewell, with Abraham employed in one of the local chert quarries.

When Peter left school he began working for a short while at Bakewell vicarage, employed by the Reverend Abrahams, Bishop of Derby and vicar of Bakewell. He then worked for several years at the DP Battery Works before finding work in Chesterfield and marrying Emily, a Chesterfield girl. They began married life at 3 Bridge Street, Derby Road, Chesterfield and it was there that a son, Peter Stanley Bond, was born. In

Peter Bond of Bakewell.
Graham Bond

earlier years at Bakewell, Peter senior had been a member of the local Church Lad's Brigade and a keen player in the football team.

When he enlisted, near the outbreak of war, he joined the 6th Battalion Sherwood Foresters and saw much active service in Belgium and France. Whilst in France, Peter acted as servant/batman to Captain Edward M. Brooke-Taylor of Bakewell, brother of Lieutenant Arthur Cuthbert Brook-Taylor, who had died at Gallipoli in June 1915.

Shortly before his death, Peter Bond had been home on 10 days leave and returned to France on Whit Monday. Official information reached his mother on June 8th 1916, that her son had died in a casualty clearing station from pneumonia and acute inflammation of the middle ear, after only two days illness. He was aged 27 years and left a widow and young child (later she remarried).

Peter was buried in grave I.L.3 Chocques Military Cemetery, 4 kilometres NW of Bethune.

The next three casualties for 1916 fell on the battlefield synonymous with that fateful year – the Somme – on the first day. The Battle of the Somme was launched on July 1st after a five day barrage by 1,573 artillery guns along a 16 mile front. 120,000 British and Empire troops dashed themselves against highly organised German defensive positions.

The Germans were by now the masters in the art of fortification and the shellfire had not fatally damaged the enemy. The German machine gun teams emerged after the conclusion of the barrage, ready to pour a withering, murderous hail of bullets into the oncoming mass of Allied soldiers. On that first day, casualties were 50%, with 19,240 killed, 2152 missing, 35,493 wounded and 585 taken prisoner. These were the worst casualties in the history of the British Army. The men who suffered

Going into the attack on the first day of the Somme, July 1st 1916.
Cliff Housley

this appalling tragedy were mainly those of Kitchener's New Armies, the cream of the country's youth, who had volunteered in droves in 1914, many forming into "Pals" Battalions, and had been two years in training for this morning and this very hour.

Despite the appalling losses of the first day, the British continued to push ahead in a series of small, limited attacks, with the Allied offensive deteriorating into a succession of minor but costly small actions. Another major offensive was launched on September 15th in which gains were made but a breakthrough eluded them. Nevertheless, the British and French continued attacking, gaining small areas of ground through mid November.

British losses in this campaign were 420,000; French 195,000 and Germany 650,000. The battles represented a watershed, for the last traces of the "early carefree spirit" of the war had gone for good. From now on the men who moved into the trenches to replace the fallen would not see the war as a wonderful crusade, but as a bloody, deadly chore, to be slogged through, and if possible, survived.

Two of the three soldiers from Bakewell and District who fell on the first day of the Battle of the Somme were from the neighbouring villages of Ashford and Great Longstone. Even more poignant was that both men were members of the same Battalion, the 11th Sherwood Foresters.

PRIVATE JAMES SHELDON NO 16106
'B' COMPANY 11ᵀᴴ BATTALION SHERWOOD FORESTERS
DIED JULY 1ˢᵗ 1916 AGED 31

James was the eldest son of Thomas and Sarah Sheldon of Fennel Street, Ashford-in-the-Water. His father was an Ashford born man, employed as a general labourer, and had married Sarah, a girl from Sutton-in-Ashfield. At the start of their married life they lived at Cressbrook, near Monsal Head, where James was born, the first of five children.

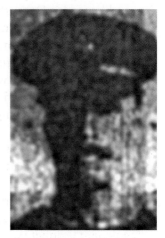

James Sheldon of Ashford.

Sometime later the family came to live in Ashford, where, by 1901, sixteen year old James was employed as a labourer in the wood yard. By 1914 he was working at Messrs Cox-Wilson's Works (Frank Cox-Wilson was a local builder and undertaker in the Ashford area) and was a keen footballer, playing at full-back for the local club.

James and his younger brother, Joseph Sheldon, enlisted at Chesterfield early in the war, with James joining the 11th Battalion Sherwood Foresters and becoming a colleague of Harold Robinson, from the neighbouring village of Great Longstone.

AND
PRIVATE HAROLD ROBINSON NO 28598
11ᵀᴴ BATTALION SHERWOOD FORESTERS
DIED JULY 1ˢᵗ 1916 AGED 25

Harold was born at Eckington, Derbyshire, just to the south of Sheffield, in 1890, the second son of George and Susannah Robinson. Their home was on Market Street, where George, a London born man, was employed as a grocer's assistant. Susannah, his wife, was from nearby Unstone. At some point just after 1901, the family, including Harold's elder brother, Robert, moved to live at Great Longstone and Harold gained employment on the Midland Railway. For some time he worked as a signalman at Bamford Station.

With regards to Harold Robinson's service in the Army in the Great War, there remains something of a problem. From newspaper reports in the *High Peak News* it is quite clear that Harold was reported missing on the opening day of the Battle of the Somme, July 1ˢᵗ 1916 and official news of his death only come to his parents in May 1917. However, the only Harold Robinson who died on July 1ˢᵗ 1916, serving in the 11ᵗʰ Battalion Sherwood Foresters, is recorded as being born at Long Eaton and living there at the time of his enlistment at Matlock.

We believe that as a railway man, it is likely that Harold Robinson from Great Longstone was transferred to Long Eaton to work at that station and a mistake occurs with regards to his place of birth. Harold joined the 11th Battalion early in the war and joined his Derbyshire colleague James Sheldon, from Ashford.

At 7-45 am on the morning of the attack (July 1st 1916), a message was received that the German Front Line was taken, and shortly after the Battalion was ordered to take over the British front line in front of Ovillers, vacated by the York and Lancaster Regiment. This was done under a fairly heavy shrapnel fire.

The Left Company filed out of a trench to occupy a bank in front of the line, but with great difficulty owing to the congestion of wounded in the trench. A very heavy machine-gun fire was brought to bear on this wave from the left flank, which had been re-occupied by use of underground galleries from the enemy second line after the assaulting Battalion had passed over.

The Second Wave then pushed forward in support. Casualties along the whole line were very heavy, and a general attempt was made to crawl forward under intense machine-gun and shrapnel fire, any available cover being made use of.

Lieutenant Colonel Watson walked diagonally across the front, collecting men as he went, and this gave a fresh impetus to the advance, but the advance died out before the first line was reached. Colonel Watson and other H.Q. Officers were wounded.

Another attempt to reach the German trenches by the sunken road on the right flank was made by 50 men under Captain Hudson, including the Battalion bombers. This attempt was brought to a standstill by heavy frontal and flank fire as they came over the brow of the hill in the last 80 yards.

The strength of the Battalion on entering the trenches on the 26th June was 27 officers and 710 men. The casualties sustained by the Battalion during the day amounted to 21 officers and 508 men. Two of the men killed in the slaughter were Harold Robinson and James Sheldon. Harold's name is commemorated on Pier and Face 10C.10D and 11A. Thiepval Memorial, for his body was never found. James Sheldon's name is commemorated on the same memorial. The two men came from neighbouring villages and fell together in battle. Almost exactly two years later, in July 1918, Harold's elder brother, Robert, would also be killed in action, in the Ypres Salient.

James Sheldon's younger brother, Joseph, had a distinguished war service with both the 1st and 2nd Battalions, Sherwood Foresters. Before the war he had served his time with Mr Nelson, the Bakewell Pork butcher. During his five years of wartime service he rose from private in 1914 to retirement as Captain in June 1919, a remarkable achievement, enhanced by winning the Military Cross with Bar and Distinguishes Service Order.

Joseph embarked with the 1st Battalion November 4th 1914 and was wounded at Neuve Chapelle (11/1/15) and again in February and April 1917.

He showed conspicuous gallantry and devotion to duty when in charge of a part of the HQ detail holding a small trench in July 1918. Under a terrific bombardment 50 per cent of his men became casualties, and he was ordered to counter-attack part of a trench which the enemy had entered. He led the attack with great courage and skill, and recaptured the trench. Later, when attacked by a vastly superior force, he established a block, and held the position, showing fearlessness and devotion beyond praise.

Joseph Sheldon of Ashford.

On September 18th 1918, in front of St Quentin, he distinguished himself in a most gallant manner. Under heavy machine-gun fire he led his Company through the wire and attacked the enemy in Dou Trench. He reorganised the survivors of all companies in his vicinity and consolidated the captured ground. Later again he went out himself under heavy machine-gun fire and succeeded in gaining touch with the battalion on his left.

On October 8th 1918, near Bohain, when in command of a Company, he showed gallantry and exceptional ability in leading his men in the advance. When the Front

George Sheldon of Ashford.
Brian Sheldon

Line, depleted of officers, came under heavy fire, he, by his personal coolness and disregard of danger, held the line, reorganised, and later put the whole position in a state of defence. Throughout the operations from the 8th to 13th he had been unfailingly cheerful in adverse circumstances, and had himself been responsible for the capture of about 200 prisoners and 15 machine-guns, located in various strong points.

James and Joseph's younger brother, George Sheldon, also enlisted, joining the Sherwood Foresters, before being transferred to a Battalion of the Welsh Regiment. Sadly, he was badly gassed in early 1918 and was honourably discharged from the Army on April 30th 1918. Although he survived the war he suffered with his lungs as a result of the gassing. George married and had a family, settling in Ashford, but in 1940, aged just 42 years, he died, another victim of the war.

LIEUTENANT JOHN BALDWIN HOYLE (MILITARY CROSS)
7TH BATTALION LONDON RIFLES
DIED JULY 1ST 1916 AGED 23

Like his brother, Geoffrey Morgan Hoyle, John was born at Knutsford, Cheshire, the third son of Edward Lascelles Hoyle and Margaret Hoyle. His father was a cotton spinner and manufacturer and the family home in 1901 was The Hall, Pott Shrigley, near Macclesfield. By the outbreak of war, however, the Hoyles were living at Holme Hall, Bakewell. We have already seen that brother Geoffrey was killed in the Ypres Salient in August 1915 and John would be killed in action on the first day of the Battle of the Somme, on July 1st 1916.

John Baldwin Hoyle was educated at Rugby School and Pembroke College, Cambridge and took the degree in June 1914. He enlisted in the Public Schools and University Corps on its formation and obtained a commission in the 7th (Service) Battalion South Lancashire Regiment in September 1914. Promoted Lieutenant in June 1915, he went to France in July of the same year. By June 1916 he was acting as Brigade Scout Officer and it was in that capacity that he was awarded the Military Cross in May 1916.

John Baldwin Hoyle of Bakewell.

On the night of 27th/28th February 1916 he made a thorough examination of the enemy wire opposite Neuve Chapelle, crawling about for three hours. He accurately noticed the position and the number of enemy sentries and selected a suitable spot for making the gap in the enemy wire. After returning to our lines and making his report he guided the party to the selected spot and covered them whilst the arrangements were being made. On several occasions Lieutenant Hoyle had carried out daring reconnaissance.

In the front line opposite Ovillers, 5km NE of Albert, with a Lance Corporal in attendance, they crept from their own lines through a sea of mud, and overcoming a number of obstacles, succeeded, after a perilous journey, in getting quite close to a German trench, acquiring valuable information. As a result of this information, a raiding party was able to go out on a successful mission.

A few weeks later, his Battalion took part in the first day's action of the Battle of the Somme and received grievous casualties. He was reported missing and during July and early August, nothing of a definite character as to his fate was forthcoming until mid August, when official notification arrived. Lieutenant John Baldwin Hoyle is buried in grave 1.B.15 Ovillers Military Cemetery, near Albert.

Private John Arthur Chadwick No: 12298
1st Battalion Sherwood Foresters
Died July 5th 1916 aged 19

John Arthur was the second son of George and Sarah Chadwick, who, in 1901 were living with their family of John, George William and Doris, on Bagshaw Hill, Bakewell. The whole family were Bakewell born and bred, with their father working in the Chert quarry. Later, he worked at the DP Battery, Bakewell, but by the outbreak of war the whole family were living at Ardwick, Manchester, where George was now employed in the Manchester Post Office.

After leaving Bakewell School, John was employed for a short period in the kennels of the High Peak Harriers at Ashford, run by Mr Tinsley at the 'Rookery'. When he went with his family to Manchester, John enlisted when he was 16 years of age and had been in training a few months before the war began. He went out with the Sherwood Foresters as part of the British Expeditionary Force in 1914 and was involved in the retreat from Mons, in which he was slightly wounded. Being a good shot, he became a sniper in the Battalion.

The Battle of the Somme commenced on July 1st 1916 and John's Battalion, the 1st Sherwood Foresters became seriously involved on July 5th. At 12-30 that morning they were told to attack, capture and consolidate a line near La Boisselle. They moved through crowded trenches to the support line near the church at La Boisselle.

*John Arthur Chadwick
of Bakewell.*
Cliff Housley

The left column was held up by strong enemy defences. The centre column was checked by a huge block of earth 12 feet high, and after several costly attempts to overcome it, the column had to give ground, as its flanks had become exposed to the attacks of enemy bombers. Meanwhile, the right column, after gaining its objectives, was driven back by bombs.

Fighting continued for some hours at close quarters but by 7 pm all the companies of the Foresters, except 'D', had been driven back. At 2 am on July 6th the Battalion was relieved (the Prussian Guards Division had been responsible for the counter-attacks).

Very heavy casualties had resulted from this action and when John Arthur Chadwick was struck down on the battlefield, his body was never recovered. He is commemorated on Pier and Face 10C, 10D and 11A Thiepval Memorial.

Sadly, we shall find that on July 1st 1917, almost exactly one year later, John's brother, George William Chadwick, would be killed only a short distance away from where John fell, whilst in February 1917, his uncle, Robert Henry Chadwick would also die in France.

SERGEANT JOSEPH REGINALD MOUNTNEY No C/567
16TH BATTALION KING'S ROYAL RIFLE CORPS
DIED JULY 15TH 1916 AGED 21

Joseph Reginald Mountney, known as Reginald to family and friends, was the third son of Albert and Agnes Mountney of Catcliffe Cottages, Bakewell (the

Albert Mountney senior on the left, at the annual camp of the "Volunteers'.
Mary Upton

Reginald Mountney with his fiancé.
Mary Upton

family had lived previously on South Church Street). His father, Albert, was a rural postman in the Bakewell district and everyone in the family were Bakewell born and bred. After leaving school, Reginald was employed on the Midland Railway at Millers Dale, on the demurrage department (amount payable by railway wagon owners for failure to load or discharge trucks within time allowed). Before the First World War, Reginald was a keen member of Bakewell Church Lads' Brigade. His father, the rural postman, was once in the old Pioneer Company (a type of Territorial unit) at Bakewell and was one of the first to join the new volunteer Corps of Bakewell. It is not surprising, therefore, that Reginald (a Territorial) and his brothers Albert and Walter all joined the colours early in the war. All three men would lose their lives whilst serving their country.

All three enlisted at Bakewell, with Reginald and elder brother Albert joining the 16th Battalion King's Royal Rifles Corps and youngest brother Walter, the Durham

LEFT TO RIGHT: *Albert Mountney, Walter Mountney, Reginald Mountney.*
Mary Upton

Light Infantry, later in the war.

Albert became a Corporal whilst Reginald rose to the rank of Sergeant in the same Battalion. They found themselves involved in the early stages of the Battle of the Somme, that began on July 1st 1916. In another 'push' on July 15th, it was reported to their parents that Albert had been wounded, whilst Reginald had been killed. News was then received that Reginald had been wounded, not killed, but this raised false hopes, for official news came a little later that he had lost his life whilst going to the help of a wounded comrade.

Joseph Reginald Mountney's body was not recovered and his name is to be found on Pier and Face 13A and 13B Thiepval Memorial. We shall find that brother Albert had indeed been wounded and taken prisoner. In May 1917, word would be received that he too had died, in a POW camp in Germany. Brother Walter was to die in 'the big' German advance in the Champagne area of France in May 1918.

PRIVATE WALTER G. HAMILTON NO 15749
11TH BATTALION SHERWOOD FORESTERS
DIED JULY 26TH (OR 28TH) 1916 AGED 30

In 1901, Walter G. Hamilton, aged 14, was living with his parents on Buxton Road, Bakewell. His father, Bernard, had been born at Ashford and was employed as a grocer's porter at Orme and Co (later he worked in the bottling department) and married Sarah Ann, a Bakewell girl. They lived first at Ashford, where Walter and his brother Charles were born, before moving to Bakewell. By 1901, another son and two daughters were added to the family.

*Walter G, Hamilton
of Bakewell.*

Eventually, Walter went to find employment as a farm labourer in the Alfreton area and it was at Alfreton that he enlisted, joining the 11th Battalion Sherwood Foresters. His younger brother Charles also enlisted and fought in the Dardanelles, before arriving in France. In August 1917 Charles would be killed in action during the Battle of Passchendaele.

Walter Hamilton enlisted at Derby and joined the 11th Battalion Sherwood Foresters. On the first day of the Battle of the Somme, July 1st 1916, the Battalion was involved in the attack near Ovillers and by July 2nd it was taken out of the line due to the severe casualties it sustained. Thankfully, Walter survived to fight another day.

Between July 3rd and 21st the Battalion was in various billets, away from the action and during those days received drafts of new men totalling 530 men, many of them arriving from England.

Between July 26th and 28th, the Battalion marched to the vicinity of Contalmaison, moving through the communication trenches to relieve a battalion that had been in the trenches for many days. It was during this relief, in which Walter and his colleagues were constantly shelled, that Walter was killed. One of many whose bodies would never be recovered, his name is commemorated on the Thiepval Memorial.

Although the main action being played by British forces was taking place on the Somme battlefield, many other battalions were in the front line on other sectors of the Western Front, mainly involved in day to day activities in the trenches. It was in such a sector, to the north of the Somme, that an Ashford man became the next casualty of war.

SERGEANT WALTER S. BRIDGE NO 27867
'B' COMPANY 17ᵀᴴ BATTALION SHERWOOD FORESTERS
DIED AUGUST 1ˢᵀ 1916 AGED 33

Eighteen year old Walter Bridge was living at Watts Green, Ashford, in 1901, together with his widowed mother Harriet, a Bakewell woman, and her grand-daughter, 10 year old Grace Lees. Walter was born at Willsden, London, but in 1901 at Ashford, he was working as a baker's apprentice.

One of his brothers was working and living at Hyson Green, Nottingham, before the start of the war, and Walter joined him at Hyson Green. He enlisted in the 17ᵗʰ Battalion Sherwood Foresters and by July 1916 had been promoted to Sergeant.

The Battle of the Somme had commenced on July 1ˢᵗ 1916, but Sergeant Walter Bridge and the 17ᵗʰ Battalion were not involved, being in the front line further north, at Givenchy, near Bethune. Between July 26ᵗʰ and July 30ᵗʰ, the Battalion was involved in routine working parties.

However, on the night of July 31ˢᵗ/August 1ˢᵗ 'B' Company carried out a raid across 'No Mans Land' into the enemy trenches at Givenchy. Three officers and twelve men were killed, three officers and forty three men were wounded and twelve men were missing. One of those killed in action was Sergeant Walter S. Bridge. His body was brought back and was buried in Grave 11.E.8. Gorre British and Indian Cemetery, 4 kilometres east of Bethune.

LANCE CORPORAL GEORGE HARTLEY VICKERS NO 18370
'E' COMPANY 9ᵀᴴ BATTALION SHERWOOD FORESTERS
DIED SEPTEMBER 27ᵀᴴ 1916 AGED 21

Six year old George Hartley Vickers was living on Mill Lane, Ashford, in 1901, together with his parents, Hartley and Mary Vickers, older brother John (9 years) and younger sister Alice Maud (1 year). His father, Hartley Vickers, was the village blacksmith, born at Ashford, and he had married Mary, a Welsh girl from Wrexham. All three children had been born in Ashford-in-the-Water.

By the start of the First World War, George was living at Brampton, Chesterfield, and working in the Mineral Managers' Depot at Chesterfield Station, on the Great Central Railway. He enlisted at Chesterfield early in the war, serving with 'E' Company 3rd Battalion whilst in training, but was posted to the 9th Battalion Sherwood Foresters on October 25th 1915.

George and the 9th Battalion were involved in various actions in the Battle of the Somme, 1916. Between September 11th and 23rd they were in and out of the front line trenches south of the Thiepval – Ovillers post, being shelled on a regular basis. (September 19th, 5 men killed and 25 wounded, September 20th several 'whizz bangs' hit Constance Trench, with 3 men killed and 5 wounded).

By the 24th September they had come out of the line and into huts and tents at a camp at nearby Mailly – Maillet, where new clothing was issued and a rehearsal held for the forthcoming attack on Thiepval. On the 25th there were bathing parades and the Battalion moved to Ovillers Post at 3pm. By 8 pm they were at Ovillers where tools, bombs etc were issued.

At 12-35 pm on September 26th the attack on Thiepval began and by 2-30 pm the 1st, 2nd and 3rd objective of the Battalion were gained, though with many casualties.

George Hartley Vickers survived the day's fighting, only to be killed in action the following day, September 27th, by shellfire, whilst in Joseph and Hessian trenches. His body was never recovered, and together with thousands of other soldiers, George's name is commemorated on the Thiepval Memorial.

PRIVATE JOSEPH MELLOR No 70626
2ND BATTALION SHERWOOD FORESTERS
DIED SEPTEMBER 29TH 1916 AGED 20

Joseph Mellor of Bakewell.
Cliff Housley

In 1901, five year old Joseph Mellor was living with his parents John and Elizabeth and six brothers and sisters on New Street, Bakewell. The parents and children had all been born in Bakewell and John earned a living for his family as a stone mason.

Joseph was living at Buxton when war was declared and the 18 year old travelled to Bakewell to enlist, being one of the first to enlist into the reserve battalion and volunteered for active service with the first batch from the Empire Barracks. Eventually he served with the 2nd Battalion in the Battle of the Somme between July 1st and end of September 1916.

During the Battle, Haig launched another major offensive on September 15th, southwest of Bapaume. The British tanks had been secretly shipped to the front, and spearheaded the attack. Despite the surprise to the

Germans, the tanks were unreliable, too slow and too few in number to gain a decisive victory. Gains were made, but a breakthrough eluded them. It also came at a cost. The 2nd Battalion Sherwood Foresters alone lost 17 officers and 421 men killed, wounded or missing. By the 19th September they had been relieved.

Somehow, Joseph Mellor had escaped the carnage, for the moment. However, by September 28th they were once more back in the front line, north-west of the Ginchy – Les Boeufs road and were subjected to heavy shelling by the enemy. On September 29th Joseph Mellor was killed by shellfire. In the absence of a body to be buried, his name was later commemorated on Pier and Face 10C, 10D and 11A Thiepval Memorial.

2ND LIEUTENANT SAMUEL STANDIDGE BODEN
14TH BATTALION DURHAM LIGHT INFANTRY
DIED OCTOBER 15TH 1916 AGED 23

Samuel Standidge Boden of Bakewell.

Samuel Boden was born at Church Gresley, near Swadlincote, Derbyshire, the second son of Life Insurance agent, Samuel Boden senior and his wife Constance. She had been born in Woodville, Leicestershire, whilst his place of birth was Clitheroe, in Lancashire, where his father had been the head-master of Clitheroe Grammar School.

They had moved around the country, living at Church Gresley, Small Heath and Worcestershire, but by 1901, Samuel Boden senior and Constance were living on Matlock Street, Bakewell, with their children, Edward, Samuel, Margaret and Norman.

Samuel Standidge Boden was educated at Lady Manners School between 1908 and 1911 and subsequently at Cheltenham College, and afterwards obtained a post as assistant school master in one of the London County Council Schools.

Just before the start of the war the family left Bakewell after 17 years in the town, but in 1915 Samuel Boden senior died and by 1916 Constance Boden was living at Church Gresley, near Burton-on-Trent.

Samuel junior was in the Officer Training Corps and received a commission in September 1914, joining the Durham Light Infantry, before being attached to the Machine Gun Corps and reaching the rank of Second Lieutenant. His brother Norman was also in the Army. Samuel had been continually on active service and was wounded in September 1915 during the Battle of Loos, where his Battalion at the time had been engaged in making an opening for the Guards to advance to the attack. He had paid a visit to Bakewell when he had recovered sufficiently from these injuries.

Samuel Boden was killed by shell fire on Sunday October 15th 1916, in the trenches during the Somme Battle, being hit on the left side of the head and killed instantaneously. He was at the time passing from one position to another with his machine gun section (he was in charge of three gun teams). There is no known grave and Samuel Standidge Boden's name is commemorated on Pier and Face 14A and 15C Thiepval Memorial.

PRIVATE JOHN ANDREWS NO 71079
17TH BATTALION SHERWOOD FORESTERS
DIED NOVEMBER 5TH 1916 AGED 31

John Edward Shield Andrews was born at Bakewell on June 24th 1885, the son of John A. Andrews, a Bakewell policemen and Sarah Andrews. At the age of 23, John Andrews junior, a quarryman, married 21 year old Emma Rose from Bakewell, her father Herbert also working in a local quarry. At the time of his wedding, on November 28th 1908, John's father, the Bakewell policeman, had died.

The couple began married life at Dagnall Terrace before living at Rock Terrace. In April 1909, a son, John, (Jackie) was born and in November 1910, a daughter, Dorothy (Dollie). On October 15th 1914, another son, Edward, was born and by this time John Andrews was serving in the Army, having volunteered at the start of the war. Sadly, Edward died aged 21 months in July 1916 when he was accidentally scalded in bath water. On November 10th 1916 another son was born and was

John Andrews of Bakewell.
Stephen Rose

named Edward Shield Andrews (Eddie). Just five days before his birth, his father was killed on the Western Front. Prior to this, John had already been wounded in battle and had spent time at a British convalescent hospital, before returning to his Battalion.

John had rejoined the 17th Battalion Sherwood Foresters and the Battalion saw action during the Battle of the Somme, especially in the latter stages. On October 27th 1916 the Battalion relieved the Royal Sussex Regiment in the front line at Authuille, near Thiepval. At 4-30 am on October 29th a small attack was carried out by the Bombing Parties on the enemy Strong Post. There was no artillery preparation and the enemy, though in great strength, were taken by surprise and offered little opposition. The Foresters took the position with great dash and the capture of this point considerably strengthened their position. One man in the Battalion was killed and John Andrews from Bakewell was severely wounded.

Mrs Andrews received a letter on Thursday 9th November 1916 informing her that her husband had been severely wounded and conveyed to hospital and on Friday

John Andrews of Bakewell holds the horse's head. He was convalescing at a hospital in England.
Stephen Rose

morning she received a second letter form Nurse Gray imparting the sad news that her husband had died from his wounds.

The nurse stated in her letter that John, when brought to the hospital, was suffering from wounds to both legs and other parts of the body, all of a serious nature. The patient asked her if she thought he would pull round, and she told him that his condition was serious, but they would do all in their power for him.

In the event of his death, he asked her to write to his wife and tell her all about the matter. He said he had a wife and three little children and he must get well to go to see them. He was conscious and brave up to the end.

John Andrews was buried in grave III.C.23 Puchevillers British Cemetery, 19km NE of Amiens, near to the casualty clearing station in which his wounds had been tended by Nurse Gray.

PRIVATE FRANCIS (FRANK) WEBSTER NO 19832
10TH BATTALION YORK AND LANCASTER REGIMENT
DIED NOVEMBER 17TH 1916 AGED 34

Frank's father, Robert Webster, was born at Sheen in Staffordshire and married Christiana, who originated from Wakefield. By 1891 they were living at Diamond Court, near Water Street, Bakewell, with their five children, including 9 year old Frank (all born at Bakewell). Robert was employed as a jobbing labourer.

By 1901, Frank Webster, now 20 years of age, was to be found as a boarder with a family at Clay Cross and working underground in a local coalmine, but later he returned to Bakewell and worked in the gas works.

By the start of the war he had been married to his wife Sarah and they had three young children, Francis Ronald, born 1908, Bertha, known as Bertie, and Nancy. They were living in the Rotherham area by the start of the war, but sadly Sarah died.

It was at Rotherham that Frank Webster enlisted, joining the 10th Battalion York and Lancaster Regiment.

The Battalion took part in the Battle of the Somme, between July 1st and mid November 1916, with Frank surviving safely. By October 12th General Haig was convinced that he could not pierce the German defences that year, but was persuaded by the French to continue the attacks through muddy terrain in a series of petty attacks until November 17th (the final attack on November 13th saw Beaumont–Hamel taken but the village of Serre remained impregnable).

It was on November 17th 1916 that 34 year old widower Frank Webster fell on the battlefield, leaving three orphaned children back in England. His body was never recovered and his name is commemorated on the Thiepval Memorial.

Frank's children were taken in and cared for by their uncle, Ebenezer Gregory (known as Eben) at his home, North View, Fennel Street, Ashford. He was a stone mason for a local firm and it was he who carved the names of Ashford's war dead on the memorial. Frank Webster's name had already gone on the Bakewell memorial, but Eben was determined to carve Frank's name on the Ashford memorial, and he was eventually successful.

The last serviceman from the Bakewell area to die in 1916 was a Sheldon man, who succumbed to wounds received in the very last stages of the Battle of the Somme.

PRIVATE JOHN BROCKLEHURST NO 8010
6TH BATTALION NORTHUMBERLAND FUSILIERS
DIED NOVEMBER 30TH 1916 AGED 23

John, or Jack as he was called, was the youngest of the two sons of John and Louisa Brocklehurst of Sheldon, a farming family living at Ash Tree View, Sheldon. His mother, Louisa, born in Ashford, was the sister of Anthony Gyte, the landlord and farmer at the Devonshire Arms public house, on Main Street. Jack Brocklehurst worked together with his brother Anthony (Tant) on the family farm, when he left Sheldon School.

In early 1915, his brother 'Tant' had volunteered for the army and had joined the Grenadier Guards. By early 1916, conscription was deemed necessary by the Government and on February 17th 1916 Sam Wilton, Jack Naylor and Jack Brocklehurst received cards about the Military Service Act (conscription). On March 14th 1916 Jack had to be at the recruiting office at 9 am and leaving Bakewell Station he arrived at York, eventually joining the Northumberland Fusiliers.

Early on June 23rd 1916 he was home on leave at Sheldon, before departing for the

Western Front. He had arrived at Ambergate Station late on the previous evening and could get no further by train so stayed overnight with a porter at his house. With the 6th Battalion Northumberland Fusiliers he became involved in action in the Battle of the Somme.

However, on Sunday November 19th 1916, John and Louisa Brocklehurst received a field post card from their son to say that he was wounded and was going on well. By November 23rd 1916 no further news had been received by his worried parents and sisters Elsie, Leah and Alice, until on November 27th they had word from their son that he was wounded in the arm and leg (by this stage, his brother 'Tant' was home on leave from the Grenadier Guards and was able to provide some support).

Jack Brocklehurst was now in the vast hospital base at Rouen because of the severity of his wounds and on November 30th John and Louisa received a telegram from there to say that their son was dangerously ill. Sadly, on the very day they received the news, Jack Brocklehurst died and his parents received a second telegram on the evening of December 1st telling of his death.

John Brocklehurst of Sheldon.
Margaret Slin

John Brocklehurst senior of Sheldon, father of John and Tant.
Tom Brocklehurst

The news proved devastating for his family and also for the small village of Sheldon, for his death proved to be the first of five Sheldon men to fall in battle.

John (Jack) Brocklehurst was buried in grave. O.III.M5 St. Sever Cemetery Extension, Rouen. Almost a year later, on October 9th 1917, his brother Anthony ('Tant') would also die, killed in action with the Guards Division during the bloody Battle of Passchendaele.

Having won the blood soaked disputed high ground, the British were now fighting their way down into the valley beyond – condemning themselves to spend a winter in flooded trenches. Nothing of any strategic value had been attained. The 'Big Push' was over and it had cost thirteen out of the twenty lives of serviceman from Bakewell and District who were killed in 1916. The sadness would be great for each of the families concerned.

1916 had shown that the British armies could not stand up to machine-gun fire interlacing a defensive zone, stretching in depth for miles. In four and half months of almost continuous attack, they were able to advance only a little more than eight miles. The casualty figures had been horrific, for on the first day of the offensive alone (July 1st) the losses easily exceeded the battle casualties sustained in the Crimean, Boer and Korean Wars, combined.

The German defensive role had been magnificent, but repeated German counter-attacks proved even more costly than Allied assaults. The German Army would never be quite the same force again.

CHAPTER FIVE

1917 – THE DARKEST HOUR

As the year 1917 dawned, the families back home in the Bakewell area would surely find it hard to imagine that it could bring a greater degree of sadness than that experienced during the previous year. Twenty men connected to the area had lost their lives in 1916. Yet, by the end of 1917, another 40 service men would become fatalities in this dreadful war, mainly as a result of the gloomiest drama in British military history, the Third Battle of Ypres, more commonly known by the name 'Passchendaele' (July 31st to November 10th). It achieved little except horrendous loss of life, whilst the seemingly inexhaustible powers of endurance and sacrifice shown by the soldiers in the hellish battlefield conditions of oozing, glutinous mud was amazing and made even more poignant by the futility of the purpose and result. Out of the 40 Bakewell and District men lost during 1917, 13 of them died in this three month period, fighting in the quagmire conditions of Passchendaele.

The German General, Von Lundendorff, aware of Allied preparations for an offensive later in the year, and fearful of over-extending German lines in the west, deliberately chose a defensive attitude. During the early spring, between February 23rd and April 5th, the Germans withdrew to a specially prepared, much shorter, highly organised defensive zone, the Hindenburg Line, some 20 miles behind the over extended line from Arras to Soissons.

Behind a lightly held outpost line, heavily manned by machine-gun posts, lay two successive, defensive positions, highly fortified. Behind these again lay the German reserves, concentrated and prepared for counter-attack. Behind the German's withdrawal, they left a scene of utter devastation, as they destroyed the crops, killed the animals, poisoned the wells, demolished the villages and blew up the bridges.

General Nivelle, the French hero of Verdun in 1916, now had command of Anglo-French forces and planned the Nivelle Offensive on the Aisne and in Champagne (April 16th to 20th). The British preliminary to this French offensive was the Battle of Arras, April 9th to 15th, a tactical victory, but without a breakthrough and resulting in the loss of men from the local area.

For the French and British, the Hindenburg Line had thus proved too great a defensive barrier to break through and more significantly, the French offensive under Nivelle had proved an expensive disaster. Elements of the French Army mutinied and large numbers of soldiers stated that, although willing to defend their positions, they would refuse any order to attack. Great pressure was therefore placed upon the British to take the fight to the enemy, and so draw German forces away from the French.

General Haig, the British Commander, had long held the aim to break out of the Ypres Salient on to the Flanders Plain and on to take the Channel ports used by the German U-boats. Sanction was given for a limited offensive to ease the pressure on the French. It would come, though, at a terrible cost.

The British Empire suffered 500,000 dead and wounded during the three months of Passchendaele. Between July 31st and early November 1917, an average of 5,000 men a day were killed or wounded, and all for the capture of a few miles of desecrated land.

The first part of the operation, however, was a complete success. On June 7th, after 17 days of general bombardment, nineteen huge mines were exploded under German positions in the southern end of the Salient and the British 2nd Army swept the enemy off the Messines–Wijtschate Ridge between June 7th and 14th.

Tragically, the following six weeks of dry weather passed before the main assault was launched on the Gheluvelt – Passchendaele Ridge. This infamous battle began on July 31st and the rains began immediately. Empire troops were expected to advance though swamp – like terrain in full view of the defending Germans on the higher ground. 80,000 Empire troops were killed and twice that number wounded before Passchendaele was taken and the Battle halted on November 10th 1917, with the Salient deepened by about five miles.

But Haig, still determined to keep pressure on the Germans to permit the French armies to recover from the mutiny, played his final card between November 20th and December 3rd, with a surprise attack on positions in front of Cambrai. The world witnessed the first mass attack of tanks, as 381 metal monsters crashed into the German lines.

It was, however, at the start of the year, on January 7th, that the death occurred of a Bakewell soldier, killed by a German sniper, whilst on routine trench duty in the Font line. It is true to say that more casualties occurred during day to day activities in the trenches, from shell fire, rifle or machine gun fire, than occurred during the large scale actions of major offensives or counter-attacks.

LANCE CORPORAL WILLIAM FIELDING BEST FINNEY NO 43068
14TH BATTALION DURHAM LIGHT INFANTRY
DIED JANUARY 7TH 1917 AGED 20

William was the only son of Thomas and Laura Finney, who lived at Orchard House, off Stanedge Road, Bakewell. Thomas was a well-known and respected farmer from the Ashbourne district, having farmed at Biggin Grange and Thorpe Cloud before retiring early and settling in Bakewell in the early years of the

20th century. He had been a member of the Board of Guardians for that area as well as being an active member of Ashbourne Rifle Club.

Their son, William, was educated at Lady Manners School on Bath Street between 1908 and 1914 and played in the School First eleven at football in 1913/1914. He was a keen member of Bakewell Church Lads Brigade and the Boy Scout Troop. After leaving school in 1914 he worked at Needham's Garage, Bakewell, as a motor engineer, intending to move onto larger works at Derby, but the war intervened.

William volunteered for the Derbyshire Imperial Yeomanry at Bakewell, early in the war, with several chums, and his Battalion or Squadron went to France in September 1915, with William becoming a despatch rider. Whilst in training in England, he was able to

William B. Finney of Bakewell.

attend the funeral of his father, Thomas, who died on July 10th 1915, aged 47 years, the body being transported for burial at Thorpe. However, he was at the Western Front when his sister, Laura Elizabeth Finney married the Bakewell chemist, Hubert Thompson, on November 25th 1915. Sadly, we shall find that his brother-in-law was killed on June 30th 1918, whilst serving as a Second Lieutenant in the Royal Garrison Artillery, as a result of gas shelling.

William was promoted to Lance Corporal in November 1915, but by the end of 1916 he was attached to the 14th Battalion Durham Light Infantry and was stationed near Bethune. On January 7th 1917, aged just 20 years, he was killed instantaneously by a German sniper whilst on routine duty in the front line and was buried in grave T.11. Cambrin Churchyard Extension, 8 kilometres east of Bethune.

The loss to the remainder of the Finney family was great, especially his sister Laura Elizabeth Thompson. Between 1915 and 1918 she would lose both her parents, her brother William and her husband, Bert Thompson.

A few days after William's death, a veteran soldier died from natural causes in his home town of Bakewell.

CAPTAIN THOMAS SWANN,
6TH BATTALION SHERWOOD FORESTERS,
DIED JANUARY 18TH 1917

A well-known personality throughout the High Peak and West Derbyshire, Thomas Swann was born at Heath House, Coteheath, Buxton, before removing to Hargate Wall. Later, he lived for many years at 'Woodhouse', on Bath Street, Bakewell. By profession, he was a civil engineer.

In the years before the war he was the Conservative (Unionist) political agent for

West Derbyshire and was involved with a number of High Peak cricket teams as a formidable fast bowler. His connection with the Volunteers and Territorials resulted in him becoming the officer commanding the administrative centre for the 6th Battalion Sherwood Foresters at Chesterfield. He was also heavily committed in making a strong and earnest appeal for more recruits during 1915 and 1916. However, his health gave rise for concern during the last six months of 1916 and he died on January 18th 1917. His funeral took place in Bakewell, being of a semi-military nature and he was buried in Bakewell cemetery.

Thomas Swann of Bakewell.

The funeral cortege wended its way slowly through Bakewell. All houses and businesses had their shutters closed or blinds drawn. The coffin was encircled with the Union flag and the dead officer's sword lay on top of it.

Service Record
Lieutenant Derbyshire Volunteers (May 5th 1875)
Lieutenant 2nd Derbyshire Volunteers (Feb 14th 1883)
Captain (July 20th 1896)
Seconded to command the supply detachment of North Midlands Brigade
Lieutenant 2nd Volunteer Battalion The Sherwood Foresters (Sept 19th 1903)
Recalled on December 14th 1914 and made Captain 6th Battalion Foresters
Was Recruiting Officer at Chesterfield.

Conditions in the trenches, especially during the winter months, were harsh and the winter of 1916/1917 was severe. Many soldiers suffered ill-health and pneumonia was prevalent. One month after the death of Thomas Swann, another Bakewell soldier died after succumbing to the virus in a hospital in France, close to the front line.

PRIVATE ROBERT HENRY CHADWICK NO 240653
6TH BATTALION SHERWOOD FORESTERS
DIED FEBRUARY 17TH 1917 AGED 37

Robert Henry Chadwick was the son of George and Charlotte Chadwick of North Church Street, Bakewell. Charlotte was born at Darley Dale and married George Chadwick, a Winster born man. He was employed as a sawyer at Smith's sawmill on Coombs Road. Robert Henry, known as 'Bob', was the second eldest of five children. Two of his nephews, the sons of his elder brother, George, would also lose their lives during the war.

By 1901, Bob's father had died and he was living with his widowed mother,

Charlotte, a charwoman, and three siblings, and was employed as a chert quarryman at Holme Bank Quarry.

He enlisted at Bakewell and joined the 6th Battalion Sherwood Foresters at the outbreak of war, the very same Battalion as his nephew, George William Chadwick. By this stage, his mother, Charlotte, had died.

By the end of 1916, the Battalion was based in the Gommecourt Sector, on the Somme front. January 1917 was a month of intense cold and heavy snow. They remained in the same sector until February 18th, but when they were relieved and moved to another area, Robert Henry did not accompany them. He had been taken ill with pneumonia and died on February 17th 1917, aged 37.

Robert Henry Chadwick of Bakewell.
Cliff Housley

Robert Henry Chadwick was buried in grave A.24 Couin New British Cemetery, 15 kilometres east of Doullens. His nephew, John Arthur Chadwick had already been killed on July 5th 1916, and we shall see that four and a half months after his own death, a second nephew, George William Chadwick, would be killed in action.

During the following month, March 1917, an assistant master from Lady Manners School on Bath Street, was killed whilst in action in the Ypres Salient, Belgium. Although his name does not appear on the Bakewell war memorial or Roll of Honour, we feel that it is appropriate to include his details.

SECOND LIEUTENANT JOHN DAVID VAUGHAN
14TH BATTALION WELSH REGIMENT (ROYAL WELSH FUSILIERS) M.C.
DIED MARCH 18TH 1917 AGED 30

John David Vaughan was born at Llangunnor, near Carmarthen, Wales, in 1886, the eldest child of Henry and Rachel Vaughan. By 1891 the family had moved to Pembrey, Burry Port, near Llanelli, on the South Wales coast, where Henry was employed as a forgeman at the local iron works.

Educated at the County School, Llanelli, he was afterwards at the University College, Aberystwyth, gaining a B.A of Wales and subsequently held teaching posts at Tollington School, Muswell Hill, London, and Elmfield College, York, for four years, from which he came to Lady Manners School, Bakewell, in 1914, staying until 1915. He was editor of the 'Peacock', the School Magazine during this period. Keen regret was manifested by the scholars and the staff of Lady Manners School when it was announced that Second Lieutenant Vaughan, Royal Welsh Fusiliers, assistant master at the school before war broke out, and was expected to resume his appointment later on, had been wounded whilst in action in Belgium by a bullet from a machine gun on Saturday March 17th 1917 and died the following morning, March 18th. He was serving in the Ypres Salient at the time.

John David Vaughan was a member of the congregation of the Bakewell Congregational Church, and on the following Sunday the pastor (the Reverend H.E. Radbourne) made sympathetic reference to his gallant death. A few months before, 2nd Lieutenant Vaughan gained the Military Cross for distinguished bravery in the field.

He was buried in grave 3.B.11 Ferme-Olivier Cemetery, 7 kilometres N.W of Ypres. His name does not appear on the Bakewell War Memorial, but does appear on the In Memoriam panel at Lady Manners School.

John David Vaughan
of Bakewell.

The next casualty from the area was an Ashford-in-the-Water man who was killed whilst taking part in a night raid on enemy positions. It is even possible that he was killed by shell fire from his own artillery.

LANCE CORPORAL SAMUEL JAMES BEMBRIDGE NO 307360
2ND/8TH BATTALION SHERWOOD FORESTERS
DIED APRIL 7TH 1917 AGED 27

The Bembridge family was living at Mount Pleasant, Ashford, in 1901. Sampson Bembridge, head of the household, had an unusual combination of jobs, for it states that he was a stone waller and also a meat maker. He originated from Monyash and having married Sarah, an Ashford girl, they were living with their children Samuel (11 yrs), Sarah (10 yrs) and Ada (1 month).

Samuel enlisted at Chapel-en-le-Frith almost at the start of the war, joining the 2nd/8th Battalion Sherwood Foresters, and they had landed in France on February 28th 1915. He had served at the Front for ten months but had been invalided home around April 1916 with a serious wound. It was only in January 1917 that he returned to his Battalion in France.

By early April 1917, Samuel and the Sherwood Foresters were stationed near the enemy held village of Le Verguier, a strongly defended position in the front line, 7 kilometres N.W. of St. Quentin. A night attack on the village was planned for midnight on April 6th.

The enemy position was strong, behind wire that

Samuel J. Bembridge
of Ashford.

was 25 feet thick, flanked by machine guns, and with the advantage of direct observation from height. 'A' and 'B' Companies of 2ⁿᵈ/8ᵗʰ Battalion were at the front of the attack, with 'D' and 'C' in support. The manoeuvring into position was difficult in the dark and one platoon, in doing so, came under heavy machine-gun fire and were practically annihilated.

The going was very heavy, owing to thaw following a fall of snow. Passing across the valley, the men were up to their knees in mud, but pressed steadily on. The British artillery were unfortunately firing short, not hitting the enemy wire at all. The left flank therefore had to halt and dug themselves in, waiting for the barrage to lift.

'A' and 'D' Companies were exposed to heavy machine-gun fire, and, with the rain falling heavily, the Germans put up a strong barrage down in the valley behind the attacking force. To add to its difficulties, the British artillery suddenly shortened the range for some reason and the whole of the Battalion suffered heavily from their own side's fire. Their own shells dropped all along 'A' Company's line and four fell amongst No 16 Platoon of 'D' Company in quick succession, killing an officer and several men. A temporary withdrawal took place and the men dug in.

The wire was too thick to cut and the whole slope was swept by machine-gun fire. 'B' Company gallantly dashed right into the enemy wire, but in trying to cut their way through, had lost terribly, with 60% of their men down. 'C' Company also suffered heavily and the Battalion being isolated, the order for withdrawal came. Even then, disaster struck as the British artillery again shortened their range and caused death from shrapnel to their own men. In the torrential rain the survivors regrouped. Five officers and 43 men were killed, 69 others wounded. Samuel's body was brought back by his colleagues and he was buried in grave II.C.42 Vadencourt British Cemetery.

On April 9ᵗʰ, British and Empire troops advanced at the start of the Arras Offensive, supported by the artillery. A Bakewell man who served in the Royal Garrison Artillery was killed on the first day of this offensive.

ACTING BOMBARDIER JOSEPH RADFORD NO 69917
124ᵀᴴ SIEGE BATTERY ROYAL GARRISON ARTILLERY
DIED APRIL 9ᵀᴴ 1917 AGED 30

In 1901 the Radford family was to be found on Castle Street, Bakewell. James Radford, aged 48, was the Bakewell auctioneer, valuer and assistant overseer to the town, and was married to Catherine, a girl from Aston, in Staffordshire.

Joseph was the seventh of twelve children of James and Catherine, all having been born in Bakewell. He attended Lady Manners School, in Bath Street, between 1902 and 1905, and was distinguished academically, having been bracketed for the silver medal for mathematics and also the Challenge Cup for athletics.

Joseph entered Lloyd's Bank, Birmingham and afterwards was promoted to the

Head Office in Lombard Street, London. Whilst there he studied at London University and passed the intermediate examination for the degree of Bachelor of Law. He was married to Kathleen and they lived at 32, Palace Road, Crouch End, North Middlesex, London.

He enlisted at Harringay, Middlesex and became a member of the 124th Siege Battery, Royal Garrison Artillery. In April 1917 the Battery was heavily engaged in supporting the Arras Offensive against the German lines east of the town. The new British gas shell was most effective in paralysing the defending artillery, for it not only compelled the gun crews to keep on their gas masks for hours at a time, but by killing off the horses like flies, prevented ammunition being brought up. There was five days of bombardment of the enemy lines in preparation for the advance, from 2879 guns, 989 of them being heavy artillery. The

Joseph Radford of Bakewell.

artillery was also involved in supplying a superbly timed creeping barrage to cover the advance of the British and Canadian infantry from 5-30 am on the 9th April, the beginning of the offensive. However, the enemy artillery was still able to respond and counter-bombard both the infantry attack and the Allied artillery positions.

One such shell took the life of Joseph Radford. His body was buried in grave III.B.6 Louez Military Cemetery, Duisans, on the N.W edge of Arras.

His brother, Lieutenant Leslie Radford, was wounded in August 1916 and was still recuperating in England.

During the actual Battle of Arras, three men with Bakewell connections were killed. One had returned from Australia to fight to protect the 'Motherland', after emigrating to seek a better life for himself.

Private Joseph Nelson No 37452 'D' Company
20th Battalion (Tyneside Scottish) Northumberland Fusiliers
Died April 10th 1917 aged 31

In 1901 the Nelson family was living at Cunningham Place, Bakewell, with Joseph's father, William Nelson, earning his living as a grocer. William and his wife Hannah (née Marsden) were Bakewell born and bred, as were all seven of their children. Their eldest son, Albert, aged 16, was working for his father as a grocer's porter in 1901.

William Nelson was the son of Horatio Nelson, the founder of Nelson's pork butchery. It is interesting to note that Joseph Nelson, who would be killed in action on April 10th 1917, was the cousin of John Francis Aitken of Bakewell, who would be killed five months later, in September 1917. Joseph was born on May 2nd 1885 and when he left school be began working in the grocery trade with this father and older brother Albert, before working for some years at R. Orme and Co Ltd, grocers. He was also a keen member of the Workingmen's Club at Bakewell. By the start of the First World War, his father, William, had died.

Joseph enlisted in the army in March 1916 and was posted to 'D' Company 20th Battalion Northumberland Fusiliers. In April 1917 the Battalion had moved to the vicinity of Arras, ready to participate in the Arras Offensive, starting on April 9th. At 5-30 am the assaulting infantry moved forward, covered by a superbly timed creeping barrage, and in less than an hour almost the whole German first-line system was captured. But to the south the German resistance,

Joseph Nelson of Bakewell.

helped by machine-gun fire from Monchy-le-Preux Hill, was so strong that it badly delayed, though could not stop completely, the advance. Thus the reserve could not pass through that day, and behind them the cavalry had moved up not only in vain but to add to the congestion.

Joseph was wounded during the later stages of the day's actions and died from his wounds the following day, April 10th. His mother received a letter from him saying that if she did not hear from him for a few days that he would be all right and he appeared very bright and cheerful, but by the second post that day she heard from the Record Office that her son had been killed. Joseph was buried in grave B.23 Haute-Avesnes British Cemetery, nine kilometres west of Arras, an area used by field ambulances. His younger brother John was a sapper in the Royal Engineers and was also out in France, but fortunately he survived the war.

2ND LIEUTENANT ALFRED FOSTER
27TH BATTERY (32ND BRIGADE) ROYAL FIELD ARTILLERY
DIED APRIL 14TH 1917 AGED 20

Alfred was the second son of Alfred Foster senior and Emily Bradley Foster, born at 'The Curetage' Bakewell, on Septmber 4th 1896. Emily was the daughter of Humphrey Davy Hudson and Harriet Hudson ad was born in 1869 at Hythe, Kent, where her father was a police constable. By 1871 they were living at Buxton, with Humphrey still employed as a constable, but by 1881 he was a hotel keeper, running the Castle Hotel, Bakewell. By 1891 he had died but the hotel was now being run by his widow and her daughters, and later by her son, William Hudson.

Alfred Foster of Bakewell.

The Castle and Commercial Hotel, Bakewell, in the mid 1880's. Humphrey Davy Hudson,
proprietor, stands in the doorway, with two of his daughters in front.
Sally Hudson

Humphrey Davy Hudson, former
policeman, and proprietor of the Castle
Hotel, Bakewell. He was the grand-
father of Alfred Foster.
Sally Hudson

Emily met and fell in love with Alfred Foster, whose occupation is often given as gentleman. In 1894 they married and for a short time lived at Aldern House, before settling down at The Curetage. In 1895 a son, George, was born, followed by Alfred in 1896 and Harriet in 1898, though sadly she died, aged six months. By this time Alfred Foster senior had taken over the coal merchant's business at Bakewell Station, but, in January 1900, he died, aged 38.

By 1901, his widow Emily and her children were living at Fairfield, Buxton. Emily Foster eventually remarried, and by 1916 was living at Allness, Rotheness, Scotland, as Emily Gaisford. The family continued to have strong connections with Bakewell, for the childrens' grandmother, Harriet Hudson, lived at Granby Croft in the town.

Alfred Foster junior, known as Alfy to his family, was educated at The College, Weymouth, and afterwards went to St. Bartholomews Hospital, London, as a medical student. He subsequently joined the Officer Training Corps and when he enlisted became a member of 27th Battery Royal Field Artillery, gaining his commission as a Second Lieutenant. He went out to France in August 1916. Alfred was killed instantly by a violent explosion whilst in action in a dug-out on April 14th 1917. Two other officers with him were seriously gassed, one had since died and the other was seriously wounded. These actions took place as the Arras Offensive (April 9th – 15th) slowed down and came to a halt on the 15th. The seven day battle cost the British 84,000 casualties.

Alfred had been home on leave in February 1917 and his brother, Private Edward Foster, was now an inmate of the Red Cross Hospital, Bakewell, having been brought home on January 18th 1917 suffering from trench feet and rheumatism.

Alfred Foster was buried in grave B.8 Athies Communal Cemetery Extension, 5 kilometres east of Arras. That village had been captured from the Germans on April 9th, the first day of the Arras Offensive.

REGIMENTAL SERGEANT MAJOR FRANK G. WILSON
13TH BATTALION AUSTRALIAN IMPERIAL FORCES,
LATER 5TH BATTALION AUSTRALIAN MACHINE GUN CORPS
DIED APRIL 15TH 1917 AGED 27

Frank Wilson was the second son of Thomas and Frances Wilson of New Street, Bakewell. His father, a general labourer, had been born at Winster and married a girl from Ipstones, Staffordshire, before settling in Bakewell. In 1901 they were living with their sons Benjamin, Frank and William.

After leaving school, Frank was a joiner by trade, employed by Messrs P and J.W Mettam of Buxton Road, Bakewell. He emigrated to Australia in 1912 but, as with so many men from the 'Empire', immediately joined the Colours at the outbreak of war and was sent to Egypt, where he was an instructor of the machine gun section for eighteen months.

Eventually he was made sergeant major. His contingent came to England, where he remained for some months and carried out his duties as instructor. In

George Francis Wilson of Bakewell.

July 1916 he was on leave in Bakewell, at his home in New Street. In November 1916 they embarked for France and he had seen many severe engagements. He had two brothers in the Army, William, a farrier and shoeing smith, stationed in Salonika with the Derbyshire Yeomanry, and Benjamin, who was in France.

Frank was involved in the Arras Offensive, his Battalion taking part in the action on the second day, April 10th. Part of the 5th Army, including the Australian Division, launched a converging assault to the south of Arras against the Hindenburg Line, in an attempt to relieve the pressure of German opposition to the 3rd Army to the north of Arras. However, there had been little time to make preparations nor to bring up the artillery necessary for a normal trench attack, far less an assault on the massive defences of the Hindenburg Line.

Eleven tanks were to be used to act as a mobile barrage and wire destroyer, leading the 4th Australian Division against the Hindenburg Line near Bullecourt, N.E of Bapaume. The Australians broke into the Hindenburg Line, but then became the target of counter-attack from all sides. Frank Wilson was wounded on the head by shrapnel shell and was removed to a casualty clearing station, where he died on April 15th. He was buried in grave 1.B.16 Grevillers British Cemetery, 3 kilometres west of Bapaume.

Eight days later, on April 23rd, a former colliery worker from Bakewell, was killed with the Sherwood Foresters on a night attack in the French colliery district between Lens and Loos.

PRIVATE JAMES COOPER NO 241159
6TH BATTALION SHERWOOD FORESTERS
DIED APRIL 23RD 1917 AGED 41

B orn in 1877, the fourth child of John and Mary Ann Cooper, James Cooper lived with his family on Mill Street, (Buxton Road), Bakewell. He was a twin, his sister being Harriet Cooper. Both parents were born at Bakewell, as were all six children.

Their father, John, was a farmer and general labourer, and by 1891 fourteen year old James was working with his father. By 1901 James had left home and for fourteen years he was employed at Clay Cross Colliery, before returning to make his home with his sister at Bakewell. In 1915 he enlisted at Chesterfield and joined the 6th Battalion Sherwood Foresters. Prior to his death he had spent fifteen months on active service on the Western Front.

Through late March and early April 1917 the Battalion were involved in severe training until April 13th at Ligny-les-Aires, before marching to billets at Noeux-les-Mines, where for three days, they were constantly bombarded with a high velocity gun.

James Cooper of Bakewell.

They were now stationed in the area of colliery villages near Lens and Loos. It was decided that the 6th and 8th Battalions, Foresters, should attempt the capture of the colliery village of Riaumont on the night of 21ˢᵗ/22ⁿᵈ April, a difficult task since its slag heaps were strongly fortified.

'A' Company attacked a group of houses at 10-30 pm. The enemy opened up a rapid rifle and machine-gun fire, falling back through the cellars of a row of houses, connected by tunnels. 6ᵗʰ Battalion men followed up the enemy from cellar to cellar. The night attack proved successful, with few causalities sustained, but in daylight, their position was difficult to maintain.

On April 23ʳᵈ a further operation was carried out to capture Hill 65. It was believed that the hill was only held by the enemy in moderate strength and that only a small force was required to capture it and only the 6ᵗʰ and 8ᵗʰ Battalions were employed. In actual fact, the position was strongly defended and machine-gun, rifle and artillery fire was great. They failed to reach their objective, sustaining casualties of 20 men killed, with 5 officers and 71 men wounded. One of those killed was James Cooper, aged 41 years. He lies buried in grave X.F.6 La Chaudiere Military Cemetery, Vimy.

Mrs David Wright, his sister, of North Church Street, Bakewell, received news of his death a few days later. Another sister was Mrs Hopkins of Coombs Road, whose husband, Sergeant William Hopkins, had won the Military Medal earlier in 1917 whilst engaged on special transport work in France.

A few days later, news arrived in Wardlow of the death of a former resident who had been killed in action fighting the Bulgarians in Salonika.

PRIVATE BENJAMIN HUBERT GREGORY NO 55783
'D' COMPANY 10ᵀᴴ (SERVICE) BATTALION DEVONSHIRE REGIMENT
DIED APRIL 25ᵀᴴ 1917 AGED 19

Three year old Benjamin Hubert Gregory was living in Gorton, Manchester, in 1901, with his parents Benjamin (27 years), a railway carter, born in Yorkshire, and Ann Eliza Gregory (30 years), born at Ashford. Young Benjamin had been born at Wardlow, where his grandparents, Mr and Mrs Alexander Gregory, of Wardlow Mires, still lived.

Eventually he began work in the Sheffield area and it was from there that he enlisted and was posted out to an obscure theatre of the Great War, Salonika, in late 1916, being attached to the 10th Battalion Devonshire Regiment.

Bulgaria had entered the war in August 1915 on the side of Austro-Hungary and her ally Germany, with its main aim of attacking Serbia and so regaining part of Macedonia which Serbia had seized from Bulgaria in

Benjamin Hubert Gregory of Wardlow.

1913. The Greeks and an Anglo-French force despatched from Gallipoli was too late to help the Serbs and were pushed back by the Bulgars on the port area of Salonika. Evacuation made good military sense but, after the Gallipoli disaster, it would have been unthinkable politically. So an allied force of Serb, British, French, Italian and Russian contingents held the Salonika area more or less passively until 1918.

The inaction of the allies made Salonika a butt for music hall jokes and even the Germans showed a little sarcasm when they referred to the enclave as their "largest internment camp". With up to half a million allied troops in the area, such a description was possibly justified. Malaria, dysentery and other diseases kept the hospitals full.

Several inconclusive Allied attacks failed in 1917 and it was in one of these actions that Benjamin Gregory was killed in action against the Bulgars. Mr. and Mrs. Alexander Gregory of Wardlow Mires heard that their grandson had been killed in Salonika, in action against the enemy. Lieutenant Dunning wrote to his grand-parents, "Dear Madam, It is with the deepest regret that I write to extend to you my most sincere sympathy (and that of the 'D' Company) in the loss of your grandson. The Battalion fought splendidly against strong opposition, and more than justified their previous reputation. Our losses were not very heavy, but all honour to those who, like your grandson, laid down their lives for their country. Your grandson was a cheerful and willing soldier and set a fine example of devotion to duty to the rest of the Company".

Benjamin's body was not recovered and he is commemorated on the Doiran Memorial in Northern Greece, close to the border with Yugoslavia, near the S.E. shore of Lake Doiran. His name is also on the Wardlow Memorial and on the roll of honour in Great Longstone Church.

A highly skilled Alpine climber with strong connections to Buxton and Manchester and whose family resided at Great Longstone at the time of his death, was killed during the aftermath of the Arras Offensive.

2ND LIEUTENANT STANLEY FERNS JEFFCOAT
22ND BATTALION ROYAL FUSILIERS (CITY OF LONDON REGIMENT)
DIED APRIL 29TH 1917 AGED 34

Stanley was the son of Archibald and Alice Jeffcoat, and had been born at Stretford, Manchester, in 1884. His father was a salesman and by 1901, 16 year old Stanley was living with his parents and younger sister Dorothy at Urmston, Lancashire, where he was employed as an estate agent's apprentice. He was known to friends and colleagues as 'Jeff'.

Some years later the family moved to live at Brown Edge, Buxton, where Stanley practiced as a surveyor. By 1906 he was a member of the Rucksack Club of Manchester and the Fell and Rock Climbing Club. By 1911 he was climbing 'guide-less' in the Alps, making an enforced stay at 700 feet below the summit of the

Aletshorn, the second highest peak of the Bernese Oberland. His climbing had started in his teens on the gritstone crags of Derbyshire and Staffordshire and his name is remembered by two climbs on the Roaches being named after him ('Jeffcoat's Chimney' and 'Jeffcoat's Buttress'). He honed his skills at Castle Naze, $2^1/2$ miles north of Buxton and $^1/2$ mile S.E. of Coombs Reservoir.

Stanley Jeffcoat
of Great Longstone.
John Wilson

By 1913 he and others had explored and climbed the central buttress on Scafell in the Lake District and was instrumental in obtaining a cottage in North Wales, which in Easter, 1914, became the first climbing hut in Britain.

By August 1914 he had volunteered for the Army and eventually joined the 22nd Battalion Royal Fusiliers (City of London Regiment). He married Ada Burton, a farmer's daughter from Brown Edge, Buxton, during his five days leave, in September 1915 and in June 1916 a son, Stanley junior, was born. At the time of his birth Stanley senior was back in England, recovering from shrapnel wounds. In October 1916, six months before his death, he and his family had moved to Great Longstone, into 'Wasdale House', near the Cross, with his parents living close by, at Holme Lea. Returning to France after his recovery, he found himself near Arras in April 1917, taking part in the Battle of Arras and its aftermath.

Stanley Jeffcoat died from wounds received on April 29th 1917 at the Battle for

Stanley Jeffcoat
of Great Longstone.
John Wilson

Mountaineer Stanley Jeffcoat practicing on 'The Scoop' at
Castle Naze, near Buxton, prior to the First World War.
John Wilson

Oppy. He led his men in the capture of a section of the enemy trenches and, with many officers and men dead or wounded, he gathered men from a different regiment, built a barricade and helped drive back repeated enemy counter-attacks. As reinforcements arrived, he sadly received a severe wound from which he died. Stanley was recommended by his Commanding Officer for a Victoria Cross, and although this did not occur, he was mentioned in despatches.

At the height of the battle in which he died of wounds he scrawled a message across the page of a book, which was eventually brought back to his wife after his death. It reads 'Goodbye wife of my heart. Have only a few minutes – and love you, think of you and Baby. Ever your true hubby – Stanley'.

Stanley Ferns Jeffcoat was buried in grave II.B.17 Roclincourt Military Cemetery, east of the road from Arras to Lens. His name is commemorated on both the Great Longstone and Buxton War memorials and on the summit of the Great Gable, in the Lake District.

Reverend C.G. Lynn-Fryer of Great Longstone Church wrote in the parish magazine for June 1917:-

"Here was a man who gave up everything in this world for his King, his country and his God, gave up a flourishing business in Manchester and now leaves a young wife and baby. Oh! How truly it may be said of him he did his duty."

In the early days of the following month, May 1917 the Mountney family of Bakewell received the dreadful news that a second of their sons had died from wounds in Germany, after being taken prisoner at the Somme, on July 14th 1916, the day on which the first of their three sons to die in the war had been killed in action. May would prove to be a terrible month for the district as five servicemen's lives were lost.

RIFLEMAN (CORPORAL) ALBERT MOUNTNEY (MM) NO C/141
16TH BATTALION KING'S ROYAL CORPS
DIED 3RD/4TH MAY 1917 AGED 27

Albert Mountney was the brother of Sergeant Joseph Reginald Mountney, who we have already seen was killed in action on July 15th 1916, aged 21. Both brothers were serving in the same Battalion of the King's Royal Rifle Corps, having joined up in October 1914, after serving in the Bakewell Territorials.

The Mountney family lived on South Church Street, with their father, Albert senior employed as the rural postmen, and Albert junior was a gardener for Mr A. Campbell Blair at Burton Closes. A former keen member of Bakewell Church Lads' Brigade, Albert was engaged to Alice Turner, daughter of Private Henry Turner, Sherwood Foresters, of 7 Catcliffe Cottages. Albert Mountney was awarded the Military Medal for gallantry on the field of battle early in the Battle of the Somme, 1916, but it was in a second major 'push' that began on July 14th that brother Joseph would be killed and Albert wounded and then taken prisoner.

On the left flank, soon after midday on the 15th July, the German resistance was clearly disintegrating, but although two squadrons of mounted cavalry worked on their flank, the infantry were a shade battle-weary. The attack slowed down and although most of High Wood was cleared that evening, the northern corner remained in German hands. Late on July 15th the wood was evacuated under pressure of German counter-attacks and it was during these actions that Joseph Mountney was killed and Albert wounded and taken as a Prisoner of War.

Albert Mountney and fiancé Alice Turner.
Mary Upton

Eventually, the Mountney family in Bakewell received the news that Albert had died from his wounds in Germany on May 3rd 1917. His body was buried in grave VI.D.7 Niederzwehren Cemetery, near Kassel, Germany.

One year later, in May 1918, the family would hear the dreadful news that a third son, Walter, had also died from wounds received in the last major German offensive of the war, in the Champagne area of France.

Meanwhile, Bakewell and Monyash residents learned of the death of a skilled worker from Needham's Garage in Bakewell, caused when his transport ship was sunk by a German U-boat in the Mediterranean Sea.

GUNNER JOHN BOULTON No 108797
188TH HEAVY BATTERY ROYAL GARRISON ARTILLERY
DIED MAY 5TH 1917 AGED 32

At the outbreak of war, John Boulton, who was born at Stoke-on-Trent, was living at Monyash with his wife Nellie. He was a skilled workman and prior to the war was in the employ of Messrs. B. Needham and Son, motor engineers, Bakewell, for seven years, and had lived at 'Calton View' in that town for a period. He was skilled at painting the bodywork of cars. John was an active worker in connection with the Primitive Methodists of the Buxton circuit. He was also a member of the Male Voluntary Aid Detachment (V.A.D.) and a keen athlete, being good at swimming and football.

John Boulton enlisted at Bakewell and joined the 188th Heavy Battery, Royal Garrison Artillery, as a gunner. In April 1917 they embarked for Salonika, north of Greece, as reinforcements for the Allied Force (British, Serbs, French etc) fighting the Bulgarians.

As they were crossing the eastern Mediterranean Sea, en route to Salonika, their transport, the troopship 'Cameronia', with 3,000 men on board, was torpedoed by a German U-boat, with the loss of many lives, including that of John Boulton. His body was never recovered and his name is commemorated on the Doiran Memorial, Salonika. When the news arrived, his wife, Nellie, was away nursing her sick mother in a severe illness at Llandudno, Wales. For some time the deceased had lodged with this brother-in-law, Mr. Palfreyman, at the Post Office in Monyash.

*John Boulton
of Bakewell and Monyash.*

The bad news was unrelenting as confirmation came five days later that the son of the Ashford schoolmaster, and winner of the Military Cross, was killed by shellfire whilst in the trenches near Lens and Loos. As was so often the case, if he had been stood a few yards to left or right at the time, he would have remained safe. Throughout his army service he had been wounded on four occasions and made a recovery each time, but his luck ran out on May 10th 1917.

2ND LIEUTENANT FREDERICK WILLIAM ARTHUR STUBBS (M.C.) 'A' COMPANY 6TH BATTALION SHERWOOD FORESTERS DIED MAY 10TH 1917 AGED 26

Arthur Stubbs, son of the Ashford schoolmaster.

Born on July 29th 1890, Arthur Stubbs was the son of William R. Stubbs, the Ashford schoolmaster (and choirmaster) and Alice Stubbs, who was also a schoolmistress. He was educated at Lady Manners School between 1903 and 1905 and then at St John's College, York, before becoming a schoolteacher, himself. Whenever he stayed in Ashford he took a keen interest in the activities of the local scout group. Arthur Stubbs had been in the Territorials before the war started and joined up at the start, in August 1914.

Enlisting as a private, Arthur got a commission on December 18th 1915, becoming a Second Lieutenant. The Battalion landed in France on February 28th 1915. By the time of his death in May 1917, two other brothers were serving in the army and another one was about to start. On July 1st 1916 he was seriously wounded on the first day of the Battle of the Somme, during the diversionary attack on Gommecourt. He came home on leave and was married to Hilda Amelia

Birks from Fenton, Stoke-on-Trent at Ashford Church on August 10th 1916. He left for France a few days later. (Arthur's father was born at Fenton and so Arthur would have known the area well).

Arthur Stubbs was awarded the Military Cross for most conspicuous bravery and devotion on 8th to 10th March 1917. On the 8th he led a patrol for 800 yards along unknown trenches to find out the exact position of the enemy. He led his men over three barricades and suddenly came upon a hostile bombing post. The patrol accounted for several Germans but were compelled by superior numbers to fall back. He and Lance Corporal Parkes covered the withdrawal with gallantry and coolness and no losses were sustained. On March 10th a small party of enemy approached the trenches under cover of mist and shot a NCO working in No Mans Land. Arthur Stubbs jumped over the parapet and tried to bring in the NCO although the enemy was only 50 yards away. He picked him up but a sniper fired at them and shot the NCO dead.

Arthur had also shown gallantry on the night of the 19th/20th September 1915 as a Lance Corporal, when, although wounded, he carried an important message to Battalion HQ through a heavy hostile artillery barrage and afterwards insisted on returning to his platoon.

It is interesting to note that Arthur was wounded four times throughout his period of service, before he was finally killed (wounded at Mont St. Eloy 26/03/1916, at La Folie (Vimy Ridge) 30/03/1916, at Cappel Fermont 03/04/1916 and Foncquevillers 01/07/1916).

In early May 1917 the Battalion was back in the trenches, east of Cite St. Pierre, in the colliery district of Lievin and Lens and for the next month they enjoyed a relatively peaceful time. However, sadly, the death of Arthur Stubbs occurred during this period. He was killed on May 10th 1917 by a shell in the Cite St. Pierre. Captain Robinson, Commanding Officer of 'A' Company, who was with Arthur Stubbs on the fatal occasion, had a very narrow escape, for he had just crossed the road and dropped into the trench on the other side when the shell came. Arthur, who had moved back a few steps to take cover at a cellar entrance, received almost the full force of the explosion and was killed instantly.

Second Lieutenant Arthur Stubbs was buried in grave II.0.4. Maroc British Cemetery, Grenay, near Lens and Lievin.

The following messages were written by his colleagues:-

From the Lieutenant Colonel:-

"His loss is very deeply felt by us all. He was a magnificent officer, and totally devoid of fear. His men were devoted to him, and we – his brother officers – had the greatest affection and respect for him. I don't think anyone could help liking and admiring him – his invariable cheerfulness had helped his company through many bad times. He was indeed a fine man, who put duty before all else."

From the Company Captain:-

"It has been a great blow to us, and I write to say how grieved we all are. I think I saw more of him than anyone else in the Battalion, and I can tell you there was no officer in the regiment who did his work better or more bravely, both in and out of the trenches. A great thing about him was that he understood the men and always knew what they wanted and how to look after them."

From another:-
"He was a splendid fellow, and I think probably the bravest man I ever knew. I shall always be proud and glad to think I have known such a man."

From his servant:-
"During my period under him, he was to me more than a brother, and I cannot express my regret enough at the loss of one so noble and kind."

During that same week in May, a second Ashford man, who had been employed at the DP Battery Works prior to the war, died from wounds received in action, whilst a third, employed as a groom at Ashford Hall, was killed whilst attacking enemy trenches.

PRIVATE VICTOR W. TURNER NO 70638
2ND BATTALION SHERWOOD FORESTERS
DIED MAY 12TH 1917 AGED 22

In 1901 the Turner family was living in Court Lane, Ashford. William Turner, a 41 year old stone mason originating from Bakewell was married to Mary Jane (42) from Ashford and with them in their cottage were their children, 19 year old May, a local school mistress, John Turner (18) a teacher, 13 year old Ainsley, 8 year old Mary and 5 year old Victor William Turner, all born at Ashford.

Victor Turner of Ashford.

When Victor left school he eventually became employed at the DP Battery Works in Bakewell, but enlisted in the Army at Bakewell in February 1916, joining the 2nd Battalion Sherwood Foresters. On Easter Monday 1916 they went to Ireland to 'put down' the Irish Rebellion and stayed until September 1916, when they embarked for France.

Between January and May 1917, the Battalion was stationed in the area between Bethune and Lens, in the coalmining area of France, with billets at Mazingarbe when out of the front line. A raid by 'C' Company on the enemy line on February 9th killed or wounded 60 enemy, with 10 Foresters killed and 30 wounded. On March 15th they took over the support line near Hulluch and on the 25th there was a German raid at 4-30 am, preceded by a bombardment, and enemy infantry infiltrated, but were beaten off.

April 1917 was a month in which both sides raided or attempted to raid each other in turn. On April 5th, 50 Germans raided Border Redoubt, but Lewis gunners and bomb throwers repulsed the attack. Two men were wounded by bombs thrown by the Germans.

On April 24th they again moved up into the trenches, the enemy shelling the road by which the Battalion was marching. Throughout the rest of April and into early May similar activities took place and casualties were rather heavy, especially in 'A' Company. Battalion casualties were 18 killed and 96 wounded for a ten day period when they were engaged in continuous fighting in the front line and there was much shelling.

Victor Turner's parents received news on a Monday morning in early May that he had been dangerously wounded in an engagement, and had been taken to the 7th Casualty Clearing Station at Noeux-les-Mines. Shortly afterwards they received fresh information that their son had succumbed to his wounds. Victor W. Turner was buried in grave I.R.21 Noeux-les-Mines Communal Cemetery, 6 kilometres south of Bethune, on the main road to Arras

Private Alfred Elliott No 203228
2ND/5TH Battalion Royal Warwickshire Regiment
died May 16TH 1917 aged 24

In 1901, eight year old Alfred Elliott was living at Greenlands, near Mill Street, Bakewell, with his widowed grandmother, Ann Noton, a farmer, uncle George Noton, a carter on the farm, aunty May Noton and siblings Ellen and George Elliott. On the occasion of the census, their parents were elsewhere. His father, Alfred senior, was a carter. Better known as Alfy Elliott, (or sometimes Fred), when he left school he was in the employ of Messrs. Thomas Allsop and Sons, the Bakewell building firm. He married 21 year old Mary Hannah Oldfield from Ashford on October 10th 1914 and they resided at Greenlands. By this time his mother was living at Rowsley. Alfy Elliott's employment by now was carter.

Alfred Elliott of Bakewell and Ashford.

When he enlisted at Bakewell he first joined the Royal Field Artillery but later transferred to the 2nd/5th Battalion Royal Warwickshire Regiment and at the time of his death he had been in France about eight months. His wife was the sister of Mrs Upton of the Bulls Head Inn, Ashford, and whilst he was serving abroad, she went to live in Ashford.

She received news from her husband on May 13th that he would be going into action (the British were attempting to distract the Germans from attacking the French, after the outbreak of mutiny in the French armies). However, a few days later she received official information that Alfy had been taken to hospital, seriously ill from blood poisoning due to his kidneys not working properly, and had died.

Alfred Elliott was buried in grave B.3 Nesle Communal Cemetery, 20 kilometres south of Peronne, on the Somme.

We find that because of his wife's strong connection to Ashford, Alfred Elliott's name is to be found on both the Bakewell and Ashford war memorials.

PRIVATE GEORGE WILLIAM BLACKWELL No 28502
5TH BATTALION SOUTH STAFFORDSHIRE REGIMENT
DIED JUNE 26TH 1917 AGED 38

George William Blackwell was born at Great Longstone in 1879, but his name is commemorated on the Ashford War Memorial. His parents, William, a general labourer, and Elizabeth were born at Longstone, as were all four children. By 1901, twenty two year old George William was a groom, employed by G.J. Marples of Thornbridge Hall. When he married Lily Doxey from Ashford in April 1903 he and his wife went to live on Ashford Grange Road, Ashford, and he was employed by Mr. F. Lees of Ashford Hall as his groom. By the time of his death in June 1917, his family consisted of four young children (William Henry 1905, George Reginald 1907, Joseph Francis 1914 and Florence Edith 1915). George enlisted at Bakewell in early 1916 and by 1917 was with the 5th Battalion South Staffordshire Regiment, to which he was attached as a horse-shoer.

George William Blackwell of Ashford.

During the latter part of May 1917 and June 16th 1917 the Battalion had spent 28 days continuously in the front and support lines in the coal mining area between Loos and Lievin, near Lens, in France.

After six days out of the line, however, they were back in the support positions of the Lievin Sector, on June 22nd. On the 24th the Battalion moved in support for the 6th Battalion South Staffs during an attack on Hill 65 and on the 28th June the 5th Battalion attacked enemy trenches east of Cite de Riaumont.

It was on June 26th, during this intense period of fighting that George William Blackwell was killed in action. He has no grave and his name is commemorated on Bay 6 Arras Memorial.

A Bakewell man whose younger brother had been killed in action on the Somme in July 1916 and uncle died of pneumonia whilst serving in France in February 1917, fell on the battlefield during night action against enemy trenches, near the coal-mining town of Lens.

PRIVATE GEORGE WILLIAM CHADWICK NO 240637
6TH BATTALION SHERWOOD FORESTERS
DIED JULY 1ST 1917 AGED 21 (AWARDED MILITARY MEDAL)

The Chadwick family was living on Bagshaw Hill in 1901. Father, George Chadwick (25 years) was a chert quarry man, married to 30 year old Sarah, both born in Bakewell. Three children completed the family, 5 year old George William, 4 year old John Arthur and 2 year old Doris. The two brothers were known by their second names, William and Arthur, and we have already seen that Arthur had been killed in the Battle of the Somme, on July 5th 1916 and their uncle, Robert Henry Chadwick had died on February 17th 1917. Now, a year after his brother's death, the Chadwick's eldest son would be killed.

George William Chadwick of Bakewell.
Cliff Housley

Some years before the First World War began, father George Chadwick, now a postman at the Bakewell Post Office and a member of Bakewell Brass Band, had taken his family to live in Manchester, where he was employed in the city's postal service. His son William had been employed at the DP Battery in Bakewell but he joined the army before the outbreak of war, joining the Sherwood Foresters.

When the British Expeditionary Force went to France in 1914 he accompanied them. Serving with the 6th Battalion he won the Military Medal in late 1916 for gallantry on the field of battle when he held a trench against enemy attack. By that stage of the war, it is interesting to note that his father, George, had also gone out to France, where he was serving in the Labour Battalion.

The 6th Battalions Sherwood Foresters were chosen to take part in an advance upon the Lens-Lievin road and a network of trenches in front of it. On the night of 30th June / 1st July 1917 the Commanding Officer was now ordered to advance his line and consolidate in order that a new line might be used as a 'jumping off place' for the attack. At 11 pm on 30th June strong patrols pushed forward to their objectives, finally taking up their positions as far forward as possible. The objectives were taken, but, being very heavily counter-attacked by the enemy, the positions gained could not be held and the town of Lens remained in the hands of the enemy. Eight men were killed, 31 men were wounded, with others missing. George William Chadwick was one of those killed during the attack, adding his name to those of his brother and uncle who had paid the supreme sacrifice.

His body was never found and his name was added to those on the Arras Memorial, on Bay 7.

The next two casualties, both from Ashford, died whilst on routine duty in the front line trenches.

PRIVATE ISAAC BOND NO 28222
'B' COMPANY 24TH BATTALION MANCHESTER REGIMENT
DIED JULY 6TH 1917 AGED 32

In 1891, 6 year old Isaac Bond was living in Ashford with his widowed mother, Harriet Bond (49 yrs) and older brothers John and George. They were living next door to John Barnett, a mason, and his sons. Harriet was supporting her family as a charwoman. Ten years later, in 1901, we find that at Mount Pleasant, Ashford, Harriet had remarried, her second husband being her previous next door neighbour, John Barnett.

Harriet was Ashford born and bred, whilst John, George and Isaac Bond had all been born at Ravensdale, near Cressbrook. By 1901 Isaac was 16 years of age and working as a gardener, whilst his brother George was employed as a shoe maker's apprentice.

A few years before the start of the First World War, Isaac Bond left Ashford to work in Oldham. He enlisted at Oldham, joining the Manchester Regiment and in 1916 married Mary Alice. They began married life at 63 Franklin Street, Oldham, although Mary saw little of her husband.

By April 1917 the 24th Battalion, Manchester Regiment, was stationed in the vicinity of Arras. The Arras Offensive of April 9th to 15th was a British tactical victory but there was no breakthrough and attention was switched to a major offensive around Ypres in June and July, to divert the attention of the Germans from the mutiny taking place in the French Army.

However, day to day life in the trenches around Arras continued and with it the danger from shell fire and enemy snipers. Casualties occurred on even the quietest days and it was on July 6th 1917 that Isaac Bond was killed in action.

Isaac's body was buried in grave I.B.8 Ecoust Military Cemetery, Ecoust-St-Mein, 16 kilometres S.E. of Arras.

PRIVATE HARRY ROBERTS NO 205910 (OR 205010)
2ND BATTALION KING'S OWN YORKSHIRE LIGHT INFANTRY
DIED JULY 14TH 1917 AGED 27

Henry (Harry) Roberts was born at Ashford in 1889, the fourth of eight children of James and Ann Roberts, who were living in a cottage on Greaves Lane. In 1901, his father, James, born in Gloucestershire, was the coachman for Mr Clifford Smith J.P. at Ashford Hall, and later he became his chauffeur, as the motor car replaced horsepower. Harry's mother, Ann, originated from Ruddington, Nottinghamshire and had met her future husband whilst in service.

By the beginning of the Great War, Harry's family had left Ashford and Harry himself was employed in Sheffield, prior to the war. By the time of his death, in 1917, he was married, with a three year old son.

After enlisting in the army at Sheffield, he joined the 2nd Battalion King's Own Yorkshire Light Infantry and by June/early July 1917, was in the line, near to the Belgian coast. Wounded by shellfire in routine, day to day trench duties, he was taken to the casualty station but died from his wounds in hospital, on July 14th. Harry Roberts was buried in Adinkerke Churchyard Extension (just inland from the coast, between Dunkirk and Ostende).

Eight days after Harry's death, a ten day continuous bombardment of enemy positions in the Ypres Salient commenced, heralding the start of the Battle of

Harry Roberts of Ashford.

Passchendaele that began on July 31st. Four days after the offensive began, a Bakewell serviceman was killed, the first of thirteen men from Bakewell and District to be killed during the 3rd Battle of Ypres (Passchendaele).

GUNNER WALTER (HARRY EDWARD) FEWKES No 142882
197TH SIEGE BATTERY ROYAL GARRISON ARTILLERY
DIED AUGUST 2ND 1917 AGED 39

Walter Harry Edward Fewkes was born at Bakewell in 1878, the son of Alfred Fewkes and Ann Fewkes. Alfred was born at Loughborough and Ann was from Shropshire, with Alfred employed on the railway. In 1871 he was the station

master at South Luffenham, Rutland, but by 1878 he had moved with his family to Bakewell, where he was the second station master. Sadly, shortly after Walter's birth at the Station House in 1878, Alfred died.

By 1881, his widow Ann was living near the Nags Head Inn, with her sons Alfred (a railway office clerk) aged 21, Walter Harry aged 3 years and Hugh, aged one year. She was supplementing her earnings as a lodging house keeper.

We have already seen that during the war, in 1915, her eldest son Albert, the railway office clerk and later piano turner, would lose his son, Hubert, killed in action. Now, in August 1917, Hubert's uncle, Walter, would also die in this terrible war.

Walter Fewkes left Bakewell for Leeds, where he was in the stock broking business. He married Rose

Walter Fewkes of Bakewell.

Eleanor, a Leeds girl, and they settled at 5 Royal Park Avenue. By the time of his death in 1917 they had four children.

Walter enlisted at Leeds and joined the Royal Garrison Artillery and by July 1917 was a gunner in the 197th Siege Battery, preparing to support the huge artillery bombardment that began on July 22nd, for ten solid days, until at 3-50 am on July 31st the infantry of 12 divisions advanced on an eleven mile front at the start of the 3rd Battle of Ypres (the Battle of Passchendaele).

The artillery continued to support the slow advance during the following days, but the gun batteries were also being continually counter-bombarded by the Germans. One such shell landed close to Walter Fewkes' gun and he was killed by shrapnel. He was buried close by in grave I.F.15 Voormezeele Enclosures, 4 kilometres SW of Ypres.

SERGEANT WILLIAM BARBER NO 27838
16TH BATTALION SHERWOOD FORESTERS
DIED AUGUST 3RD 1917 AGED 23

William was a native of Nottingham, the son of John Barber. Before the start of the Great War he began work at Messrs. Burgons' Ltd in Bakewell, the grocers and provisions shop and lodged at the home of Mrs. Williams of Lumford House. William became well-known in the Bakewell district through his position at Burgons.

He joined up early in the war at Matlock, and rose in the ranks to become sergeant in the 16th Battalion (Chatsworth Rifles) Sherwood Foresters. The Battalion had been involved in the first few days of action in the Battle of Passchendaele, beginning July 31st 1917.

On the evening of the 2nd August 1917 they once more moved into the front line of action to take over the sector, in and behind the St Julien defences. There was torrential rain throughout the relief, with conditions underfoot proving to be horrendous. The next day, August 3rd, they contrived to make shelters with water-proof sheeting but the conditions were extremely dangerous because of German shelling.

William Barber of Bakewell.

Tragedy struck at Battalion Headquarters, established in a disused German gun-pit. During the relief, a high velocity shell dropped right through the entrance and three officers and thirty men were killed or wounded. One of those killed was Sergeant William Barber, whose body was never recovered. His name was commemorated on the Menin Gate at Ypres.

PRIVATE JAMES RENWICK TIMM No 43213
9TH BATTALION ROYAL IRISH FUSILIERS
DIED AUGUST 16TH 1917 AGED 25

*James Renwick Timm
of Little Longstone.*
Michael Stuart

Nine year old James Renwick Timm, the fifth eldest of the eight children of John and Mary Hannah Timm, was living with his family, close to the Pack Horse Inn, Little Longstone, in 1901. His father, John Timm, was born at Longstone and had married Mary, who originated from Darwen, in Lancashire. He made a living as a carter in the Longstone area and when his son James left Longstone School, he too became a carter.

When James enlisted in the army at Bakewell on December 4th 1915 he joined the 3rd Battalion Sherwood Foresters, its training battalion, and went to France with the Foresters on July 23rd 1916. However, he was slightly wounded and when he recovered he was transferred to the 9th Battalion Royal Irish Fusiliers on August 30th 1916 (it is interesting to note that whilst with the Irish Fusiliers he was put on a charge for smoking on parade on May 4th 1917 and served 3 days field punishment).

John Timm, the Little Longstone carter, stands on the main street of the village. He was the father of James Renwick Timm who was killed during the Great War.
Ian Cox

By June 1917 he was serving with the 9th Battalion in the Ypres Salient, where the Battalion held a supporting role in the Battle of Messines (they still managed to lose 19 men killed). This Battle had been the preliminary action to the bloody 3rd Battle of Ypres (Battle of Passchendaele), which began on July 31st and attempted to eliminate the northern half of the Ypres Salient, the southern position having been won in the Messines attack.

The 9th Battalion was held in reserve, since it was destined to take part in the assault at Langemarck on August 16th. Yet they still suffered in the frightful mud (in which many men were swallowed up and drowned, as in a quicksand), from the shelling and the bombing by aircraft. The result was that they were not fresh for the attack on August 16th.

At zero hour, 4-45 am, enemy shells rained down upon them, crouching in the British front line, causing the loss of 50 men before leaving the trenches. At last they climbed over the parapet to follow behind a creeping barrage. The leading companies received few losses from the enemy artillery but those that came after suffered heavily. 'A' and 'B' Companies in the lead were met by gusts of machine-gun fire from pill-box posts, especially from a little knoll called Hill 35. The hill was rushed and taken, but the creeping barrage had gone on ahead of them. The 9th Battalion tried to dig in on Hill 35, but the C.O., Lieutenant Colonel Somerville, was killed and there were too few officers and men left to hold the ground. The survivors retired little by little, exposed to fire that resulted in further heavy losses. By the end of the day they were back in their original trenches and were relieved the next day.

Nine officers were killed, 11 were wounded, 143 men were killed and many more wounded. One of those killed in action in the attack on Langemarck was James Renwick Timm. His body was not recovered and he is commemorated on Panel 140 to 141 Tyne Cot Memorial. Sadly, we shall find that during the Second World War, his nephew, James Renwick Timm (named after his uncle) would also be killed in action, whilst fighting in Italy.

PRIVATE WILLIAM ARTHUR WRIGHT NO G/43408
16TH BATTALION MIDDLESEX REGIMENT
DIED AUGUST 18TH 1917 AGED 24

William's very early background is somewhat unclear to us. However, we do know for sure that before the First World War, William and Sarah Wright and family were to be found in Bakewell, living first at Rock Terrace and then at Acre Wall Terrace, Monyash Road, with his father, William senior, employed at Holme Bank Chert Quarry. William Arthur, the second son, had been a member of the Church Lads' Brigade and after leaving school was first employed in the drapers and outfitters in the Clothing Hall in Bakewell Square. Later, he moved away to become a waiter in a large hotel at Westgate, near Margate, on the Kent coast.

William enlisted at Margate in May 1916 and eventually joined the 16th Battalion

Middlesex Regiment. He embarked for France in late November 1916 and we find that in June 1917 he was home on leave in Bakewell, just two months before his death in August 1917.

On July 5th 1917 the Battalion moved into the Ypres Salient, west of the Yser Canal. The enemy's shell fire was heavy, for even in support they lost 10 men wounded on the 7th and throughout the rest of July lost 11 killed and 71 wounded.

Early in August the 16th Battalion were S.W. of Langemarck, going into the front line on the 9th/10th August, west of the stream called Steenbeek. An attack was made on the 12th August by three platoons of 'A' Company, forming up in three lines west of the Steenbeek, and at 4-20 am, under an artillery barrage, Passerelle Farm, east of the stream, was attacked. This

William Arthur Wright of Bakewell and Over Haddon.

'push' was successful, with prisoners, two machine-guns and a howitzer captured. The position was consolidated and held, but a second attack was necessary, during which the farm was recaptured. On the night of August 13th the Battalion was relieved and marched back to camp. Causalities had been heavy. Two officers and 30 men were killed and 4 officers and 83 men were wounded. Fortunately, William Arthur Wright survived to fight another day.

However, the Battle for Langemarck began at 4-45 am on August 16th. In this battle, three Battalions of the Middlesex Regiment (2nd, 7th and 8th) took an active part, whilst two more, the 12th and 16th Battalions, were in reserve. The conditions on the battlefield were made worse by the surface being a sea of thick mud after days of torrential rain. Between the 16th and 18th August the three Battalion received heavy casualties before being withdrawn on the 18th.

It was during this relief that enemy shelling was even directed onto the Battalions in reserve, including the 16th Battalion Middlesex Regiment. One man was killed by shell fire, William Arthur Wright, and in the horrendous conditions underfoot, his body was never recovered. William's name is commemorated on Panel 113 to 115 Tyne Cot Memorial.

Sergeant Charles Edward Hamilton No 10794
9th Battalion West Yorkshire Regiment
Died August 27th 1917 aged 28

Charles was the second eldest son of Bernard and Sarah Ann Hamilton of Buxton Road, Bakewell. We have already seen that Charles' elder brother, Walter, had been killed in the Battle of the Somme, on July 28th 1916.

Charles was employed as a gardener at Grenston Park, Tadcaster, near York, prior to which he was on the gardening staff at Renaston Hall. He had been engaged to be married to Miss Webster, who was on the staff of Renaston Hall.

He enlisted on August 26th 1914 and saw service with the West Yorkshire Regiment at the Dardanelles, in Egypt and in France, by which stage he had been promoted to sergeant. Charles was wounded in the thigh during the Battle of the Somme, in August 1916, and was invalided home, and after being in a Surrey hospital, spent a short period of sick leave with his parents in Bakewell. Just before Christmas 1916 he went back to France for the second time.

Charles Edward Hamilton
of Bakewell.

The 9th Battalion West Yorkshire Regiment was involved in the bloody Battle of Passchendaele, beginning on July 31st 1917. The second blow of this long battle fell on August 16th. The left wing was again advanced across the shallow depression formed by the little valley of the Steenbeek and past the ruins of what had been Langemarck. The horrendous muddy conditions, caused by days of torrential rain, and the enemy's skilful resistance resulted in severe casualties for little gain.

One of those casualties was Charles Edward Hamilton, who died in action on August 27th 1917. In the oozing mud of the Passchendaele landscape, his body was never recovered and his name is also commemorated on Panel 42 to 47 and 162 Tyne Cot Memorial.

2ND LIEUTENANT JOHN FRANCIS AITKEN
6TH BATTALION LANCASHIRE FUSILIERS
DIED SEPTEMBER 7TH 1917 AGED 26

John Francis Aitken was born near Avondale in Alabama, United States of America, in 1891, the only son of James and Harriet Ann Aitken. His father, James, was born in Mississippi and was a cotton planter in the state of Alabama. He had married Harriet Nelson, the daughter of Francis Nelson, owner of Nelson's pork butchery in Bakewell and a daughter, Dorothy, completed the family.

In July 1896, James Aitken died and Harriet returned to Bakewell, to live at Castle Street with John and Dorothy. John was educated at Lady Manners School, between 1900 and 1907 and both there and in later life was a keen cricketer and fond of athletics and football, playing in the 1st eleven of Bakewell Football Club. He was also a member of the church choir and choral society.

John Francis Aitken
of Bakewell.

After leaving school he was employed as a clerk in William Deacon's Bank, first at Bakewell, then Buxton and afterwards Matlock (to and from which he motor cycled). At the time of his death, John was engaged to Miss Blanche Taylor of Chesterfield.

Before the start of the Great War, John Aitken was already a trooper in the Derbyshire Imperial Yeomanry at Bakewell and joined up with his squadron in Bakewell at the start of the war. He saw service with them in Egypt, beginning 27th April 1915 and went with them to Salonika, where he was a despatch bearer, and gained the rank of Lance Corporal, before receiving his commission on December 6th 1915.

However, he transferred to the Lancashire Fusiliers 6th Battalion, and in England he had taken a course on signalling, spending his leave at his mother's house in March 1917. He had been away two years. By early September 1917 the 6th Battalion was in the Ypres Salient, Belgium, taking part in the bloody Battle of Passchendaele. On September 6th 1917 they attacked German pillboxes at Iberian, Borry and Beck House Farms.

John Aitken was acting as the Battalion Signalling Officer and in the course of his duty to communicate with Brigade Headquarters, was hit in the throat, opening up a large blood vessel and died within three minutes. He is buried in grave I.G.3. Brandhoek New Military Cemetery, Belgium.

Private George William Furniss No.36426
11th Battalion Sherwood Foresters
died September 16th 1917 aged 24

In 1901 George William Furniss, aged 7 years, was living with his widower grand-father, William Furniss, a farmer, at Gritstone Cottage, Great Longstone. With them were his uncles and aunties, Anthony, Nellie and Ada. He had been born in Manchester, the son of William and Alice Furniss, but at the 1901 Census, his parents were probably still in Manchester.

George was brought up in Great Longstone, attending the village school and later becoming a member of the Inkerman Lodge of the Oddfellows Society, which met at the White Lion. However, shortly before the start of the Great War, he went to live with his parents and brothers, who now resided at Haydn Road, Sherwood, Nottingham. He enlisted at Derby in January 1915, joining 'D' Company 3rd Battalion Sherwood Foresters by February 1916 and was posted to the Royal Scots in April of that year. However, he eventually became a member of the 11th Battalion Sherwood Foresters.

Early September 1917 found George and the Battalion in the Ypres Salient, during the Battle of Passchendaele. Between September 2nd and 13th they were in various billets behind the lines, training in preparation for an attack on September 16th. On September 15th they moved from the camp at Dickebusch to relieve the Royal Fusiliers on the front line astride the Menin Road, with Battalion HQ at Clapham

T he photograph shows the terrible conditions in which the men fought at Passchendaele.
Duckboards were often the only means of crossing the swampy ground in relative safety.

Junction. The casualties of the Battalion moving into their positions were very heavy. In conjunction with the Division, they carried out a raid on a hostile strong point opposite the junction of their front line, on September 16th. 36 prisoners were taken and the left Company killed a number of the enemy who retired across their font.

However, during the raid, further casualties were sustained and we find that George Furniss was one of those killed in action. The ground conditions, due to the days of torrential rain and the terrible pounding of artillery shells, were such that George's body was never recovered and he is commemorated on the Tyne Cot Memorial.

George's brother, Private Jack Furniss, of Sherwood, Nottingham, serving with the 5th Battalion Sherwood Foresters, was taken prisoner by the Germans, but thankfully survived the war.

PRIVATE ERNEST DRABBLE TWYFORD No 241778
2ND/6TH BATTALION SHERWOOD FORESTERS
DIED SEPTEMBER 30TH 1917 AGED 22

The Twyford family lived at Barn Cottage, Nether Haddon, in 1901. George Twyford was the wood steward on the Haddon Estate. He was born at Pilough and married Elizabeth, a Bakewell girl. Three of their six children had been born at Stanton Lees, but Ernest Drabble Twyford, the second youngest child and two of his siblings were born at Haddon.

Prior to the war, Ernest was a joiner and pupil forester under his father. He joined up on February 4th 1916, at Bakewell, being posted to the 2nd/6th Battalion Sherwood Foresters. Shortly afterwards they went through the Irish Rebellion, being finally drafted out to France in February 1917. At the end of April 1917, his parents received a letter from their son telling that he had been wounded, having received a bullet just below the shoulder. Ernest recovered from the wound and returned to active service, in time to take part with his Battalion in the September stages of the Battle of Passchendaele (3rd Ypres).

By September 23rd they were in the vicinity of Vlamertinghe, 2 km west of Ypres, and making preparations for the next 'push' that was planned for the 26th. At 10 pm on September 24th they relieved the South Staffs in the front line running from Grafenstafel Road to Downing Trench, whilst on the 25th the Battalion was heavily shelled, with two men wounded.

At 5-50 am on the 26th, after a heavy artillery barrage, the Battalion advanced and the objective was reached about 7-30 am with a number of prisoners being taken. The Battalion positions were heavily shelled during the

Ernest Drabble Twyford of Bakewell and Haddon Hall.

27th, with numerous casualties resulting, and at 9pm on the 29th/30th September the Battalion was relieved by the Anzacs. Total casualties for the period 24th to 30th September were 11 officers and 220 other ranks killed, wounded or missing.

At the end of September, Ernest's parents received a letter from one of the nurses at Base hospital, stating that Ernest had been grievously wounded in the abdomen by a gunshot. There was little hope for his recovery and the following day the sad news was received that he had passed away.

Ernest Drabble Twyford was buried in grave VIII.E.16 Dozingham Military Cemetery (a casualty clearing station) N.W. of Poperinge.

LANCE CORPORAL FRED MORTON NO 9966
9TH BATTALION SHERWOOD FORESTERS
DIED OCTOBER 4TH 1917 AGED 32

Fred Morton was born at Great Longstone on 29th June 1885, the fifth of the nine children of Jonathan and Rose Morton of 4 Victoria Terrace, a group of cottages backing onto the walkway through the village churchyard. Jonathan was born at Great Longstone and married Rose, a Sheffield girl, and he was employed as a stonemason for most of his life. Fred left school in August 1899 to train as a butcher, but in 1905 he became a regular soldier in the army. As a career soldier he served for nine years in India with the 1st Battalion Sherwood Foresters. In 1914 he was discharged from the army but rejoined at the commencement of the war and joined the 1st Battalion on December 7th 1914, serving with 'A' Company, as part of the British Expeditionary Force.

Fred was wounded in the arm by a German bullet on January 24th 1915 and went to hospital, followed by a period of recuperation in England on February 14th. When he recovered, he transferred to the 9th Battalion, serving in Gallipoli, then Egypt, before returning to France by July 27th 1916. He saw action on the Somme at both Flers and Courcelette and at Thiepval.

In early June 1917 he paid a visit to his parents at Great Longstone, before returning to take part in the Battle of Messines Ridge. He won the Military Medal for gallantry when on a patrol on July 23rd 1917 towards the German positions at Canadian Trench, north of Ypres.

When the Battle of Passchendaele was launched on July 31st he actually saw further action around St. Julien and Langemarck by August 1917.

Between September 17th and 30th, the Battalion was in training for a planned assault on the village of Poelcappelle on October 4th. By October 3rd the 9th Battalion were in position, before the village.

*Fred Morton
of Great Longstone.*

At 5-30 am on October 4th the enemy began to shell the back area, causing considerable casualties in the Reserve Company. The advance began and small parties of Germans were cleared out of some consolidated shell holes after slight resistance, and two machine guns captured. 'A' Company, on topping the rise, came under machine-gun fire and a number of men were hit. After the first quarter of an hour rifles began to jam with mud and wet, otherwise more of the retiring enemy would have been hit.

The Company found a large concrete emplacement occupied by 2 machine-guns on the top and two on the flank outside. Two NCO's rushed forward and threw a bomb inside and men inside surrendered. 'A' Company now dug in under fire of snipers and machine guns.

'D' Company advanced on the second objective and came under machine-gun

*Fred Morton
of Great Longstone.*

fire, resulting in the loss of officers and men, but the enemy machine-gun and Trench Mortar Battery were overpowered. During these actions Fred Morton was killed but in the atrocious conditions underfoot, his body was not recovered and his name is to be found on the Tyne Cot Memorial.

Of Jonathan Morton's five sons, four were serving in the army. Fred had sadly been killed and we shall see that in 1919, another son, Arthur Morton, would die in hospital in France.

Five days later, the Guards Division launched another attack. A Bakewell man in the Coldstream Guards and a Sheldon man in the Grenadiers were both killed during this action, on the first day of the advance,

October 9th. Their names are both inscribed on the same panel of the Tyne Cot Memorial.

PRIVATE GEORGE SKIDMORE NO 16051
2ND BATTALION COLDSTREAM GUARDS
DIED OCTOBER 9TH 1917 AGED 25

In 1901, nine year old George Skidmore was to be found with his parents, George and Ellen Skidmore and five siblings at their home on Monyash Road, Bakewell. George senior, a Bakewell man, was employed by the building firm of Allsops as a stone mason and had married Ellen, who came from Monyash. In 1901, their eldest son, Stanley, aged 20, was an apprentice slater.

George Skidmore of Bakewell.

For a period before the war, George Skidmore junior had been learning farming, although he also worked for Charles Critchlow, the Bakewell cab proprietor. He enlisted early in the war, not locally, but at Mexborough, and being a tall man, joined the 2nd Battalion Coldstream Guards. By the time of his death he had spent two years in France and Belgium. By this time, both his parents were dead.

The Coldstream Guards were involved in the 3rd Battle of Ypres (Passchendaele) between July 31st and November 4th 1917. On October 4th a resumption of the offensive on an eight mile front gave the British possession of a main ridge east of Ypres, despite the torrents of rain, which made the battlefield a worse morass than ever.

However, by the time of the next attack on October 9th the whole of the battered front was held by fresh German troops. There had been rain each day from the 4th October and on the 8th it became torrential. Yet they pressed on with the start of the attack on October 9th on an eight mile front, and it proved a tragic fiasco. The Guards Division, including the Coldstreams, were to advance across the Broembeek stream and occupy the southern edge of Houthulst Forest.

At the time of his death, George Skidmore was attached to Brigade Headquarters, some distance behind the lines from which the advance was to be made that day. He was in a dug-out on which a hit was made by an enemy shell and he was killed instantly. He had been on leave in Bakewell in August, but now news was received in the town of his death. There was no known grave and George Skidmore's name is commemorated on Panel 9 and 10 Tyne Cot Memorial, Belgium.

It was reported in the *High Peak News* in June 1918 that a J. Skidmore had been repatriated in May 1918 after being wounded in October 1917 and taken prisoner. He was now in a hospital in England. This could likely be John Skidmore, a younger brother of George.

GUARDSMAN THOMAS ANTHONY BROCKLEHURST NO 22332
3RD BATTALION GRENADIER GUARDS
DIED OCTOBER 9TH 1917 AGED 26

Known as Anthony or 'Tant' to family and friends, he was the eldest of the two sons and second eldest of the five children of John and Louisa Brocklehurst of Sheldon (his other siblings being Elsie, John, Leah and Alice). His father was a farmer, born at Sheldon, who had married Louisa Gyte, an Ashford born girl and the family lived at Ash Tree View, Sheldon, halfway along the main street. Educated at Sheldon School, Anthony worked for his father on the farm and also for Sheldon farmer, John Frost. A tall, athletic lad, he was good at sport and played for Sheldon cricket team.

Anthony (Tant) Brocklehurst of Sheldon.
Margaret Slin

On January 23rd 1915 Anthony, his cousin Fred Brocklehurst and Sam Wilton were fetched by motor car to Buxton to enlist in the Grenadier Guards and then be drafted to Caterham, Surrey. By November 1915, Anthony and Fred, who were both serving in the 3rd Battalion, went to France and on December 30th 1915 they came out of the trenches and were resting 5 miles behind the lines. (On December 16th the Gyte sisters at the Devonshire Arms, Sheldon, were packing presents to send to Anthony and Fred).

The Battalion took part in the Battle of the Somme and, in a major 'push' on September 15th, the two lads became casualties, Fred being wounded in the shoulder by a bomb and Anthony in the thigh, with both requiring treatment in hospital. Anthony continued his recuperation in Herefordshire and on October 21st he came home for 10 days leave. On October 31st Anthony Brocklehurst returned to his regiment in Chelsea but was back in Sheldon, on leave, by November 26th 1916. Sadly, he and his family received the news that his brother, John Brocklehurst junior, had died of wounds on November 30th, whilst serving with the Northumberland Fusiliers.

On December 26th 1916 Anthony went back to Chelsea, together with Joe Handley and Joshua Millington, leaving from Bakewell Station. By September 1917 the 3rd Battalion was taking part in the Battle of Passchendaele and between 9th October and the 12th, the Guards Division took part in the crossing of the Broembeek (a flooded water course) and the occupation of the southern edge of Houthulst Forest. On October 9th the 3rd Battalion advanced in the second wave. Barring the way was a concrete blockhouse and Sergeant Rhodes was awarded the VC for securing the surrender of the garrison. The Germans who took refuge in the dug-outs were a constant trouble to Fred and Anthony Brocklehurst and the rest of the Battalion.

The objective was secured and consolidation was at once begun. In the afternoon the enemy was seen advancing and were dispersed by machine gun fire.

When it was dusk, the sad task of burying the dead was undertaken, under heavy shell fire at times.

During the 10th October the 3rd Battalion remained in the line they had captured. About 4-30 am the Germans put down a heavy barrage on the Battalion positions, but no infantry attack developed and the remainder of the day was quiet. On the night of October 10th the Battalion was relieved by the 4th Battalion Grenadiers. In the two days of battle, especially on the 9th, they had lost 16 men killed, 63 wounded and 3 missing. During the action of the 9th October they captured 2 field guns, 4 machine-guns, 2 trench mortars and 93 prisoners.

However, on that first day of the battle, Anthony Brocklehurst had been killed by a shell burst, close to his dug-out, and a piece of shrapnel entered his lungs, causing instant death. His cousin, Fred, sent word to Clarice Brocklehurst at Sheldon, and the sad news arrived on October 17th. In the letter he asked her to

Fred Brocklehurst of Sheldon.
Margaret Slin

Anthony Brocklehurst, on the green at Sheldon c1913. He and his brother, John, would be killed whilst serving in the Great War.
Ralph Lord

break the news to 'Tants' parents, John and Louisa. They, of course, were devastated to find that this dreadful conflict had now claimed the lives of both of their sons.

Thomas Anthony Brocklehurst's body was never recovered from the battlefield and his name is commemorated on Panel 9 Tyne Cot Memorial.

Sadly, 24 days later, we shall find that Anthony Brocklehurst's cousin, Tony Gyte from Sheldon, died on November 2nd from wounds received during the last stage of the Battle of Passchendaele.

LIEUTENANT WILLIAM H. HILL
ROYAL FIELD ARTILLERY
DIED OCTOBER 25TH 1917 AGED 34

William, or Billie as he was known to his family, was the third son of Mr. J.E. Hill, a master tailor on Matlock Street, Bakewell. The news of his death was received by his parents on his 34th birthday. He was struck on the head by a shell. The deceased had written to his wife, in Bakewell, stating that it was directed that he should go to an observation post which was considered very dangerous. He tossed up with another officer as to who should go and the lot fell upon him, and so, in company with four men, they proceeded to their objective.

They had nearly reached the point on October 25th 1917 when they were seen by the enemy, who opened fire on them, killing Lieutenant Hill and another man and so deadly was the fire that the other three men were wounded. Unfortunately they could not secure the body of Lieutenant Hill that night and a party was told to make an effort the next morning but again they failed and up to 31st October the body had not been recovered.

Prior to the war, William was in business with his father as a tailor and had been educated at Lady Manners School from 1896 to 1898. He was a prominent member of Bakewell Conservative Association, the town's football club and was keen on all athletics. He married the daughter of Mr. Dawson of Pineapple Farm, Baslow Road in 1910 and they had a little girl by the time of William's death.

He joined the army within a month of the outbreak of war and rose rapidly from the ranks in the Royal Field Artillery. He first went to Ireland and afterwards sailed to India but had not been in that country long before they received word to return to England and proceed to France.

William Hill's wife had received a cheery letter on Sunday morning from her husband but an hour later the telegram announcing his death was delivered.

PRIVATE ANTHONY GYTE NO.79156
17TH BATTALION SHERWOOD FORESTERS
DIED NOVEMBER 2ND 1917 AGED 19

In 1901, three year old Anthony Gyte, known to family and friends as Tony, was living at the Devonshire Arms Inn on Sheldon Main Street with his parents

Anthony senior and Maria, and elder siblings Mary (13), Tom (12), Emily (10), Ethel (8) and Evelyn (6).

Anthony Gyte senior was both the landlord of the public house and a farmer at the same premises. Although born in Ashford parish, his family had run the farm and inn for many years. He was a well-respected member of the community, being both a councillor and a member of the Board of Guardians, responsible for the well-being of the poor of the parish.

On April 14th 1886, 22 year old Anthony had married 28 year old Maria Brassington at Youlgreave Parish Church. She had been born at Bradford, Youlgreave, the youngest of six children of John Brassington, a farm labourer, and Mary Ann Brassington.

Maria became a school teacher, and when Sheldon village school (nowadays Hartington Memorial Hall) was built in 1878, she became its first school mistress. She lodged with Elizabeth

Tony Gyte of Sheldon.
Margaret Slin

Brocklehurst, a widow, and her son Edwin, the village joiner. However, when she married n 1886 she had to give up her position as the village school mistress and helped her husband run the village inn.

Sadly, as time went by, Maria Gyte suffered increasingly from rheumatoid arthritis, causing her to become almost immobile by 1913. She had to be carried about indoors by means of a wooden chair with shaft handles (known as her 'rick-shaw'), whilst out of doors she was conveyed along the village street in a bath chair.

Anthony Gyte senior and his sons Tom and Tony worked the farm, helped by William Gould, a farm labourer who 'lived in' and Vincent Hallows.

The 'Devonshire Arms' was one of the main focal points in the social life of the village, with regular dances held in the loft of the barn next door (nowadays converted into the present day pub known as the 'Cock and Pullet'). Work for Tony's sisters, Mary, Ethel and Evelyn, was hard, for there were domestic duties in the home and public house and work to be done in the dairy, whilst they also had to look after their sister Emily, who did not enjoy good health (including arthritis).

Being loyal members of St. Michael and All Angels Church at Sheldon, the family attended regularly on Sundays, with the younger members often walking to Ashford, Longstone or Monyash churches for evening service. Tony's brother Tom was a fine cricketer, being captain of the Sheldon Cricket Team and often took many opposition wickets on match days. On June 15th 1912 he had taken all ten of Chatsworth wickets for 34 runs at Sheldon.

Tony Gyte, a 'gentle sort of lad', was the youngest child in the family and had a special place in his mother's heart. His parents tried desperately to put off the

The Gyte family of Sheldon c1894. (Evelyn and Tony were not yet born.)
LEFT TO RIGHT: *Mary Gyte, Anthony Gyte, Tom Gyte, Maria Gyte and Ethel, Emily Gyte.*
Margaret Slin

The Devonshire Arms Inn, Sheldon, was the home of Anthony and Maria Gyte and family.
They were the parents of Tony Gyte, who died of wounds in 1917.
Margaret Slin

moment when Tony had to start his training in the army, but with little success. We have already seen that in 1914, as VAD trained Red Cross nurses, his sisters Ethel, Mary and Evelyn were playing their part in the war effort as Voluntary Aid Detachment nurses at the Red Cross Hospital in the Workhouse Infirmary at Bakewell.

Tony's sister, Mary, had married Clement Wager, a gamekeeper from the Longstone area, in April 1914. Clement had been born at Rowdale House. By June 1916 he had enlisted and joined the North Staffordshire Regiment, before going with them to France in September.

On December 16th 1916, Mary and his young son, Anthony, received news at their Grindleford home that Clem was posted missing since an attack on November 18th/19th. By February 1917 news came that he was a P.O.W. of the Germans at Cambrai

Clement and Mary Wager (née Gyte) with their son Anthony c1916.
Margaret Slin

hospital, with a bullet wound in the shoulder, before being moved to a P.O.W. camp in Germany. It would not be until December 7th1918 that Clement Wager returned home to his family in Grindleford.

Meanwhile, Anthony Gyte had successfully contested the call-up of Tom Gyte, who was allowed to continue working on the family farm, but Anthony and Maria's efforts were less successful with regards to young Tony Gyte.

On June 5th 1916, a miserably wet day, Tony's father took him in the horse and float to Bakewell, where he attested and drew 2s 7d. On October 9th 1916, his papers arrived calling him up for the army on November 2nd. He went before the Medical Board at Derby and passed for General Service on January 10th 1917.

Tony received his calling-up papers on February 16th 1917 and that same day, his father went with the milk to Longstone Station and then with Tony to Bakewell, until the train departed with the new recruits. 77 men marched off and people cheered them. However, Anthony travelled with Tony on the train to Normanton Barracks, Derby, to put his case forward and Tony was allowed another two weeks exemption.

On April 16th 1917 Tony went by train to Normanton Barracks, and came back the same day in khaki. Maria wrote to Colonel Brooke-Taylor at Bakewell, asking for another extension because they were backward on the farm because of poor weather, but there was no joy and Tony went back to Normanton Barracks on April 17th. He was drafted to Cleadon Camp, Sunderland, for initial training with the 3rd Battalion Sherwood Foresters and found difficulty settling into army life. On July 1st 1917 Tony came home on leave for the last time. He arrived at Longstone Station by the milk train from Derby. He had arrived at Derby at 2am and stayed at the Y.M.C.A. He went cycling on his sister Evelyn's bicycle to Monyash and Bakewell with James Frost, and on July 3rd to Middleton with Evelyn, George Brocklehurst having lent him his bicycle. He returned to his unit on July 5th, with sisters Ethel and Evelyn seeing him off at Bakewell Station.

After only seven weeks proper training Tony Gyte went with the 17th Battalion Sherwood Foresters (Welbeck Rangers) to the Western Front, via Folkestone, on July 11th 1917.

After more training at Base Camp during August, Tony went into the front line in the Ypres Salient, Belgium, during September and experienced action in the trenches during the later stages of the Battle of Passchendaele.

On October 19th his Battalion went into the trenches at Tower Hamlets and Bodmin Copse, east of Zillebeke, where they were busily employed burying cables and carrying equipment to dumps at the front line. October 22nd saw No.7 Platoon making a raid into enemy lines but the objective was not gained.

The Battalion left the trenches on October 24th, arriving at Vyverbeek Camp, where they were able to bathe and clean up over the next few days. Musketry classes and respirator drill was carried out but at 2-30pm on November 1st, Tony was in a party of 300 men which proceeded to Larch Wood Tunnels. Three parties of 100 each worked till 9pm digging and throwing up breastworks, draining the land and carrying materials in atrocious conditions, due to the glutinous mud and enemy shelling with high explosive and gas shells.

It was on this day that Tony Gyte was wounded by shrapnel in the stomach, leg and arm. He was taken by stretcher bearers to the Casualty Clearing Station but did not live for long, succumbing to his wounds in the early hours of November 2nd 1917. He was originally buried in Bodmin Copse but later his burial place became Special Memorial A.11 Larch Wood (Railway Cutting) Cemetery, 4 kilometres S.E. of Ypres.

On November 7th the family heard in a letter from a Bakewell colleague of Tony's that he had been severely wounded, but it was not until November 13th, on the day that Tony would have reached his twentieth birthday, that they received official news that he had died in a field ambulance. On November 18th a memorial service was held for Tony in Sheldon Church.

The family, especially Maria, were devastated by Tony's death. She records in her diary entry for January 24th 1918, "I feel awfully bad over the loss of my dear Tony and I can scarcely hold up when I think of him, my loved lad whom I shall never see in this world again. It is too dreadful to think of the thousands of young men who have laid down their lives in this terrible war."

On the first anniversary of Tony's death, November 2nd 1918, Maria had beribboned cards printed, with the following verse:-

> "Gone from our home, oh! how we miss him,
> Loving him dearly, his memory we keep;
> Never while life lasts shall we forget him,
> Dear to our hearts in the place where he sleeps.
> In a land of strangers our dear lad does lie,
> Not one of us there to bid him "Good-bye!"
> But the Angel of GOD keeps guard o'er his soul
> Till we meet him again at the call of the roll."
>
> (*Verse courtesy of Margaret Slin*)

(Maria died in 1934, Anthony in 1945 and daughter Emily in 1928 at the age of just 37. The Devonshire Arms Inn and farm passed to Tom Gyte, who had married his cousin, Alice Brocklehurst. Tom managed the farm whilst the public house was run by his sisters Evelyn Gyte and Ethel Hallows (Ethel had married farm worker Vincent Hallows), until it closed 31st December 1972.

As the main action continued in the Ypres Salient, at Passchendaele, British service-men were on duty in other sectors of the Western Front, either involved in routine guarding of the front line or in occasional small scale raids and incursions. It was on such a raid in an area to the north of Arras that a Wardlow man was killed by shell fire, whilst the same fate was suffered by a Bakewell serviceman. One day later a Sheldon man died from malaria and fever in Salonika, in the eastern Mediterranean.

PRIVATE WILLIAM HASLAM NO.267447
2ND/7TH BATTALION SHERWOOD FORESTERS
DIED NOVEMBER 4TH 1917 AGED 21

William, or Willie as he was known, was the fourth of six children of Stephen and Sarah Haslam, and in 1901, five year old Willie was living with his family at Mount View, Main Street, Wardlow. His father, who originated from Darley Dale, was married to Sarah, a Bakewell girl and earned his living as a scrap iron dealer. The parents had lived first at Bakewell, then Ashford, where Willie was born, returned to Bakewell and then moved to Wardlow in 1900.

When Willie enlisted at Bakewell in September 1916, he was living and working in the Buxton area, employed at the Feather Quarry.

He joined the 2nd/7th Battalion Sherwood Foresters and embarked for France just after Christmas 1916. In early October 1917 his parents received the news that he was in the 7th General Hospital suffering from gunshot wounds but he quickly recovered and a month later he was back with his Battalion in the front line, just to the north of Arras, in France.

Again his parents received bad news, this time telling them that their youngest son had been killed in action on November 4th 1917. He had only lived a few hours after being wounded. His Company Sergeant wrote to them that he went forward unflinchingly, but, unfortunately was struck in the chest by a portion of a German shell. Willie's last words were for his mother, he reported.

William Haslam was buried in Sucrerie Cemetery, Ablain-St. Nazaire, 13 kilometres north of Arras.

William Haslam of Wardlow.
Tony Hill

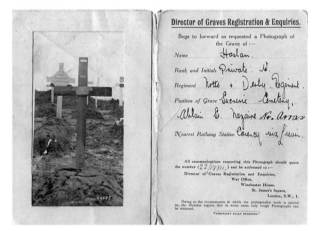

The original grave and wooden cross of William Haslam.
Tony Hill

LANCE CORPORAL JOHN LOVATT KNIGHT No.240512
'B' COMPANY 6TH BATTALION SHERWOOD FORESTERS
DIED NOVEMBER 14TH 1917 AGED 22

John Lovatt Knight was born in Openshaw, South Manchester, in 1894, the son of John Lovatt Knight, senior, and Isabelle Knight. His father was a Staffordshire man, having been born at Newcastle-under-Lyme, whilst Isabelle came from Manchester.

John Knight was employed in Openshaw as a gas engine worker. Sadly, Isabelle died in 1906, aged 55 years and in 1908 John remarried to Alice, a local girl and they lived at 48 Hanbury Street, Miles Platting, Manchester.

A few years before the First World War started, John Lovatt Knight junior came to live and work in Bakewell. He enlisted in late 1914, at Bakewell, joining 'B' Company 6th Battalion Sherwood Foresters. He landed in France with his colleagues on June 26th 1915.

Three times he was wounded and recovered, before his death in November 1917. He was first wounded on November 25th 1915 at Richebourg, France, secondly on

June 3rd 1917 at Lieven, France and shortly afterwards, on July 1st 1917 at Cite St. Pierre. Fortunately he survived, but only to be killed four and a half months later.

On November 4th 1917 a raiding party was sent into the enemy trenches. Three prisoners were brought back, twelve Germans killed and twenty wounded. Of the raiding party, two men were killed, fourteen others wounded and five were missing.

The Battalion relieved the 5th Battalion in the Verquin and Cambrin sector, just south of Bethune, between the 9th and 15th November and was involved in action on Hill 70. On the 15th November they were relieved by the 4th Battalion Lincolnshire Regiment, but during their time in the trenches they had received casualties from shell fire and snipers. One of those who was killed was John Lovatt Knight, who was buried in grave III. A. 27 Philosophe Cemetery, Mazingarbe, between Bethune and Lens.

John Lovatt Knight of Bakewell, working as a sanitation orderly for his Company in November 1916.
Cliff Housley

We have already seen that on April 25th 1917, a Wardlow man had been killed in action against the Bulgarians, fighting in Salonika, to the north of Greece, in a relative 'backwater' of the Great War. Seven months later, in November 1917, a Sheldon man was also buried in a Salonikan cemetery.

Private Alfred Wildgoose No.24272
12th Battalion Lancashire Fusiliers
Died November 15th 1917 aged 39

Alfred (Alf) Wildgoose was born in 1877, the fifth of seven children of Thomas and Jessie Wildgoose of Main Street, Sheldon. Their home, Hope Cottage, was just below the schoolhouse. Thomas and Jessie were Sheldon born and bred, with Thomas employed as a general labourer, working on the roads for the council. Jessie was the daughter of Samuel Housley, who had been a farmer and beer seller in Sheldon.

By 1901, Thomas aged 80 and Jessie aged 63, were living in the same house but all their children had left home except for 18 year old Beatrice, who was employed as the school caretaker (she resigned from the position in 1915). Her brother Alf was by now living at Chorlton in Staffordshire, boarding with George Wright and his wife (who came from Sheldon). George was a carter on a farm and 23 year old Alf Wildgoose was working on the land.

However, at the time of the Great War he was back, living and working in Sheldon, where by now his parents were both dead. Alf was a member of the village cricket team, together with Tom Gyte.

Alf Wildgoose enlisted at Buxton, but on January 28th 1915, a cold and frosty morning, the Recruitment Officer came in a car for Alf as he departed for Derby, to join the Sherwood Foresters. The night before, a collection was made for him in the 'Devonshire Arms' and 5s 9d was raised.

By June 29th 1915 Alf was on leave in the village, where landlord Anthony Gyte provided him with cigars and Billy Naylor gave him cigarettes. The next day he returned to the Foresters' training base at North Shields. He embarked with his regiment to fight at the Dardanelles but he went down with fever and returned to England and by December 28th 1915 he was recovering in Edgbaston Hospital, Birmingham. By September 9th 1916, having transferred to the 12th Battalion Lancashire Fusiliers, Alf was back in the village from training at Withensea, on the east coast, on what would prove to be his final leave before being drafted overseas to Salonika, as part of the Salonika Expeditionary Force, fighting against Bulgarian forces.

A year later, he was dead, not from action in the front line, but from the effects of the conditions of poor sanitation, heat and insects experienced in that area of the world.

News arrived at Sheldon on November 22nd 1917 that Alfred Wildgoose had died of malaria and fever on November 15th.

He was buried in grave 1277 Salonika (Lembet Road) Military Cemetery, on the northern outskirts of Thessalonika.

CORPORAL GEORGE DUFFORT PRICE NO.43397
1ST BATTALION NORTHAMPTONSHIRE REGIMENT
(FORMERLY 6TH BATTALION NORFOLK REGIMENT (CYCLISTS)
DIED NOVEMBER 18TH 1917 AGED 32

George Price was the youngest child of the Over Haddon schoolmaster, William Price and his wife Frances (Fanny). William was born at Cannock, Staffordshire, and Fanny at Solihull, Warwickshire. In his work as a schoolmaster, William and his family had lived in a number of different parishes. Two children were born at Whitmore, Staffordshire, another at Cannock, one in Shropshire and George Price had been born in 1885 at Bruntingthorpe, between Lutterworth and Market Harborough, in Leicestershire.

In 1888 the family came to live first in the 'Church House' and then the schoolmaster's house in Wellgate Lane, Over Haddon. William Price continued to be the headmaster at the village school until the beginning of the Great War period, when he left to live at Ballidon, near Parwich. Between 1896 and 1900 George had attended Lady Manners School in Bath Street, one of the first scholars at the newly-built school. In 1901, fifteen year old George was living with his sister, 24 year old Catherine Price at the Schoolhouse, Bruntingthorpe, Leicestershire, where she was employed as the schoolmistress.

By 1914, George Price had long since left Derbyshire and was employed as head forester on the Gunthorpe Estate, Norfolk, between Holt and Fakenham. He gave up this position and volunteered for the army in October 1914. George enlisted at Fakenham and joined the 6th Battalion Norfolk Regiment (a Cyclist Battalion) before transferring to the 1st BattalionNorthamptonshire Regiment and spent the period up to July 1916 serving on guard duty on the East Coast. Eventually, his regiment was ordered to the Western Front, with George having risen to the rank of Corporal.

He was given leave of absence and arrived back home at Ballidon, Derbyshire, on Friday November 2nd 1917, ready for his marriage. His bride was Ada Constance Hardy of Gunthorpe, Norfolk and they were married at All Saints Church, Ballidon, by Rev. Pitts Tucker, vicar of Parwich, on the following Monday, November 5th 1917. After spending his brief honeymoon at Parwich he returned to join his section of the machine-gun company of his Battalion in Flanders. His wife of a few days and his family would never see him again.

His Battalion was involved in the latter stages of the Battle of Passchendaele. Progress had been trifling, except in the loss of life, partly explained by the exhaustion caused in pushing forward over a morass of mud, by the enemy's use of mustard gas and by his tactics of holding the bulk of his troops well back for a counter attack. When, on Wednesday 4th November 1917, the Canadian Division gained the empty satisfaction of occupying the site of Passchendaele village, it brought an end to the tragedy of 'Third Ypres'.

George Duffort Price had survived the 'hell hole' that was Passchendaele, but only a few days later he was killed on Sunday November 18th by shell explosion during day-to-day activity in the trenches, as the Germans shelled the new forward line of the British forces. He was buried in grave B.27 Buffs Road Cemetery, NE of Ypres, leaving a young widow back in Gunthorpe. His name is commemorated on the war memorials at Lady Manners School, at Over Haddon and Gunthorpe, Norfolk.

As the Battle of Passchendaele came to an end in early November 1917, news came from a more distant theatre of war, telling of the death of the vicar of Bakewell's son. Stationed in Egypt with General Allenby's forces, his battalion was engaged in fighting the Turks, as Allied forces attempted to march on Jerusalem. The city would be captured on December 9th 1917 but the vicar's son had been wounded during the 3rd Battle of Gaza and died on November 19th.

Captain Geoffrey William Pepperall Abraham 24th Battalion (Pembroke and Glamorgan Yeomanry) Welsh Regiment died November 19th 1917 aged 22

At Bakewell Vicarage in 1901, the 43 year old Right Reverend Charles Thomas Abraham, vicar of Bakewell and Bishop of Derby, resided with his wife Mary, his father, a retired Bishop, and their six children, including five year old Geoffrey.

Born in Auckland, New Zealand, Reverend Charles Abraham had married Mary, who came from Staines, in Middlesex. The eldest child had been born in Shrewsbury, but the rest of the family were born in Lichfield.

The family had arrived at the vicarage in 1897 and their father remained the vicar of Bakewell until 1918. Educated at Stoke House, Stowe, and at Cheltenham College, Geoffrey Abraham, the second youngest child, chose a business career after studying to become a mechanical engineer and joined Messrs. E. and A. Robinson's business at Redcliffe, Bristol, paper manufacturers.

On the day that war was declared, 5th August 1914, he enlisted as a trooper in the Pembroke and Glamorgan Yeomanry. We have already seen that on that first day of war, his father was speaking to a large crowd in Rutland Square, talking about the justice of the fight Britain was embarking on. Eventually all five sons served in the Army, including two who hurriedly returned from running an ostrich farm in East Africa.

Another son, Lieutenant Michael Abraham, had been captured by the Germans in 1914, when fighting with the BEF. After two years of captivity his health deteriorated and in August 1916 he was one of 500 soldiers exchanged by the Germans in neutral Switzerland. His father travelled to Murren, in Switzerland, to spend five days with his son before he began his treatment with the Swiss doctors.

Meanwhile, Geoffrey Abraham had received his commission three months after volunteering in 1914 and had been in Egypt withAllenby's forces since January 1916.

Determined to take the important town and fortress of Gaza, Allenby secretly moved first against the inland town of Beersheba, attacking on October 31st 1917. Whilst the infantry assailed the Turkish defences in frontal attack, the Desert Mounted Corps, including Captain Geoffrey Abraham, swung wide to the east, then turned on the city, capturing it after an all-day battle. However, during the attack Geoffrey was wounded.

Despite the wound, he continued in action. Allenby struck north on November 6th, splitting the two Turkish armies, and launched the Desert Mounted Corps across country towards the sea and against Gaza. The Turks evacuated Gaza to avoid the trap. On the same day, November 6th, however, Geoffrey was again wounded, more seriously on this occasion and was evacuated to a hospital at Port Said, in Egypt. It was here that Captain Geoffrey Abraham died on November 19th and was buried in grave F. 42 Port Said War Memorial Cemetery.

(We find that in late April 1918, his brother, Captain Jasper Abraham, Royal Field Artillery was severely wounded in the German 'push' and was in hospital at Boulogne, where his parents visited him. He was one of the two brothers ostrich farming in East Africa, and, being part of the Special Army Reserve, had quickly returned to England. Thankfully he made a good recovery.)

The final casualty for 1917 occurred on the last day of the year, when a Bakewell member of the Royal Flying Corps was killed as his troopship hit a mine and sank in the eastern Mediterranean.

Airman Third Class George William Daffern No.93460
56th Kite Balloon Section Royal Flying Corps
died December 31st 1917 aged 40

George William was the eldest of the four children of James Daffern and Mary E. Daffern. James had been born in Winkley, Leicestershire, whilst his wife, Mary, was from Sheffield. By 1891, they and their four children, all born in Bakewell, were living on Mill Street, Bakewell, with 35 year old James employed as a labourer in the stone quarry. Fourteen year old George William was working in the same quarry as a labourer.

We have been unable to trace George William and his family in the 1901 Census, except for the youngest child, George's sister, Sarah Jane Daffern. The family must have been in somewhat straitened circumstances for we find that eleven year old Sarah Jane is living in the Poor House (Newholme, Bakewell), as an inmate in 1901. Where the other members of the family are at this time we do not know.

However, when George William Daffern enlisted during the Great War, both he and his father, James, were back in the Bakewell area. George was unmarried and had followed no regular employment for the previous few years. He joined the

A kite balloon, similar to the type used by George William Daffern's Kite Balloon Section of the Royal Flying Corps. They were used for artillery spotting and aerial reconnaissance.

Royal Flying Corps and by December 1917 he was an airman 3rd class in the 56th Kite Balloon Section. The balloons, when raised just behind the front line, were used for artillery spotting and reconnaissance. They performed a great service, but the work of those men observing from the basket slung underneath the balloon itself, was dangerous, for they were the target for attack by enemy aircraft.

George William Daffern was home on embarkation leave in November 1917, for the Balloon Section was due to leave England shortly, their destination Egypt. They set sail on the troopship H.T. 'Osmanieh'. On December 31st 1917 the ship was entering the port of Alexandria in Egypt when it struck a mine. 76 officers and men were lost, including George William Daffern. His body was not recovered and he is commemorated on the Chatby Memorial, Alexandria, Egypt.

Sadly, when news of his death reached Bakewell, his father, James Daffern, was in the Whitworth Hospital, Darley Dale, seriously ill and was not expected to live.

As the last servicemen from the Bakewell area to die in 1917, George Daffern's death brought the total of local servicemen who had been killed in action or died during the year to forty. Their loved ones suffered pain and heartache but there would be no noticeable "let-up" during 1918, for, during the last year of the war, a further 35 lives were lost before the armistice on November 11th brought the conflict to a conclusion.

CHAPTER SIX

WILL IT NEVER END?

In February 1918 the death occurred of a Bakewell man serving in the Army in England. Sadly he would be the first of thirty five servicemen from the Bakewell area to die during the final year.

PRIVATE EDWARD WOOD NO.78353
7TH BATTALION DURHAM LIGHT INFANTRY
DIED FEBRUARY 7TH 1918 AGED 22

Edward's father, Thomas Wood, was a gardener, born in Sheffield in 1871. Married to Frances, a Lincolnshire girl, they were to be found on Monyash Road, Bakewell in 1901. Their eldest child, Minnie (7 years), had been born in Sheffield but Edward, John and Frederick were born in Bakewell.

Edward had been a Sunday School scholar at the Wesleyan Chapel and was a sidesman. Prior to the war he was employed by Messrs. Hunter, grocers of Bakewell, as their traveller.

He joined up in February 1917 and joined the Durham Light Infantry (the *High Peak News* reports that it was the 7th Battalion Lincolnshire Regiment). After serving only seventeen days he had to go into hospital at Rugeley, Staffordshire, where he was training, and was in hospital until his death.

Edward Wood's body was transported by train, arriving at Bakewell Station, from where it was conveyed to the Wesleyan Chapel. A detachment of wounded soldiers from the Bakewell Red Cross Hospital at Newholme attended.

March 1918 was the month in which Ludendorff launched the German offensive which he hoped would overwhelm the Allied forces on the Western Front, before the manpower of America arrived in Europe to play a crucial role in proceedings. However, eight days before the offensive was launched, a Bakewell sailor lost his life at sea, off the coast of the Isle of Wight.

SIGNALMAN Z/6199 ROBERT CARR
S.S. 'TWEED' ROYAL NAVAL VOLUNTEER RESERVE
DIED MARCH 13TH 1918 AGED 19

Robert Carr, or Bob as he was known, was born in 1898 at Nether Hallam, Sheffield, the third child of John William and Edith Annie Carr. His father was a druggist and grocer at Sheffield and also had a druggist shop at Bakewell. By 1914, the parents lived at Ecclesall, Sheffield, but Robert was engaged in his father's wholesale druggist business and spent much time in Bakewell.

Bob Carr volunteered for service, joining the Royal Naval Volunteer Reserve and trained as a signalman. By February 1918 he was serving on the S.S. Tweed, a 1,025 ton British steamship.

On February 13th 1918 the ship was off St. Catherines Point, 10 miles south west of the southern coast of the Isle of Wight (in the outer approaches to the Solent), when she was torpedoed by a German submarine UB-59, without warning.

She sank with the loss of seven lives, one of the sailors being Bob Carr. His body was not recovered and his name is commemorated on Panel 30 Plymouth Naval Memorial.

Seven days later, on Wednesday March 20th, an interesting ceremony was held at the church in Great Longstone, in connection with the deaths of two soldiers with strong village ties.

We have already seen that on March 12th 1915, Captain Hubert B. Dixon had been killed in action. On April 12th 1917, Hubert's nephew, Lieutenant William Bernard Shaw, was also killed.

Bernard Shaw was the only son of William Longsdon Shaw and Martha Fletcher Shaw of 'Longstone', Bristol Garden, Brighton and the 'Outrake', Little Longstone. He was born at Whitebough Hall, Chinley, and his early years were spent at the Manor House, Little Longstone. He was a great grandson of the late James Longsdon of the 'Outrake' and grandson of the late Mr. and Mrs. Pitt-Dixon. He was educated at St. Edmund's Hall, Oxford University, where he studied for Holy Orders, but when the war broke out he at once joined the Officer Training Corps, the Inns of Court Regiment and was gazetted 2nd Lieutenant in 'B' Company, 9th Battalion Royal Sussex Regiment.

He was in charge of the machine-gun section and was wounded in the head at the Battle of Loos, September 1915, likewise receiving injuries to his back and having his ankle shattered. He was taken to Lady Evelyn Mason's Hospital for Officers, where he made a rapid recovery.

Bernard Shaw subsequently returned to the firing line in August 1916 and secured his step to full lieutenant that same year.

Between April 9th and the 14th 1917, General Haig launched the Battle of Arras. Between the 9th and 10th April the Canadians attacked and captured the main section of the dominating Vimy Ridge. There still remained the main stronghold on the northern tip to be captured, known as 'The Pimple', as well as the Bois en Hache on the eastern slopes of the Loretta Ridge.

The Canadians attacked the 'Pimple' on April 12th, whilst the British 1st Corps, including the Royal Sussex Regiment, attacked the Bois en Hache, in driving sleet and snow. Both objectives were captured, but in the process, Bernard Shaw lost his life attacking German machine-gun positions on the Bois en Hache, Vimy Ridge. He was just 23 years of age.

His body was not recovered and his name is commemorated on Bay 6, the Arras Memorial.

Hubert Dixon's brother, Mr. R. Pitt-Dixon of Great Longstone, and William and Martha Shaw of Brighton, wished to commemorate the lives of their loved ones, as well as honour the names of the other men from Great and Little Longstone who had lost their lives. The splendid lych gates at the churchyard were therefore commissioned by the two families.

Wednesday March 20th 1918 witnessed a large congregation present at the dedication service of the two lych gates and a war-time shrine, on opposite sides of Church Lane. The one nearest the old churchyard was commissioned by Hubert Dixon's brother to honour Hubert's name and memory, whilst the one leading into the new cemetery was provided by Mr. and Mrs. Shaw and included a war-shrine in the form of a crucifix and the names of the men from the villages inscribed into the wood.

One of the two war memorial lych gates at Great Longstone's St. Giles Church. This one is dedicated to Captain Hubert Bradshaw Dixon, and both lych gates were dedicated in March 1918.
Keith Taylor

Lych gate to the cemetery at St. Giles Church, Great Longstone, dedicated to
William Bernard Shaw. Inside the gate (shown below), is a war shrine (crucifix) dedicated
to the men of the village who were killed in the Great War.
Keith Taylor

Both gates were made of English oak of local growth, covered in with hand-made Staffordshire tiles and was erected by local builder W.J. Eyre. The congregation assembled first in the church, a procession being formed, headed by the Reverend C.G. Lynn Fryer, accompanied by a surpliced choir. A dedication prayer was said at the gates and the names of the fallen were read out.

Meanwhile, on April 6th 1917 America had declared war against Germany, but with her small army of 210,000 men, it would take some while before the manpower resources could become a decisive factor. During the winter of 1917/1918 General Ludendorff realised that Germany's only hope of winning the war lay in a decisive victory in the West in 1918 before the weight of American man power began to tell. The Bolshevik Revolution of 1917 in Russia had resulted in that country being knocked out of the war.

Ludendorff therefore shifted most German forces from the Eastern Front and prepared for an all-out offensive to be launched as early as possible in the Spring, using "shock troops" as spearheads for the assault. He planned to smash the Allied armies in a series of hammer blows, driving a wedge between the British and French forces, and then destroy the British in subsequent assaults. Preparations were made for the massive attack in the Somme area to begin on March 21st between St. Quentin and Arras towards the goal of capturing Amiens.

Eight servicemen from the district would die during the "Kaiser's Battle", when overwhelming German forces would roll forward and swallow them up in the desperate weeks of late March and early April 1918. The British were well aware of German intentions and made preparation for the inevitable attack. One of the most ironic re-deployments was to abandon the Passchendaele Ridge and form a tight defensive line around Ypres. All the sacrifices of the previous Autumn seemed as naught.

Liddell Hart, the military historian, wrote: "At 0430 hours on March 21st the sudden crash of some 6,000 German guns heralded the breaking of a storm which, in grandeur of scale, of awe and destruction, surpassed any other in the World War. By nightfall a German flood had inundated 40 miles of the British front; a week later it had reached a depth of nearly 40 miles and was almost lapping the outskirts of Amiens, and in the ensuing weeks the Allied cause itself was almost submerged. Germany came desperately near to regaining that last chance of victory which she had forfeited in early September 1914."

On the first day of the offensive, two soldiers from Bakewell would be the first men from the area to be "swallowed up' in the German tidal wave.

PRIVATE JOHN STEPHEN HOPE NO.42441
2ND/7TH BATTALION MANCHESTER REGIMENT
DIED MARCH 21ST 1918 AGED 25

In 1901, John Stephen Hope, aged seven years, was the youngest of four children living with their parents, John and Mary Jane Hope, at their home at West End, Elton. Their father, born at Stanton Lees, was a general labourer and their mother came from Winster. All the children had been born at Elton.

John Stephen Hope enlisted at Bakewell, where he lived and worked at the time of the Great War, but by then, his father, who had lived for some years at Haslin Row, Harpur Hill, Buxton, had passed away.

He joined the 2nd/7th Battalion Manchester Regiment and by mid-March 1918 they were stationed near Albert, in the path of the planned advance of Ludendorff's offensive, due to begin on March 21st.

Ludendorff's best units were developed into 'shock troops', to be spearheads of the planned assault. His intention was to smash the Allied armies in a series of hammer blows, with overwhelming superiority in manpower and artillery support. The Germans began their drive at dawn on March 21st 1918, in heavy fog, on a 60 mile front between Arras and La Fère. The objective was to break through, dislocate, and roll up the British.

Following a surprise five hour bombardment by more than 6,000 artillery guns, the German 'shock troops' rolled through the fog, infiltrating behind a rolling barrage. The forward units of the British army, including the 2nd/7th Battalion, although putting up a stiff resistance, were overwhelmed and suffered severe casualties as they withdrew. One of the casualties was John Stephen Hope, whose body was never recovered from the battlefield and whose name is commemorated on Panel 64 to 67 Pozieres Memorial, 6 kilometres N.E. of Albert.

LANCE CORPORAL JOHN WILLIAM FROST NO. 58719
2ND BATTALION SHERWOOD FORESTERS
DIED MARCH 21ST 1918 AGED 21

John William Frost, known to family and friends as William, was born at Stavely, near Chesterfield, the second child of John Henry Frost and Beatrice. John Henry came from near Hull, in Yorkshire and married Beatrice, a Stavely girl. It was at Stavely that daughter Beatrice and son William were born, but their second son Fred was born in Bakewell. John Henry Frost had brought his family to live in the town, on North Church Street, when he became employed at the DP Battery works as an electrician attending dynamos.

William Frost was also employed at the DP Battery works. He was a member of the Church Choir, the Boys' Brigade, Boy Scouts and was also a Sunday School teacher.

He enlisted at Bakewell and eventually joined the 2nd Battalion Sherwood Foresters, whilst a younger brother, Henry Frost, joined the Royal Navy. William rose to become a Lance Corporal in his Battalion and became a Lewis gun instructor. Two months before his death he was home on leave in Bakewell, in January 1918.

On March 21st 1918, the day of the German 'push', the 2nd Battalion Sherwood Foresters were in the line to the right of the village of Lagnicourt. At 5 am a terrific bombardment began, including gas shells, until 9-30 am. This bombardment annihilated the garrisons of the forward system and few survivors came back to the reserve lines.

The Germans attacked 'C' Company in the mist and dust, overrunning them, and 'A' Company were nearly all killed by shell fire, whilst 'B' Company held on grimly, thirty yards from the German attackers.

It was at 5 am, early in the bombardment, that William Frost was killed as a result of shell fire. As with so many of his colleagues, William's body was never recovered and his name is recorded on Bay 7 Arras Memorial.

PRIVATE JOHN SHERWIN No.34544
11TH BATTALION LEICESTERSHIRE REGIMENT
DIED MARCH 22ND 1918 AGED 30

In 1891 four year old John Sherwin was living with his parents, 28 year old John Sherwin senior and 26 year old Margaret Sherwin in Hyde, Cheshire. All three members of the family were born in Hyde, where John senior was employed at nearby Denton as a hat curler. Denton hat factory was world-famous for the making of bowler hats and John helped to make the curved brims.

However, young John, known to his family and friends as Jack, had a connection to Sheldon, near Bakewell. We find that in 1901, fourteen year old Jack was now living in Sheldon with his uncle, 57 year old Abraham Clarke Manderfield and aunty, 61 year old Selina Manderfield, at Rose Farm. Abraham had been born at Cromford but lived and worked in Sheldon as a forester and farmer, whilst Selina Hancock had been born in Sheldon (in 1861, before her marriage, she was working as a servant at Taddington).

Jack Sherwin's future wife, Mary Banks, was born in 1890, at Ludwell Grange, in Hartington Town Quarter, on the narrow road between Hartington and Pilsbury. She was the second youngest of four children (all girls) of 44 year old William Banks, a Hartington born farmer and 30 year old Emily, a Cheshire girl.

By 1907, Mary was working at Sheldon and had become acquainted with William Wager, a farmer employed in the Monyash area at the time. At 34 years of age he was sixteen years older than Mary. He too came from a well-established Hartington farming family, which farmed the 400 acre Moor Farm, employing a governess for the young children and four other servants. William's father, Andrew Wager, originated from Longstone, whilst his mother Emily came from Longnor.

On November 7th 1907, William Wager, aged 34, married 18 year old Mary Banks at Sheldon Church (though she records her age as 21 in the marriage register). A witness at the ceremony was Abraham Manderfield of Rose Farm, the uncle of Jack Sherwin, and already we see a connection between Jack and Mary.

The newly-married Mary Wager returned with William to live at Hard Dale Farm, in the dale leading down into Hartington. Sadly, William Wager was not in good health, having suffered from chronic bronchitis for 30 years. In February 1910 he went down with pneumonia, haemorrhaged, and died on February 28th 1910, at the age of 37.

Jack Sherwin had been working for Willliam Wager at the farm. After his death, Jack and Mary became close and in April 1911 they were married at the Primitive Methodist Chapel in Ashbourne. Mary was already pregnant and on October 29th 1911, their first child, Arnold Sherwin was born at Hard Dale Farm.

In the spring of 1913, a second child, Gladys Sherwin was born at the farm, though she was always known as Betty. September 21st 1915 saw the birth of their third child, Arthur John Sherwin, with Jack still running Hard Dale Farm.

However, when conscription came into force in early 1916, Jack was called up into the army and eventually joined the 3rd Battalion Leicestershire Regiment, although when he was killed in 1918, he was serving in the 11th Battalion.

On Jack's enlistment, Mary and the three children went to live with Jack's uncle, Abraham Manderfield, by now a widower, at Rose Farm, Sheldon, and the children went to Sheldon School. (Selina Manderfield had died in 1906.)

Jack Sherwin and the 11th Battalion found themselves at the forefront of the German offensive on March 21st 1918 and on the following day, March 22nd, Jack was posted as 'missing'. On Sunday April 21st 1918, Mary Sherwin received official news that her husband Jack was missing, but throughout the next year she had no confirmation that he had been killed. It was only on May 16th 1919 that official news of his death arrived at Rose Farm. Sadly, eight days later, Jack's uncle, Abraham Manderfield, was found dead in one of his fields, from a heart attack,

Arnold Sherwin, eldest child of John and Mary Sherwin, taken at Hand Dale Farm, Hartington, in late 1912.
David Sherwin

Sheldon School c1919. Arthur Sherwin sits on the ground, to the left of the slate.
David Sherwin

after attending his cattle.

Jack Sherwin's body was never recovered and his name is commemorated on Bay 5 of the Arras Memorial. His widow, Mary Sherwin, and their three children remained in the village, at Rose Farm, but early in 1921 she married for a third time, her husband being a farm worker, Frederick Carson of Rose Cottage, Sheldon. He joined Mary and his three step children at Rose Farm and a son, Frederick (Sonny) was born.

Betty (Gladys) Sherwin at school in Sheldon, c1919.

Ken Brocklehurst

However, when Mary was expecting another child, she and the infant died on March 6th 1923, Mary being just 32 years of age. The three Sherwin children, Betty, Arnold and Arthur left Sheldon to live with their grandmother, Mrs. Banks, at Buxton, and eventually with their aunty, Mrs. Pickford, in the same town.

PRIVATE LAWRENCE DOUGLAS No. 39307
4TH SPECIAL RESERVE BATTALION SOUTH STAFFORDSHIRE REGIMENT
DIED MARCH 24TH 1918 AGED 30

It is likely that Lawrence Douglas, whose name is commemorated on the Bakewell Memorial, was born at Leawood, near Lea, in 1887, the son of John Douglas from Bonsall and Clare Douglas, born at Lea. Lawrence's father was employed at the Smedley's Hosiery Mill, near Holloway, as a book-keeper. It may be that Lawrence Douglas' connection with Bakewell lies in the fact that he probably came to work in the market town. He enlisted at Bakewell and joined the 4th Battalion South Staffordshire Regiment.

By March 12th 1918 the 4th Battalion was stationed at Achiet le Grand, just north of Bapaume, where training took place until March 21st, the day of the German offensive. By 11-30 pm on March 21st the Battalion went up and dug in behind the Army line on the left of the road between Fremicourt and Beugny, remaining in this line during 22nd March.

By the 23rd, this line had become the front line, with casualties being taken as the Germans pushed hard against the defensive positions.

At 2am on the 24th, the Battalion retired to a position between Fremicourt and Beugnatre and dug in there. By 3pm they reorganised in a sunken road just north of the railway line, as they came under fierce artillery, machine-gun and rifle fire. By 6pm they had to take up fresh positions as they retired to a trench west of the Bapaume – Arras road, but were forced further back as they retired across the main road at 8pm and dug in 400 yards due east of Biefvillers.

It was during the desperate fighting on March 24th, as retirement followed retirement, that Lawrence Douglas lost his life. There was no possibility of a burial, his body being left on the battlefield, and his name is commemorated on Bay 6 of the Arras Memorial.

PRIVATE WILLIAM ARTHUR CRAWFORD SIMS NO. S/22504
2ND BATTALION SEAFORTH HIGHLANDERS
DIED MARCH 28TH 1918 AGED 29

William Henry Sims, the father of William Arthur Crawford Sims, was a furniture dealer and pork butcher on Bridge Street, Bakewell. He was a Bakewell man who had married Sarah Jane Duggan, a Liverpool girl whose family had Irish connections. Emily, Florence, William Arthur (known as Arthur), Elsie, Harry and Doris completed the family.

Before the Town Hall was built in Bakewell in 1890, there were pig sties there and William Henry kept pigs for his pork butcher's business. His furniture shop was nearest the present-day Information Centre whilst the furniture store is now the Wheatsheaf Inn's kitchen area. Eventually he concentrated on the furniture side of the business and kept a number of horses and carts for this purpose.

William Henry died before the start of the war, but Sarah Jane continued the furniture business, with her son Arthur providing help. Later in life, the shop became a newspaper shop, run by the Sims family.

During the First World War, Arthur Sims enlisted in the army at Bakewell and first joined the Army Service Corps, where they could make use of his experience with horses. Later he was transferred to the infantry, serving with the 2nd Battalion Seaforth Highlanders and wearing the kilt as part of his uniform.

Arthur wrote home during the severe winter weather of January 1918 for ointment to be sent out to him by his mother, so that he could apply it to his knees and legs. The icicles hanging from the bottom of his kilt were cutting his legs.

William Arthur Sim's sister, Elsie, at the Sherwood Forester's panel of the Menin Gate, Ypres in 1927.
Bill Sudbury

When Ludendorff launched his offensive on March 21st 1918 the Seaforth Highlanders were caught up in the desperate withdrawal, of attack and counter attack amidst the following days of confused fighting. On March 28th Ludendorff ordered a fresh 'push', a direct attack against the high ground near Arras. However, the nine German divisions collapsed under a storm of fire from the expectant defence, including the men of the 2nd Battalion Seaforth Highlanders. This reverse helped to bring the advance to a halt in early April, but on that fateful day of March 28th, Arthur Sims was killed in action on the heights near Arras. He has no known grave and his name is commemorated on Bay 8 Arras Memorial.

In 1927, Arthur's sister, Elsie Sudbury, travelled to France with her husband and visited the Arras Memorial to pay tribute to her brother, as well as visiting other battlefield memorials such as the Menin Gate. Sarah Jane Sims received news in September 1916 that her youngest son, Harry, in the Sherwood Foresters, was wounded in the thigh and right wrist and was now in a Liverpool hospital. Thankfully he survived.

PRIVATE JOHN WARD NO. 241456
6TH BATTALION STAFFORDSHIRE REGIMENT
DIED APRIL 5TH 1918 AGED 28

John was born at Church Street, Ashford in the Water, in 1890, the son of Joseph Ward, a gardener, born at Bonsall and Margaret, born at Matlock. However, the family was living in Great Longstone by the start of the Great War and it would be on that village's war memorial that John's name would be inscribed.

John left Great Longstone around 1913 to work in Staffordshire, in the employ of Tamworth Rural District Council. He enlisted in the army in November 1915 and joined the 6th Battalion North Staffordshire Regiment, being gassed in April 1917.

We have just seen how the German attack against Arras collapsed under a storm of fire from the expectant defence. The town of Amiens now became the main German objective but the surge was almost stagnant, its impetus being slackened because of the exhaustion of the German troops and the difficulties of supply, as well as the resistance of the Allied Forces, including John Ward and the 6th Battalion.

Roads were blocked, transport was scuppered and German reserves harassed by the British air attacks. When the attack was renewed on March 30th it had little force and made little progress in face of a resistance that had been afforded time to reorganise and harden.

Nearly a week passed before, on April 4th, a further German effort was made by fifteen divisions, of which only four were fresh. Meeting a reinforced defence, including the 6th Battalion North Staffords and John Ward, this attack had still less success. Seeing that his new effort was too late, General Ludendorff then suspended the attack towards Amiens by the end of April 5th.

However, it was on that fateful day that John Ward was killed. His body was recovered and buried in grave II.E.19 Aix-Noulette Communal Cemetery Extension, 13 kilometres south of Bethune.

PRIVATE HERBERT ELLIOTT NO. 97692
29TH BATTALION MACHINE GUN CORPS (INFANTRY)
DIED APRIL 12TH 1918 AGED 23

In 1901, Herbert Elliott was a six year old, living with his parents, William and Margaret and seven other siblings, at Little Longstone. They had only moved to the hamlet in 1900, since all the children, including a nine month old son, had been born at nearby Wardlow. Both parents had also been born at Wardlow and William was employed as a general labourer.

By the start of the First World War, Herbert had left Little Longstone to find work and was living at Ambergate when he enlisted in the army, travelling to Derby to do so. He joined the Sherwood Foresters.

However, in October 1915, the Machine Gun Corps had been created, using mainly Vickers machine guns. By the time of the Battle of Messines in June 1917, machine gunners were also employing creeping barrages, with fire falling ahead of the artillery barrage, to catch troops moving to the rear. They would concentrate on specific targets, or sweep the enemy ground behind his front. For these tasks, the guns were placed 1,000 yards behind the advancing infantry and were moved up as soon as the enemy positions were captured. Machine gun tactics had in fact become more like those of the artillery than of the infantry. However, being the target for every enemy weapon, they well earned the nickname of the 'Suicide Club'.

When Ludendorff's offensive of March 21st 1918 failed to capture Amiens and take the Channel port, a second major 'push' was made by the Germans, this time to the north in Flanders, along the Lys valley and in the Messines area, south of Ypres. The offensive was launched on April 9th and British forces were overwhelmed by superior numbers in the first few days. General Haig's 'Backs to the Wall' order, forbidding retirement, issued on April 12th, galvanised resistance and the German drive was halted by April 17th, after a ten mile advance which included the recapture of Messines Ridge.

It was in the area of Messines Ridge that Herbert Elliott was killed on April 12th, the very day on which Haig issued his order to resist at all cost. His body was not recovered from the battlefield and his name is commemorated on Panel 11 Ploegsteert Memorial, just to the south of Messines, and on the Great Longstone war memorial.

PRIVATE JAMES SIDNEY HEWITT NO. 37206
10TH BATTALION EAST YORKSHIRE REGIMENT
DIED APRIL 13TH 1918 AGED 19

The Hewitt family lived at 6 Sunny Bank, Great Longstone. In 1901, James Hewitt senior was employed as a plate layer on the Midland Railway between Hassop Station and Monsal Head. He was 54 years of age, was born at Rowland, and was married to Alice Furness, a Great Longstone girl, aged 36. Their children, Maude (7 years), and James Sidney Hewitt (2 years) completed the family.

In early 1917, James, or Jimmy as he was known, went to Bakewell to enlist and joined the 10th Battalion East Yorkshire Regiment. He was on leave for a few days at Great Longstone in December 1917, but was with his Battalion in France, when Ludendorff launched his offensive on March 21st 1918. Over the following days of withdrawal, the Battalion lost many men, but Jim Hewitt survived. (Four officers and 207 men became casualties.)

*James Sidney Hewitt
in earlier days, c1906.*
Olive Mead

*James Sidney Hewitt
of Great Longstone.*
Olive Mead

*James Hewitt, father
of James Sidney Hewitt.*
Olive Mead

Plate layers on the stretch of line between Hassop Station and Monsal Head c1910.
LEFT TO RIGHT: *Isaiah Gilbert, James Hewitt, X.*
James Hewitt was the father of James Hewitt, junior, who was killed in the Great War in 1918.
Isaiah Gilbert was responsible for the examples of topiary at and near Hassop Station,
which were such a feature of that stretch of line prior to the First World War.
Noel Green and Olive Mead

Between April 2nd and April 9th, the 10th Battalion were at Monchy-Breton, where new drafts of men arrived to make up the numbers and training began. The men were exhausted from the previous days of battle.

When news arrived of the second German 'push' in the Flanders and Lys area on April 9th the Battalion embussed for that area on April 10th arriving at Vieux Berquin, to the east of Hazebruck, and marched to Haute Maison. For the following three days they were involved in desperate fighting.

On April 12th Haig issued his historic order of the day: "There is no other course open to us but to fight it out. Every position must be held to the last man. With our backs to the wall and believing in the justice of our cause, each one of us must fight on to the end." By 11th April the breach in the Allied line was thirty miles in

James and Alice Hewitt, parents of James Sidney Hewitt.
Olive Mead

width, and by the 12th its depth was doubled. This was the crisis. Less than five miles seperated the Germans from Hazebruck junction. On the 13th, British and Australian reserves began to arrive from the south, and the German pressure showed signs of slackening.

Ploegsteert Memorial in Belgium.
Olive Mead

However, in the desperate fighting to the east of Hazebruck, as the 10th Battalion fought with their backs to the wall on April 13th, James Sidney Hewitt was struck down on the battlefield. As with so many men, including Herbert Elliott, his colleague from Little Longstone, serving in the Machine Gun Corps, James Hewitt's body was not recovered and his name joined that of Herbert on the Ploegsteert Memorial, on Panel 4.

James Hewitt was the seventh and last Bakewell and District servicemen's death resulting from the German offensive of March – April 1918. However, it was to be during a period of normal day-to-day trench duty that an Ashford man lost his life due to gun-shot wounds near the beginning of May.

PRIVATE GEORGE HILL No. 28514
2ND BATTALION SOUTH STAFFORDSHIRE REGIMENT
DIED MAY 9TH 1918 AGED 36

George Hill of Ashford.

The Hill family were living at Hill Cross, Ashford in 1882. One year old George was born at Ashford, his parents being Thomas, a general labourer and later a carter, who was born at Longstone, and Mary Ann (née Bolsover), an Ashford girl. His eleven year old brother, Charles, and five year old sister Sarah Ann completed the family.

By 1901 Mary Ann was now a widow, living with sons Charles, aged 30 and working as a farm labourer and 19 year old George, a marble sawyer and mason at the Ashford Marble Works. The family was still living at Hill Cross.

However, when the Ashford Marble Works closed in 1905, George became a gardener until he later went to work in Messrs. Arthurton's spar mines at Great Longstone. By the time that he enlisted in the army in 1916 he was married to his wife Annie and had three children, the family living at Hill Cross. He married Annie Elizabeth Redfern, the daughter of an Ashford painter, in September 1908. Their children were George William 1908, Beatrice 1911 and Thomas 1912.

After enlisting at Bakewell, George eventually joined the 2nd Battalion South Staffordshire Regiment and during the German offensive that began on March 21st 1918, the Battalion was heavily engaged, sustaining many casualties.

By mid-April they were stationed in the Blairville and Bois leux-au-Mont sector, half way between Bapaume and Arras, spending time in and out of the front line trenches.

The Battalion came out of the line on May 5th and attended church parade but in the evening of the same day they relieved the Royal Fusiliers in front of Bois leux-au-Mont. May 6th was a typical day of trench warfare, with heavy artillery shelling during the afternoon and torrential rainfall during the night. The following day, the trenches were under water, whilst on May 8th the artillery shelling was extremely heavy. It was on this day that George Hill was seriously wounded by gunshot and was taken to the casualty clearing station in an unconscious state. The following day, May 9th, George died without recovering consciousness, leaving a widow and three young children.

George Hill was buried in grave II.B.2 Bagneux British Cemetery, Gezaincourt, two kilometres south west of Doullens.

It was to be on English soil, in a Lichfield hospital, that the next death occurred, but on this occasion it was the result of natural causes.

SERGEANT EDGAR JAMES MELLON NO. 68985
ROYAL DEFENCE CORPS
DIED MAY 16TH 1918 AGED 37

Edgar James Mellon, known as James to his colleagues, was born in Halifax and in the 1901 Census he was a 20 year old professional soldier serving with the North Staffordshire Regiment in their Whittington Barracks, near Lichfield. His father had been a professional soldier, reaching the rank of sergeant major in the same regiment. Edgar James Mellon joined the army as a drummer boy at the age of 14 years.

His death took place in a Lichfield hospital on May 16th 1918, following an operation for appendicitis. During his service in the army he saw action in India. After returning to England he was placed on the Reserve List and served as a police constable at Bakewell before the Great War, as well as at Buxton and Ilkeston. It was in Buxton that he met his future wife and by 1918 they had three children, Jessie, Norman and Peggy.

Edgar James Mellon, formerly a policeman in Bakewell.

James was on the Reserve List when war broke out and was recalled to the Colours, serving with the North Staffordshire Regiment as a sergeant. In the earlier stages of the war he was twice wounded, once in the foot. After recovering, he became instructor to a Cadet Corps and was later in the Royal Defence Corps.

Maria Gyte, in her diaries, reports on January 19th 1915 that Policeman Young who went from Ashford to join his regiment (Grenadier Guards) called at the Devonshire Arms, Sheldon, with Policeman Mellon. She reports that James Mellon had been to the front and got wounded and had been in hospital and had come back to Bakewell on furlough. He expected to go back the following day.

His funeral was held at Lichfield with full military honours. The cortege was half a mile long and included 500 cadets who had passed through the hands of Sergeant Mellon. It is interesting to note that his father had died in the same Lichfield barracks.

Six days later, an Ashford resident, whose family was living at Churchdale Hall, and who had recently won the Military Cross for gallantry, was killed in France whilst on reconnaissance.

LIEUTENANT COLONEL ERNEST JOHN WALTHEW
(ROYAL ENGINEERS) COMMANDING 46TH DIVISION (WON M.C.)
DIED MAY 22ND 1918 AGED 42

Ernest John Walthew was born at Stockport, the third child of George Walthew, a cotton spinner and doubler manufacturer, and his wife Annie. By 1901, 25 year old Ernest was living at Stockport Road, Cheadle, and was running the family business. His 24 year old wife, Maude Clegg was the daughter of Sir William Clegg of Sheffield.

Eventually they came to reside in Buxton and in 1910 he was elected a member of Buxton Urban District Council until 1914. He was a member of the Freemasons at Buxton and of the Conservative Party. Ernest was a keen follower of the High Peak Hunt and was Secretary of the Hunt Steeplechases, his horse 'Wiseman' being the winner of the point-to-point steeplechase in 1912 and 1913.

Ernest John Walthew of Ashford.

By the outbreak of war they had left Buxton to reside at Churchdale Hall, Ashford, with their daugther and son. Ernest Walthew served with the Royal Engineers, attached to the Sherwood Foresters. It was in May 1915 that Lieutenant Walthew left Sheffield with the local engineers. By June 1915 he had risen in rank to captain and by 1917 to major.

In January 1918 he was awarded the Military Cross for gallantry on the battlefield and was later promoted lieutenant-colonel. Lately he had received an appointment to Divisional Headquarters and it was while discharging his duties that he met with instantaneous death. He was killed whilst carrying out a reconnaissance with his adjutant, who was also killed, and his body was buried in Fouquieres Churchyard Extension, 1 kilometre south west of Bethune.

He left a widow and two children, who had left Ashford to reside at the White House, Salcombe, Devon. Whilst residing at Ashford, Maude Walthew had become the first commandant of the Bakewell Red Cross Hospital, based at the Workhouse.

The next casualty, a Bakewell man, found himself at the forefront of the next major German offensive, launched in the Champagne area of France.

Private Walter Mountney No. 79557
6ᵀᴴ Battalion Durham Light Infantry
died May 28ᵀᴴ 1918 aged 18

Walter Mountney.
Mary Upton

Walter Mountney of South Church Street, Bakewell, was the youngest of the three sons of Albert Mountney to be killed in the First World War. His father was a Bakewell person, as was his mother Agnes, and Albert worked as a rural postman for the area.

By the time Walter enlisted at Bakewell in 1917, we have seen that two of his brothers were already dead. He was posted to the 6ᵗʰ Battalion Durham Light Infantry after his initial training.

We have already seen that on March 21ˢᵗ 1918, Ludendorff launched his massive offensive against the British positions, the aim being to take Amiens and then the Channel ports. The weight of superior German numbers forced the British forces back, resulting in severe casualties being sustained.

The German advance was halted before reaching Amiens, but in April, a second major 'push' was made in the area of the Lys valley, further to the north. This too eventually ground to a halt. The German plans were thwarted but at a great cost. Many British Battalions had been decimated, and as a result, the British Parliament passed a law permitting 18 year old soldiers to serve abroad, in order to make up the numbers in the depleted battalions (prior to this, soldiers had to be 19 before being allowed to fight overseas).

Eighteen year old Walter Mountney therefore found himself with the Durham Light Infantry in France during the closing scenes of the German offensive. In late April, early May, a number of the British Battalions that had been engaged in the ferocious fighting of March/April 1918, including the 6th Battalion Durham Light Infantry, were sent to recuperate and train in a supposedly 'quiet' sector of the French front line, in the Champagne area of France, between Reims and Laon.

Unfortunately, this area on the Aisne and Marne rivers was the exact place chosen by General Ludendorff for his next (and last) major offensive, to begin on May 27ᵗʰ 1918. About 1am the enemy bombardment opened with every kind and calibre of shell, including gas, and heavy casualties were caused in the forward posts on the plateau, and nearly all the rearward communications were cut within a very short time. The ordeal was made more trying by crouching, semi-suffocated in gas masks. At 4am the grey waves of German soldiers advanced out of the swirling mist and reached the crest of the ridge, forcing many of the survivors to fall back down the slope. All attempts to organise any defence at this point had to be abandoned and the retreat was continued.

During the desperate fighting that took place on May 27th and 28th, Walter Mountney was severely wounded and died on May 28th. He is buried in grave K. 14 Sissonne British Cemetery, Between Reims and Laon.

PRIVATE WILFRED ALDGATE NO.242145
16TH BATTALION ROYAL WARWICKSHIRE REGIMENT
DIED MAY 30TH 1918 AGED 25

In 1901, at Gilchrist Yard, near Fennel Street, Ashford, seven year old Wilfred Aldgate was living with his 26 year old mother, Annie Aldgate, at his grandparent's, Thomas and Mary Brocklehurst's farm. The Brocklehurst's originated from Sheldon but Wilfred and his mother, Annie Aldgate, had been born at Ashford. Annie was working as a domestic servant when she gave birth to Wilfred at Ashford in February 1894 and was unmarried.

Prior to the war Wilfred was employed as a forester on the Duke of Devonshire's estate. When he joined up at the start of the war he first became a member of the Sherwood Foresters but after being in hospital wounded, he was transferred to the 16th Battalion Royal Warwickshire Regiment. (He had been wounded by shrapnel shell in the right side and taken to a Canadian hospital in France in May 1917.)

Wilfred was a runner in connection with Brigade work and with some other colleagues had his headquarters in a sandbagged hut. Here they were sleeping on May 30th 1918, when a shell burst underneath the hut and blew them all up. All were killed or badly wounded, with Wilfred being killed outright.

Wilfred Aldgate is buried in grave 4.A.4 Tannay British Cemetery, Thiennes, between Bethune and St. Omer. His mother, Annie, still resided at Ashford, and had a memorial stone erected in the cemetery at Orchard Hall.

A Bakewell resident, hit by shellfire whilst a member of a night-time working party, was the next to die.

PRIVATE OSWALD WILLIAM WHITTAKER NO. 52059
8TH BATTALION LINCOLNSHIRE REGIMENT
DIED JUNE 28TH 1918 AGED 18

The Whittaker family lived on Matlock Street, Bakewell. The head of the household in 1901 was 36 year old William Henry Whittaker, who was born at Pear Tree, Derby and acted as a mineral agent. His wife Miriam, 35 years old, and Sheffield born, was a baker and confectioner. Daughters Coletta (14), May (13) and one year old Oswald, completed the family. When Oswald left school he was apprenticed to the J. W. Stewart drapery business. He had been a member of the Boy

Scouts and Church Lads' Brigade, was a chorister and had put in work with the 'Volunteers'.

Oswald joined up on October 27th 1917 and proceeded to France on April 10th 1918. Just two weeks later he would die from the wounds he received. He had first been with the Leicestershire Regiment but was transferred to the 8th Battalion Lincolnshire Regiment, and in June 1918 was near the front line east of Doullens, north of Amiens.

Private Whittaker's officer wrote to his parents, "As you know, he was my 'batman' and I was with him on a working party on the night of 26th/27th June. We had nearly finished when suddenly the enemy shelled us and your son Oswald was hit in three places. Stretcher-bearers attended him immediately, but found him unconscious and he was hurried down to the dressing station. He never regained consciousness and passed away very shortly afterwards. I got to know him very well and am deeply grieved at his loss, as he was a very hard-working, conscientious man."

*Oswald W, Whittaker
of Bakewell.*
Sandra Taylor

Oswald William Whittaker, 18 years of age, (he would have been nineteen on September 28th) was buried in grave E.1 Couin New British Cemetery, 15 kilometres west of Doullens.

2ND LIEUTENANT HUBERT ROBERTS THOMPSON
99TH SIEGE BATTERY ROYAL GARRISON ARTILLERY
DIED JUNE 30TH 1918 AGED 28

Hubert, or Bert as he was known, was the youngest son of John Roberts Thompson, a chemist and druggist, and Ellen Agnes Thompson. John was born in Bakewell at the Thompson family home and shop on King Street, the business having been established in 1780, whilst his wife, Ellen Agnes Sherwin, was born in Derby. By 1901 the family consisted of John junior (19 years), Ellen May (18 years and known as May), Frank (15 years) and twelve year old Bert.

Bert Thompson attended Lady Manners School in Bath Street from 1898 to 1905, leaving at the age of sixteen to join his parents and older brothers in running the family shop. The brothers did their training under the eye of their father, but the shop was more than a druggist store, for it sold many other items, including alcohol and spirits.

In 1905 Bert married Laura Elizabeth Finney, the daughter of Laura and Thomas Finney of Orchard House, Bakewell on Thursday November 25th. Bert's older brother, John, had married a sister of Laura Elizabeth Finney and sadly, we have already seen that her younger brother, William Fielding Finney had been killed in

LEFT TO RIGHT: *Frank Thompson, John Thompson, Bert (Hubert) Thompson.*
Ian Bright

Hubert Thompson of King Street, Bakewell. LEFT TO RIGHT: *May (Ellen Mary) Thompson, Hubert (Bert) Thompson, Ellen Agnes Thompson.*
Ian Bright

The chemist and druggist shop of John Roberts Thompson c1905, in King Street, Bakewell.
Ian Bright

action on the Western Front on January 7th 1917, aged 20.

Bert Thompson joined the forces in April 1916 as a gunner in the Royal Garrison Artillery, as a member of a siege battery, whilst his elder brother Frank joined the Royal Field Artillery, looking after the team of horses. Bert proceeded to France in September 1916. He then returned to England to join a school of cadets for training, having been recommended for a commission, which he gained as a second lieutenant in November 1917. In mid-April 1917 he was home on leave in Bakewell and again in October of that year, when he was able to meet his brother Frank, who had returned from France.

Sadly, family and friends received news of the death of Second Lieutenant Hubert Thompson, which took place in a French hospital on Sunday June 30th 1918, aged 28. He had been the victim of a gas attack by German artillery shells and suffered badly from the effects of the gas. Taken first to a casualty clearing station, he was quickly transferred to a main medical hospital in the area close to St. Omer. He died at the hospital and was buried nearby in grave III.G.4 Aire Communal Cemetery, 14 kilometres SSE of St. Omer, leaving a young widow to grieve in Bakewell.

A regular army man from Bakewell, with a fine record of military service for his country, died at home in Bakewell and was buried in the local cemetery.

Sergeant Benjamin Kay
Royal Garrison Artillery
Died July 4th 1918 aged 47

The death of Sergeant Benjamin Kay took place at his home in Bakewell on July 4th 1918, aged 47 years. He was a professional soldier who had served in India, Gibraltar, Egypt (Port Said), Hong Kong, South Africa (Boer War) and in Ceylon. He was 19 years old when he joined the Colours and served for the full 21 years, being present at the taking of Pretoria during the Boer War.

He took part in the Tirah Expedition 1887-1898 on the North West Frontier of India and served on the Punjab. Benjamin was connected to Lord Robert's staff during the Boer War and afterwards proceeded to China with the Royal Garrison Artillery. In 1911 he retired on a pension to Bakewell but at the outbreak of war went straight to London and offered his services.

He was regarded as too old but was attached to the British Embassy in Petrograd, Russia, as a courier, where he came into contact with the Tsar and members of the Russian administration. He remained there for 18 months and the Tsar awarded him the Order of St. Stanislaus. But then his health broke down and he returned to civilian life. Since returning to England he had worked at Tilbury Docks but suffered with an affliction of the heart.

Benjamin Kay had been ill for two months at Bakewell before he died at the age of 47, and was buried in Bakewell Cemetery.

Three days later, a Bakewell soldier who had been captured during the Ludendorff offensive of March 21st 1918, died as a prisoner-of-war in Germany.

PRIVATE JOHN THOMAS CARROLL NO. 235058
NORTH STAFFORDSHIRE REGIMENT
DIED JULY 7TH 1918 AGED 35

John Thomas Carroll was born at Bakewell in 1883, the eldest of the ten children of Richard and Annie Carroll. By 1901 the family was living at Rock Cottage, Undercliffes, Endcliffe Rocks, off Buxton Road, Bakewell. Richard had been born in Bakewell but Annie was a Greatorex from Tansley, before her marriage. He was a self-employed stone carter, using his horses and carts on hire to the local council and carried chert from Holme Bank Quarry. He also transported coal from Bakewell railway station and hired his carts to transport hay at harvest time. In 1901, both John Thomas Carroll, aged 17 years and William Carroll, aged 14 years, were working as carters for their father, whilst a boarder, William Nuttall from Youlgreave, also worked for them.

John Thomas Carroll enlisted in the army in 1916, joining first of all the Lincolnshire Regiment, before transferring to the North Staffordshire Regiment. By this stage, two other brothers were also serving in the army.

During June 1917 he was reported to be in hospital in England, suffering from wounds, but was progressing satisfactorily. On making a full recovery, it was likely that at this stage he joined the North Staffordshire Regiment.

Sadly, it was reported to his parents that he was missing in action from the first day of the Ludendorff offensive, on March 21st 1918. Unknown to his parents, he was being held as a prisoner-of-war at Stendal Camp, between Magdeburg and Wittenberge, in Eastern Germany, where he died on July 7th 1918, aged 35. His parents still received no official news about him, even though he had been buried in grave III.B.19 Berlin South-Western Cemetery. Official confirmation of his death was not received by his parents until the end of February 1919.

Meanwhile, a railwayman from Great Longstone died two weeks later whilst taking part in a small-scale raid on enemy lines in the Ypres Salient.

PRIVATE ROBERT ROBINSON NO. 91432
'D' COMPANY 2ND BATTALION SHERWOOD FORESTERS
DIED JULY 23RD 1918 AGED 29

Robert was born at Eckington in Derbyshire, to the south of Sheffield. He was the eldest son of George and Susannah Robinson and in 1901, twelve year old Robert and his eleven year old brother were living with their parents on Market Street, Eckington. Their father, George, who was a grocer's assistant, had been born in London, but his wife Susannah came from nearby Unstone, Derbyshire.

Seven years later, the family moved to live in Great Longstone. Robert was first employed as a porter at both Hassop and Millers Dale Stations, on the Midland Railway, but then became a shunter on the railway at Matlock. By the time of his death in July 1918, he had a young wife, 29 year old Charlotte Frances Robinson, and two children (including Hilda Mary born 1915), their family home being at Sunny Bank, Great Longstone. Charlotte Frances Beresford was the eldest of the five children of Joseph Beresford, a carpenter born at Leek and Harriet Beresford from Great Longstone. All five children had been born in the village and the family home was at Spring Bank, Great Longstone.

Robert Robinson of Great Longstone.

Robert joined the army midway through 1917, training as a signaller in the 2nd Battalion Sherwood Foresters. He went to the front in April 1918, but survived for only three months. His brother, Harold, had already been killed whilst serving in the army in July 1916.

In the last week of June 1918 the Battalion relieved other units in the Dickebusch sector of the Ypres Salient. It proved an unpleasant front, where the dominating position of the enemy on Kemmel Hill made movement impossible by day. Most work had to be done at night.

After a short break from front line duty, they were back in the Salient during July. They successfully attacked the enemy, recapturing Elzenwalle. The Battalion kept the enemy on its front alert by carrying out several small raids. On the night of 23rd July, 'D' Company organised a small raid under Second Lieutenant Tombazis with ten men; a German post was rushed and the occupants bolted so that no prisoners could be captured. Machine-gun fire opened up on the party from a neighbouring post and the Foresters retired, but Robert Robinson was hit and died.

He was buried in grave XV. B. 13. Nine Elms British Cemetery, just to the west of Poperinge.

The next to die was an Ashford man who was wounded whilst winning the Military Medal, and died from these wounds whilst being treated in England.

Private Jasper Johnson No. 27263
(won Military Medal) 2nd Battalion Hampshire Regiment
died August 1st 1918 aged 21

In 1901 the Johnson family was to be found at Torrs Farm, Hassop, where Jasper Johnson senior was a farmer. He had been born at Great Longstone and married Annie, an Eyam girl. One child had been born at Foolow, three at Rowland, and two at Hassop, as Jasper worked on different farms. In 1901 Jasper Johnson junior, aged

5 years, was staying with his grandfather, 60 year old Thomas Davis and family at Foolow. Thomas Davis was a farmer and mining engineer, born at Foolow. By 1914 the family were living at Woodland View, Ashford.

Jasper junior helped his father on the farm, but his main employment was with Walter Tinsley of the 'Rookery', Master of the High Peak Harriers and Hunt. It is interesting to note that in the Diary of Maria Gyte, from Sheldon, she records that on September 30th 1914 on their farm, a young bull was killed. Jasper Johnson, known to friends and family as 'Jess', was fetched from Ashford and it was skinned and dressed.

When Jess (Jasper) enlisted, he joined the South Staffordshire Regiment, but was later transferred to the 2nd Battalion Hampshire Regiment. With this Battalion he was in action at La Creche, when he received wounds to his back, right knee and left lung. For his gallant action in this battle he received the Military Medal.

Jasper (Jess) Johnson of Ashford.
Peter Johnson

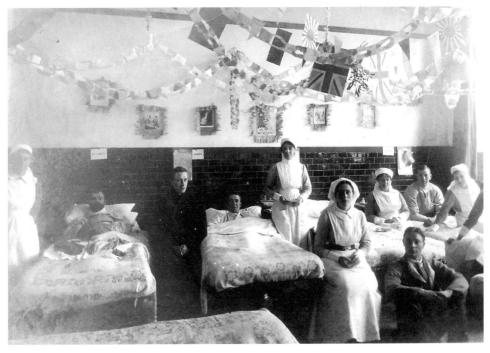

Nurses and wounded servicemen at the Newcastle Hospital in which Jasper Johnson died in 1918.
Peter Johnson

However, the wounds were severe and he was brought home to England and received medical attention at Newcastle Hospital. It was there that he succumbed to his wounds on August 1st 1918. He was brought by train to Hassop Station and laid in rest at his home 'Woodland View'. From there he was conveyed on a gun carriage drawn by a number of the 'Volunteers' for burial at Ashford Parish Church at 2pm on August 5th. Reverend H. E. Sherlock officiated, three volleys were fired over the grave and the 'Last Post' was sounded.

One day after Jasper Johnson's funeral, a Bakewell man was killed in action on the second day of a four-day attack on enemy positions near Bethune, France.

PRIVATE CECIL CLARK No. 57606
2ND BATTALION LANCASHIRE FUSILIERS DIED
AUGUST 6TH 1918 AGED 22

Cecil Clark of Bakewell.
Harry Hutchinson

Cecil was the third eldest of nine children of Fred and Mary Clark of Cunningham Place, Bakewell. Fred and Mary were both born in Bakewell, with Fred employed by Thomas Allsop, the Bakewell builder, as a stone mason and carver. He was involved in the building of the new Post Office in the town in 1894 and shortly afterwards in the construction of the new Lady Manners School, on Bath Street. Fred actually carved the peacock on this building. His fine stone carving work can be seen on the City Hall, Sheffield. A fine musician, Fred was a virtuoso on the melodeon. Sadly, he died in 1908, at the young age of 42.

Before the First World War began, Cecil Clark was employed at Holme Bank Chert Quarry. Cecil's older brother, Douglas, enlisted and joined the Royal Field Artillery and shortly afterwards, in 1915, Cecil joined up and became a member of the Sherwood Foresters, before later transferring to the 2nd Battalion Lancashire Fusiliers.

By August 5th the French and Americans had pushed the Germans back on the Marne and on August 8th General Haig was to launch the Amiens offensive against the Germans. However, Cecil and his Battalion were further north of these operations, in the vicinity of Bethune.

They faced the German trenches at Cantrainne and Busnettes, 10 kilometres east of Bethune, with an attack planned against Pacault Wood on August 5th. The fighting for the wood continued into August 6th with attack and counter-attack in the German trenches. The fighting went on throughout the 7th and 8th August, with the final objective, L'Ecleme, being taken on the 8th. However, Cecil Clark had been killed on 6th August. Since arriving in France in 1916 he had escaped injury, but now his luck had run out.

His body was recovered and he was buried in grave D.14 Le Vertannoy British Cemetery, Hinges, 2 kilometres NW of Bethune. Mary Clark received news that her second eldst son, Cecil had been killed. Some month before, she had learned that her eldest son, Douglas, had been severely wounded and gassed, but thankfully he recovered. Sadly, we shall find that Cecil Clark's nephew, also called Cecil, after his uncle, would be killed in action at the Battle of Imjin, during the Korean War.

Cecil Clark and sister Lizzie.
Harry Hutchinson

Two weeks later, as the Germans slowly retreated, and the British continued their major push, known as 'The Advance to Victory', a guardsman from Little Longstone, who worked at Thornbridge Hall, lost his life south east of Arras.

GUARDSMAN FRED COWAN SLACK No. 25187
1st BATTALION GRENADIER GUARDS
DIED AUGUST 24th 1918 AGED 37

In 1891, Fred's father Joseph, aged 57, was working locally as a groom and assistant gardener at one of the large houses in the Little Longstone area. Fred was nine years old and his brother Frank was also a gardner, whilst brother Harry was working as a railway porter on the Midland Railway. Their father Joseph was a native of Wormhill, whilst their mother Margaret came originally from Tideswell. The family was living four dwellings away from the Pack Horse Inn, Little Longstone, run by William and Sarah Taylor, and young Fred had been born in the village.

By 1901, Joseph was working as a road labourer, but 19 year old Fred was now employed as a gardener at Thornbridge Hall, Great Longstone, the home of George Jobson Marples. During the next fourteen years, Fred Cowan Slack became first a footman at the Hall and then rose in position, to become a butler for the wealthy businessman.

A tall man, Fred joined the 1st Battalion Grenadier Guards when he enlisted at Bakewell in 1915 and became a bomb thrower with his Battalion. In August 1917 he was injured during the Battle of Passchendaele and was returned to England, where, in September, after being in hospital, he spent ten days leave with his wife and young son.

Aged 34, Fred had married 20 year old Lucy Ruth Grassick at Great Longstone Church on August 4th 1916, whilst on leave from his unit. Lucy was born at Ashover, into a farming family and in 1901 her father John was farming and also working in the coalmine in the Clay Cross area. It is likely that Lucy Grassick came to work at Thornbridge Hall, where she met Fred Slack. In September 1916 a son, Fred Cowan Slack junior, was born to Lucy and Fred.

After the Germans launched the last major offensive in the Champagne area on May 27th 1918, the Allies finally rallied and on July 18th Marshall Foch began his counter-stroke and drove the enemy back over the River Marne. Although in full retreat, the Germans continued to offer a stubborn resistance and counter-attacked all along the line, whilst

Fred Cowan Slack in footman's uniform at Thornbridge Hall. He later rose to the position of butler.
Alastair Slack

This photograph was taken in the grounds of Thornbridge Hall in 1916, and shows the guests at the wedding of Mary Ann Taylor to Ernest Edward Gilbert, son of Isaiah Gilbert. The bride, who was the game cook at the Hall, and groom, are at the centre of the front row. To the left is Sarah Ann Gilbert, Noel Green's grandmother. Noel's grandfather, Isaiah, to the right of the groom, first worked with horses and drugs and later as a ganger on the railway line between Longstone and Hassop. He was, however, most famous for his topiary and speeding passengers would gaze with amazement at the birds, animals and other wondrous shapes he created. The child at the front is Noel's sister, Cecily, and her mother Rossellen is fourth from the left at the back. The tall man to the centre is Fred Slack, who died in the Great War.
Alastair Slack

in August the British struck across the Somme in their 'Advance to Victory'.

The British pursued the Germans who were slowly retreating. On August 21st, at the start of a fresh British advance, the Germans put down a heavy barrage of shells on the trenches occupied by Fred and the 1st Battalion. Patrols were sent out and encountered the enemy, capturing two Germans. A strong party of the enemy which tried to recapture them, was beaten off. On August 22nd the Battalion was relieved and proceeded to Boiry St. Martin, a few kilometres south east of Arras.

On August 23rd they reached a little further south to Moyenneville. The 1st Battalion was to move forwards towards Ervillers and help to capture an objective known as Mory Switch.

On reaching the Ervillers – Hamelincourt road, the leading companies came under a light field gun barrage and long range machine-gun fire, forcing them to deploy gun and rifle fire, leaving fifty men as prisoners.

Fred Cowan Slack, on the extreme right, with other members of Mr. Marple's staff at Thornbridge Hall.
Alastair Slack

Three more companies swept on to the next objective, which was carried successfully. By 5-45pm the position was completely in the hands of the Battalion, which had sustained 45 casualties.

At 7am on August 24th the attack was continued. A shrapnel barrage had been put down by British artillery, but it was too far in advance to be of assistance and as the attack developed the Germans opened an intense machine-gun and shell fire from Mory Copse and Hally Copse. The situation was such that all they could do was cling on.

During the morning Germans could be seen dribbling forward small parties to Mory Copse, and the sniping and machine-gun fire became more concentrated and intense. At 10-45am the Second Division made an attempt to come up on the right but suffered considerable casualties.

The 1st Battalion casualties were high during that day (155) and one of these was Fred Cowan Slack, who was killed by shell fire. His body was never recovered and his name is to be found on Panel 3 Vis-en-Artois Memorial, 10 kilometres south east of Arras.

The original grave of Fred Cowan Slack.
Alastair Slack

Even though the Germans were now on the retreat and had lost all chance of winning the war, they fought tenaciously over the next few months, resulting in many more casualties to servicemen from Bakewell and district as the war gradually came to a close.

SECOND LIEUTENANT HENRY BYRON
10TH BATTALION MANCHESTER REGIMENT
DIED SEPTEMBER 2ND 1918 AGED 30

Mr. C. E. Bennett, draper, Matlock Street, received a letter from Mrs. Wharmby of Stalybridge stating that her brother Henry (Harry) Byron of the Manchester Regiment, had been instantaneously killed on September 2nd. He was a native of Stalybridge.

Before the war he was a traveller for Bennetts, and was found dead on the battlefield with gunshot wounds to his head. He was buried close by in grave B. 9. Manchester Cemetery, Riencourt-les-Bapaume, 3 kilometres south of Bapaume, which had been captured three days before his death. Convalescent comrades formed a guard of honour and a big gun sounded the 'Last Post'.

The occasion of his death occurred during the second phase of the Amiens offensive launched by Haig against the enemy forces (August 21st to September 4th) which caused the retirement of the German army to their final position, the Hindenburg Line.

Aged 30 years and married, Henry Byron had lived in Bakewell for about fifteen years, being first apprenticed to the former firm of Messrs. Booth and Wright, drapers of King Street, and subsequently, for several years was with Mr. Bennett and his former partner, Mr. Sheldon at their shop on Matlock Street. He had shown a keen interest in sports and was a member of the Working Men's Club Committee.

Joining the Sherwood Foresters in 1916, he made rapid progress with them, rising to sergeant and by April 1917 had obtained a commission as Second Lieutenant and was transferred to the Manchester Regiment. He only returned to France on August 14th and had previously been in hospital in Cornwall, recovering from wounds received a few weeks before.

Three days after Henry's death in France, a Great Longstone man succumbed to wounds he had received a year earlier and was buried in the village churchyard.

PRIVATE ARTHUR WARD NO. 50777
8TH BATTALION (DEPOT) NORTH STAFFORDSHIRE REGIMENT
DIED SEPTEMBER 5TH 1918 AGED 37

Arthur Ward was born at Great Longstone in 1882, the third eldest son of Thomas and Frances (Fanny) Ward, of Mill Lane. Thomas was a chert miner in 1891, whilst his son Herbert was a farm labourer, George was a gardener and groom at one of the large houses and Arthur, aged nine years was at school. Their brother Charles had died in 1882, aged ten years.

We know that Arthur became a Territorial soldier in his spare time, whilst living at Great Longstone. By 1903, aged 21, he was a member of 'A' Company 2nd Volunteer Battalion Sherwood Foresters, based at Bakewell, which, in 1908 became the 6th Battalion (Territorials) Sherwood Foresters.

During the First World War Arthur enlisted at Sheffield and eventually joined the 8th Battalion North

Arthur Ward of Great Longstone.

Staffordshire Regiment. By this time, both his parents were dead, father Thomas passing away in 1911 and mother Fanny in 1912. His brother, George, was still farming at Longstone. Prior to the war, Arthur was employed by Messrs. Vickers of Sheffield and was married.

During the Battle of Passchendaele, Arthur was severely wounded in the left hip in late September 1917, and spent time in hospital in France. Eventually he was brought to a hospital in England and from there to his home. Sadly, complications occurred and Arthur Ward died at home on September 5th 1918, aged 37 years. He was buried in St. Giles Churchyard, Great Longstone.

The headstone of Private Arthur Ward in Great Longstone churchyard.
Keith Taylor

PRIVATE FRANK THOMAS WILLIAM SUTER NO. 53791
23RD BATTALION CHESHIRE REGIMENT
DIED SEPTEMBER 8TH 1918 AGED 19

Sidney John Suter, a 32 year old electrical and mechanical engineer (born at Chatham, Kent) was living in the St. Pancras area of London in 1901 with his London born wife, Catherine Annie Suter, and their four children, including one year old Frank Thomas William Suter.

By the year of the First World War, Frank's parents had arrived in Great Longstone, living at Thornbridge Villas, with Sidney employed as electrical engineer for G. J. Marples at Thornbridge Hall. Frank Suter enlisted at Lewisham, London, joining the Essex Regiment in 1917. By the time of his death, in September 1918, however, he had transferred to the 23rd Cheshire Regiment.

At some point in August 1918, Frank Suter, was severely wounded, being attended to at the Casualty Clearing Station, and then being taken to one of the numerous hospitals to be found at St. Omer, one of the main military bases in France. It was there that Frank Suter died from his wounds on September 8th 1918 and was buried in grave V. E. 19. Longuenesse (St. Omer) Souvenir Cemetery.

It was to be in the Russian Caucasus, far away from the more well-known theatres of war, that the next fatality occurred, the son of a future vicar of Bakewell.

CAPTAIN ERIC MINOR SPINK
7TH BATTALION NORTH STAFFORDSHIRE REGIMENT
DIED SEPTEMBER 14TH 1918 AGED 24

In 1901, six year old Eric Minor Spink was living at Hanley, an area of Stoke-on-Trent in Staffordshire, where his father, the Reverend Edmund Spink was the rector of St. Jude (1895-1908). Edmund had been born at Ripon, whilst his wife, Frances Ann originated from Shropshire. In 1901, Eric was the youngest of three siblings.

The Spink family had no connection with Bakewell until after the death of Eric in 1918, when, in early 1919 the living at Bakewell and rural deanery was offered to the Reverend Edmund Spink, and he took up the appointment in March 1919 (he remained the vicar of Bakewell until 1931). Between 1908 and 1919 he had served as the vicar of Leek and from 1917 to 1919 as Rural Dean of Leek and took over the living at Bakewell from the Reverend Abraham, who we have seen, had also lost a son during the Great War. The Bakewell War Memorial was unveiled and dedicated in August 1920

Reverend Edward Spink, vicar of Bakewell from 1919. His son was killed during the First World War.

and therefore the name of the new vicar's son was included on the memorial.

Eric Spink eventually became a captain in the 7th Battalion, North Staffordshire Regiment and by September 1918, he and the Battalion were helping in the fight against the Turks at Baku, in the Azerbaijan region of the Caucasus. Situated on the western shore of the Caspian Sea, the port was an important centre of the oil industry.

On January 27th, British troops under Major General Dunsterville moved north-east from Baghdad, reaching Enzeli (Pahlevi) on the Caspian Sea on February 17th. An advanced Battalion, the 7th North Staffs and Eric Spink crossed the Russian border and entered Baku on August 4th 1918, the Turks being driven out on August 6th.

Baku was in the charge of the Armenian Socialist Revolutionary Government after the fall of the Russian Czar in 1917, with the Bolsheviks in opposition. The British had been invited in to help with the defence of Baku and the oil fields, though this was opposed by the Bolshevik Party.

Arriving in the town, the 7th Battalion found billets at the Hotel Metropole and the Hotel Europe. By August 13th, their numbers had reached 500 men and they were accompanied by a force of armoured cars.

The condition of the local army, upon which the whole expedition would depend, was appalling. They did not seem to realise the perilous position and made little effort to help in preparing a defence. Ex-Russian officers in the town refused to help because of their hatred of the Armenians, who were in power. The North Staffs took up a defensive position, including on 'Dirty Volcano', a hill forming a Salient in the line. On August 19th, the 9th Battalion Royal Warwicks arrived and by August 25th the British force was 1,000 men strong.

The first Turkish attack was launched on August 26th on 'Dirty Volcano', with a detachment of the North Staffords providing a gallant defence against great odds, the men fighting to the death. Despite heavy losses, the Turkish force took the position. Another Turkish attack was launched on August 31st and further withdrawal took place, the Armenian forces providing little support for the British. All hope of saving Baku now appeared to be shattered. However, the Baku government refused to allow anyone to leave, threatening armed force.

The Turks were very quiet during the next ten days, except for artillery bombardment of the town. All British sick and wounded were evacuated by ship.

About 4am on September 14th the final Turkish attack began, with infantry and cavalry crossing the railway valley and advancing in mass to attack the ridge west of the town. The North Staffords suffered heavy casualties but counter-attacked, incurring further losses.

The Turks now made a determined effort to cut off the troops from the town itself and made a massed attack on the North Staffords, who were guarding the left flank with forty five men under two officers, Major Beresford Havelock and Captain Eric Spink, who were killed almost at once, gallantly directing their men to the last. Most of the men became casualties, fighting to the last.

At 8-30pm, orders were given for the British to withdraw from the line and the Brigade was embarked on two ships. The horses were shot, the armoured cars run into the sea and the engines of the Ford vans were smashed up and burned. The ships left Baku port at 11pm.

Eric Minor Spink was buried at Baku, Azerbaijan (Armenia).

It was not until November 1918 that a British flotilla on the Caspian Sea drove the Turks from Baku.

LANCE CORPORAL CLEMENT ALFRED STEVENS (WON M.M.) NO.27836
2ND BATTALION SHERWOOD FORESTERS
DIED SEPTEMBER 18TH 1918 AGED 25

George Briddon lived on Bagshaw Hill, Bakewell, in 1901, and worked as a smallholder. His daughter, Ellen, aged 29 and born in Bakewell, had married Herbert Stevens, who had arrived in the town from Frome, Somerset, to work as a painter and paper-hanger. They were living with Ellen's father, George Briddon, together with their three children, including Clement Alfred Stevens. Later, the family was to live on Stanedge Road, Bakewell.

After leaving school, Clement Stevens was employed as a gardener by Mr. Dennis, Headmaster of Lady Manners School. He enlisted at Matlock and joined the 2nd Battalion Sherwood Foresters and rose to the rank of Lance Corporal. In August 1917 he was wounded in the leg and sent home to a hospital in Newcastle. He had already been wounded twice.

General Haig launched the Amiens offensive on August 8th 1918, taking the attack to the Germans. By August 22nd the Germans were ordered to withdraw from the Amiens area and the Lys Salient, but as Peronne was captured and St. Quentin threatened, the entire German situation deteriorated, necessitating retirement to the final position, the Hindenburg Line, by September 4th.

Clement A. Stevens of Bakewell.

The Sherwood Foresters were involved in this offensive and although the 'push' slowed down by September 4th, due to shortage of reserves, the 2nd Battalion was involved in fierce fighting during the middle of September.

By September 17th they were in position near Holnon village, just to the west of St. Quentin, ready for an attack the following day on a German strongpoint called 'The Quadrilateral'. At 5-30pm on the 17th, the Battalion position was heavily shelled, causing thirty casualties and six horses were killed.

At 5-23am on September 18th the Battalion advanced to the attack. The right company was held up by heavy machine-gun fire, with the remainder of the Battalion still trying to push on and gain the Quadrilateral. By 8-35am the enemy were still holding certain strongpoints and a nest of machine-guns failed to be put out of action. By 11-45am the order came for a fresh attack on the Quadilateral, with enemy aircraft active over the Battalion front lines. The planes were fired on, in the darkness, by heavy guns. At 1am on September 19th the orders for the attack were cancelled.

However, during the fighting on September 18th, Clement Alfred Stevens was killed. His body was recovered and he was buried in grave D. 12. Trefcon British Cemetery, Caulaincourt, near St. Quentin.

On May 14th 1919 it was reported in the *London Gazette* that Lance Corporal Clement Stevens had been awarded the Military Medal for a gallant action on the feld of battle.

PRIVATE JAMES ELLIOTT NO. 71307
'D' COMPANY 1ST BATTALION SHERWOOD FORESTERS
DIED OCTOBER 7TH 1918 AGED 21

James Elliott was born in Bakewell in 1897 and lived with his parents James and Ellen Elliott and four siblings at Cemetery House, Cemetery Road, in the town. His father was employed as the superintendent of the parish church cemetery and originated from Rowsley, whilst his mother, Ellen, was a Sheffield girl.

James, known as Jim to his friends, enlisted in the army in 1916, joining the Sherwood Foresters. Whilst on the Western Front he suffered from trench fever, but had made a good recovery and became a member of 'D' Company, 1st Battalion Sherwood Foresters.

In September 1918 the Battalion was in an area near Oppy Wood, spending twenty two consecutive days in the trenches up to September 15th before being relieved.

During the latter part of September and the first few days of October, officers and men were engaged in carrying out several important raids against the German positions, with the view to obtaining identification and information about in what strength the enemy was holding his front line. Considerable opposition was met with, for the Germans were still inclined to put up a stout resistance, and casualties were by no means light.

A major attack went in on October 6th against the line just NE of Arras, near the village of Oppy. 'D' Company captured several trenches and helped to surround Oppy village, which, after some stiff fighting, was entered in the evening. That same evening, 'D' Company drove the enemy further back. In the face of considerable opposition they established a strong post and during the night the enemy counter-attacked and was successfully repulsed.

However, during the later actions, Jim Elliott was severely wounded. Information for his family came from the chaplain and matron of one of the casualty clearing stations that he was wounded in both arms and died shortly after entering the emergency hospital.

James Elliott was buried in grave B.38 Duisans British Cemetery, Etrun.

At the time of his death, his parents, James and Ellen, were living at Sherwood House, Haddon Road, Bakewell.

PRIVATE GEORGE WILLIAM BLAGDON NO. 238946
408TH AGRICULTURAL COMPANY, LABOUR CORPS
DIED 8TH OCTOBER AGED 36

By 1901 the Blagdon family was living on North Church Street, with 19 year old George William being the eldest of seven children of William and Selina Blagdon. William, a Bakewell-born quarry worker had married Selina Nadin from Buxton. With money from Selina's side of the family, William purchased a horse and cart and supplemented his income by transporting people in his 'horse bus'. Sadly, Selina died before the start of the First World War and some of the younger members of the family were split up.

By the outset of the War, George William Blagdon, who was employed in the chert quarry at Holme Bank, was married, with his wife employed in the home of Charles Critchlow, a shopkeeper in Rutland Square. George enlisted in the early days of the war and joined the 6th Battalion Sherwood Foresters. Shortly afterwards, his brother Harry joined up, becoming a Sherwood Forester, as did his brother Edward, some time later.

In 1916 George wrote to his wife that he had had a very narrow escape. They had gone into the trenches, when one night, just after midnight, and after their supper had been brought in, the trench in front was

Harry Blagden, brother of George William Blagden.
Mrs. M. Stewart

blown up by a terrific explosion. Men were shot up into the air. George and several others were almost buried for over a day, with nothing to eat, before they were eventually got out. As a result of their experiences and the wounds he received he was brought to England to recuperate.

When George William had recovered sufficiently, he was deemed unfit to return to active service with the 6th Battalion and instead he joined the 408th Agricultural Company of the Labour Corps. By September 1918 they were busy working on the land in the Halifax area when he was taken ill and he died in the town. His body was returned to Bakewell and he was given a military funeral when he was buried in the town's cemetery.

Although his brother Harry was gassed a number of times whilst serving on the Western Front, he thankfully survived the war, as did his brother Edward.

Headstone of Private G.W. Blagden in Bakewell Cemetery.

PRIVATE JOHN WILLIAM ROWLAND NO. 40097
5TH BATTALION LANCASTER REGIMENT
DIED OCTOBER 10TH 1918 AGED 19

John William Rowland, known as Jack to his family and friends, was born in 1900 at Cunningham Place. His father, Harry, a Bakewell man, had married Eliza Slater from Matlock and in 1901 Harry was working as a section builder in the electric works at Bakewell (almost certainly the DP Battery Works).

As the family grew, with the additions of Percy, Hilda, Vera and Joan, Harry began farming at Castle Hill Farm (now a housing estate), where he became a milk retailer. The farm was part of Castle Hill Estate, owned by Mr. Blake. His home, Castle Hill, later became the boarding school for Lady Manners. To earn extra money, Eliza did the laundry for Mr. Blake.

Jack Rowland enlisted in 1917 at Bakewell and joined the Leicestershire Regiment, before being transferred to the 5th Battalion Lancaster Regiment. It was whilst the Battalion was following up the German retreat from the Hindenburg Line in October 1918, that Jack Rowland was killed in action by shrapnel wounds, 5 kilometres SW of Armentieres. He was buried in grave I. E. 49. Rue-Petillon Military Cemetery, Fleurbaix.

John (Jack) William Rowland of Bakewell.

Harry Hutchinson

TROOPER WILLIAM KENNEDY No. 75261
HOUSEHOLD CAVALRY (DERBYSHIRE YEOMANRY AND LATER ESSEX YEOMANRY)
DIED OCTOBER 25TH 1918 AGED 33

William was born at Levenshulme, Lancashire, the second child of John and Edith Kennedy. By 1901 his father, John, who originated from Ireland, was employed as a traveller for a hosiery shop in the Levenshulme area, whilst his mother, Edith, was an assistant in a draper's shop. 17 year old William was employed as an apprentice warehouse man.

However, some years before the start of the First World War he came to live and work in Bakewell, together with his wife Bertha. He was almost certainly involved with the Derbyshire Imperial Yeomanry before the war, because when he enlisted, it was with the Yeomanry that he served, eventually becoming a member of the Essex Yeomanry, in the Household Cavalry.

Near the close of the war, in September/October 1918 he was attached to the No.2 Line of Communication Eastern Area Reinforcement Camp, and it was here, in October 1918 that he was taken ill with pneumonia/influenza. He died in hospital near Dieppe, aged 33, and was buried in grave I. R. I. Janval Cemetery, Dieppe.

After the war, his wife remarried and went to live in Castleton.

GUNNER ALFRED FRANCIS MARSDEN No. 309123
2ND/1ST (LANCS.) HEAVY BATTERY ROYAL GARRISON ARTILLERY
DIED NOVEMBER 3RD 1918 AGED 31

In 1891, at Haddon Grove Farm (now called Mill Farm), between Over Haddon and Monyash, two year old Alfred Francis Marsden was living with his parents, Benjamin and Isabella Marsden. Benjamin, a 43 year old farmer and leadminer had married Isabella, a native of Callow, Wirksworth. However, some time before 1901, Benjamin left his wife and family to live in Chesterfield.

Alfred worked on his mother's farm at Haddon Grove, whilst his brother worked the neighbouring farm, Organ Ground Farm (the ground had been sold by Bakewell Parish Church to pay for a new church organ). Alfred, William and his other brothers were all farmers and cattle dealers.

Alfred travelled to Derby to enlist and joined the Royal Garrison Artillery, serving as a gunner with the 2nd/1st (Lancashire) Heavy Battery. He was engaged in a great deal of action, being wounded late in the war and was sent to the large hospital centre of Etaples, on the coast, 27 kilometres south of Boulogne. He was recovering well, but caught pneumonia and succumbed on November 3rd 1918, aged 31 years, just eight days before the end of the war.

Alfred Francis Marsden was buried in grave LXIX.A.5 Etaples Military Cemetery.

SERGEANT JOHN HENRY SHERRATT No. 46916
164TH PROTECTION COMPANY, ROYAL DEFENCE CORPS
DIED NOVEMBER 7TH 1918 AGED 34

Headstone of Sergeant J.H. Sherratt in Bakewell Cemetery.

John Henry Sherratt's father, John Henry senior, was born at Langly in Derbyshire and married Priscilla, who came from Derby. They settled in Bakewell and by 1891 were living at Rock Terrace, together with eight year old John Henry junior and his four siblings. In 1901, seventeen year old John Henry was still living in Bakewell parish, but away from home. He was boarding at the home of John Carrington, a farmer, and his sister-in-law, and John Henry was employed on the farm as an agricultural servant.

He was a member of the Derbyshire Imperial Yeomanry and was involved with them near the out-break of war. Eventually, due to wounds received and medical ill-health, he joined the 164th Protection Company, Royal Defence Corps, as a sergeant, in England.

However, his medical condition worsened and he was discharged from the army and returned to live with his parents at Diamond Court, Bakewell. He continued to be medically attended.

The sudden death came as a considerable surprise to friends and family in and around Bakewell. His mother last saw him alive around 10 o'clock the previous night, November 6th, and nothing was heard during the night. About 8am next morning, Priscilla, on visiting her son's bedroom, found him dead, he having apparently passed away in his sleep on November 7th.

John Henry Sherratt was buried in Bakewell Cemetery.

Inspired by the Communists and sparked by a mutiny of the German High Seas Fleet, disorder, revolts and mutinies flared inside Germany between October 28th and November 10th. A new Socialist government took power and proclaimed a Republic on November 9th, whilst the Kaiser fled to Holland on the 10th. A German delegation negotiated an Armistice at Compiegne, France, at 5am on November 11th and hostilities ceased at 11am. After nearly four and a half years of fighting the war had come to an end.

Celebrations took place throughout Bakewell and district. In the market town, Armistice celebrations continued through to Saturday night, when the soldiers and sailors of the district, with the utmost ceremonial, burnt an effigy of the Kaiser in the Cattle Market, after dragging him round the town in a bath chair and 'shooting' him at the stake with fireworks.

However, between the Armistice of November 11th 1918 and 1920 nine more servicemen from Bakewell and district would die from wounds received during the war or from the effects of the flu pandemic. News of the death of loved ones as a result of the flu virus must have been very hard for their families to accept. They had survived against the odds on the battlefield only to succumb to the killer virus. I find that one of the sad points of some of these men's deaths is that though they had connections with Bakewell and district, some were not included on any war memorial. Four cases simply have a Commonwealth War Graves headstone in Bakewell Cemetery.

PRIVATE ERNEST ARTHUR SMITH NO. 84101
3RD BATTALION SHERWOOD FORESTERS
(LATER TRANSFERRED TO 501ST AGRICULTURAL COMPANY, LABOUR CORPS)
DIED NOVEMBER 14TH 1918

Through illness or wounds received in battle, it was deemed in 1918 that Ernest was no longer fit for action on the battlefield and was transferred from the Sherwood Foresters to the Labour Corps. By late 1918 he was working on a farm at Ticknall, Derbyshire. Ernest was married, with two children, although some years after his death, Jane Smith remarried and lived at Barratt's Yard, Bakewell.

Ernest Arthur Smith died as a result of a bout of pneumonia. He received a military funeral, with a firing party from the 'Volunteers', Sadly, his name is not on the Roll of Honour in Bakewell Parish Church or on the War Memorial in Rutland Square.

PRIVATE (DRUMMER) FRANK PULLEN NO. 72661
'B' COMPANY 1ST BATTALION SHERWOOD FORESTERS
DIED NOVEMBER 15TH 1918 AGED 19

Frank Pullen of Hassop.
G.W. Hewson

Frank's father, George Edward James Pullen, was born in 1873 at Bath but came eventually to live at Chesterfield. George enlisted in the 1st Battalion Sherwood Foresters in 1890, aged 17 years and was promoted to Corporal in 1892 and Sergeant in 1895.

Whilst stationed at the Curreagh Camp, Dublin, he met his future wife, Ellen Fane, and married in Dublin in November 1896. Shortly afterwards he joined the 2nd Battalion and in December 1896, George and his wife Ellen, together with the 2nd Battalion, sailed for India and by mid-January 1897 were stationed at Bareilly, to the east of Delhi, beginning active service on the North West Frontier.

On September 22nd 1897 the Sherwoods joined the

Pullen Family group, March 1918.
STANDING: *Mary Elizabeth, Edward James (Ted), Frank.*
SEATED: *George Edward James, Florence Genevieve, Ellen Margaret, Ellen Margaret.*
G.W. Hewson

Tirah Expedition in the Punjab, to protect India's North West Frontier and saw action at the Khyber Pass. It was on this expedition that the young Winston Churchill made a name for himself with his accounts of the exploits. The Battalion returned to Bareilly in April 1898.

Their first child, Edward James Pullen (Ted), was born at Bareilly in 1897, but in November 1898 the Battalion embarked for Aden, which was reached on November 14th. Their second son, Frank, was born at Aden on 12th July 1899. A few months later the Battalion embarked once again, this time for Malta, where they stayed until January 1901.

Certain men of the 2nd Battalion, including George Pullen, embarked for Gibraltar and then onwards to South Africa, as part of the 5th Malta Mounted Infantry Company. At this stage George was promoted to Colour Sergeant and saw action in Transvaal, Orange Free State and Cape Colony during the latter states of the Boer War.

However, his family was no longer with him because they had gone their seperate ways at Gibraltar, returning home to Regimental barrack life at Normanton, Derby, where, in June 1901 the first daughter, Ellen Margaret (Eileen) was born.

The Battalion returned from South Africa in March 1902 and the family was re-united. Mary Elizabeth (Maisie), a second daughter, was born at Derby in 1903 but the family then lived for two years at Aldershot before proceeding to Ireland in November 1906 and it was there, in November 1909, that George was promoted to Regimental Sergeant Major. In Ireland a daughter, Gene (Florence Genevieve) was born in 1909.

Further service was undertaken on Salisbury Plain and Sheffield. By the outbreak of the Great War George was permanent staff instructor to the 6th (Territorial) Battalion of the Sherwood Foresters at Bakewell, having been the local 'terriers' instructor for a number of years, and would have been greatly involved in the scenes in Rutland Square, Bakewell, when the Territorials marched off to war in August 1914.

On February 18th 1915 he received promotion to Warrant Officer 2nd Class and the Battalion proceeded to France in March and thence into Belgium, where they went into the Ypres Salient and remained there until the end of July 1916.

In August 1916 they moved onto the Somme front and were engaged in battle from September. During the six weeks on the Somme the Battalion suffered a total casualty list of 805 men.

Further actions continued throughout 1917 and 1918 and in June 1918 George was promoted to Warrant Officer 1st Class whilst in France. Thankfully George Pullen survived the war, a truly remarkable feat. During 1918/1919 the Battalion marched into Germany (it was in this period that he missed the funeral of his youngest son, on November 15th 1918). On January 26th 1919 he returned to England and was eventually demobilised in February 1919.

By 1917 the family was living at the Dower House, Hassop, and remained there until 1927, with George Pullen eventually working for Colonel Francis Stephenson, who had purchased Hassop Hall in 1919 (George later went to work for the Duke of Rutland as a 'night watchman' at Haddon Hall, with the family home becoming Butts Cottage, Bakewell). Just before and during the Second World War he gave drill instruction at Lady Manners School and kept everyone on their toes. He died on January 24th 1948 and was buried at Hassop Church graveyard, where his son Frank had been buried in 1918.

Frank Pullen's elder brother, Edward (Ted), joined the Sherwood Foresters on Boy Service in 1913 as a drummer and served with 'A' Company 1st Battalion, disembarking with the BEF in France on November 4th 1914. On October 30th 1917 he was transferred to the Royal Flying Corps as an aerial gunner and promoted to Corporal in February 1918 in France. On demob in 1920 he joined the Manchester City Police.

By 1935 he had been promoted to Inspector, then to Chief Inspector, before joining the army on September 29th 1943 as a Major in the 8th Army, fighting in Italy and receiving the MBE for gallantry during the Italian campaign. At the end of his army career he was a Lieutenant Colonel and was seconded to the Overseas Police Corps (Allied Military Government Police Force) in Vienna. He held a senior position with the transitional government in Austria after the war.

Returning to England he had an important governmental job, dealing with political security at the Westcott Rocket Propulsion Establishment.

Frank, the youngest son of George Pullen, was a weighing office clerk at Hassop Station when he joined 'B' Company 1st Battalion Sherwood Foresters on December 6th 1917 as a drummer. It seems strange that he ever managed to join the army since we know from medical records that from the age of sixteen he suffered from glandular tuberculosis. However, with a proud military background and both his father and brother serving their country, it may have been that his father's influence within the Sherwoods might have prevailed over the doctor's notes.

On April 30th 1918 Frank was hospitalised but returned to duty and his Battalion in France on May 10th 1918. After suffering severe losses in the battles of March and April 1918, the Battalion had been sent to a 'quiet' sector on the front in the Champagne area of France in May to recuperate and reorganise. It was to be here, however, that the next German offensive was to be launched on May 27th. During the opening day of the offensive Frank was wounded whilst engaged in the retiring fight from Ventelay to Montagne de Guyencourt.

Not only was Frank wounded and suffering from glandular tuberculosis, but for several months he had been suffering from pulmonery tuberculosis. Returning to England he spent the last two months of his life at Derbyshire Sanatorium, Walton, Chesterfield, where he died from influenza (Spanish flu) on November 15th 1918, aged 19. His funeral took place with full military honours at the Hassop Roman Catholic Cemetery, although his father could not attend because of Battalion duties in France. Frank Pullen's name is also commemorated on the roll of honour in Great Longstone Church and on the war shrine on the churchyard lych gate.

PRIVATE WILLIAM H. HOWARD NO. 26517 1ˢᵗ BATTALION AND 16ᵀᴴ BATTALION SHERWOOD FORESTERS DIED FEBRUARY 18ᵀᴴ 1919 AGED 30

William H. Howard was living at Calton Lees, Edensor, in 1901, with his parents, Edward and Margaret and three other siblings. His father was a stone mason on the Chatsworth Estate. A Bakewell-born man, he had married Margaret, a Sheffield girl, and all four children from the marriage were born at Bakewell.

The 16ᵗʰ Battalion, the Chatsworth Rifles, had been decimated by the Ludendorff offensive of March 21ˢᵗ 1918. By March 30ᵗʰ only two companies had survived, and together with stragglers, formed a composite Battalion, used to fill a gap in the line in the north, in Belgium, where the second German thrust came. Many more casualties resulted when they fought at the Battle of Wytschaete Ridge.

Afterwards, the remnants of the 16ᵗʰ Battalion, including William Howard, spent the rest of the war training the newly-arrived Americans for active service conditions. More men left in drafts to fill in the other units and so the numbers became even lower. It now consisted of just a cadre, used as a training staff.

They remained in France, at Le Havre, on the coast, and then at Rouen, until April 1919. Freshly arrived units were passed on for duty in Germany, in the newly occupied region of the Rhine. It was here, in February 1919 that William caught influenza, one of many to be caught up in the flu pandemic sweeping the world. He succumbed to the virus and died on February 18ᵗʰ 1919, aged 30. William Howard was buried in St. Peter's Churchyard, Edensor.

CORPORAL ARTHUR MORTON NO. M2/113489 MOTOR TRANSPORT ROYAL ARMY SERVICE CORPS ATTACHED TO 38ᵀᴴ SIEGE BATTERY DIED MARCH 8ᵀᴴ 1919 AGED 30

Arthur Morton was born on May 17ᵗʰ 1888 at 4 Victoria Terrace, Great Longstone, the sixth of nine children of Jonathan Morton, a stone mason, and Rose Morton. Arthur was the brother of Fred Morton, who we have already seen was killed in action at Passchendaele on October 4ᵗʰ 1917.

Arthur left Great Longstone School in November 1900 and became a labourer. On December 31st 1910 he married Maud Mary Turner from Wardlow, in Great Longstone Church. Three children were born (Arthur 1912, but sadly drowned in Monsal Dale 1925; George born 1915 and Elsie in 1917).

Arthur joined up in 1917 and served in the Motor Transport section of the Army Service Corps, seeing service in France during the last months of the war, in 1918. The fighting was intense, even in the days just prior to the Armistice of November 11ᵗʰ. Arthur, whose Motor Transport was assisting a Siege Battery of the Royal Horse Artillery in its actions, was wounded during the capture of Lille in October 1918, and entered one of the town's hospitals.

It is almost certain that Arthur Morton was afflicted by the Spanish flu pandemic sweeping the world during 1918 and 1919. On March 8th he died and was buried in grave I. B. 45. St. Andre Communal Cemetery, on the northern outskirts of Lille.

The news of Arthur's death brought great sadness to Jonathan and Rose in Great Longstone. After the death of their son Fred in 1917, they might have thought they would be spared further loss with the ending of the war. It was not to be and Rose suffered further grief when, on July 5th 1919, her husband Jonathan died, aged 64 years. Although a stone mason throughout his life, he had spent the last year or so as a roadman, working for the Rural District Council.

PRIVATE THOMAS HICKS No. 307084
5TH BATTALION SHERWOOD FORESTERS
DIED MARCH 27TH 1919 AGED 37

Thomas was the youngest son of Philip Charles Hicks (known as Charles) and Jane Hicks and in 1901 the family was living on Matlock Street, Bakewell, where Charles was a cab proprietor. His two eldest sons, Philip and James, were also cab proprietors with their father, whilst 19 year old Thomas was a groom, employed by his father.

However, by 1901, Thomas's mother, Jane, was dead and by the end of the war, his father, Charles, had also died. Thomas had served in the army from near the start of the war, from which he was invalided in early 1918, owing to an injury received during active service.

Since that time he had been in the employ of Mr. E. Wood, proprietor of the Rutland Arms Hotel, as his chauffeur, and was living on Bridge Street, but on March 27th 1919 he too died of pneumonia. He received a full military funeral, was buried in the cemetery and his name is also found on the Bakewell War Memorial.

PIONEER E. H. SMITH No. 192243 ROYAL ENGINEERS
DIED MAY 14TH 1919

It has been impossible to find any details , with certainty of accuracy, about Pioneer Smith. His headstone is to be found in Bakewell Cemetery, but his name is on neither the war memorial or the roll of honour. We are pleased to include Pioneer Smith in our account of Bakewell.

PRIVATE THOMAS EDWARD TURNER No.202586
5TH BATTALION SHERWOOD FORESTERS
DIED JUNE 4TH 1919 AGED 40

Thomas Edward Turner was born in 1878 and the family were living in New Street, Bakewell. His father had Irish connections, but his mother Emma was Bakewell born and bred. By 1881, two year old Thomas' father had died and his mother Emma, was the housekeeper for Frank Dawson, a stone mason. In 1901, however, 58 year old widow Emma Turner is at 15 Catcliffe Cottages, working as a laundress from home, together with her daughter Harriet, aged 25. Thomas, aged 22, was earning a living as a stone mason, brother Robert was a book binder, whilst sister Lily was a general servant.

Thomas Edward Turner married Elizabeth Ann Turner (no relation), who had come from Ashton-under-Lyme to visit her relatives, Mr. and Mrs. Agguter, of Catcliffe Cottages. She met Thomas and they married and by the time of his death in 1919, they had six children, Jim, Tom, Elizabeth, Frances, Agnes and Edith.

Thomas enlisted at Bakewell and joined the 5th Battalion Sherwood Foresters. Sadly he was badly gassed and returned home, but never recovered and died on June 4th 1919, aged 40 years, just before the Peace Celebrations were held across England. He was buried in Bakewell Cemetery.

His wife, Elizabeth Ann, was left with six young children to raise by herself and had to take in other people's washing to support them.

AIR MECHANIC 2ND CLASS TYRRELL FREDERICK WEBB
No. 6649 ROYAL AIR FORCE
DIED JULY 8TH 1919 AGED 35

Little information has been found on the life of Tyrrell Webb before the Great War or his wartime service in the RAF. It is known that he was the son of E.T. and F. Webb and husband of R. G. Webb of Hillmorton, on the side of the A6 running through Ashford parish. He was admitted to hospital in 1919 and died in the Buxton registration district, his body being buried in Derby (Nottingham Road) Cemetery. Tyrrell Frederick Webb's name is commemorated on the Ashford War Memorial.

CORPORAL FRANK HOLDER No. 75149
DERBYSHIRE IMPERIAL YEOMANRY DIED MAY 17TH 1920 AGED 31

The death of Frank Holder of Monyash Road, Bakewell, took place at Derby Royal Infirmary, Derby, on Monday May 17th 1920.

In 1891, two year old Frank was living on Monyash Road, Bakewell, with his father William (born at Crofton, near Wakefield), a butler at one of the large houses in Bakewell, and mother Ann Holder, born at Stanton-in-the-Peak. Frank was the youngest of seven children. By 1901, however, his father had died and by the time of Frank's death in 1920, his mother was also dead.

Frank had been ill for some weeks and was taken to the Infirmary only a few hours before his death. He had mobilised with the Derbyshire Imperial Yeomanry at the outbreak of war and served with them in Gallipoli, Egypt and with the Salonika forces, and like so many other soldiers who served in Salonika, had suffered from severe bouts of malaria.

Frank's illness and death would not have occurred if he had not served in the forces during the First World War. It seems a shame to the writer that Frank Holder, and indeed three other servicemen mentioned, are not to be found on Bakewell's war memorial or roll of honour.

Finally, it is worth noting that although on the Wardlow War Memorial tablet inside the village church, the names of Benjamin Gregory and William Haslam are commemorated, and, as we have already seen, the names are also on the roll of honour in Great Longstone Church, there are other servicemen with Wardlow connections who lost their lives during the Great War. The names of five other men are included on a roll of honour in Wardlow Church, commemorating those who passed through the village school next door. It seems right that I should supply details of these men as we close the chapter on the First World War and those who made the supreme sacrifice.

Headstone of Corporal F. Holder in Bakewell Cemetery.

Keith Taylor

PRIVATE EDWARD BIBBY NO. 242448
6TH BATTALION SHERWOOD FORESTERS
DIED OF WOUNDS MARCH 11TH 1917 AGED 23

In 1901, Edward was living with his parents, William and Mary Ann Bibby, at Wormhill, where William was a shepherd on a stud farm. His father came from Lancaster and mother from Kendal, and most of the children were born at Lancaster. By 1914 he was living in the Litton area, near Tideswell. For several years Edward was in the employ of Messrs. Cooper Brothers of Wardlow (farmers), whilst by 1914 his parents resided at Elton, where his father was a farm bailiff for Mr. Prince.

In 1914, Edward joined the Tideswell branch of the Derbyshire Yeomanry and with the Company went through the Gallipoli campaign. He was afterwards invalided home suffering from enteric fever (typhoid). Edward was transferred to the 6th Battalion Sherwood Foresters after recovery, but broke his thigh whilst playing football at Derby on Easter Monday 1916. Later he went to Ireland with the Battalion and in late December 1916 was sent to France.

By the 26th February 1917 the Battalion had marched to Simoncourt, a village to the south west of Arras, then marched to Achicourt. The Germans were in the process of retiring to their freshly prepared defensive positions called the Hindenburg Line and the Battalion noticed them retiring from the nearby village of Gommecourt.

The 6th Battalion marched to take over the old German line at Gommecourt and from there, on March 6th, they attacked Kite Copse and the Burg, the former being captured and held; the Burg was however found to be very strongly occupied and the position had to be evacuated. During these operations eight men had been killed, two were missing and forty three men were wounded.

One of the wounded was Edward Bibby who was taken to the 1st South Midlands Casualty Clearing Station at Warlincourt Halte British Cemetery, Saulty, between Arras and Doullens. It was here that Edward died and was buried in grave VI. C. 14.

PRIVATE JOHN HENRY BIRLEY NO. 56088
13TH BATTALION ROYAL WELSH REGIMENT
DIED AUGUST 1ST 1917 AGED 31

John Henry's father, James Birley, was a Wardlow man who became a coachman and groom. He married Grace, a Sheffield girl, and he brought up his family at Upper Hallam, Sheffield, although John Henry was born at Wardlow. The Birley's were a very old local family, associated with Wardlow, Ashford and Bradwell.

At Sheffield, John Henry was apprenticed with Samuel Hancock, monumental mason. Eventually he settled in Bamford as a monumental mason in the village and married a local girl, Olivia Froggett, residing at 4 Fair View, where they raised a family.

He enlisted at Buxton, joining the Leicestershire Regiment, before transferring to the Royal Welsh Fusiliers. In July, the Battalion was stationed at Ypres, and took part at Passchendaele. A soldier wrote to Olivia Birley, "Whilst in action I picked up a wallet

John Henry Birley of Bamford, with connections to Wardlow.

containing the enclosed photographs. I didn't know who it belonged to, as no one was near it, and it was soaking wet with rain and mud. I saw the address on one of the cards, so I thought it my duty to send them on, as they may belong to someone dear to you." The next day, Olivia received the following letter, "Dear Madam, I very deeply regret to inform you of the death in action of your husband, He went into action with the Battalion on July 31st and took part in the great victory of the Welsh over the Germans. On the following day he was struck on the head by a piece of shell and was killed. He was a fine soldier and I know from his letters home, which I always censored, that he was a devoted husband and father."

John Henry's body was lost in the mud of Passchendaele and he is commemorated on Panel 22 Menin Gate.

Private Samuel Redfearn No. 57299
9th Battalion Sherwood Foresters
died March 10th 1918 aged 39

Samuel was the only son of Samuel Redfearn senior and Grace Redfearn, both Foolow born and bred. His father was a farmer at Brosterfield, Foolow and all his life he assisted his father on the farm, except for a short period before enlisting in July 1916, when he was employed in work on the roads by the County Council. By this time he had a wife, Mary Alice, and five children under 12 years of age, living at Town Head, Eyam. Samuel joined the 9th Battalion Sherwood Foresters and was killed in action in France on March 10th 1918. He was buried in grave III.B.46 Philosophe British Cemetery, Mazingarbe, between Bethune and Lens.

Corporal William Lomas No. 240841
2nd/6th Battalion Sherwood Foresters
died March 21st 1918 aged 26

William was born at Newmills, the fourth of five children of George Lomas, a bleachworks labourer, and Hannah Lomas, both of Newmills. William enlisted at Newmills, and was with the Sherwood Foresters when they were over-whelmed by superior numbers in the Ludendorff offensive on March 21st 1918. His body was not recovered and his name is commemorated on Bay 7 Arras Memorial.

For the fifth person on the Wardlow Roll of Honour, Samuel Allsop, Sherwood Foresters, I am sorry to say that no information on his background or service record has been forthcoming.

There has probably never been a more prolonged and appalling experience for ordinary soldiers in all the history of the British Army than the four years of trench warfare, 1914-1918. And now, after living through such nightmarish conditions, the survivors looked forward to returning home.

Though victory had been achieved, the cost was enormous in both manpower and material, with 900,000 Empire troops killed and a further two million wounded. Those who survived came back to a 'land fit for heroes'and were promised that the Great War had been 'the war to end all wars'. The sentiment seemed appropriate at the time but history would make a mockery of them

As a silence fell over the battlefields, Bakewell and the surrounding villages of Ashford, Great and Little Longstone, Hassop, Over Haddon, Rowland, Sheldon and Wardlow counted the loss of so many local men (120 in total). Those who arrived safely back gave thanks that they had survived the horrors of war. However, with-in the space of nineteen years, they would once again find themselves confronting the prospects of conflict against Germany and the possibility of world-wide conflagration.

During early 1919 there were signs in Bakewell of a sense of normality returning. The wartime Red Cross Hospital at Newholme Infirmary closed in April 1919, over 1,100 patients having passed through it and the last of the Belgian refugees left Bakewell in March of that year. London House on Matlock Street, which had been occupied, was taken over by the local branch of the Red Cross.

Maria Gyte of Sheldon reported in her diary that the younger members of the Gyte and Brocklehurst families attended a Victory Ball at Bakewell Town Hall on Tuesday March 4th 1919 and did not get back until 4am the following day. The music was provided by Messrs. Barnes' Orchestra (Matlock) and Mrs. Philcox of Bakewell on pianoforte.

On an even brighter note, a national holiday was held on July 19th 1919 when Peace Celebrations were held in towns and villages throughout the land. However, some villages appear to have chosen their own time to celebrate. 'Welcome Home' celebrations for the servicemen had already been held before the date of the Peace Celebrations. The *High Peak News* records the events in Ashford on Saturday June 21st 1919, when the Ashford servicemen were 'Welcomed Home'. The paper reads:

"It was not without a thrill of pride that Ashford heard Captain Joe Sheldon DSO, MC and bar, 2nd Battalion Sherwood Foresters, 'fall in ' some forty local men on the Bakewell Road just outside the Ashford boundary. Only some half-dozen of the men were in khaki, but there was an alertness and soldierly bearing about these sons of Ashford which no one could help noticing. Much as these men had grumbled at parades in the past, there was no murmur of disapproval at this one, and everything was overshadowed by the feeling of thankfulness that they had been spared to take part in it. They all hoped it would be their last, for the average Englishman, while a good fighter, as has been proved, is not a born soldier, and, while quick at adapting himself to varied conditions of life, he is much more comfortable in his suit of 'civvies' than otherwise.

"Captain Sheldon, an Ashford boy who joined the Regulars some years ago, has won his way through the ranks by sheer Derbyshire 'grit'.

"Ashford has not forgotten her boys, and the right royal welcome home they gave them will be long remembered. Punctually at 3pm the men fell in and marched through the village and back again. Streamers had been hung across the road and flags were flying from the windows of many houses. The streamers declared 'Welcome Home' and 'Good Luck to our Boys'. The procession was headed by the Union Jack, carried by Mr. G. W. Oldfield, the boys holding the corners being Masters Eric Boden and Francis Wilson. Following were the Chairman of the Parish Council (George Boden), G. G. Thorpe and T. W. Wilson. Then came the Youlgreave Brass Band, four VAD nurses (Mrs. Poe, Miss Lees, Mrs. Kenworthy and Miss E. Flewitt), and then the men under Captain Sheldon, with the Ashford Boy Scouts (troop leader E. Marsden) and Girl Guides (Miss Pitchford) marching on each side as a guard of honour. The Scout Master, Mr. Ernest Stubbs, the schoolmaster's son, was in the ranks with the other returned soldiers.

"Standing just outside the churchyard, a touch of pathos was added to the scene by the placing of a wreath on the grave of Private Jasper Johnson who died in England from wounds received on active service.

"Proceeding to the Hall Orchard, a thanksgiving service was held and public presentation of medals made. A platform had been erected in the field, and on this were the Rev. H. E. Sherlock (vicar), Rev. J. Newbould (Wesleyan Minister), Mr. F. Lees (Ashford Hall), Mr. C. H. Britton (Great Longstone) and Col. H. Brooke-Taylor (Bakewell). The Ashford schoolmaster, Mr. Stubbs, who had lost his son during the war, was at the organ. The roll of honour was read out by Mr. T. W. Wilson, with many wet eyes among the large company.

Afterwards the Colonel went around the ranks and spoke to each man individually, before tea in the schoolroom followed. The band played in the village during the evening and also for dancing which took place in the Hall Orchard, and afterwards in the Schoolroom."

Three weeks after Ashford's 'Welcome Home', Bakewell and the surrounding villages each participated in their 'Peace Celebrations'; on Saturday July 19th.

At Ashford, a tea, a tent and sports had been organised by the committee and it was fitting that the tea should take place on a spot where, within the recollections of one inhabitant, there had been feastings on at least six different occasions of national rejoicing previously – at the end of the Crimean War, King Edward's Wedding Day, the Jubilee, the Diamond Jubilee, King Edward's Coronation and King George's Coronation. One of Ashford's oldest inhabitants, Mr. Charles Downs, could well remember the Scots Greys as they went through the village on their way to the Crimean War in 1853.

At this spot, near the bridge end, a tent 70 feet by 15 feet had been erected, where the whole village could be fed. The street was decorated. Celebrations started in the afternoon with the sports in Rowside Field, in front of The Rookery (kindly lent by Samuel Furness). The paymaster for the running competitions was E. Gregory, who presented each prize-winner with a souvenir he had brought from Germany.

Tea for all was served in the tent. The children were also provided with another meal during the evening. There was an open-air impromptu concert in the evening, with Mrs. Fairholme of Churchdale Hall being at the piano. Half a dozen lads were dressed as pierrots, and calling themselves a 'jazz band', also added to the amusement, and dancing took place during the intervals.

At 8-30pm, on account of threatening rain, an adjournment was made to the schoolroom, where dancing continued to midnight, the music being provided by Mrs. Mullins and Mr. Upton. About 10pm there was a splendid display of fireworks, which had been given for the occasion by Mrs. Fairholme.

Longstone and district also welcomed home the servicemen. In delightful weather they were entertained to dinner at the Headstones Hotel, Monsal Head at 5-30pm and the proceedings, including two concerts in the hotel and open-air music and dancing was continued with much zest until midnight.

A large number of returned servicemen, with their wives and friends, assembled at the old cross in Great Longstone and, headed by Youlgreave Brass Band, marched

The returned soldiers of Great and Little Longstone, Monsal Dale, 1919.
STANDING LEFT TO RIGHT: *Jack Bridge, Fred Nuttall, Harry Jupp, X, X, Harry Hurst, X, Mr. Barnes,*
John Thornhill, X, X, George Bennett.

Seated: X, X, X,
  X, Charlie Ward?
    ? Beresford, X, Sam Furniss, Tom Smith, Martin Oliver, X, X, Joe Hambleton,
Jack Berresford, Charles Brihgtmore, Ernest Holmes, Jack Turner.

Longstone Local History Group

in procession to the Headstones. It was marshalled by Colonel Herbert Brooke-Taylor, assisted by Regimental Sergeant Major E. Pullen of Hassop. The route was lined by cheering villagers.

Just over a hundred had dinner, served by Mr. J. Barritt, the licensee. At the hotel the words 'Peace – we owe it to our brave boys; God bless them all', was placed in a conspicuous position. Another inscription was 'Let us never forget the memory of our fallen heroes who gave their all for our Peace and Victory', displayed near the entrance to the hotel, overlooking the Dale. On each side of the inscription was placed a large laurel wreath in memory of the fallen.

After dinner there was dancing for an hour on the spacious green near the hotel, the programme being supplied by the Youlgreave band. Reassembling in the hotel, an excellent concert was given by several Manchester artistes. Later in the evening, the soldiers and sailors held a concert at which the programme was taken part in by Messrs. Harry Hurst, C. Brightmore, J. Morton and J. Solder. Towards 11pm a splendid display of fireworks was given in a field near the hotel by a Manchester firm!

Peace Day celebrations at Sheldon on July 19th were very low key, for their celebrations were to be held on July 24th. Maria Gyte, at the Devonshire Arms in Sheldon, who had lost her son Tony in the war, records in her diary on July 19th, "A few flags out at Sheldon and a garland made by Bertha Brocklehurst." She wonders how people could think of the sorrowing hearts of those who had lost their loved ones being expected to look on or join in any festivities. Miss Grover, from Ashford, was providing an excellent ham tea etc. for everyone next Thursday July 14th, grown ups and children as well, the food supplied by Mr. Marsden, proprietor of the Ashford Hotel.

On the day of the celebrations she reports that in dull weather, the men were busy fixing up a flag on the church and making other arrangements. A cricket match between the ladies and gentlemen was to be the first on the list of sports. The children were to be given commemorative mugs, provided by Miss Grover and a motor arrived with them about dinner time. A very impressive service was held in the church by James Stephenson, the lay reader. The people and children of Sheldon walked in procession behind the returned soldiers, and at the front G. Ward carried a laurel wreath which had been made by Mr. Stephenson (gardener at Churchdale Hall) and deposited on the altar. The service was in remembrance of the fallen lads. Sports were held during the evening, after a tea had been taken in the schoolroom.

Peace Day festivities at Rowland were held in a field kindly lent by Mr. J. T. Trickett and commenced early in the afternoon with sports. Tea was prepared in a marquee which had been tastefully decorated and 65 villages and friends sat down to the meal.

Sports were resumed after tea and the remainder of the evening was spent in music and dancing. At a few minutes to twelve a volley was fired and rockets let off, and although the rain poured down, the people of the village turned out and saw the bonfires and flares on the hills around.

At Wardlow the schoolchildren paraded the village and sang suitable songs. After an excellent meat tea, sports were held and prizes distributed. After the sports the children were served with cake and milk and the day was finished by all proceeding to the top of Wardlow Hey Cop to watch the display of fireworks and to see the bonfire lit by the oldest inhabitant, Mr. John Allsop. Another tea was given on Monday to about a hundred people and the evening was passed in games and other amusements.

On Thursday 21st August 1919 there was a splendid 'Welcome Home' celebration for Bakewell Servicemen. The Square was a blaze of colour due to flags and bunting, whilst Haddon Estate provided large fir trees to be placed around the Square. At night time many houses were brilliantly illuminated by fairy lamps. Near the lamp in the centre of the Square (later to be the site of the war memorial) was a huge Union Jack flying from a flag pole 50 feet high and near this a platform had been erected for the band, this being draped with red, white and blue.

On the Bath Garden causeway a cenotaph, over 14 feet high, and taking the form of a cross, was erected. Half covering it was a Union Jack and surmounting it was a laurel wreath, with the words 'To our glorious dead'.

At 10am, the ex-servicemen assembled in Coombs Road, with Colonel Brooke-Taylor in charge of the parade, which numbered about 250 men. The first three

'Welcome Home' celebrations for Bakewell servicemen on Thursday August 21ˢᵗ 1919.
The message on the banner hanging from the Rutland Arms reads, "Let us never forget the
memory of our fallen heroes who gave their all for Peace and Victory". One can see part of the
50 foot flag pole erected next to the lamp standard in the square. The large fir trees were
provided by the Haddon Estate. Included on the platform are the Bishop of Derby (Reverend
Abrahams), the vicar of Bakewell Reverend E. Spink and Mr. A. Buxton, Chairman of the
Urban District Council.

R. Richmond

platoons consisted of men in uniform, followed by three platoons wearing 'mufti'.
On Bakewell Bridge they were met by the Chesterfield Old Comrades Band and
they continued in their march throughout the town, with Brigadier-General
Goodman of the Sherwood Foresters taking the salute at the end of Rutland Terrace.
The streets were thronged and, at the salute, there was a hearty cheer.

The company formed up in close column of platoons facing the Rutland Arms
Hotel. On the platform were Mr. A. Buxton, Chairman of the Urban District Council
Brigadier-General Goodman, Colonel H. Brooke-Taylor, the Bishop of Derby
(Reverend Abraham), Reverend E. Spink (Rural Dean and vicar of Bakewell) and
Methodist ministers. The choir of the Parish Church was also present and a speech
was given by the Bishop of Derby (who had lost a son during the war). Colonel
Brooke-Taylor then read the names of the seventy fallen men. Following the reading
of the names the bugle sounded 'The Last Post' and 'Reveille'. The National Anthem
was sung and the parade was dismissed.

725 guests were afterwards entertained to dinner at the various hotels and eating
places in the town. 'No speech making' was the order of the day and the only toast
given was 'The King'.

In the afternoon, a military sports programme was gone through on the

Recreation Ground, the crowd numbering between three and four thousand. The ex-servicemen had themselves arranged the programme which consisted of tug-of-war, slow bicycle race, mixed wheelbarrow race, bun-eating competition, pillow fight over the water, chariot race, football contest and boat race.

During the evening a large gathering in the Square danced to the strains of the band. Brilliant flares at four different points outside the town brought the official proceedings to a close.

At Bakewell the Peace Day Celebrations commenced with the ringing of a merry peal on the church bells. At 10-15am the children assembled at their various Sunday Schools, and from there they proceeded to Portland Square, where a procession paraded to a service for children at the Parish Church. Before moving off, the children all sang the National Anthem. Leading the procession were Mr. V. R. Cockerton (churchwarden) and Colonel Brooke-Taylor (Chairman of the Peace Celebrations Committee) and following were the choirboys, the Reverend E. Spink and F. Sloman and the bugle band of the Church Lads' Brigade (under Mr. S. Allcock).

In the afternoon an evening of sports took place on the Recreation Ground, with a fancy dress parade during the interval. There was also a Punch and Judy show on the ground and later in the evening six flares were set off at various parts of the town. It is interesting to note that a temporary war memorial had been erected on the railings of Bath Gardens, with flags and a wreath dedicated to the men of the Derbyshire Imperial Yeomanry.

Apart from the official celebrations, the township had their own celebrations around the area in which they lived. The streets were gaily decorated and in the

The temporary war memorial created on the Bath Garden railings, Bakewell, on July 19th 1919. The wreath and ribbons are commemorating members of the Derbyshire Inperial Yeomanry who died in the war. A permanent war memorial for Bakewell would be unveiled in August 1920.

Old House Museum, Bakewell

festivities New Street took one of the leading parts. A garland across the one end bore the inscription 'Unto us peace is given' with a laurel wreath on each side, while at the other end a huge Union Jack covered practically the width of the street and across it were the words, 'Our motto is 'All Unite together'.' Tea was partaken of at the Castle Hotel, by permission of Mr. Marriott, followed by dancing at the hotel and in the street. The celebrations were continued on Monday, when, with the morning over, a tea was provided for a number of school children and old people and dancing again took place.

Matlock Street decorations were tasteful and effective, those at the Royal Oak Hotel, on which appropriate inscriptions together with wreath and anchor, were suspended. About 170 were provided with a tea which had been laid out in Thacker's Avenue on tables.

About 90 sat down to a meal at the Oddfellows Hall, whilst the residents of Monyash Road and neighbourhood, to the number of about fifty, met in Mr. Thacker's field and enjoyed a meat tea in the open.

North Church Street and the immediate district assembled at the Devonshire Arms, where Mrs. Wilson provided a meat tea to which forty sat down. A social and dance took place in the large club room afterwards, Mrs. Phillips and Mrs. Poole, two of Bakewell's oldest residents, leading off the dance.

Forty sat down to tea in Mr. Charles Wilkinson's premises in Water Street whilst the tea for 75 residents in the Catcliffe district took place on the lawn at West Bank. After tea, cigars and cigarettes were handed round to the men.

Buxton Road residents had a tea in the yard of Mr. Bailey's Mill, about sixty being present. The green stuff for the decorations was sent by Mr. G. Twyford, of Haddon, and over the entrance to the yard was the inscription 'Thanks be to God, who giveth us the Victory'. Mr. Frank Lomas lent some vases made from shell cases for the table decorations. After tea, cigars and cigarettes were provided for the men, and chocolate and sweets for the children. A musical evening was afterwards spent, Frank Lomas playing the organ and Mr. Harrison lending his gramophone.

Needham's Garage in Back Mill Street presented a party spectacle, and here over a hundred sat down to tea, including Mrs. Spink, the vicar's wife. They decorated the tables and provided each person with a buttonhole of red, white and blue flowers, and also allowed them to roam round the gardens at Milford House afterwards. At the tea table a collection amounting to £1 13s 2d was made for the fund for Bakewell's monument to the fallen. Dancing took place in the evening, with the garage walls and the bridge over the mill stream illuminated by coloured electric lights.

At the Town Hall an enjoyable tea and social evening had been arranged by the Post Office Staff, about 120 guests attending.

Everything went off smoothly at Great Longstone, where the village had been tastefully decorated. The cross had been decorated by Mr. J. Thornhill, and suspended on the village green was a fine model of the airship R34, the work of the same gentleman. Appropriate references were to be seen all over the village to the

Peace Celebrations on Great Longstone village green, Saturday July 19th 1919.
STANDING LEFT TO RIGHT: *X, X, X, Harry Hurst, X, X, X, X, X, John Thornhill, X, X, X,*
Len Bennett, X, Mr. Timm (Little Longstone).
SEATED LEFT TO RIGHT: *X, X, Charlie Morton, Jack Turner, X, X, X, X, X, Joe Hambleton, X,*
W.J. Eyre, X, George Bennett, X, X, X.
Longstone Local History Group

John Thornhill with his model of the airship R34 in 1920.
It was sent by rail to London to be put on display in Gamages, the toy store.
Peter Thornhill

gallantry of the soldiers and sailors, and a streamer with 'Welcome Home' was hanging across the entrance to Church Lane.

The ringing of the church bells in the morning commenced the day's festivities. A service was held in the church at mid-day, a procession having been formed at the cross, headed by the returned soldiers (including three from Little Longstone) in charge of Lieutenant W. J. Eyre, Royal Engineers, and following were Red Cross nurses, the Parish Council, the Oddfellows club with their banner, the Boy Scouts and the Girl Guides (under Mrs. Boam).

The Guides carried a laurel wreath with the inscription, 'To the glorious memory of the fallen; Greater love hath no man than this, that a man laid down his life for his friend'. This was afterwards placed on the Cross, and another wreath from the returned soldiers inscribed, 'In memory of our fallen comrades' on the lych gate of the churchyard. The returned soldiers were afterwards photographed on the green, following which they were entertained to dinner at the White Lion, about forty sitting down. The toast of The King and the Returned Soldiers was given and the proceedings enlivened by songs from Messrs. Harry Hurst, Leonard Bennett and Charles Brightmore. The school children sang patriotic songs around the Cross and were also photographed there. They had been trained for the occasion by Miss Allcock.

In the afternoon, children's sports were held in Church Croft, kindly lent by Mrs. Cox, the entrance to which had been decorated by William Redfearn, who had also decorated the entrance to the White Lion.

Hassop Peace Celebrations were held in the Hassop Roman Catholic schoolroom, beautifully decorated by the young ladies of the village. The celebrations consisted of a meat tea, sports and a dance. Prior to tea, cricket and other various entertainments were indulged in. After tea, sports for the young ladies and children commenced. Afterwards a cricket match between married and single men took place.

After this, dancing until midnight followed in the schoolroom, Mr. Bennett supplying the music with his gramophone. Peace mugs were presented to all the children attending school and all others resident in the parish. The celebrations closed with the singing of 'The end of a perfect day' and, 'Auld Lang Syne', followed by 'God Save The King'. (Earlier in the year, Longstone's soldiers had been entertained by their former schoolmaster Mr. H. A. Spanton, and later they received a treat in August from the Committee of the Christmas Parcels Fund.)

It was during the years just after the war that Bakewell and district parishes raised money, mainly by contributions and parish events such as whist drives and dances, to provide some sort of memorial to honour the names of those who had died.

In January 1919 Sheldon chose to erect a marble tablet commemorating the fallen on the wall of the church. William Shimwell of Youlgreave was asked to provide the monument and the £65 it would cost was to be met by public subscriptions.

The unveiling and dedication of the war memorial took place on February 11th

1920, a very rough and showery day, with snow, rain and sleet in the air. The words of Maria Gyte, recorded in her diary sets the scene:

'Anthony (her husband) took the gig and fetched Mr. Spink, the vicar of Bakewell, who had a nice chat with me before going to church. The tablet was dedicated and unveiled. After waiting for some time for Mrs. Grover, who did not arrive at the time stated, Mr. Stephenson, lay reader, drew the Union flag aside. Just as this had been done, both Misses Grover drove up. The service was most impressive. Mr. Spink could feel for our poor lads as he had also lost his only son in the war (in Mesopotamia).'

Bakewell decided to raise money for the erection of a war memorial cross and also provide a facility that the town had always been without, a hospital, to be named the Bakewell and District War Memorial Cottage Hospital. Contributions for the latter would be raised in all the parishes throughout the Bakewell district.

The war memorial in Sheldon Church, unveiled and dedicated on February 11th 1920.

The parishes involved in contributing to its erection were Ashford, Bakewell and Over Haddon, Baslow and Bubnell, Beeley, Curbar, Calver and Froggatt, Edensor, Eyam, Longstone, Hassop and Wardlow, Monyash, Rowsley, Sheldon, Stanton and Birchover, Stoney Middleton, Youlgreave and Middleton.

All of these parishes had lost men during the Great War, besides those I am dealing with in detail within the covers of this book. As a random representative for all the other parishes who lost loved ones and which contributed to the hospital building fund, I provide a note on a Beeley inhabitant who was killed in action on the Western Front in March 1918.

LANCE CORPORAL JESSE HARRISON No. 89138
35TH BATTALION MACHINE GUN CORPS (INFANTRY)
(FORMERLY No. 377 OF THE ARMY SERVICE CORPS)
DIED ON TUESDAY MARCH 26TH 1918 AGED 32

Jesse was born on March 29th 1884 at Beeley, the son of a single woman, 28 year old Emma Rebecca Harrison, who lived with her parents and siblings at Moor Farm, Chesterfield Road, Beeley. Jesse's grandfather, Thomas Harrison, a stone mason and farm labourer, originated from Sheldon and married Emma Grafton, a Beeley girl.

Their daughter, Emma junior, was one of eleven children and when Jesse was born, Emma was working as a domestic servant (in later life she married and lived for some time at Church View, Beeley). Two of her siblings, elder brother Samuel and younger sister Charity, were sadly born deaf and dumb.

By 1901, 17 year old Jesse was still living with his family at Moor Farm and was working as a carter, a job he was involved with until he enlisted in the army during the Great War.

The Harrison family had a long history with involvement in horses and therefore it is not surprising that when Jesse enlisted at Chesterfield he joined the Army Service Corps, which was mainly employed in the transportation of supplies, equipment and

Jesse Harrison of Beeley.
Pauline Harrison

ammunition to the front line soldiers, using horse-drawn vehicles as well as motorised transport.

It was dangerous work but Jesse wished to be involved in first line fighting and was transferred to the Machine Gun Corps, supporting the infantry in defence and attack. By this stage he had risen to the rank of Lance Corporal.

In March 1918 he was stationed with his Battalion on the Somme and they found themselves overwhelmed by the superior forces of the German army in the first few days of the Ludendorff offensive, commencing on March 21st. Throughout the following days they attempted to stem the German advance, rallying then retreating, rallying again and then continuing their withdrawal until on March 26th, just three days after his 33rd birthday, Jesse Harrison was killed by shell fire. His body was never recovered and he is commemorated on Panel 90 to 93 Pozieres Memorial, 6 kilometres NE of Albert.

By January 1920 a sum approaching £10,000 had already been subscribed or promised towards the hospital (although £3,000 still had to be raised). The first sod on the Butts Road site was cut in May 1920.

During the last week of June 1920, the Jubilee lamp in Rutland Square, the site for the memorial cross, was taken down. The war memorial, it was hoped, would be unveiled and dedicated on August 6th, the day before the stone-laying ceremony of the War Memorial Cottage Hospital.

In early July 1920, a German field gun, which had been presented to 'C' Company Sherwood Foresters and had been lying at Bakewell Station for two weeks, was brought into town on Saturday evening, July 3rd, under the direction of the officer commanding the Company, Captain E. Brooke-Taylor. It had been hoped that a number of ex-servicemen would have helped to drag the trophy into the Square, but only a handful turned out (torrential rain was falling). However, a large crowd assembled. The gun was to remain in the Square for a few days.

The following week, it was reported that an unsuccessful effort was made by a few ex-soldiers to pitch the gun into the pit nearby, which had been made for the foundations of the war memorial.

Friday evening, August 6th 1920, witnessed a huge crowd in the Square, which was closed to traffic. The half-hour service was sad, impressive yet inspiring. (The memorial, 24 feet in height, consisted of 20 tons of stone, and 50 tons of concrete was used for the foundations.)

Prior to unveiling, a half-muffled peal was rung on the bells of the Parish Church. 'O God Our Help in Ages Past' was sung, accompanied by Bakewell Brass Band. After a prayer, the Chairman of the Memorial Committee, Reverend E. Spink, requested Mrs. Margaret Hoyle to unveil the memorial, the plinth of which was covered with the Union Flag. She then recited the names of the men from Bakewell who had fallen (she herself had lost two sons). The vicar then blessed and dedicated the memorial. The Congregational Minister, Reverend Radbourne, then read the lesson.

During the singing of the next hymn, nearly eighty wreaths were placed on the steps of the memorial by relatives and friends of the dead men. Colonel Herbert Brooke-Taylor then addressed the gathering (he too had lost a son in the war):

"The site on which it stood was almost an historic site in the history of this little town. It was here that they had bade farewell to the men of the Sherwoods when they marched off to their mobilisation centre. They were the advance guard of hundreds of men who went from amongst them to take their place in the fighting line. Five years later, on the same spot, they welcomed home the men who had saved them so well.

"It was a day that would be remembered to the end of their lives. That night they were dedicating that memorial to the men who would never come back. It was their bounden duty to ever remember the men who had laid down their lives, and it was only right that they should have in their midst such a memorial that their names might never die, and that for generations, when we were passed away, the children would spell those names out, and say to themselves, 'These are the men who died that England might live'.

"It would also be a memorial to the nobility of the women – of the glorious way in which the women acted during that great crisis. They had let their husbands, brothers and sons go with their blessing. Their's was a glorious part in the history of the country. He would offer to those who had lost boys in the war his most grateful sympathy, and congratulate them on the way they behaved in that awful crisis."

The sounding of 'The Last Post' and the 'Reveille' by Mr. J. H. Fletcher appropriately concluded the proceedings. (The memorial was constructed of Stancliffe Quarry stone and was erected by J. W. Wildgoose of Matlock. It was designed and inscribed by Mr. Advent Hunstone of Tideswell.)

The stone laying ceremony for the Bakewell and District War Memorial Cottage

Remembrance Day 1920 in Bakewell. The war memorial was erected on the site of the 1897 Jubilee lamp standard and was unveiled and dedicated on Friday August 6th 1920.

R. Richmond

Hospital took place off Butts Road, on Saturday afternoon, August 7th, with the Duke of Rutland participating.

A procession formed in Rutland Square and proceeded to the site, headed by Bakewell Brass Band under B. W. Duckmanton, followed by ex-servicemen, Bakewell Men's VAD with their stretchers, the Boy Scouts, Ashford Girl Guides under Miss Avena Callodine, Bakewell Girl Guides under Miss Dickson, the collectors of funds from the various parishes, the Loyal Devonshire Lodge of Oddfellows (Great Longstone), and council members.

A number of schoolchildren in charge of S. Allcock and teachers had previously been marched into the site. In the rear of the procession were 200 Freemasons, headed by brethren of the 'Dorothy Vernon Lodge' of Bakewell. Waiting at the ground was the Duke of Rutland and members of his family. The names of 263 men from the Bakewell district were inscribed on a plaque in the entrance to the Hospital.

The Wardlow memorial consisted of a tablet in the church and was dedicated in late 1919. Ashford's memorial was to be a cross on the south side of the church tower, made of Cornish granite and about 11 feet high and to be erected by Beresfords of Belper. Money had been contributed by the villagers and it would cost around £100. During early 1920, Over Haddon residents were still holding whist drives and dances to raise funds for the village war memorial, to be erected on the main street of the village. The local war memorial committee was led by Joseph Oldfield.

For some years after the war, Great Longstone had raised money for a memorial through many social events, including carnivals.

A fancy dress parade and sports, in connection with the local War Memorial Fund, were held at Great Longstone on Whit Monday. Preceded by the drum and bugle band of the Pendleton Troop of Boy Scouts, who were then in camp at Monsal Head, a procession consisting of decorated vehicles, many parishioners in costumes representing various nationalities, paraded the Longstones to Monsal Head and back. In the evening, sports were held in a field near the parish church lent by Mrs. Cox. From 8-30pm to 2am there was dancing in the Social Institute, Miss Oliver of Longstone being the pianist.

On Sunday July 22nd 1923 the Duke of Devonshire unveiled Great Longstone's War Memorial, situated on the village green, opposite the schools.

The war memorial cross commemorating the names of those who died whilst serving their country 1914-1919, in the churchyard at Ashford in the Water.
Keith Taylor

The War Memorial Institute at Ashford is opened by the Prince of Wales in 1932, accompanied by the Duke of York (later to become George VI) and the Duke of Devonshire.
J. Duncan

These cottages, thatched at the time the photograph was taken, were formerly on the site of Ashford War Memeorial Institute. The old A6 road, which used to pass through the village, runs by the side of them.

Alastair Slack

Over a thousand people were present. The Grecian column, eight feet three inches tall in Stancliffe Stone was designed and erected by J. W. Boden of Matlock, at a cost of £132.

Ex-servicemen lined up on three sides, with a special place in front reserved for relatives of the fallen. On the other sides were Longstone Girl Guides under Mrs. Armitage, Boy Scouts under C. Wyse and members of the Loyal Inkerman Lodge of Oddfellows. Six of the thirteen men to fall were members of the Lodge and the Lodge's wreath was placed on the memorial by their oldest member, James Hewitt, who himself lost a son.

The service commenced with the singing of the National Anthem, accompanied by Bakewell Brass Band. A prayer and hymns followed, with the unveiling undertaken by the Duke of Devonshire. The 'Last Post' concluded the proceedings.

The war memorial in Main Street, Over Haddon.

Keith Taylor

Unveiling and dedication of Great Longstone War Memorial on Sunday 22nd July 1923.
Ian Cox, the Longstone Local History Group and Olive Mead

Unveiling and dedication of Great Longstone War Memorial on Sunday 22ⁿᵈ July 1923.

Ian Cox, the Longstone Local History Group and Olive Mead

The war memorial plaque to the First World War dead inside the entrance porch to Little Longstone Congregational Chapel.

Keith Taylor

In Memoriam board in the entrance hall of the War Memorial Library at Lady Manners School, Bakewell.

Keith Taylor

These memorials to those who had died whilst serving their country in the armed forces were completed during the 1920's. Tragically, however, events around the world during the 1930's were conspiring to increase international tension between certain nations, especially in Europe, and the prospects of war were building up once again.

CHAPTER SEVEN

THE SECOND WORLD WAR 1939 – 1945

The everyday lives of the inhabitants of Bakewell and the surrounding villages were rudely overshadowed by the increasing prospects of war in Europe during the later stages of the 1930's. Tensions on the international diplomatic scene rose dramatically from 1936 onwards as the political climate in Europe changed and "war clouds" loomed on the horizon.

Fascist and Nazi regimes had won favour as the democratic institutions of certain European countries had been found wanting. The strains imposed by economic collapse during the years of the "Depression" and the bitterness caused by the outcome of the Versailles Peace Treaty, settled in 1920, had been too great for the young, untested democratic institutions introduced in Germany, Italy and other countries in middle and eastern Europe. These regimes (especially Hitler's in Germany and Mussolini's in Italy) were determined to push their aggressive foreign policies, in the belief that the remaining democracies were ill-prepared to defend their rights.

The Fascist forces of General Franco gained the ascendancy during the Spanish Civil War 1936-1939 and a German ultimatum led to the appointment of several Nazi German ministers in the Austrian cabinet. On March 11th 1938 German troops entered Austria and the Anschluss, or forbidden union of Austria and Germany, was established.

Tension increased in other areas of Europe, especially in Czechoslovakia, where Hitler demanded further concessions by October 1st 1938, in default of which, Germany would "march". The Czech Army mobilised on September 23rd, France on the next day.

In Britain, Territorial AA and coastal defence units, the Observer Corps and Auxiliary Air Force were called up on September 26th 1938 and the British Fleet was mobilised on the 28th. Gas masks were distributed to civilians in all parishes and provisional air-raid shelters were dug in London parks.

Prime Minister Neville Chamberlain visited Hitler at Bad-Godesberg and Berchtesgaden, without result, and on September 28th Hitler invited the British and French Premiers to meet with Mussolini at Munich next day. At this meeting, it was agreed that German occupation of the areas demanded should proceed in stages between October 1st and 10th. Chamberlain was able to return to London, claiming "Peace in our time". Appeasement had apparently "won the day".

The Munich Conference of 1938. Mussolini, Hitler, Dr. Schmidt (interpreter), Chamberlain.

During this period of tension, the Bakewell district had joined in the preparations for a possible war. In March 1938 Territorial units of the Anti-Aircraft Company were training in the drill halls and on Sunday March 13th three searchlight positions were taken up in the vicinity of Monyash and a plane was hired to travel above the area, first with lights on and then without, as the AA Company used their sound locator. During the Munich crisis large numbers of men offered their services as Air Raid Wardens and gas masks were stored in Bakewell.

Relief turned to concern, however, when in March 1939, Hitler occupied Bohemia and Moravia, in Czechoslovakia, without British or French intervention. Sensing a weakness of resolve throughout the European democracies, Hitler turned his attention to Poland during the summer months. War clouds gathered ever larger as Chamberlain spelt out clearly in Parliament British condemnation of Hitler's latest aggression and made it clear that an attack on Poland would not be tolerated. On April 26th, Britain reintroduced conscription and the first of the young men from Bakewell, Over Haddon, Ashford, Rowland, Hassop, Sheldon, and the Longstones were "called up".

The weakness displayed by Britain and France in Munich was Hitler's most powerful incentive to plan the attack on Poland for September 1st 1939. He believed that Poland, too, could be defeated in isolation, especially when on August 23rd, Germany and Soviet Russia signed a Non-Aggression Pact. Hitler's way to Poland seemed open, but on August 25th the signing of the Anglo-Polish Alliance was announced in London and Hitler realised that his attempt to isolate Poland had failed.

At 11-15a.m. on Sunday September 3rd 1939, Neville Chamberlain announced to a hushed nation that Britain was at war with Germany. It was the beginning of the greatest conflict the world has yet seen.

The biggest contrast between the Great War and the Second World War was the unprecedented fear in 1939 of devastating air attacks and that there would be immediate danger and horrors in store. The Government therefore began to plan for the evacuation of women and children from the industrial areas into the more rural districts.

THE EVACUEES

As the might of Germany's armed forces swept across the Polish frontier on Friday September 1st, and Britain still remained at peace, the reality of the situation was brought home to the people of Bakewell and district with the arrival of special trains at Bakewell and Hassop Stations, bringing evacuee school children from the industrial cities to be billeted in the Bakewell area.

The organisation of the civilian defence forces in the Bakewell district had reached a high state of efficiency and for over a week, hundreds of people had been helping. Splendid assistance had been given at Bakewell by the local troop of Boy Scouts, who had been attached to many activities as messengers.

Bakewell itself had been warned to expect children and adults to the total number of 600, but the number which eventually arrived was short of this figure. On Friday morning a special train arrived at 11-10 a.m. and this brought over 300 from the Manchester and Salford areas, the party including a number of teachers and helpers.

They were received at the station by the Chairman of the Bakewell Urban District Council, A.R. Brand, J.P., and the Reception Officer, Arthur Aves. Numerous voluntary helpers assisted in preparing rations for the evacuees and 25 minutes after the arrival of the train, all the adults and children had been supplied, and they were on their way to the Church of England School, where C.R. Allcock, the Chief Billeting Officer and his assistants, who included a goodly number of school teachers, commenced the arduous task of billeting the children.

On the first day (Friday) 265 children and 45 adults arrived, against the 400 they had expected. On the second day (Saturday) they expected 200 mothers and young children, but the number which arrived was 30 mothers and 47 children.

Requests were made for people who could lend mattresses, camp beds or single bedsteads, whilst it was stated that the organisers would be pleased to hear from householders who were willing to give facilities for baths to those children billeted in houses where no baths existed.

The Chief Billeting Officer for the Bakewell Rural District Council was B.G. Cadge, assisted by reception officers at Millers Dale, Hassop and Rowsley Stations. On Friday September 1st, 545 evacuees arrived at Millers Dale and on Saturday a further 205 (Tideswell received 313 of these, Taddington 17, Litton 75, Great

Continued on page 326 ☛

Penrhos College pupils learning to skate on the Long Lake, Chatsworth, during the evacuation to Chatsworth House from Colwyn Bay, between September 26th 1939 and March 21st 1946. The pupils wore olive green uniforms.
Derbyshire County Council, Local Studies

The Painted Hall, Chatsworth House, during the war years. It was here that the Penrhos College pupils assembled for morning and evening prayers and church services during their stay as evacuees, when their school at Colwyn Bay was requisitioned by the Army. The school's senior girls' choir sat on the stairs, on the cushions shown in the photograph.
Derbyshire County Council, Local Studies

Penrhos College pupils dined in the Servants's Hall, Chatsworth House, during the war years.
Derbyshire County Council, Local Studies

Wartime for the Devonshire family at Edensor House 1943-1944.
BACK ROW: *Lady Anne Hunloke, Lady Anne Cavendish, Lady Elizabeth Cavendish,*
The Duchess of Devonshire.
FRONT ROW: *Nicholas Hunloke, Lady Andrew Cavendish with daughter Lady Emma Cavendish.*
DOGS: *Benjy, Studley and Bootle.*
The Dowager Duchess of Devonshire

WOMEN'S LAND ARMY

*The Duchess of Devonshire
encouraging recruitment of
women into the Land Army,
at Bakewell Show, August
1939, just days before the start
of the Second World War.*

*The Marquis (Andrew Cavendish) and Marchioness of Hartington with their children, Peregrine
and Sophie Cavendish, at The Rookery, Ashford, 1945. Andrew succeeded to the title of the 11th
Duke of Devonshire on the death of his brother, and Peregrine is the current Duke.*

Jean Blackwell and The Dowager Duchess of Devonshire

Fred Turner leads the horse and cart carrying the Mitchell children (evacuees) into the yard of Gregory Farm, March 28th 1940. Mrs. Davis' shop is on the left side of the road.

Stanley and David Fearn

Sylvia Mitchell, evacuee from Manchester, drives the shorthorn cattle down Wardlow main road in 1942, towards Gregory Farm. Wardlow School and Church stand in the background.

Stanley and David Fearn

March 28ᵗʰ 1940. The Mitchell children were evauees from a Manchester school. The two lads were billeted with George and Ethel Davis, who kept 'The Shop' (today called Galena Cottage) at Wardlow, next door to Gregory Farm. Their sister was billeted with Mr. and Mrs. Fred Turner at Gregory Farm.
LEFT TO RIGHT: *Neil Mitchell, Sylvia Mitchell, Geoffrey Mitchell.*
The sign reads: 'You get 5/- dividend when you fill up a Brooke Bond Dividend card.'
Stanley and David Fearn

C1951. Isaac Bond, farm worker for Sam Gillott of Birley Farm, Wardlow, collecting water in barrels from the standpipe near the Bulls Head Inn, in order to water the beasts in the field.
Frank Robinson

Hucklow 10, Little Hucklow 5, Foolow 9, Wardlow 6, Bradwell 158, Flagg 12, Chelmorton 34, Eyam 83 and Ashford 28).

At Hassop Station, Train No. M203 with 105 evacuees arrived at 11a.m. on the first day and 218 arrived on the second. They were sent to Great and Little Longstone, Hassop, Rowland, Grindleford, Curbar and Calver (Billeting officers for the Longstones included brothers Robert and John Thornhill and headmaster, Percy Buggins). The remainder, for distribution in the southern part of the district, came to Rowsley Station, and amongst those places which received them were: Rowsley, 25; Beeley, 18; Winster, 106; Aldwark, 2; Baslow, 75; Grange Mill, 1; Birchover, 16; Chatsworth, 8 and Elton, 28. Others were continuing to arrive daily, including mothers and babies.

Chatsworth House was vacated by the Duke of Devonshire and his family, who moved to Churchdale Hall, near Ashford, when a girls' boarding school arrived for the duration of the war. Penrhos College, founded in 1880, was situated on the sea front at Colwyn Bay and in 1939 housed 320 female boarders, 250 of them being Senior and Middle School pupils. The 250 Senior and Middle School pupils, ranging in age from 11 years to 18 years, together with 36 members of staff and their headmistress, Miss Constance Smith, arrived at Chatsworth House on September 26th 1939 and the school would remain on site until March 21st 1946.

Lady Manners School, Bakewell, shared its buildings with a large party of boys from the North Manchester Municipal High School, with morning lessons for one, the afternoon for the other, then reversing the arrangements the next week. Most of these High School boys returned to Manchester after five months. Meanwhile, a Manchester Roman Catholic School received its education at the Brigade Hall in Bakewell.

When war broke out, the headmaster at Great Longstone School was Percy Buggins, with the juniors taught by Miss Lomas and the infants by Miss Robinson, but the number of children increased dramatically with the arrival of the Manchester evacuees, led by their teacher, Miss Urtika, who lodged with Mrs. Doddemeade on Longreave Lane. Some evacuees were billeted with Mrs. Hambleton on Sunny Bank, whilst a number of girls stayed with Mrs. Herrington. Again, a part-time system of education was devised because of the numbers, and later the barn at "The Elms" (now Church Lady House) was used for classes.

An orphanage from London was housed on the top floor of Longstone Hall, the home of Mr. and Mrs. Plowright, with the girls, in their grey and yellow uniforms, attending the local school. Air raid alarm practice was held, with children having to go home or to a friend's house when the actual alarm was sounded.

When the Army requisitioned the Ashgate Children's Home, Chesterfield, for their own use, the orphans arrived at Little Longstone for the duration of the war and beyond, being housed at the "Outrake", Little Longstone. Miss Hudson was their teacher and Mr. and Mrs. Batty the master and matron.

Birkdale, a small prep school from Sheffield, also moved to the Longstone and Ashford area. The first and second forms, aged seven to nine years, stayed at the

The Outrake, Little Longstone, home of Lieutenant William Bernard Shaw's parents. During the Second World War it became the home for the Ashgate Orphanage, from Chesterfield.

Keith Taylor

Evacuees from the Ashgate Orphanage, Chesterfield, at The Outrake, Little Longstone during the Second World War. The army had requisitioned the Chesterfield orphanage.
Cicely Gilbert stands second from the left.

Noel Green

farm at Thornbridge, whilst the ten to thirteen year olds were housed in the stables at Hassop. Others were moved to Thornbridge Hall, with some sleeping in the main hall and others accommodated in the large garage.

Little Longstone Institute (Social Club and Reading Room, demolished in 1976), a wooden building purchased for £333 in 1924, and sited between Parva and Christmas Cottages, was first of all used as a school for evacuee children, until the numbers diminished. It was then taken over for awhile by the Columbia Picture Corporation, a film company, that had escaped the dangers of the London Blitz by being housed at Cressbrook Hall. The London members of staff were billeted in Longstone, Tideswell and Ashford. The films were stored in the Hall's stable block and lorries would arrive to collect the film for nation-wide distribution. The Company provided splendid war-time social evenings, especially at the Monsal Head Hotel and the Bull's Head, Tideswell. In 1943 the film company returned to London.

The Sullivan family from Pimlico, London, came as evacuees to Over Haddon, to escape the Blitz. Mr. Sullivan, a shop keeper, is with his wife Carrie and two sons (one called Anthony) and they were billeted with the Oldfield family at Mona View.
Carolyn Pearce

In February 1941, Little Longstone Institute was rented and taken over by Wright and Sons, leather merchants, who had been bombed out of their factory at West Bar, Sheffield. The workers came from Sheffield every day in a lorry. They collected shoes and boots from villages in North Derbyshire and South Yorkshire, stitched and nailed on new soles and returned them to the village shops that had provided them. The firm remained in the village until 1946.

THE ARMY ARRIVES IN THE DISTRICT

In Bakewell itself, during the early days of the war, the 26th Mobile Light Anti-Aircraft Regiment, Royal Artillery (Territorial Army) were recruiting in the Bakewell district, having opened a recruiting office at Devonshire Chambers. Recruitment was for Home Defence and recruits between the ages of 27 and 50 were being accepted. Lorry drivers, cooks and mechanics were especially required.

September 11th 1939 saw three companies of recruits arriving on a troop train at Bakewell Station. The men marched down Castle Hill to requisitioned premises and billets at Burton Closes and Haddon House. The Glossop area had provided two companies of recruits and Chesterfield a third, to form the 4th Corps of the Royal Corps of Signals. Their billets were spartan and overcrowded and resulted in the outbreak of an influenza and meningitis epidemic. Volunteer nurses tended to the

Glossop Company of the Royal Corps of Signals stationed at Burton Closes, Bakewell during the early days of the Second World War.
P, Mosley

soldiers' needs in improvised hospital wards set up in the Union Workhouse (Newholme) and the Co-operative Hall in King Street.

Both houses had been densely crowded with soldiers. They had no mattresses, only one bowl each and two blankets to sleep on, on the wooden floor. Latrines consisted of white-washed telegraph poles placed over open trenches three feet deep, with chlorine of lime added. By this time there were 700 soldiers in the town and the "Society of Friends" (Quakers) turned their Meeting House into a splendid canteen.

The 4th Corps of Royal Corps of Signals departed with the British force that attempted to dislodge the Germans from Norway in 1940, without success. They were replaced in Bakewell by the 6th Corps of Signals. "Brooklands" on Coombs Road was used as the Officers' Mess and the accommodation problem was eased by Nissen Huts being erected behind Burton Closes.

Billets were also found in the town for the soldiers in Bath Street, Bridge Street, Buxton Road and Haddon House. Most of the public houses also took in soldiers. The Rutland Arms Hotel became the first Officers' Mess, before moving to Rowsley, at Stanton Woodhouse, and finally to Burton Closes and Brooklands.

By 1941/1942 the Royal Army Service Corps had replaced the Royal Corps of Signals, with their bases at Wirksworth, Matlock, Whitworth Institute (Darley Dale) and Bakewell (when, in 1944, the invasion of Europe occurred through Normandy, the Nissen Huts at Burton Closes housed German prisoners of war, with the men performing farm work, clearing snow in winter and acting as foresters on the Chatsworth Estate).

A contingent of the RASC was stationed at Hassop. Ammunition came to Hassop Station by rail and was stacked alongside the wide verges of the roads in the Sheldon, Monyash and Buxton areas. Bombs, shells and grenades were stored in boxes on the verges, stretching for miles along these country lanes. They lay in the open past Wheal Lane on the way from Sheldon to Flagg and Taddington and in the opposite direction on Magpie Flats, as well as on the approach to Bole Hill. The green lane running off the Bakewell to Monyash road was used, as well as the road to Haddon Grove and on Barker Lane, past Red House, towards Monyash. The munitions lay unattended and the farmers would drive their cattle along these roads, attempting to keep them clear of the munitions boxes.

The first transports for the RASC were impressed vehicles such as furniture vans and haulage lorries. Three out of ten were out of service when they were brought in but eventually they obtained better quality vehicles. A number of the early driving instructors were London bus drivers who had been drafted into war work, with the promise that they would not see overseas action.

The trainee drivers always drove in convoys of approximately 20 vehicles, nose to tail, and practised both day and

A German Prisoner of War called Laurence, helps out the Pearce family of New Close Farm, Over Haddon, during the latter part of the war and into 1947-1947. The POW camp was in Nissen huts at Burton Closes, Bakewell. The child with the bicycle wheel is Noreen Pearce.

Carolyn Pearce

night time driving. Many of the walls in the area received their fair share of knocks, especially during night operations. In the blackout, lead vehicles drove on side lights, as did the rear vehicle, whilst the others had none showing, except a small spotlight fitted underneath, shining onto the rear white axle casing. Instructors sat in the lorries with their trainees, whilst sergeants rode ahead on motor cycles.

In the Longstone area, a much used route was the steep incline from Monsal Dale to Monsal Head, with drivers also getting into difficulties when slipping backwards driving up the "Headstones". Two soldiers were sadly killed when their lorry over-turned going down Beggarway Lane, Great Longstone.

THE HOME GUARD

During the anxious, dark days of 1940, Bakewell and district folk rallied to the cause, when, on May 14th, Anthony Eden broadcast to the nation that volunteers were required for a new force called the Local Defence Volunteers (nick-named "Look, Duck and Vanish"), later to be re-named the Home Guard.

Ashford Home Guard Platoon was part of "A" Company of the Sherwood Foresters, based at Bakewell. Their C.O. was Lieutenant Sinclaire (a recent incomer to Ashford, who worked in Sheffield) and his second in command, Second Lieutenant Walter Wild, was an Ashford shopkeeper. Their H.Q. was in the Club Room at the Devonshire Arms Hotel (nowadays the Ashford Arms). Guard duty was at this post every night, with two hours on and four hours off, and included patrolling the village. The Quartermaster's store was near the Bull's Head Yard, with Private Jack Fletcher senior, the manager of Burgon's shop in Bakewell, acting as Quartermaster.

Manoeuvres were held on Longstone Moor and Edge, as well as at Chatsworth, with weapons training and firing at the Butts on Coombs Road, Bakewell, at a miniature range inside Bakewell Drill Hall and on a small range off Duke's Drive, Ashford.

Sheldon Home Guard members included Arthur Bramwell, brothers Ernest and Joe Andrews from Johnson's Lane Farm, Stanley Brocklehurst from Ash Tree View Farm, Ben Sheldon of Town Head Farm, Tom Gyte of the Devonshire Arms, Sonny Carson and George Eaton. They were led by Lieutenant Sinclaire of the Ashford Platoon, together with Mr. Swift, who lived on Duke's Drive, Ashford.

Mrs. Swift would sometimes attend with her husband and show the members how to bandage wounds. As a young child, Kenneth Brocklehurst remembers that she demonstrated by practising on the Sheldon children, including Kenneth. Both Ashford and Sheldon Home Guard units would often go on manoeuvres together.

Sheldon Home Guard had their headquarters in the Village Hall (previously, the old school, which had closed in 1933). There were only three telephones in the village at that time and Home Guard communications came via the telephone at the Frost's farm, Manor Farm.

Information and directions were phoned through to the farm, where a buzzer connection had been fitted that could be sounded in the Village Hall. At the sound of the buzzer, a Home Guard member ran to the farm to receive the instructions.

Regular army soldiers also made use of the Village Hall, Primitive Methodist Chapel and the end section of Yew Tree House, for accommodation and places to meet. Eventually these soldiers left Sheldon to be stationed in huts on Wheal Lane, near Taddington, close to Over Wheal Farm.

The view from Sheldon was wide ranging, especially towards Buxton and Sheffield, as well as across to Monyash and one guard duty post was the water tank for the Sheldon Water Works, at the top end of the village. On nights of inclement weather, the inside of the stone base provided shelter from the wind and rain.

The H.Q. of Longstone Home Guard Platoon was at Longstone Hall, the home of James Plowright, with Mr. Plowright as Commanding Officer and Captain Wood his second in command. Two men from the First World War, Bill Bowers and Mr. Coniham, acted as sergeants and it was often the former Great War soldiers who helped with training.

Longstone Home Guard were put through their paces on training exercises and manoeuvres on Longstone Moor, with the RASC units based at Bakewell taking the part of the enemy. On one occasion the regular army units were guarding a farm on the Moor, when members of the Home Guard crept to within a short distance and threw a smoke grenade, causing a great deal of panic.

Each Sunday morning they would meet on parade at Longstone Hall and each night, six members would be taken by car onto Longstone Moor to a cottage, which would be their guard post. Again, they would be at their post 2 hours on and 4 hours off, and would walk from the cottage to the top of Betney Kop, the highest point on Longstone Edge. They practised their shooting along Moor Road.

Wardlow Home Guard members practised manoeuvres with colleagues from other platoons in the council depot yard at Calver, where mock rescues were practised on a large chimney. The tale is told of Private Molloy being sent up the outer wall of the chimney to fix a dummy on the top but, becoming scared by the height and his precarious position, froze, and great difficulty was found in talking him back down.

Over Haddon's Home Guard Head Quarters was in a hut at the top end of a field called Castle Ho, on the Bakewell side of New Close Farm, and it was also used as a lookout point. A hand cranked field telephone was kept in the hut and was manned before sunrise and after sunset. Members included Joe Pearce, Warren Pearce, Jack Thurlby, Joe Sherratt, Jim Mellor, Jim Taylor and 16 year old Joe Oldfield.

A detachment of Bakewell Home Guard.
BACK ROW: *X, Harold Higgins, Jack Blackwell, Billy Bramwell (electrician), Joe Smedley (clock repairer), Colin Elliott, Herbert Lomas.*
SECOND ROW: *X, Eddie Darnell, Dennis Fletcher, Mr. Smith, Tommy Linnet (blacksmith), Vic Littlewood, X, Edgar Mansfield (fishmonger), Jack Gannon (bus driver).*
FRONT ROW: *Joe Mansfield, Arthur Bramwell (coal merchant), Mr. Sutton (Suttee – manager of the Rutland Arms), Major Towler (Attendance Inspector for Derbyshire Schools), Mr Lees (Williams Deacons Bank), X, Walter Heathcote.*
B. Wild and Sylvia Marsden

Over Haddon members also had to be on duty in Bakewell at the weekend, from Saturday evening until Sunday morning. Two man patrols operated between Bakewell and Ashford, Bakewell and Hassop Station or Bakewell and Over Haddon. They also took their turn in guarding the Bakewell Home Guard Telephone Exchange, situated above Bakewell Post Office.

Home Guard Head Quarters at Bakewell was situated in the loft of a building adjacent to Bakewell Infant School, Bath Street. Safety was not assured, however, even when the men were resting in this building. On one evening, members were playing cards when there was the sound of an explosion as a member's rifle went off and the bullet passed close above their heads. From that point on, the man responsible was only allowed to patrol and be on parade armed with a bayonet.

ACTIVITY IN THE SKIES, THE AUXILIARY FIRE SERVICE AND THE ARP

We have seen how the evacuee school children came to the rural areas to escape the bombing in the towns and cities. Inhabitants in Bakewell district, especially those in the Longstone, Sheldon and Wardlow areas, could often see from a distance the terrible pounding that Sheffield was taking in the Blitz. During the blackout, the glow from the burning ruins of the city and the arc of tracer bullets were clearly visible. This was especially the case on the nights of Thursday December 12th and Sunday December 15th 1940, when the German Luftwaffe mounted its severest raids of the war on the city of steel. Whole rows of streets were flattened and tram cars became mangled wrecks. Over 400 people were killed during the first raid, whilst almost the same number perished on December 15th. It was during this period that conditions became unbearable for Wright and Brothers, leather merchants, who were to arrive in Little Longstone in February 1941.

Bakewell's one and only air raid began at 6p.m. on December 23rd 1940 when a German aircraft circled the town and dropped two high explosive bombs. The Air Raid Prevention wardens were alerted at their centre in the Town Hall and the town's fire brigade arrived at the DP Battery Works, Lumford, to find that the bombs had narrowly missed the mill dam, leaving two large craters. Houses in the Lakeside area were slightly damaged. On that same evening incendiary bombs fell on land between Youlgreave and Conksbury around 8-30p.m. but fortunately there were no casualties and only one farm was damaged.

After losing its way returning from a raid over Europe, a Wellington bomber crashed into Lathkill Dale, close to Conksbury Bridge. The airmen had parachuted to safety and one who landed knocked on the door of Mrs. Nuttall of Manor Cottage, Monyash Road, near Over Haddon. He was handed over to Bill Bibby, a Special Constable, who kept him under observation as a suspected enemy because of his strange accent. He was only released when another member of the crew arrived to tell them that the arrested man was in fact a Scotsman.

Whenever the air raid siren was sounded, the Penrhos College girl boarders sheltered in the Chatsworth beer cellar, especially on the occasions of the blitz on Sheffield. Cream crackers and bovril were passed down the rows of girls sitting on forms, until the "all-clear" was given.

It was to the beer cellar that the girls retreated in the summer term of 1942 when two German planes attacked Chatsworth House as they flew by. The girls were in the Painted Hall for evening prayers, after having supper, when the attack began. The north side of the house received a few machine-gun bullet marks. It was believed that the two planes were shot down later in Lincolnshire.

The younger members of staff and prefects shared in the fire-watching role. Each night, one staff member and one prefect slept in a hut on the roof of Chatsworth House, while another pair slept in an alcove on Bachelor's Corridor. Each pair had a telephone at hand.

On another occasion a Wellington Bomber crashed in the park on Lindup Low, between the Beeley traffic lights and Edensor.

One stick of 12 incendiary bombs was dropped near Great Hucklow, in a lane between Wardlow Mires and Grindlow, and others landed near Stoney Middleton, in the quarry at the junction of the Eyam and Stoney Middleton road. It was believed that the German pilots had flown from Great Hucklow Gliding Club before the outbreak of war, and knew the area well. They had decided to jettison the bombs in open countryside. Searchlight Companies were stationed in Coplow Dale, near Little Hucklow, and at Taddington, tracing the journeys of the droning German bombers on their way to Sheffield and the western ports. Whenever there was an air raid on Sheffield, steam trains had to wait in the local tunnels or in the cutting by Longstone Bridge, to prevent the glow from their fires providing help for the planes in plotting their position.

At Great Longstone, buildings such as St. Giles Church were sandbagged for protection against bombs and ladders were placed inside, making access to the roof readily available. During the Munich Crisis of 1938 large numbers of men offered their services as Air Raid Wardens and gas masks were stored in Bakewell Town Hall and in the outlying villages. Unfortunately, by July 1939 it was being reported that there was a shortage of Air Raid Wardens because of a lack of interest and few were undergoing training now. At the end of July an ARP exercise took place in the whole district to test the blackout, Wardens and special constables were called out at midnight on Thursday 20th July 1939 and patrolled the areas.

At 3-30am on Monday 4th September, the day after war was declared, air raid sirens went off in the district and the Air Raid Warden system was tested in action. It was a false alarm but it revealed the need for a more adequate siren warning in this hilly and scattered area.

From early days, wardens were issued with helmets and uniforms, stirrup pumps, stretchers and partially shaded torches to prevent the upward glare of light. By November 1940 earplugs, issued by the Government to reduce the effect of air raid noises, had been distributed. Decontamination drills were practised in case the Germans dropped gas bombs and mobile gas vans or sheds were taken around the villages. ARP Wardens could practise crawling through the enclosed space with gas masks on, after smoke canisters had been tossed inside.

An Auxiliary Fire Service was set up in most villages. In Great Longstone the fire station was established in a small wooden shed in the field between Flaxdale and John Thornhill's poultry farm. Here were stored a manual pump, stirrup pumps, buckets and tools and it was the meeting place for local firemen E. Holmes (Captain), G. Holmes, E. Holmes junior, Tom Hurst and B. Sales. Fire Service stirrup pumps were also stored at Flaxdale (R. Thornhill), Poultry Farm (John Thornhill) plus

All that nowadays remains (year 2007) of the Auxiliary Fire Service headquarters of the Second World War period in the village of Great Longstone (in Flaxdale Field). Amongst the equipment stored here was a pump on wheels. Dragged by firemen to the scene of any fire, it was operated by rocking a bar in a see-saw motion.

Keith Taylor

extending ladder, at the police house, in the parish church porch and with F. Herrington of Sunny Bank and H. Bennett at Croft Lodge. A considerable number of private homes also possessed their own stirrup pumps, whilst wardens had distributed bags of sand to every house in the village. Air Raid Wardens at Great Longstone included Robert Thornhill from Flaxdale, John Thornhill from the poultry farm, F. Herrington of Sunny Bank and Herbert Bennett from Croft Lodge.

Practise was taken very seriously as can be seen with an incident in the Hope Valley. The Chief Air Raid Warden in one of the villages in the Hope Valley had an electric bell installed in his house, by means of which he could be called immediately an air raid warning was received.

One night during September 1939, needing to rise very early the next morning, he set his alarm clock accordingly. At the appointed time the alarm clock "did its stuff", with the result that the Air Raid Warden jumped out of bed in a great hurry. Hastily donning some clothes he made a quick dash around the village, calling on his other wardens and telling them to get to their stations owing to an air raid warning having been received. It was not until some minutes afterwards that he realised the mistake he had made.

SUPPORTING THE WAR EFFORT ON THE HOME FRONT

During the month of July 1940 the Bakewell district responded to the call by Lord Beaverbrook, "Women of Britain, give us your aluminium. We will turn your pots and pans into Spitfires and Hurricanes, Blenheims and Wellingtons". Railings disappeared from many properties and areas, especially in Bakewell itself, as scrap metal was sought. In 1939 the Government had issued the message, "Let dig for victory be the motto of everyone with a garden", and by 1945 Britain was importing one third of its food instead of two thirds as before the war.

Throughout the war years, the market town and surrounding villages contributed significant sums of money to fund raising, whether for comforts for the servicemen, Red Cross parcels, relief for the Russians or raising money for war weapons.

At the Bull's Head, Wardlow, darts and dominoes evenings were held to raise funds for comforts for the servicemen. Three Wardlow women, including Ida Sellers, were sent with other women who normally worked at the Progress Knitting Works in Bakewell, to perform war work at Eccleshall, near Sheffield, packing gunpowder into shells, with many receiving powder rash for their troubles.

In the Longstone area, Mrs. Lilian Reeves, wife of the previous vicar of St. Giles, who produced plays for the St. Giles Players, organised an entertainment towards the end of 1940 to raise money for the local Spitfire Fund, with half the proceeds going to the war weapons fund. There were dances held in Longstone Institute to

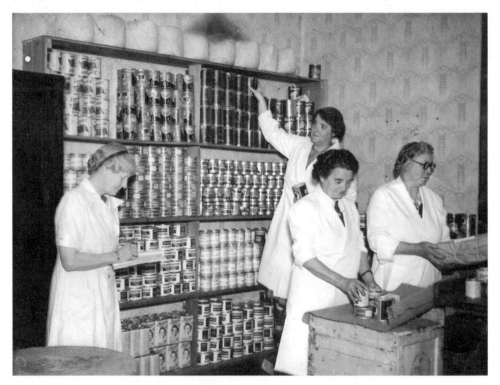

The Women's Institute wartime canning factory Great Longstone c1940-1941. The factory was in the garage and Guides and Brownies room at the Vicarage, Great Longstone.
Stocking the shelves is Alice Maud Knight. Checking the list is Mrs. Goodwin (she ran the local Choral Society). At the desk are Mrs. Bramwell and Mrs. Nuttall.
Olive Mead

Lady Manners School pupils singing in the Bath Gardens, Bakewell, during 'Wings for Victory' campaign: 'Salute the Soldier', 1943.

Lady Manners School

raise money, with soldiers from the Rifle Brigade lodging in Monsal Dale attending. The Women's Institute organised a joint Christmas party for evacuees and village children, whilst these same children practised knitting and made khaki balaclavas and scarves for the servicemen.

Surplus fruit and vegetables were bottled and canned, with the canning taking place in premises at both Longstone Hall and especially the Vicarage. The Vicarage garage and the Guides and Brownies meeting room in the Vicarage became the main focus of canning operations, with Mrs. Trendell, wife of the vicar of Great Longstone, playing a prominent role in proceedings.

The Women's Institute was very much involved in this process and tended their own allotment. Beans were salted to preserve them and eggs were pickled in isinglass, whilst, as in so many wartime communities, Pig Clubs were encouraged and multiplied. For the Longstone area, the main slaughterman who arrived to kill the pig was the appropriately named Mr. Bacon, from Little Longstone.

Children in the village, especially the Girl Guides, led by Miss Arning, gathered rose hips from the hedgerows for syrup, berries and plums for jam making. Land Army girls also came to work at Thornbridge Hall and on some of the local farms.

Continued on page 343 ☛

Potato pickers on John Thornhill's farm, Great Longstone, 1942.
BACK ROW: *John Thornhill, Chris Bennett, Tom Hurst, Percy Buggins, Joan Bebbington,*
Sheila Hurst, Jenny Pickford, Stella Holmes (Barnes), Mary Ward, Herbert Bennett, Nellie Birkhead.
FRONT ROW: *X, Martin Oliver, Colin Slack, Michael Jeacock, Alfred Furniss, Betty Udale,*
Joan Barnes, Annie Garrett, Betty Barnes.
Peter Thornhill

Bill Pickford and Peter Thornhill in Coarse Low Field, Great Longstone, August 1940.
Peter Thornhill

Despatching eggs from Thornhill's poultry farm to Longstone Railway Station on a sledge in January 1940, a very severe winter.
LEFT TO RIGHT: *Bill Pickford, John William Thornhill, Peter Thornhill.*
Peter Thornhill

Drilling oats on Coarse Low Field, Great Longstone, April 1940. Jimmy Fearn, Bill Pickford and John Thornhill junior.
Peter Thornhill

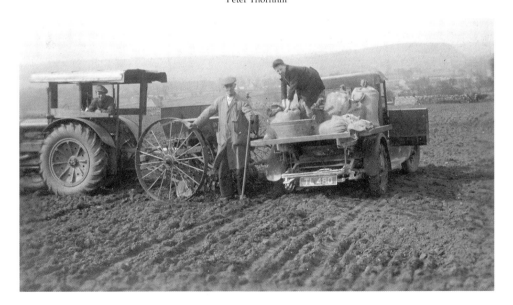

Threshing and baling oats in Coarse Low Field on John Thornhill's farm, Great Longstone,
September 1ˢᵗ 1949.
Peter Thornhill

Harvest time, August 1940, on John Thornhill's farm, Great Longstone.
Bill Pickford (senior), Peter Thornhill, Rachel Greaves (land girl)
Peter Thornhill

Bringing home the harvest, Great Longstone, August 1940.
Peter Thornhill

Harvesting on John Thornhill's farm during the Second World War.
Jimmy Fearn driving and brother Ted on the binder.
Peter Thornhill

Potato planting on John Thornhill's farm, Great Longstone, May 3rd 1943. Herbert Bennett driving and Chris Bennett in light-coloured coat.
Peter Thornhill

Jimmy Fearn discing in Coarse Low Field, Great Longstone, April 1940.
Peter Thornhill

Potato planting on John Thornhill's farm, Great Longstone, May 3rd 1943. John William Thornhill driving, Herbert and Chris Bennett on the left. Peter Thornhill and another on the right.
Peter Thornhill

One such girl lodged with the Sandersons at the Pack Horse Inn, Little Longstone, whilst others were dropped off from a lorry that came from a hostel at Chapel-en-le-Frith. However, children from Great Longstone School were also sent out to do light work on the farms, including potato picking, stone gathering and clearing the fields before seeding. Potato picking by the children occurred at Thornhills and turnip thinning at Long Roods Farm, whilst one October some children were even taken across to Breton Clough to work alongside Italian Prisoners of War.

During March 1942 a "WARSHIP WEEK" National Savings Campaign was held throughout the country and the event was a success in Bakewell. As a result, a Hunt Class coal burning mine sweeper, HMS "Derby", was adopted by the civil community of Bakewell.

Launched in 1918, by 1939 it was in Reserve Status and laid up at Singapore, but was re-commissioned and re-fitted. During 1940 it took part in convoy and escort work from Aden, sailing in the Red Sea and Persian Gulf. 1941 saw it doing similar work and sweeping for mines in the Eastern Mediterranean, from its base at Alexandria, whilst in 1942 and 1943 it saw action off the coast of North Africa. By 1944 it was operating in Adriatic waters, but, in September 1944, it was placed in reserve and laid up in Gibraltar.

In Sheldon village, Ethel Plumtree (née Frost, of Manor Farm) was a young school girl during the war years and recalls;

"I remember the pitch darkness of the blackout, and at Manor Farm we only had candles, lanterns and paraffin lamps, no electric. We took gas masks to school at Ashford each day and had trial practices with them at school.

"There were only three tractors and four cars in Sheldon during the war, bearing in mind that there were a lot more farms and small-holdings in Sheldon then. Most farmers milked cows and provided milk for the villagers.

"During war time farmers had to grow a compulsory 10% acreage of grain crops and potatoes according to the acreage of their farms and with no modern machinery and most of the farms still using horses, the machinery which was available had to be operated manually. Lady Manners school children were released to help with the potato picking at Sheldon but my father used to say this was a mixed blessing as they spent a lot of time throwing potatoes at each other.

Sheldon during the Second World War. (Note the hooded lamps on the car because of the blackout.) Henry Frost from Manor House Farm is with his nieces and nephew.
LEFT TO RIGHT: *Ethel Frost, Phyllis Frost, John Frost.*
Ethel Plumtree

"As we had a tractor at Manor Farm, it was commandeered and my uncle, Henry Frost, had to tow the snow plough (a wooden triangular construction) in the winter time. The winter of 1939/1940 was especially severe with heavy falls of snow and much drifting and there were no cabs on tractors then.

"Dad was a member of Sheldon Home Guard Platoon and was often on duty. However, on the nights when not on duty, he would still walk down the plantation side near the farm and look around for any signs of danger. However, one night he had a real fright. One of the regular army soldiers stationed at the Village Hall lost his way and came through the plantation, jumping over the wall behind father, without him hearing anything. I don't know who had the biggest fright!"

THE FIRST CASUALTIES OF THE WAR 1939

When Neville Chamberlain had announced to the nation that Britain was at war with Germany on September 3rd 1939, it was not long before the people of Bakewell and district learned that they would not be spared the loss of life of their servicemen. Any false hopes were dashed when news came to the people of the market town that one of their men had lost his life whilst serving in the Royal Navy, to be followed in December 1939 by news that an army man had been killed in a motoring accident in the blackout. The loss of these two men were the first of thirty five servicemen to lose their lives during the Second World War.

ABLE SEAMAN JOHN (JACK) CLEMENTSON NO. P/SSX20373
HMS "ROYAL OAK", ROYAL NAVY,
DIED OOCTOBER 14ᵀᴴ 1939 AGED 19

Bakewell district had its first casualty of the war on October 14th 1939. Able Seaman Jack Clementson lost his life when the battleship, "Royal Oak" was sunk. Official confirmation of his death was received by his parents by telegram from the Rear Admiral, Royal Naval Barracks, Plymouth, on Monday. Jack was 19 years of age and the only child of Mr. and Mrs. E. Clementson, of "Gate House", Haddon Hall.

Jack's father was a retired police-officer of the Derbyshire Constabulary, who had served 25 years in its service, latterly near Dronfield, at both Greenhills and Coal Aston, where Jack attended school.

The family came to live at "Gate House", Haddon, on his father's retirement in 1935. Jack Clementson had always been very keen on going to sea, joining the Royal Navy aged sixteen and a half in 1937 (for a short while prior to this he was employed on the Haddon Estate).

Jack served on HMS "Aurora" in the Mediterranean Fleet before the war, then on HMS "Courageous", an aircraft carrier, before he was commissioned to the

Able Seaman John Clementson of Bakewell.

battleship "Royal Oak" in June 1939 (3 months later, on September 17th, cruising

Battleship HMS Royal Oak on manoeuvres 1938.

Part of the crew of HMS Royal Oak at Scapa Flow, 1939.
Jack Clementson of Bakewell was part of the crew.

with four escorting destroyers off SW England, on anti-submarine duties, the carrier "Courageous" was torpedoed at dusk by U-29, sinking immediately with the loss of 515 lives).

By October 1939 HMS "Royal Oak" was in "safe" anchorage at Scapa Flow in the Orkneys, the naval base of the British Home Fleet. On the night of October 14th German Lieutenant Commander Guenther Prien, commanding U-47, daringly threaded elaborate anti-submarine defences and treacherous tide rips to enter Scapa Flow, where the British Home Fleet lay concentrated. Firing two spreads of four torpedoes each against the nearest large vessel, he scored several hits on the battle-ship "Royal Oak". She went down in two minutes, taking with her 786 officers and men, including Able Seaman Jack Clementson. Guenther Prien then brought his submarine safely out of the harbour and escaped. Jack's body was never recovered and his name is to be found on Panel 33, Column 2 of the Portsmouth Naval Memorial.

GUNNER HERBERT ASKEY NO. 1481454
115 BATTERY 26TH LIGHT ANTI-AIRCRAFT REGIMENT ROYAL ARTILLERY
DIED DECEMBER 8TH 1939 AGED 39

We know little about Herbert (or Bert as he was known) Askey's background. He was born in 1900, his mother being Martha Askey, whilst an uncle, Thomas Askey, lived at Harpur Hill at the time of Bert's death. Bert was well-known in the Bakewell area, having worked as a farm labourer on a number of local farms. He joined the Royal Artillery at Bakewell, early in September 1939, as war was declared.

Bert was in training as a gunner on light anti-aircraft guns, in the Hertfordshire countryside, when he was knocked down and run over by a motor vehicle in a Hertfordshire village on a Friday evening. The blackout was in operation, bringing a pitch darkness to which none of us nowadays are accustomed to. The increase in the number of road accident casualties rose dramatically in those early days of the war.

Bert was taken to Hatfield House, belonging to the Marquis of Salisbury, which, from September 1939 was used as a military hospital. It was there that Bert Askey died and was buried in Grave 1 Hatfield Park War Cemetery, Hertfordshire, in the small cemetery attached to the temporary hospital.

THE YEAR 1940

In the Autumn of 1939 the British Expeditionary Force (BEF) had embarked for France, together with men from the Bakewell area, but no hostile action was pursued as the opposing sides faced each other across the Siegfried and Maginot Lines during the bitter, freezing winter of 1939/1940, in the period known as the "Phoney War".

However, this "Phoney War" came to a shattering close on May 10th 1940 as the German Armed Forces invaded the Low Countries in their plan to defeat France and eliminate the BEF. As the might of the Wehrmacht and Luftwaffe drove the British back in their retreat to the Channel coast and Dunkirk, Bakewell and district were fortunate that no fatalities from these areas occurred during the bitter, desperate fighting, and indeed, it would be January 1941 before the next fatality occurred, of a serviceman from Ashford.

The people back in the Derbyshire Dales witnessed the sad plight of the British Army, however, when the troops began arriving home after their evacuation from the beaches of Dunkirk. For a two week period in early June, exhausted, dirty, bedraggled members of the army arrived by train and lorry in Matlock, Darley Dale and the Bakewell district. They sat forlornly on the grass verges near the Whitworth Institute at Darley Dale, in the Hall Leys Park at Matlock, where they washed the grime from their faces in the boating lake, whilst similar scenes occurred at Bakewell. For a fortnight they were accommodated locally, some under canvas, as reorganisation took place and they could be sent home on leave and then back to their units, that were re-equipping as best they could. Many locals helped by inviting soldiers into their homes for tea and biscuits, or even for a meal.

We have already seen that it was during these dark, tension filled days of the war that the Home Guard was brought into existence. By June 4th 1940 the evacuation of Dunkirk was completed and 338,000 men had been lifted from the beaches. On June 5th Hitler had decided on the invasion of Britain and Operation "Sea Lion" was begun. Having no adequate surface force to oppose British naval strength, the Luftwaffe's task was first to defeat the RAF and then to neutralise the Royal Navy.

In the first phase of the Battle of Britain, August 8th to 18th, the Germans planned to coax the British into combat by attacking sea ports and fighter bases. Aided by radar, Fighter Command still dominated the air space over Britain. Phase two, August 24th to September 5th, saw the German attack shift to concentrate against the main inland RAF bases and by sheer weight of numbers came close to cracking Fighter Command. The British were partly saved by a change of plan by the Germans. London now became the target for incessant aerial bombardment and Fighter Command was able to concentrate its dwindling forces.

By mid October the Battle of Britain had been won and Hitler cancelled Operation "Sea Lion" on October 12th.

During 1940, Bakewell, Over Haddon, Ashford, Sheldon, the Longstones, Rowland, Wardlow and Hassop had thankfully escaped the grim news of the loss of local men in the conflict on land, sea and in the air. Sadly, this position was to change in 1941 as news was brought to Ashford that one of its men had died in hospital whilst in training with the Army in Scotland. He would be the first of five service-men to lose their lives during this year.

THE YEAR 1941

PRIVATE SAMPSON LYNES GRATTON NO. 4980382
2ND/5TH BATTALION SHERWOOD FORESTERS
DIED JANUARY 21ST 1941 AGED 25

Sampson Gratton, known to family and friends as Sam, was born in 1915, in Ashford in the Water. The family, consisting of Sam, his sister Doris and parents Thomas Furniss and Minnie Gratton, lived at "Wyedene", a house on Betty Lane, just before the old Ashford Post Office.

Sam's father, known as Furniss Gratton, worked for the Council, helping to maintain the local roads as lengthman and as part of a road gang. The surface of the roads was laid with "slurry", a mixture of crushed stone, limestone dust and water and Furniss Gratton became known in the locality as the "Slurry King". When he retired he became caretaker of Ashford Village Institute.

Sampson Lynes Gratton (Sam) of Ashford.
Nigel Hare

Furniss Gratton's brother, Jabez Benjamin Gratton, had helped his father Benjamin Gratton run a printing works and photography shop in Bakewell in earlier days and made

Sam Gratton with his sister Doris, at Ashford.
Nigel Hare

use of his photographic skills to produce post cards showing local scenes. Their father, Benjamin, also ran the post office at Ashford, but by the 1930's it was Jabez and his wife who ran the shop, whilst continuing using his skills as a photographer and book-binder.

His nephew, Sam, left school and began working for R. Orme and Company in Bakewell, the main grocery and provisions store in the market town, and it was from there that he was called up in October 1940, becoming a member of the 2nd/5th Battalion Sherwood Foresters.

The Sherwood Foresters were training on Brigade exercises, practising attacking enemy positions, in the Galashiels and Melrose area of the Scottish Borders during December 1940 and January 1941. Later they would be sent to North Africa. However, they would leave without Sam Gratton. Sam only possessed one kidney, an even more serious health condition than it is

Benjamin Gratton's printers and photography shop on Matlock Street, Bakewell c1900.
He was the grandfather of Sam Gratton.
J. Duncan

nowadays. In mid January 1941 he became seriously ill and entered Peel Hospital, at Clovenfords, near Galashiels, where he died of pneumonia on January 21st, aged 25. Peel Hospital had been built by and for the military, consisting of wooden Nissen huts, and situated in the "middle of nowhere", seven miles to the west of Galashiels (surprisingly, after the war it was operated for civilian use until the late 1980's).

The first notice his parents received of his death was in a letter from a Scottish

Sam Gratton of Ashford, an employee
of R. Orme and Co. of Bakewell.
N. Hare

lady, whose family had "befriended" Sam and another army colleague. Sam's body was returned to Ashford and he was buried in the village cemetery, the first Ashford man to die whilst in service.

Despite the convoy system operating during 1940, the toll of British ships sunk by the roving German submarines kept mounting. By August 1940 two and a half million tons of shipping had been destroyed. Britain just did not have sufficient light warships to provide adequate protection for her merchant ships, nor could the shipyards produce sufficient replacements.

By 1941, under the direction of Admiral Karl Doenitz, German operations developed into the "wolf-pack" pattern: groups of as many as 15 to 20 U-boats spread over the sea lanes approaching Britain. Convoys were tracked by the discovering submarine until the pack could be assembled for simultaneous assault.

One method used by the British was to train Royal Naval gunmen to operate guns fixed aboard Merchant ships and it was a Royal Navy seaman from Bakewell operating such a gun who was next to lose his life, in the stormy, grey February waters around the coast of Britain.

Thomas Furniss Gratton and his son Sampson (Sam) Gratton of Ashford.
Nigel Hare

ABLE SEAMAN FRANCIS CECIL CLARKE No. P/J80303
HMS "PRESIDENT III" ROYAL NAVY,
DIED FEBRUARY 23RD 1941

Francis Cecil Clarke was the son of Henry and Mary Clarke and husband of Dora Clarke, and was connected to the market town of Bakewell.

Joining the Royal Navy he trained as a gunner at the Royal Navy shore base of HMS "President III" at Bristol. The base trained gunners to man the guns attached to merchant ships, to provide some means of defence against aircraft or submarines (the ships were known as Defence Equipped Merchant Ships or DEMS). If a gunner from the Royal Navy was killed in action on one of these merchant ships, his name would appear under the name of the Royal Navy base, in Francis Clarke's case, HMS "President III".

This means that on February 23rd 1941, the date of his death, he was aboard a merchant ship attacked and sunk on the High Seas. Although we cannot be sure, completely, if we have traced the action in which he was killed, we know that on February 18th 1941 Convoy OB288 departed Liverpool with 46 ships. This convoy was only to be escorted for the first stage of its journey. Thirteen German U-boats and seven Italian submarines were operating in the Atlantic during February 1941.

The convoy had already been attacked by enemy aircraft, but early on the 23rd the last escort left the convoy. Six submarines converged on the target of 46 merchant ships and over the next two days, seven merchant ships were sunk. We cannot be sure whether Francis Cecil Clarke was on one of these merchant vessels but we do know that on February 23rd he was lost at sea on a Defence Equipped Merchant Ship.

His body was not recovered and he is commemorated on Panel 47 Column 2 Portsmouth Naval Memorial and on Bakewell War Memorial.

In January and February 1941 General Wavell's Western Desert Force in North Africa advanced 500 miles, taking Tobruk, destroying nine Italian divisions and capturing 130,000 prisoners, 400 tanks and 1290 guns. British casualties amounted to 500 killed and 1373 wounded. However, by March, the Luftwaffe had sent an Air Corps to nearby Sicily, General Erwin Rommel had landed in North Africa with the Afrika Korps, whilst Wavell's best combat troops were sent to fight in Greece and Crete. The British position was considerably weakened as Rommel launched his first offensive, March to May 1941.

An officer in the British Army with Bakewell connections was with Wavell's forces in North Africa in 1941 and was to be the next victim of the war, as the British forces attempted to stem Rommel's advance.

CAPTAIN ROBERT WILLIAM JONAS NO. 106952
ROYAL ARMY SERVICE CORPS
DIED JUNE 20TH 1941 AGED 30

Robert William Jonas, known to everyone as William, was a Sheffield man who, during the war, had brought his family to live in Bakewell, away from the dangers of German air attacks. His parents were Robert and Mary Elizabeth Jonas, who lived at 59 Slayleigh Lane, Fulwood, Sheffield, and he was their elder son.

He was educated at Eastbourne and Uppingham Schools and at the latter was connected to the Officer Training Corps. After leaving school he eventually became an official of George Bassett and Company, confectionery manufacturers, of Sheffield and during the war married his wife, Edith Isabella Gray (known as Isa). At the time of his death they had an infant son. William was a member of Hallamshire Golf Club but as

Robert William Jonas of Bakewell and Sheffield.

soon as the war began he joined the forces and was posted to the Royal Army Service Corps.

The Blitz on Sheffield, the city of steel, became severe in December 1940 and many Sheffield people were sent away for safety. William Jonas brought his wife and child to live at "Morelands", Merriall Close, Bakewell.

By 1941 William Jonas was serving with the British forces in North Africa, fighting against General Rommel's Afrika Korps and the Italian forces. Between April and December 1941 General Wavell, leader of the Allied forces in the Western Desert, was determined to hold the North African port of Tobruk at all costs, to deprive Rommel of a base port to support further advance into Egypt. On April 10th, Rommel mounted an ill-prepared assault and was thrown back after a three day attack. Advancing part of his force to the Sollum escarpment, east of Tobruk, Rommel invested the fortress, while overhauling his tanks and bringing up reinforcements.

Forced by political pressure from home to attempt the relief of Tobruk, Wavell launched a "shoestring" offensive against the Halfaya-Sollum passes held by Rommel. One infantry division and an armoured division participated between the 15th and 17th June. Split into six semi-independent task forces and committed piece-meal, the British attack was repulsed by Rommel after some minor successes. Captain Jonas was wounded and died on June 20th 1941.

His body was buried in grave 15.H.3 Halfaya-Sollum War Cemetery, Egypt.

Three and a half months went by before news was next received in Bakewell of another death, that of a Royal Navy seaman, but unlike Cecil Clarke, he was not engaged in battle on the High Seas when he died but was in hospital at the time and died from natural causes. He was brought back home to Bakewell to receive a military funeral.

LEADING SEAMAN REGINALD WALTER POWELL NO. C/JX152955 HMS "EASTBOURNE" ROYAL NAVY DIED OCTOBER 5TH 1941 AGED 20

Reginald and his brother Vernon were the sons of Frederick Powell, living at Sellers Yard, North Church Street. Reginald's mother died when he was at a young age and Frederick married his second wife, Lilian. Reginald had been a member of the 1st Bakewell (Parish Church) Troop of Boy Scouts and later of the Rovers, playing in the Rover Scouts' Band. As a boy he also sang in the Parish Church Choir.

His father, Frederick, had served twelve years in the Royal Navy, but at Bakewell, he worked for the Council on the sanitation wagon. Most houses in Bakewell did not possess flush toilets, having earth closets instead. A bucket or simple pit was placed beneath the wooden seat, which had a cut out hole, and ashes and cinders were placed in layers in the space below. The sanitation wagon, with its metal container on the back, arrived usually late at night or early in the morning, and the waste had to be carted away.

At the age of 16 years, Reginald joined the Royal Navy in May 1937, following in the footsteps of his father. He progressed to become a leading seaman and at the time of his death he was a member of the crew of HMS "Eastbourne", an anti-sub-marine frigate used as a convoy escort.

During the early stages of the war he was on board the vessel whilst it escorted a number of convoys, but Reginald was invalided out of the Navy and was on his month's leave pending his discharge, dated October 20th 1941. While on leave, the disability for which he was discharged became worse and he died on October 5th, aged 20.

The funeral took place at Bakewell Cemetery on the Wednesday, the Union flag of the British Legion in Bath Gardens being flown at half mast. Overnight, the coffin had rested in the Parish Church. The "Last Post" was sounded by Messrs. T.H. Frost, H. Strutt, J. Wigley and A. Walker of the Bakewell Rover Scouts.

The fifth and final casualty from the Bakewell district for the year 1941 was that of another naval man, with connections to Wardlow, who died on board a battleship which was sunk in the Eastern Mediterranean.

ORDNANCE ARTIFICER 5TH CLASS WILLIAM LESLIE BLEARS
NO. C/MX65829 HMS "BARHAM" ROYAL NAVY
DIED NOVEMBER 25TH 1941

William Leslie Blears, known to his friends as Leslie, is to be found on the Roll of Honour (not the War Memorial tablet) in Wardlow's Church of the Good Shepherd. His connection to Wardlow is that he was engaged to be married to a Wardlow girl, Pat Bramwell, whose family lived at "The Leeches", Wardlow., but sadly he was killed in the Mediterranean Sea.. He visited Pat in the village on numerous occasions, looking very smart in his naval uniform.

By 1941, Leslie was a member of the crew of HMS "Barham", a First World War battleship, which was part of Admiral Cunningham's cruiser-carrier force in the Eastern Mediterranean.

With the arrival of the Luftwaffe Corps in Sicily and Rommel's Afrika Korps in Libya, Allied surface and air activities were disrupted and Malta bombed incessantly. Shipping from England to North Africa had to be re-routed via the Cape of Good Hope and the Red Sea.

In anticipation of German intervention in the Balkans and Greece, the British sent their best troops from North Africa to Greece in March 1941. Due to the Germans' rapid progress, these forces withdrew to the coast and Royal Navy ships evacuated 43,000 troops, 14,000 of these being landed on Crete to prepare its defences. A total of 24 Royal Navy vessels were lost to German air attacks.

Whilst German air-borne troops assaulted the island of Crete on May 20th, the Royal Navy routed a German amphibious operation bringing reinforcements, with the loss of 5000 German lives. Naval forces managed to evacuate 15,000 hard pressed defenders from Crete but many vessels were lost, with naval casualties totalling 2000 men.

The arrival of twelve more U-boats into the Mediterranean complicated the British naval situation. The submarines soon had a devastating effect on Royal Navy strength, for on November 12th HMS "Ark Royal", with her complement of aircraft, was sunk by torpedo and this was the beginning of a series of grievous losses to the Fleet.

At 4-25p.m. on November 25th 1941 HMS "Barham" was hit by three torpedoes from submarine U-331, 200 miles WNW of Alexandria. The salvo, fired at close range, struck "Barham" on the port side, between the funnel and after turrets. She immediately took a heavy list to port and when she was on her beam end, about four minutes after being hit, her magazine blew up. She sank with the loss of 861 officers and men, including Leslie Blears.

More was to follow. On the night of December 18th an Italian submarine launched three "human torpedoes" against Alexandria. Penetrating the harbour boom, time bombs were fixed to the battleships "Queen Elizabeth" and "Valiant", which were put out of action for months. In the course of a few weeks the whole of the Eastern Fleet was eliminated and Rommel's position in the Western Desert was rapidly strengthened.

No bodies were recovered from HMS "Barham" and Leslie Blears is commemorated on the Chatham Naval Memorial and on the Roll of Honour at Wardlow.

THE YEAR 1942

In just over two years of warfare, seven servicemen from the area we are dealing with had lost their lives, but during 1942, as the spheres of conflict widened, seven more servicemen would die in this year alone. Three men perished whilst serving in the Royal Navy, two in the Mediterranean and one in the North Atlantic, whilst three airmen also lost their lives. Two were members of Bomber Command, brought down over Europe, whilst an Ashford man was a fighter pilot based in Egypt and the Western Desert. The first serviceman to die in 1942, however, was a regular army man from the Ashford/Longstone area, who was killed in the defence of the island fortress of Singapore against Japanese forces.

On December 7th 1941, Japanese aircraft made a surprise attack on the United States Pacific Fleet moored in Pearl Harbour, causing great damage and resulting in both America and Japan entering the war. One day later, December 8th, Japanese forces invaded Malaya, whilst on the 10th, the British Navy lost the battleship "Prince of Wales" and battle cruiser "Repulse" to Japanese air attack. British forces in Malaya were forced to retreat southwards and as the year ended, the demoralised British were driven back relentlessly upon Singapore itself, now a naval base without a naval force. By the end of January 1942, the remnants of this force crossed the causeway to Singapore Island and then demolished it.

Two unpardonable deficiencies brought about the fall of this so-called impregnable fortress-naval base: its fixed defences and artillery were sited to repel naval attack only, and its field forces were shockingly ignorant of the terrain and of jungle fighting.

It was in late January 1942 that George Ernest Neal, the regular army man with connections to the Ashford and Longstone areas, arrived at Singapore by convoy to shore up the defences of the island fortress.

WARRANT OFFICER CLASS II GEORGE ERNEST NEAL No. 4967912
5TH BATTALION SHERWOOD FORESTERS
DIED FEBRUARY 12TH 1942 AGED 38

George Ernest Neal, known as Ernest to family and friends, was born at Broughton in North Lincolnshire, between Scunthorpe and Brigg. He was part of a large family, and with employment scarce, Ernest joined the army in the 1920's, eventually rising to the rank of Warrant Officer II in the 5th Battalion Sherwood Foresters. He was a good sportsman and played for both the Battalion football and cricket teams.

Army football team 1930's. George Ernest Neal stands second from the right on the back row.
David Neal

In the late 1930's Ernest Neal was stationed at Ripley Drill Hall House and lodged with Mrs. Dolly White, a relative of the Shimwell family who farmed at Long Roods

The wedding of George Ernest Neal and Nora Shimwell.
LEFT TO RIGHT: *Maud Sanderson, Herbert Sanderson, George Ernest Neal, Nora Shimwell, Isaac Shimwell, Hilda Shimwell, Mabel Shimwell.*
David Neal

Farm, Ashford, just below Monsal Head, on the road leading down into Ashford.

Dolly's niece, Nora Shimwell, from Long Roods Farm, often visited her aunty and so came to meet Ernest Neal at Ripley. After a courtship and engagement, they were married on Boxing Day 1940, in Ripley. On October 21st 1941, a son, David Neal, was born at Long Roods Farm. One day later, his father, Ernest, arrived to see his new born son, before setting off with his Battalion for embarkation to Singapore.

As a regular army man, Ernest had been with the Foresters in France as part of the British Expeditionary Force in May 1940. They were involved in the with-drawal from Belgium as the German Armed Forces invaded the Low Countries and France on May 10th, but instead of making a fighting retreat to Dunkirk, the 5th Battalion withdrew to Le Havre and then Cherbourg, before embarking at Brest, arriving at Southampton on June 18th.

The Battalion remained in Britain as part of Home Forces until Autumn 1941, when they embarked at Liverpool and made the long voyage to Bombay, in India, via Halifax, Nova Scotia, Trinidad and South Africa, arriving on December 27th 1941. Leaving Bombay on January 19th, they arrived at Singapore on January 29th, an un-successful Japanese air attack being made on the convoy as it approached Singapore.

The total strength of the garrison was 85,000, though many were non-combatants. Very little had been done to put the Island's defences in order, morale was low owing to defeats on the Malayan mainland, whilst Japan had air and sea superiority.

On arrival, the 5th Battalion helped to take over the Eastern Sector of the northern coast, organising the defences and patrolling the coast. On February 5th, shelling of their positions began in earnest and on the 8th, news came that the Japanese had gained a foothold on the NW of the island and were advancing.

On February 10th the Foresters were ordered to make up a force called"Tom Force", which, on February 12th advanced from its position with a view to clearing the area around the village of Bukit Timar. This advance was met with very heavy aerial attack. Japanese bombers were diverted from attacking the harbour to bomb the advancing "Tom Force" counter-attack. The 5th Battalion advanced up the left side of the Bukit Timar road and in savage fighting got to within 400 yards of the village, where they were stopped by heavy fire and were forced to retire.

It was in the savage fighting on February 12th that Warrant Officer George Ernest Neal was killed in action. His body was never recovered from the battlefield and his name is remembered with honour on the Singapore Memorial.

Sadly, despite his connection to Ashford and Little Longstone, Ernest's name is not found on either the Ashford, Little Longstone or Great Longstone war memorials, although his name is to be found on a stone in Little Longstone Chapel graveyard. He is commemorated on the Broughton war memorial, Lincolnshire, and on the Roll of Honour in Ripley Church.

On the 50th Anniversary of VJ Day (Victory over Japan) a pleasing ceremony took place at the war memorial in Great Longstone. On August 20th 1995 a wreath laying ceremony was undertaken by David Neal in tribute to his gallant father, killed in action at Singapore.

20th August 1995 VJ Day Service (50th Anniversary) at the War Memorial, Great Longstone.
A wreath laying ceremony was undertaken by David Neal in tribute to his gallant father,
killed in action in the defence of Singapore, February 12th 1942.
David Neal

20th August 1995 VJ Day Service (50th Anniversary) at the War Memorial, Great Longstone.
David Neal

ABLE SEAMAN JAMES WILLIS FIRN No. D/JX254743
HMS "LIVELY" ROYAL NAVY
DIED MAY 11TH 1942 AGED 24

James was the third son of Jack and Mary (Polly) Firn of Buxton Road and later Granby Croft, Bakewell. His mother, Polly, was a member of the Gladwin family from Birchover before her marriage and the other children included Frank, George and Annie. By the time of James' death in 1942, his father Jack had died.

James Willis Firn served on board the destroyer HMS Lively.

Before joining the navy, in March 1941, James was employed by the DP Battery Limited. He expressed a preference for the navy and had been on HMS "Lively", a Class L destroyer, since May 1941, being recently promoted to Able Seaman.

Of the other three sons of Polly Firn, one was serving with the RAF in the Middle East, another was in the Royal Engineers in the same part of the world, whilst the third was a member of Bakewell Home Guard. Frank, a sergeant in the RAF, had joined as a regular in 1932, and in his last letter home, James told the story how Frank and he had met after many years, Frank visiting James' ship when it was in port.

By November 1941 James Firn and the "Lively" were part of the British Force "K" in the Mediterranean Sea, made up of the light cruisers HMS "Aurora" and HMS "Penelope" and destroyers HMS "Lance" and "Lively" (Commanding Officer Lieutenant Commander Hussey). On November 9th 1941 they intercepted an Italian convoy some 130 miles SW of Calabria, bound from Naples to Tripoli, North Africa. In the resulting battle the Italian destroyer "Fulmine" was sunk as well as the German transports "Duisburg" and "San Marco" and five Italian transports.

On November 24th 1941 Force "K" intercepted an Axis convoy some 100 miles west of Crete, the convoy being bound from the Aegean Sea to Benghazi, in North Africa. Two German transports in the convoy, "Maritza" and "Procida" were sunk by "Penelope" and "Lively", despite the presence of two Italian torpedo boats.

On December 19th 1941, while on their way to intercept an Italian convoy bound for Tripoli, Force "K" ran into a newly laid Italian minefield. A light cruiser and a destroyer sank, whilst another light cruiser was badly damaged, but the destroyer HMS "Lively", with James Firn on board, escaped damage.

However, she was not so fortunate on May 11th 1942. At 20-00 hours on May 10th four destroyers of the 14th Flotilla (Jervis, Lively, Jackal and Kipling) sailed from Alexandria, Egypt, to intercept an Axis convoy en route from Taranto, Italy, to Tripoli. It was hoped to intercept the convoy off Benghazi on May 12th, providing the destroyers could escape detection.

However, they were sighted by an Axis aircraft, although the ships' radar failed to spot the aircraft. At 1553 hours on May 11th the monitoring service at Alexandria warned the force that air attacks could be expected. Reluctantly, Captain Poland on board HMS "Jervis", gave the order to turn back. From 1600 hours onwards fierce air attacks were made on the ships.

Three or four bombs scored direct hits on or about Lively's waterline abreast "A" mounting. She listed to starboard as a second salvo of bombs fell alongside. A few seconds later she was on her beam ends. At 1645 hours there was an explosion forward and HMS "Lively" sank immediately. Her survivors were rescued by HMS "Jervis" and "Jackal".

Although James' body was recovered he was dead. His body was brought to the nearest landfall and he was buried in grave XX.A.13. Alamein War Cemetery.

SERGEANT FRANK SQUIRES No. 1108725
(WIRELESS OPERATOR/AIR GUNNER)
149 SQUADRON ROYAL AIR FORCE VOLUNTEER RESERVE
DIED JUNE 30TH 1942 AGED 22

Frank was born at Bakewell on July 22nd 1919, the third son of Frank and Ada Squires (there were six sons and six daughters). His parents had both been born at Worksop and when they married they lived with Frank senior's brother and wife at Ripley, at their green grocer and fishmongers' business.

At some point the family moved to Over Haddon and then to a house at Lumford, on Buxton Road, Bakewell., where Frank senior was one of the managers of the DP Battery Works.

After leaving school Frank Squires junior was employed by the firm of M. Broomhead and Sons, plumbers, of Rutland Street. He enlisted in the services, joining the RAF in July 1940. By 1941 he had qualified as a wireless operator/air gunner with the rank of sergeant and was operating on Stirling bombers with

Frank Squires of Bakewell.
Sandra Holland

149 Squadron, Bomber Command, from RAF Lakenheath, in Suffolk. Meanwhile, Frank had become engaged to Jessie, a local girl from the Bakewell district and would have married if it had not been for the death of Frank in 1942.

Frank was home on leave in mid June 1942, just a few days before his death, and during his stay he visited his old school, the Church of England Senior School and gave a talk to the pupils there. He had been presented to the King and Queen, together with others who had taken part in the first 1000 bomber raid on Germany, when the royals had paid a visit to the aerodrome at which he was stationed.

He had been on numerous raids over Germany and was in one of the first planes to attack Cologne in the 1000 bomber raid. He described how the Germans had lit decoy fires away from the city. They got through the flak without harm, but in the following 1000 bomber raid on Essen, their plane had been damaged, but managed to get home.

On June 24th 1942 he had arrived back at Lakenheath from his leave and wrote to his parents:

"Well, I've landed down here OK. I had a little trouble round these Suffolk country lanes, my chief trouble being the number of railwaymen I had to knock up in the middle of the night to open their many gates. Five of them, and I landed here at 25 past 3 in the morning, a little tired, but I enjoyed it.

"The ground crew have had my car engine to bits and she is running lovely now and Tony and I are going to Norwich this evening as we have a stand down. We had an easy but boring trip last night. I'm sorry to say that good old "B-Bill" is now a mass of wreckage as we had to crash land her owing to slight engine and under carriage trouble.

"Will you ask McEwan to hurry up with my cover note for the car insurance."

Cheerio, your loving son,
Frank.

Frank Squires.
Sandra Holland

Frank Squires and his fiancé Jessie.
Sandra Holland

Ada Squires, mother of Frank, at Volendam, Holland, during her visit to see Frank's grave, just after the end of World War Two.
Sandra Holland

Sadly, a few days later, flying a fresh aircraft, he and the crew were reported missing on the 29th/30th June. Stirling bomber BF310 OJ-H took off at 0025 hours on 30th June from Lakenheath on a mission against the German port of Bremen. It was shot down by a night fighter and crashed into the Ijsselmeer (the large fresh water lake in Holland), south of Hoorn. Unusually, the pilot in charge was an American from North Carolina, who had joined the Royal Canadian Air Force in order to enter the war. All the crewmen perished and Frank Squires was buried in grave 69.E.3. of Amsterdam New Eastern Cemetery.

Frank had been one of three brothers serving in the forces, with Ronald in the RAF Military Police and Harold in the Army. After the war, Jessie moved away and married, becoming Mrs. Poole and having a son, but she always carried with her a tremendously strong feeling for her first love, Frank Squires.

SERGEANT ROBERT STEWART CRICHTON PLOWRIGHT NO. 622703 (AIR-GUNNER) SQUADRON 21 OPERATIONAL TRAINING UNIT RAF DIED SEPTEMBER 14TH 1942 AGED 34

Robert was the son of James Stewart Crichton Plowright and Elizabeth Plowright. Robert's father was a partner in the firm of Plowright Brothers Ltd., engineers, iron and brass founders of Brampton, Chesterfield. The firm made mining machinery, coal screens, storage bunkers, coal hoppers and haulage gear for the coal mines at their Brampton Iron Works on Shepley Street. Robert's mother, Elizabeth Gaunt, came from a coal merchant's family in Chesterfield. The Plowright family lived on the outskirts of Chesterfield, between Brampton and Holymoorside.

The Plowrights arrived in Great Longstone in 1938, when they came to live at Longstone Hall. Robert's brother, Owen, eventually went into business as a potter in the Chesterfield area. Their father took a keen interest in Great Longstone people and the community and later became President of Bakewell Show in the year 1950.

When the war began, Robert was already married. He enlisted and joined the RAF, eventually serving as an airgunner. In September 1942 Robert was flying with 21 Operational Training Unit based at RAF Edgehill, Oxfordshire. At 2340 hours on September 14th 1942 Wellington bomber HE116, piloted by a Canadian, took off on a raid against the German port of Bremen. It was presumed lost somewhere over the North Sea.

Two weeks later, three of the crewmen's bodies, including that of Robert Plowright, were washed up on a beach on the small island of Schiermonnikoog, the most northerly of the Frisian Islands, eleven kilometres north of the Dutch mainland.

Robert Plowright is buried in grave 87 Schiermonnikoog (Vredenhof) Cemetery, the date of his internment being September 30th 1942.

Noel Green, a 17 year old member of Longstone Home Guard Platoon at the time of Robert's death, remembers the day that the parents received the telegram reporting his death. James Plowright was the leader of the Home Guard Platoon and it was meeting for exercise in the yard of the Hall on the Sunday morning when the sad message arrived.

SERGEANT ROBERT HARRIS NO. 1195323
RAFVR 73 SQUADRON
DIED OCTOBER 22ND 1942 AGED 20

Robert Harris was the son of Major (retired) Thomas Avaran Harris and Harriet Bessie Harris. Around 1920, Major Harris, a regular army man, who had fought in the Great War, brought his family to live at "Parkfield", a house on Ashford Lane, on the way towards Monsal Head.

The Major was a keen and noted archaeologist in the area. Amongst other sites that he explored was the Roman remains in Dimonsdale, just outside Ashford, on the way towards Taddington. Many of his finds from there and from other Stone Age sites, are to be seen in one of the Sheffield museums.

When Robert enlisted, he joined the RAF and trained as a pilot. By the middle of 1942 he was serving with 73 Squadron, a fighter squadron operating Hurricanes from their base, landing ground 85, thirty miles SW of Alexandria, Egypt.

73 Squadron was part of the Desert Air Force (DAS) and the year 1942 was a crisis year in the Mediterranean and the Western Desert. German and Italian forces under Rommel were at the gates of Egypt and except for Malta, the Mediterranean Sea was virtually under German control. And yet, by August 1942, the Desert Air Force had achieved a degree of superiority it never relinquished. The DAF had become a greatly expanded force with American built Tomahawks, Kitty Hawks and Maryland bombers added to the Hurricanes and Wellingtons. An ever increasing force was now concentrated against enemy storage and supply dumps and enemy shipping.

Throughout October 1942 General Montgomery made preparations for the Battle of El Alamein and 73 Squadron, its Hurricanes armed with "tank busting" cannons, became increasingly involved in attacks on supply depots and preventing aerial reconnaissance by the Luftwaffe. On October 22nd, just one day before the launch of

*The type of fighter plane flown by Robert Harris of Ashford
in the Western Desert and over the Mediterranean.*

the Battle of Alamein, Robert Harris took off from Landing Ground 85 in Hurricane BP167 on another mission, from which he never returned. His body was never recovered and he is commemorated on Column 261 Alamein Memorial.

The following day, the Battle commenced, and with it the end of Rommel's dream of entering Cairo and securing Egypt.

TELEGRAPHIST GEOFFREY GILBERT NO. C/SSX32419
DUTCH SHIP "ISAAC SWEERS" ROYAL NAVY
DIED NOVEMBER 13TH 1942 AGED 22

Geoff Gilbert was the eldest of ten children of Charles Henry and Alice Gilbert. Charles was born at Pineapple Cottage, near Newholme, Bakewell and married Alice Goodwin, a Bakewell girl. They set up home on Buxton Road.

Around 1933 the Gilbert family moved to Baslow, where they lived at Alma House (a converted pub), a large dwelling on School Lane, which could accommodate a big family.

Charles Gilbert was working on the Chatsworth Estate as a woodsman (later he would work for Glebe Mines at Eyam) and when Geoff left Baslow School, he joined his father as a woodsman.

Geoff Gilbert was called up early in the war and joined the Royal Navy, in which he trained as a radio telegraphist. In June 1941 he joined the crew of a former Dutch destroyer, the "Isaac Sweers", at Southampton, the ship leaving for trials at Greenock, before entering Scapa Flow in the Orkneys, where her crew got their training throughout July.

Geoffrey Gilbert of Bakewell.
LEFT TO RIGHT: *Lily Fern (aunty), Geoffrey Gilbert, Mary Gilbert (wife).*
Peter Gilbert

As part of the 19th Destroyer Flotilla, the "Isaac Sweers" was involved in escorting troopships in convoy, southwards, usually to a position near Spain, throughout August and September 1941.

On September 17th she left for Gibraltar as part of Force "H", to help escort merchant ships through the Mediterranean Sea to Malta. The destroyer had a narrow miss by a torpedo dropped from one of twelve torpedo planes which attacked the convoy. The "Sweers" had two men wounded by shell fragments, one

Geoffrey Gilbert was telegraphist on the destroyer Isaac Sweers.
The ship is shown entering Valetta Harbour, Malta.

being Geoff Gilbert.

Throughout October and November 1941 the "Sweers" was part of a Freetown convoy, before returning to escort Malta convoys once again, including one to transport 37 Hurricane fighters to the besieged island. It was during this period that the aircraft carrier "Ark Royal" was sunk by a torpedo, close to Gibraltar. During December 1941 and January 1942 other major actions were fought with Italian naval units and aircraft, and convoys were escorted to Malta.

On January 23rd 1942 the "Isaac Sweers" left for the Netherlands East Indies where the Japanese were gaining successes. The destroyer received minor repairs at Colombo, before being attached to the British Eastern Fleet. After the Japanese fleet attacked Trincomalee, Ceylon (Sri Lanka) on April 9th 1942, sinking the carrier "Hermes", the fleet left for Bombay, the Seychelles and finally Mombassa, Africa. It was here that the "Isaac Sweers" left for England and an overhaul in Southampton through June to September.

It was during this period of shore leave that Geoff was married to his fiance, Mary Woodward, from Carr Vale, near Bolsover, Chesterfield. Shortly after the marriage, Geoff returned to his ship and this was the last occasion that his new bride and his family saw him.

In October 1942 the "Isaac Sweers" left for Gibraltar as part of the escort of HMS "Furious" and then made a rendezvous with the troop convoy KMF-1, bound for the beaches of Algeria, and the landing of American, British and French forces in the invasion known as "Operation Torch".

By November 1942 the destroyer was part of Force"H" at Gibraltar, during these invasion days. On November 12th, she was at sea to rendezvous with Force "H", the plan being to refuel underway from Force "R" (two oilers with four escorting armed trawlers), and by midnight, in the night of 12th/13th she was ready for action, to the north of Algiers.

At about 0500 hours on November 13th, two torpedoes hit the starboard side of the "Isaac Sweers", and they put the whole ship ablaze from bow to stern. The first torpedo hit a fuel tank and burning oil spread over the water, the second hitting the longroom and officers' quarters. All 13 officers were asleep at the time and all perished.

The ship had escaped many attacks from aircraft and submarines in the past, but she could not survive the damage now sustained. The "Isaac Sweers" sank due to a U-boat attack by Kapitan-Leutnant Wilhelm Dommes on U-431. Only 86 men survived from a crew of 194. The trawler Loch Oskaig tried to come alongside the burning destroyer, but had to abandon her plans due to the heavy fires and exploding ammunition.

One of those who was killed was Geoffrey Gilbert. His body was not recovered and his name is commemorated on the Chatham War Memorial and on the Bakewell War Memorial (Geoff's name is also read out on Remembrance Day at Baslow).

LEADING STOKER JOHN GEORGE BRUCE NO. C/KK97353
HMS "FIREDRAKE" ROYAL NAVY
DIED DECEMBER 17TH 1942

We believe that John George Bruce may have lived on Monyash Road, Bakewell, but any other information on his background has not been forthcoming. It is also possible that he was in the navy before the start of the Second World War. Whether this is the case or not, we do know that by late 1942, John was a leading stoker serving on board HMS "Firedrake", a F Class destroyer.

On the night of December 16th 1942, HMS "Firedrake" was the escort leader to Convoy ON153, with 43 ships bound for Canada.

They sailed in a force 12 storm, the worst the Atlantic had seen for a long time. At

John George Bruce was on board the destroyer HMS Firedrake.

about 1700 hours, when just outside the range of aircraft based in Iceland, the ASDIC operator picked up a contact. HMS "Firedrake" tracked the contact to about five miles south of the convoy, when, at 2010 hours she was hit by a torpedo fired by U-boat

U-211, commanded by Kapitan Leutnant Karl Hause. The ship broke in two, the bow section sinking immediately, with the stern just managing to stay afloat.

Lieutenant Dampier had a tally up and found there were 35 still on board. He quickly got the men to work shoring up the bulkheads of No. 3 boiler room, and making safe and jettisoning the depth charges and torpedoes. The gun crew were ordered to fire star shells to attract the attention of the other escorts, because all the radio and signalling equipment had gone with the bow part of the ship.

At 2200 hours, HMS "Sunflower", a corvette, made towards them, firing star shells herself. The skipper first thought that the stern section of "Firedrake" was a U-boat and was about to fire at it, but then realised his mistake.

The weather was so bad and the sea too rough to get alongside. The skipper decided to stand by and hope the weather would get better. At about 0040 hours on December 17th the weather worsened and the bulkheads started to give way. The stern of "Firedrake" started to sink, so the men had no option but to take to the water, and at 0045 hours the stern sank.

The "Sunflower" moved in quickly to pick up the men in the water. Twenty seven men were lifted on board, although one died later. 168 crewmen from HMS "Firedrake" perished that night, including John George Bruce.

His body was never recovered from the Atlantic and his name is commemorated on the Chatham Naval Memorial, as well as on Bakewell War Memorial.

THE YEAR 1943

For British servicemen in 1943, the main theatre of operations was North Africa (especially Tunisia), Italy and the Mediterranean Sea, where four of the seven Bakewell and district men to be killed during 1943, perished. In Northern Europe, the sole means of striking at the enemy had to come from the air and one airman with Bakewell connections was killed over Germany. Meanwhile, the surrender of Singapore on February 15th 1942, Britain's main fortress in the Far East, had resulted in the capture of thousands of prisoners by the Japanese forces. Two prisoners of war from this district, one a native of Bakewell and the other from Over Haddon, died as a result of the inhumane treatment provided by their Japanese captors and perished during 1943.

The first fatal casualty of the year was a member of Bomber Command, who, in the 1930's had been a boarder at Lady Manners Grammar School.

SERGEANT (AIRGUNNER) ARTHUR SANDERSON BLAGDEN
No. 944213 12 SQUADRON ROYAL AIR FORCE VOLUNTEER RESERVE
DIED JANUARY 23RD 1943 AGED 22

Arthur was born in 1920 at Dore, near Sheffield, the son of Arthur and Mary Hannah Blagden. The family lived at "Sherwood", Cavendish Avenue and Arthur Blagden senior was the Managing Director of John Fowler (Don Foundry)

Ltd., situated in the Attercliffe Bridge area of Sheffield, its industrial heart. They produced ingot moulds of all designs and special alloys of strong quality. We also believe that Arthur Blagden and his wife had strong connections to the Indian sub-continent and had spent time there. Arthur Blagden junior was sent as a boarder to Lady Manners School, Bakewell, in 1931, at the age of 12 years.

In 1931, the school was on Bath Street, with other buildings in the town used as extra premises because of the rise in the number of pupils. Boarders stayed at School House, which was housed in the old Vicarage. Arthur Blagden became a member of IIb. During the 1930's, Mr. and Mrs. Harvey were in charge of the boarders. A poem by the 12 year old was included in "The Peacock", the school magazine, in 1931:

Arthur Sanderson Blagden shown as a 16 year old boarder at Lady Manners School, Bakewell, in 1936.

The Wayside Inn

I halted at a pleasant Inn
As I my way was wending;
A golden apple was the sign
From Knotty bough depending.

Mine host – it was an apple tree –
He smilingly received me,
And spread his choicest, sweetest fruit
To strengthen and relieve me.

Full many a little feathered guest
Came through his branches springing,
They hopped and flew from spray to spray
Their notes of gladness singing.

Beneath his shade I laid me down
And slumber sweet possessed me;
The soft wind blowing through the leaves
With whispers low caressed me.

In the School House, at the Vicarage, on the evening of December 6th 1934, the boarders put on an entertainment. Arthur Blagden and Leonard Arthur were the leading lights in the School Scout Troop production of Dickens' "Christmas Carol".

Arthur was interested in sport and proved to be a fine rugby player for the school

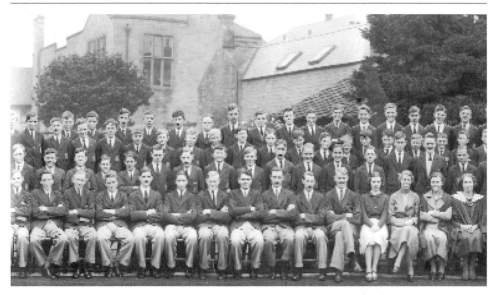

A section of the school photograph showing Lady Manners pupils in Bath Gardens, July 1936. The school was in Bath Street, Bakewell, but already the foundation stone had been laid for the new school on Shutts Lane, earlier in 1936. The new school would be opened in 1938.

Bill Sudbury

The School House group of boarders from Lady Manners School, Bakewell, 1934, at the School House (in the old Vicarage). Seated in the centre of the front row is Mr. R.A. Harvey, the schoolmaster in charge. Arthur Sanderson Blagden is standing second from the left, second row from the back.

Lady Manners School

team. By the 1932/1933 season he was playing in the Colts team. In the 1936 season he was also playing for the cricket team and the magazine mentions that his batting style was good generally, but he must correct his tendency to play a "cross-bat". His highest score that season was 17, against Chesterfield Grammar School, at home.

At rugby he gained his colours in the 1936/1937 season and during 1937/1938 he became the vice-captain, playing at fly-half. The magazine records that he had been the mainstay of the backs, was a real opportunist with a fine, natural swerve, although too often he allowed himself to be tackled. He scored 4 tries for the team that season, Lady Manners winning seven of the ten matches played.

It was on May 20th 1936 that the laying of the foundation stone of the new Lady Manners School on Shutts Lane was undertaken by the Duke of Rutland, appropriately on the tercentenary of the foundation of Lady Manners School by his ancestor, Grace, Lady Manners.

The opening ceremony of Lady Manners School was held on February 24th 1938, with the Marchioness of Hartington the chief guest, although the school was in occupation by staff and pupils since the beginning of term in January.

During the year 1937/1938, Arthur Blagden was Head Boy at the School House. During Saturday evenings, friends of the school sometimes came to entertain the boarders. Miss Boulsover brought her episcope and a bundle of post card views to recount her latest holiday abroad. Mr. Snow, also a faithful visitor with his portable gramophone, came to give musical talks, whilst Arthur's father, Arthur Blagden senior, delighted everyone with his lectures on life in India, where he had spent some years.

The new Lady Manners School nears completion in 1937. The foundation stone was laid by the Duke of Rutland on May 20th 1936.
Peter Thornhill

The opening ceremony of Lady Manners School took place on February 24th 1938,
with the chief guest being the Marchioness of Hartington.
LEFT TO RIGHT: *Marchioness of Hartington, X, Headmaster Mr. Filsell.*
Peter Thornhill

Lady Manners School playing fields.
Sally Hudson

As Arthur left Lady Manners in 1938 he offered his services in the Royal Air Force Volunteer Reserve, as war approached. After acceptance, some time later, he became an air-gunner, and was posted to RAF Wickenby, between Lincoln and Market Rasen. Lancaster bomber ED386, with Arthur Blagden on board, took off at 1725 hours from Wickenby, on January 23rd, 1943, its target being Dusseldorf. At Wickenby, they had just completed the conversion programme to the Lancaster.

Arthur's plane crashed, due to enemy action, near Grevenbroich, between Cologne and Monchengladbach, Germany. A funeral service was held for the airmen at the Stadtfriedhof in Monchengladbach on January 27th, but since the end of the war their remains have been taken to Rheinberg War Cemetery, where Arthur Blagden is buried in grave 2.C.12.

Three months after Arthur's death, another Bakewell man was killed in action, fighting in the latter stages of the conflict in Tunisia, North Africa, against German and Italian forces.

Lance Sergeant Norman Shimwell No. 6981648
"C" Company Royal Iinniskilling Fusiliers
Died April 27th 1943 aged 27

Norman's father, Joseph Shimwell, was born at Youlgreave, whilst his mother, Lydia Twyford, came from nearby Alport. They lived first at Prospect Terrace on Stanedge Road, Bakewell, and it was here that Norman, his brother Stanley and sister Elsie were born.

Their father worked first as a driver for Baileys Corn Merchants from their mill on Buxton Road, delivering corn to outlying farms. He was then employed at R. Orme and Company, grocers, in the area dealing with the supply of corn. Finally, by the time war broke out he was working at the DP Battery Works. By this time the Shimwell family was living at Undercliffe, on Buxton Road.

When Norman left school he began working at R. Orme and Company, in the warehouse, whilst brother Stan was employed in Orme's bottling store on Water Street. Much of Norman's leisure time was spent at the British Legion Club, where he took an interest in the billiards team (it is interesting to note that Nigel Bond, the world class Bakewell born snooker player is closely related to Norman).

Both Norman and Stan were called up fairly early in the war. Stan became a sergeant in 339 Heavy Anti-

Norman Shimwell of Bakewell.
Graham Bond

Aircraft Battery, Royal Artillery, and served in Northern Ireland, Dover and the Orkneys. They were frequently machine-gunned by the German aircraft as they passed over the Cliffs of Dover. Norman, meanwhile, joined the infantry, becoming a member of "C" Company, Royal Inniskilling Fusiliers and did part of his training in Northern Ireland.

Norman Shimwell (centre) with two colleagues.
Graham Bond

In early November 1942, Montgomery's Eighth Army had defeated Rommel's Afrika Korps at Alamein and pursued them westwards across Libya and into Tunisia. On November 8th 1942, Operation "Torch" saw a combined American/British/French force land in Algeria and push eastwards towards Tunisia. The plan was to squeeze the Afrika Korps between the two armies in Tunisia and force its surrender.

It was to be in Tunisia that Norman Shimwell died. In October 1942 he was back in Bakewell on embarkation leave, but on November 22nd his Battalion, as part of the First Army, had landed in Algeria and was pushing eastwards. At this stage he was a Lance Corporal, but was promoted to Corporal on January 18th 1943 and to Lance Sergeant by April 6th, just three weeks before his death.

Between April 22nd and May 3rd the final offensive began in North Africa. General Alexander planned a power thrust by the First Army, with the Eighth Army on the right and the Americans on the left. The Germans had been reinforced but the Allies had air superiority. The First and Eighth Armies inched forward against determined resistance, and it was in the severe fighting against German positions on Tangoucha Hill on April 27th that Norman Shimwell died.

His friend, Lance Corporal Bird of "C" Company wrote to Norman's parents, a week after his death, telling them what he believed to have happened to Norman. It appears that Norman and fellow members of "C" Company were shelled by the Germans on a ridge and Norman was rendered unconscious, lying in a pool of blood. Two colleagues were going to do their best to bring him back, but the Germans came in at the back of them and those left behind were taken prisoner, including the two fellows who were with Norman.

His body was never recovered from the battlefield, with his parents receiving the news that he was presumed missing. It was only on June 1st 1944 that they received news from the War Office that Norman was officially presumed to have died of wounds. Later, Norman Shimwell's name was commemorated on Face 19 of the Medjez-el-Bab Memorial in Tunisia.

A year later, on April 27th 1944, his brother Stanley wrote the following letter to his parents, Joseph and Lydia, from Dover, where he was stationed:

"Well, I received the wire this morning and I've no need to say how sorry I am, but look mother, try and not take it too hard, always remember it was for his country and he was so proud of his country, so try and think that you are not the only one and be proud of him, because if it wasn't for him and thousands like him, things would be really terrible, so please try and remember that Mother."

The late summer of 1943 witnessed the death of an Over Haddon man and one from Bakewell, both resulting from the inhumane treatment they received from Japanese forces after their capture at the fall of Singapore.

Bombadier Leo Kay No. 398459
3 Heavy Anti-Aircraft Regiment Royal Artillery
died August 20ᵀᴴ 1943 aged 34

Leo Kay was born at Over Haddon, near Bakewell, around 1910, a son of William Kay, who worked as a tailor for Quail and Mellor, the outfitters in Bakewell Square, next to the Red Lion Inn. William's first wife died, leaving a family consisting of siblings Laurie, Leo and Marjorie. William married a second time and children Michael and Philip were born. Eventually the family lived in the old Schoolmaster's house on Wellgate Lane, Over Haddon.

Laurie Kay became a regular army man before the start of the Second World War and was serving in the Military Police in Palestine when war began. His brother, Leo, a large, ginger-haired lad, worked on a number of local farms after leaving school. As war began he joined the Royal Artillery, like his Bakewell compatriot,

Leo Kay's father, William Kay, of Over Haddon, worked at Quail and Mellor of Bakewell, drapers and outfitters.

D. Lane

Lieutenant-General Arthur Percival, General Officer Commanding Malaya (on the extreme right)
marches out with the British flag-of-truce party to surrender Singapore,
accompanied by Japanese officers, on February 15th 1942.

Harry Heathcote, but served in a Heavy Anti-Aircraft Regiment.

The Regiment was stationed at Singapore by December 1941 and, as we shall see with Harry Heathcote, was involved in the desperate defence of Singapore in early February 1942. Like Harry, he was taken prisoner by the Japanese when Singapore surrendered on February 15th 1942.

It was reported to his father William that he had been officially reported missing at Singapore on March 23rd 1942. It was three years later that William received news from the War Office in April 1945 that information had been received from a member of his unit that Leo was wounded during an air attack in February 1942. He was evacuated to the Regimental Aid Post and appeared to be progressing favourably when last seen by the informant. News about Leo then comes to an end. It would appear that after his recovery he eventually began work for the Japanese.

Due to the harsh punishment, heavy work schedule, poor food and lack of adequate sanitation, Leo Kay became seriously ill and succumbed to beri-beri (a vitamin deficiency disease) on August 20th 1943. There is no official grave for Leo Kay. Instead, his name is commemorated on Column 8 Singapore Memorial, together with 24,000 other men.

GUNNER HARRY HEATHCOTE NO. 815143
5 FIELD REGIMENT ROYAL ARTILLERY
DIED SEPTEMBER 5TH 1943 AGED 31

Harry was born in 1912, the second and youngest son of Samuel (Sam) and Martha Heathcote of New Street, Bakewell. His elder brother was James Walter Heathcote, better known as Walter. There had been other children in the family but these had died at an early age. Sam Heathcote, the boys' father, was employed in the building trade in Bakewell.

Both children passed the exam to attend Lady Manners School but the family could not afford to send them and they completed their education at Bath Street School.

When war came in 1939 Harry enlisted and joined the Royal Artillery, becoming a member of 5 Field Regiment. There is a possibility that he was a regular army man before the war. We know for certain that by December 1941 the Regiment was based in the Far East, at Singapore, the main military outpost in that part of Empire. The base would play a crucial role in the likely event of entry by the Japanese in the world conflict. Events moved quickly after the Japanese attack on Pearl Harbour on December 7th 1941.

Harry Heathcote of Bakewell with his mother Martha.

Joe Hoskins

Singapore was a protected naval base from which a powerful fleet could operate and was defended against attack from the sea by fixed coastal defences. Unfortunately, these guns could not be turned to combat a Japanese attack on the city from the Malayan Peninsula. When Japan launched its invasion of Malaya on December 8th 1941, a British naval force, consisting of the battleship "Prince of Wales" and battle cruiser "Repulse" plus four destroyers, left that evening to intercept Japanese transports. With no fighter escort cover, both capital ships were sunk the next day.

By the end of January 1942 British forces had been pressed back to the southern tip of the Malayan Peninsula and onto Singapore Island. A Japanese landing was

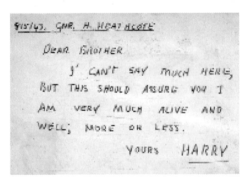

Harry Heathcote's note home to his brother Walter in Bakewell, from the Japanese POW camp he was incarcerated in, 1942-1943, in Burma.

Joe Hoskins

Envelope in which the short note was posted from Burma to Harry's Brother, Walter.

Joe Hoskins

effected in early February and on the 15th the British Commander surrendered after the Japanese captured the main water supplies for the island.

The Malayan campaign cost the Japanese 3507 dead and 6150 wounded. The Allies lost 9000 dead and 130,000 as prisoners of war, one POW being Harry Heathcote. The captured Allied forces were treated with appalling cruelty and inhumanity by their captors, who regarded them as unworthy of honourable treatment because they had chosen surrender rather than death.

Harry Heathcote was amongst the POW's who were set to work on constructing the dreaded Burma Railway that linked Burma with the Siamese rail network.

In October 1942 the Japanese conquerors of Burma decided to reconstruct the line for military

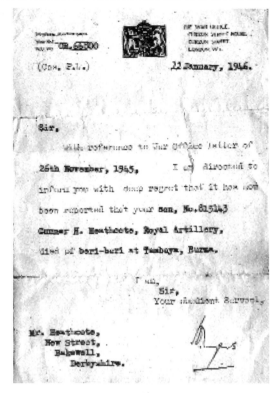

Official notification of Harry Heathcote's death.
Joe Hoskins

reasons, using labour of mainly Dutch and British POW's and conscript Asian labourers. They worked in appalling conditions, were treated with great brutality and lacked adequate food and medical attention. The railway, over 280 miles long, was completed in November 1943 at the cost of over 63,000 lives (13,000 Allied

The temporary cross marking Harry Heathcote's grave at Thanbyuzayat Military Cemetery, Burma.
Joe Hoskins

prisoners and 50,000 Asians) out of a labour force of 150,000. One of those workers who suffered dreadfully and eventually died, was Harry Heathcote, joining his colleague from Over Haddon, Leo Kay, who had also worked on the construction of the railway.

During his captivity, Harry managed to write a short note to his brother Walter, who was serving in Bakewell Home Guard. He assured his family that he was alive and well, "more or less". The last three words covered over the terrible ordeal he and others were going through.

Although Harry died on September 5th 1943, his family was unsure about his fate until after the end of the war. It was not until January 22nd 1946 that Sam

Heathcote received official notification from the War Office that his son had died of beri-beri at Tambaya, Burma, in 1943.

Harry Heathcote's body was eventually brought to be buried in grave B1.D.12. Thanbyuzayat Military Cemetery, 37 miles SSE of Moulmein, Burma. Harry's mother, Martha, had died some time before her son's death, being spared the sad news of what had happened to him.

Action now switched to the Eastern Mediterranean, where a naval officer with connections to the Storrs-Fox family at St. Anselms Private School, Bakewell, was lost with his ship.

COMMANDER STUART AUSTEN BUSS (MVO AND DSC)
HMS "DULVERTON" ROYAL NAVY
DIED NOVEMBER 13TH 1943 AGED 43

In 1900, one year old Stuart, the second son of George Buss (35 years) and Clare Evelyn Buss (22 years), was living with his parents and elder brother Ronald (2 years) at the Manor House, Littlebourne, six miles east of Canterbury, Kent. George Buss came from Kent farming stock, but as a young man had worked in the London Stock Exchange for a short while, before buying Manor Farm, Littlebourne, in about 1890. The family was completed when a third son, Humphrey, was born in 1903.

The eldest son, Ronald, enlisted in the Army towards the end of the Great War, serving with the 2nd Battalion, 10th Ghurka Rifles. He remained in the Army after the war ended, served in Iraq in 1924 and then was killed in a road accident near Quetta in 1926 (in present day Pakistan).

Commander Stuart Austen Buss, Royal Navy. He is standing on the bridge of his destroyer HMS Punjabi, 1941-1942, whilst the ship was on escort convoy duty, taking supplies to Russia on the Arctic convoy route.
John Buss

Stuart was educated at Haileybury College, leaving school to join the Royal Navy in July 1918. He was a midshipman on HMS "Royal Sovereign" in 1919-1921 in the Mediterranean Fleet and by 1929 he had risen to the rank of Lieutenant.

At the wedding of a mutual friend, he met Sylvia Storrs-Fox, the daughter of William and Mary Storrs Fox. Her father was the retired headmaster and founder of St. Anselm's School, Bakewell, and when she met Stuart, she was working as a teacher in Scarborough.

Commander Stuart Austen Buss was in charge of the destroyer HMS Dulverton.

On March 2nd 1929, Stuart, aged 28, and 25 year old Sylvia were married at Bakewell Parish Church. Stuart Buss continued his naval career, commanding HMS "Vimiera" in Hong Kong and China in 1932-1934. In March 1933 their daughter, Joy Austen Buss, was born at Hillside, Bakewell, with Stuart now a Lieutenant Commander.

By 1935 he was in command of HMS "Tiverton", which had the honour of being the guard ship of the Royal Yacht "Britannia" at Cowes in 1935. This was the last time that George V was at Cowes, before his death in 1936 and Stuart Buss was awarded the MVO (Member of the Victorian Order) for his service to the King at Cowes (the MVO is a direct gift of the Sovereign).

Between 1937-1938 Stuart served at Chatham. On October 2nd 1936 a second child, John Austen Buss, was born at Littlebourne, near Canterbury, where the family was now living.

After Dunkirk, the danger in Kent from possible German bombing meant that Sylvia Storrs Buss moved with the children, first to Yelverton, Devon, and then to Darley Dale, in Derbyshire in 1941, before moving to Bakewell in 1942.

Meanwhile, Commander Stuart Buss served on HMS "Electra" and HMS "Foxhound", seeing service in Norway, on Russian convoy operations as escort and in the Mediterranean Sea.

By mid 1943, Stuart was in command of HMS "Dulverton", a Royal Navy Escort destroyer, in the Eastern Mediterranean. In September 1943, with Italy having capitulated, the British decided to take over the islands of the Dodecanese group in the Aegean Sea, off the coast of Turkey. The occupation of the islands of Kos, Leros and Samos was carried out between September 15th and 18th, taking over from the Italians. The island of Rhodes, however, with its airfield, had been taken over by a German garrison on September 11th.

The Germans reacted to the British action with a vigour that came as a complete surprise and by October 3rd, German landing craft from the sea and paratroopers from the air, stormed the defences of Kos and overwhelmed the British and Italian garrison.

By November 1943, the Germans were planning the capture of the neighbouring island of Leros by sea and air. It was during the attempt by British naval forces to resist this effort that Stuart Buss lost his life.

Throughout 1942 and 1943, HMS "Dulverton" had been involved in actions in the Mediterranean Sea. Her battle honours for 1942 included naval actions off the coast of Libya and in the Gulf of Sirte, protecting the Malta convoys and helping to sink the German U-boat U-559 by depth charge NE of Port Said on October 30th 1942. She had used her guns off -shore in the landings on Sicily and at Salerno in 1943 and was now attempting to come to the assistance of the hard-pressed garrison on Leros Island, invaded by the Germans on November 13th. Commander Buss on the "Dulverton" was in command of the 5th Destroyer Flotilla and on November 13th the cruiser "Phoebe" and destroyers "Dulverton", "Belvoir" and "Echo" were sent into the Aegean north of Rhodes to look for landing forces.

At 0130 hours HMS "Dulverton" was sailing off the neighbouring island of Kos when it was struck by a remote-controlled glider bomb from a Dornier 217 aircraft and sank two hours later. The bomb struck the ship abreast the bridge, inflicting serious damage and starting extensive fires.

The destroyer sustained heavy casualties, but sister ships took off six officers and 114 ratings before she was scuttled two hours later by HMS "Belvoir". Three officers, including Commander Stuart Austen Buss of the 5th Destroyer Flotilla, and 75 ratings were lost with HMS "Dulverton". Stuart Buss' body was not recovered and his name is commemorated on Panel 78 Column 1 Plymouth Naval Memorial and on the Bakewell War Memorial. He was awarded a posthumous DSC for his action.

After his death, the family lived with an aunt and uncle in Baslow for a few months before returning to Bakewell. Stuart Buss' son, John, trained as a doctor, and for some years practised in Bakewell, before returning to Canterbury, Kent.

The last two local casualties for 1943 both fell in action in Italy in the last few months of that year, as Allied forces attacked the German Winter Defensive Line (the Gustav Line) in the mountains and ravines just inland from the Adriatic coast of Italy.

TROOPER JAMES RENWICK TIMM NO. 5050917
"A" SQUADRON 50TH ROYAL TANK REGIMENT, ROYAL ARMOURED CORPS
DIED NOVEMBER 30TH 1943 AGED 25

James, or Jim as he was known, was the youngest of the three sons of Joseph William Timm, known as William to family and friends, and Hannah Jane Timm (née Jackson) of Little Longstone. The two elder brothers were Leonard and John. The family lived in a cottage next to Rose Cottage, close to the Pack Horse Inn, their father working on the Midland Railway as a plate layer, on the stretch between Hassop Station and Monsal Head, as well as maintaining a smallholding.

William was the son of John Timm, the Little Longstone carter, and brother of

James Renwick Timm, who we have seen was killed in action during the First World War. When he had left school, William had started work at 14 as a farm boy, before working on the railway. Hannah Jane Jackson came from nearby Cressbrook and had worked at the Cressbrook Cotton Mill before her marriage to William.

Leonard Timm worked the smallholding for his father, William. It consisted of outbuildings and fields behind "Outrake", fields alongside Chertpit Lane and also in the area known as "Up Scratter", adjacent to the road leading from Monsal Head towards Wardlow. Pigs were raised and slaughtered in pig sties behind the family cottage on Main Street, whilst the milking was done in the "Outrake" buildings. Leonard was often helped in this task by children from the "Outrake" Children's Home, during and after the war. His brother, John, worked as a plate layer on the railway, on the same section as his father, during the inter-war years, before working first at Eyam Quarry and then at Glebe Mine after his demob from the Army in 1945/1946.

*James Renwick Timm
of Little Longstone.*
Andrew Lomas

*William Timm, father of James Renwick Timm, is on the left, helping to cart and spread lime
on the fields around Longstone.*
Andrew Lomas

James Renwick Timm, known as Jim, was born in 1918, a year after the death of his uncle, James Renwick Timm, during the Great War, and was named after him. Leaving Longstone School, he began work at Home Farm, Hassop, before working for a local building firm and became the fiancée of Iris Fletcher, a girl from Eyam (after Jim's death, she married Harold Webb from Eyam). Before the war, brothers Jim and John, would cycle over to Eyam on a tandem to court Iris Fletcher and Stella Bramwell, respectively.

Jim Timm enlisted in the army early in the war and is believed to have first served with the Royal Corps of Signals. His brother John enlisted in the Royal Engineers a little later, whilst Leonard remained at Little Longstone, working on the smallholding.

John Timm, brother of James Renwick Timm of Little Longstone.
Andrew Lomas

Eventually, Jim transferred to the Royal Tank Regiment, joining "A" Squadron of the 50th Royal Tank Regiment and serving as a trooper and driver. He went out to North Africa as part of a draft of men to make up the numbers of the 50th RTR, in the later stages of the battle against Rommel's Afrika Korps in Spring of 1943. It was just before his embarkation from Glasgow that his brother John managed to meet him in Scotland and this was the last time anyone from the family saw him.

Trooper Jim Timm was involved in the last actions against the Germans in Tunisia and then began training with newly arrived Sherman tanks for the invasion of Sicily, which began on July 10th 1943.

After Sicily, the 50th Royal Tank Regiment landed at Taranto on the Italian mainland on September 26th as part of the Allied invasion. In support of the 8th Indian Division, they moved northwards up the Adriatic coast, through October and November, as the Germans retreated to their winter defensive position, the Gustav Line, stretching from the River Garigliano in the west to the Sangro River in the east.

In atrocious rainy conditions, a bridgehead had been established across the River Sangro by November 24th and by nightfall of November 30th the whole ridge overlooking the river was in Allied hands. However, the fighting on that day had been desperate and severe and during these actions, James Renwick Timm was seriously wounded and succumbed to these wounds.

The terrain in which they fought was extremely difficult, especially for armoured vehicles, with steep cliffs and ridges on either side. At midday on November 30th, "A" Squadron and Jim Timm advanced with the Indian infantry up the axis road, heading for a key position overlooking the whole Sangro valley. While in close support of the infantry, Four Troop, commanded by 23 year old Lieutenant Kenneth Pillar, was dealing very effectively with mortar and machine-gun positions. Near the top of the ridge, Lieutenant Pillar's tank was hit by a shot from a German tank which was sited 400 yards away. Without pausing, Pillar continued to advance and fight his tank; it was then hit a second time, putting the gun out of action.

As the crew baled out, they were fired upon by tank and infantry machine-guns. One of the crew was wounded in the process and Pillar returned to the wounded man and carried him to a sheltered position, under intense fire. Lieutenant Pillar then realised that his driver, Trooper Timm, was still in the tank, so he returned yet again to the vehicle, which was still under fire from the enemy. As he climbed onto the vehicle, it was hit a third time, throwing him to the ground. He climbed back on and as he raised the driver's hatch he was killed by another shell. For Pillar's actions he was recommended for a posthumous Victoria Cross, but instead was mentioned in despatches (Kenneth Pillar came from Barrow-in Furness and had gained a Bachelor of Arts degree at Canterbury).

William and Hannah Jane Timm, parents of James Renwick Timm of Little Longstone, on the occasion of their 60ᵗʰ wedding anniversary.
Andrew Lomas

The Medical Officer, Captain Brandon Lush, heard a plaintive cry over the radio from Trooper Timm saying that he was alive, though badly wounded. He cried out for help and Captain Lush got together some volunteers from the Friends' Ambulance Unit (a Quaker unit) and set out with a stretcher towards the German lines. They found the destroyed tank with Jim still alive and conscious within it. The body of Kenneth Pillar was lying alongside.

Original grave of James Renwick Timm, in Italy.
Andrew Lomas

Members of the rescue party were all wearing Red Cross armbands and the German infantry watched them from a distance without firing, while they got Jim out with difficulty and took him back to an infantry regimental aid post. Unfortunately, he died on the way back and was eventually buried in grave XIV.E.32., Sangro River War Cemetery.

When Jim was killed, the War Office sent a telegram to his parents but when the postman delivered it to the cottage in Little Longstone, it somehow got caught underneath the carpet and lay hidden. His mother was profoundly deaf and had not heard the postman's knock. It was not until around Christmas time that the family discovered it and realised that their son was dead and not posted as missing.

The news devastated Jim's parents and his mother,

Hannah Jane, never really recovered from receiving the information. In Little Longstone Chapel, two commemorative wooden offertory plates were commissioned by the family and carved by Advent Unstone of Tideswell, whilst Cicily Gilbert of Little Longstone made a communion cloth in Jim's'memory.

One day after Jim Timm's death, an officer with Bakewell connections was killed a short distance away from where James Renwick Timm had fallen.

Major Sidney James Bunch (Military Cross) No. 65744
Lincolnshire Regiment, (6th Battalion Inniskilling Fuseliers)
died on December 1st 1943 aged 33

The name of Major Bunch is to be found on the Bakewell War Memorial but sadly we have been unable to find his connection to the town. We do know that he was the son of Reverend Joseph Arthur Bunch and Lila Bunch of East Twickenham, Middlesex, and husband of Vera Evelyn Bunch, who, in the late 1940's was living at Congleton, Cheshire.

During the Second World War, Major Sidney Bunch had won the Military Cross whilst serving with the Lincolnshire Regiment, but by September 1943 he had been attached to the 6th Battalion Inniskilling Fusiliers, an Irish Regiment.

During that month the Battalion had landed in Italy as part of the Eighth Army and fought its way up the Adriatic coast of Italy, being engaged in heavy fighting at Termoli in October and at San Salvo by November..

The next river to cross was the Sangro at the Adriatic terminus of the German Winter Line and the enemy positions were extremely strongly held. The river was wide; the plain beyond it about 2000 yards across, with its first escarpment rising to 100 feet. Then came a much higher ridge, strongly fortified and, in front of it, mine-fields, wire entanglements and underground entrenchments.

At 6-30a.m. on November 29th, "B" and "D" Companies of the 6th Inniskillings led the way, supported by tanks. The tanks came to a standstill in the minefields and the 6th Battalion came under heavy fire from German posts. Methodically, the Battalion tackled houses and dug-outs one by one and when the tanks were able to join them, they secured their part of the ridge.

During the night of November 30th the 6th Battalion and the County of London Yeomanry did a circuitous night march via Fossacesia and San Maria and fell on the town of St. Vito along the Treglio Ridge at first light on December 1st. The town was taken by the 6th Battalion by 4p.m., together with their armoured support. However, the Germans had made a determined stand in the town and the 6th Battalion was involved in some desperate street fighting before the job was done. Among their casualties was Major Bunch, who was killed whilst leading his men from house to house.

Sidney James Bunch was buried in grave VIII.E.42. Sangro River War Cemetery, the final Bakewell and district casualty for the year 1943.

THE YEAR 1944

At the beginning of 1944 the U-boats still menaced the Atlantic and Arctic sea lanes, whilst the embattled German economy was producing war materials at ever increasing rates, despite the ravages of Allied bombing. The war was far from a decision, especially as the Japanese were fighting tenaciously in the Far East theatre of war.

Despite this, the Axis Powers were now on the defensive. The Eastern Front in Russia was crumbling as Hitler's Russian gamble proved to be lost. Italy's capitulation had taken her forces out of the war, whilst North Africa had been cleared and the sea lanes in the Mediterranean were open. Above all, the burgeoning power of America was now coming to the fore.

The Allies held the priceless advantage of strategic interior lines as they looked across at Europe from their bridgehead in the British Isles. They could, in principle, attack Germany at any point. The invasion of Western Europe, code-named Operation "Overlord", would come in Normandy on June 6th 1944, whilst the difficult assault on the mainland of Italy continued against well-led and motivated German forces.

The ever widening campaigns of 1944 witnessed the largest number of deaths of servicemen from the Bakewell district in any one year of the war. Eight servicemen would pay the supreme sacrifice. Normandy claimed three lives, two would die whilst serving in the RAF, one died in Egypt, another in Italy, whilst the eighth died just over the French border, in Belgium.

LANCE CORPORAL ALFRED KIRKBY N0. 4984446
5TH BATTALION SHERWOOD FORESTERS
DIED JANUARY 11TH 1944 AGED 37

Alfred Kirkby was the only child of Alfred and Louisa Kirkby of Holme Lane, Bakewell. Both he and his father worked as gardeners for the Hoyle family at Holme Hall. A quiet man, who played cricket for a local team, Alfred junior enlisted during the war and joined the 5th Battalion Sherwood Foresters.

There is a problem with the date and whereabouts of Alfred's death. The Commonwealth War Graves Commission report that he died on January 11th 1944 and he is commemorated on the Medjez-el-Bab Memorial in Tunisia, North Africa. The problem is that the fighting in North Africa had ended seven months earlier, in May 1943, and therefore Alfred could not have been killed in action in that area on January 11th 1944. Even on January 11th 1943 the 5th Battalion were not in that area of Tunisia.

We do know, however, that between January 5th and 15th 1944, the 5th Battalion was involved in desperate fighting in the mountains of Italy. Having consulted with the Sherwood Foresters Museum's former curator, it is believed that Alfred Kirkby was with his Battalion in Italy when he was killed and that a mistake has been made with regards to the commemorative inscription on the memorial in North Africa.

Alfred and the Sherwood Foresters had landed on the beaches of Salerno, Italy, on September 10th to 14th 1943, where the fighting was intense and severe, but by September 17th the Germans began a deliberate disengagement, retiring northwards. Between October 12th and November 14th, the Sherwoods were involved in the assault across the Volturno River and the foot by foot progress over abominable trails in mountainous country, north of Naples.

By December 1943 the Germans had established a formidable defensive zone called the Winter Line or "Gustav Line", which the Allies, including the Foresters, attacked during December but the year ended in blizzard bound stalemate.

Between January 5th and 15th 1944 the Allies made stubborn assaults through the mountains NE of Naples, advancing seven miles to the final "Gustav Line" along the Rapido River, with Monte Cassino the key obstacle.

During these assaults, the 5th Battalion was fighting on the slopes of Mount Maggiore. On January 8th there was severe shelling and mortaring of the Battalion area during the morning. At 2200 hours there was again very severe shelling, mortaring and heavy machine-gun fire from Cedro. On January 9th there was more shelling as the Battalion moved forward and began to dig in, in new positions. Patrols were sent out over the spur and were fired on, with casualties reported. The 10th and 11th January were spent on Maggiore with more patrols sent out on the 11th, meeting with a German patrol.

It was during this period on the slopes of Mount Maggiore that we believe Alfred Kirkby lost his life on January 11th.

SERGEANT ERNEST WILLIAM HAMILTON NO. 1238004
(WIRELESS OPERATOR/AIRGUNNER) ROYAL AIR FORCE VOLUNTEER
RESERVE 103 SQUADRON RAF DIED FEBRUARY 20TH 1944

Ernest Hamilton, or Ernie as he was known to everyone, lived at Sunny Bank, close to the butcher's shop at Great Longstone and attended Longstone School. His mother was a single woman and they lived with Ernest's grandmother. Sadly, his mother died young and by the time of the Second World War, his grandmother was also dead and he was living with his aunt and uncle, Mr. and Mrs. Blackwell of Sunny Bank.

Ernie volunteered to join the RAF and when he was called up he trained to be a wireless operator and air-gunner in Bomber Command. He eventually joined 103 Squadron, which in February 1944 was stationed at RAF Elsham

Ernest Hamilton whilst attending Longstone School 1933.

Wolds in Lincolnshire, between Scunthorpe and Immingham.

Lancaster bomber JB745 PM-1 took off at one minute past midnight on February 20th 1944 from Elsham Wolds, its target being Leipzig. All seven crewmen were killed.

Over 800 aircraft took part in the raid over the German city. The planes had been given a wind speed reading that was hopelessly incorrect. The Luftwaffe also located the bomber streams at an early stage and it was a stiff fight onwards from the Dutch coast. It proved to be a hazardous flight back as well, as combat followed combat, most ending with a fiery trail of flames as yet another bomber crew plunged earthwards.

Seventy eight aircraft failed to return (with seven air crew per plane), Bomber Command's worst night of the war to date. Three of the Lancasters shot down were from 103 Squadron, including that of Ernie Hamilton.

Ernest William Hamilton was buried in a collective grave 6.J.14-18 Hanover War Cemetery.

The number of fatalities in bomber crews was frighteningly high. Of the 125,000 airmen who passed through Bomber Command, roughly 55,000 or 44% were killed. But if you remove from the picture those who were still in training when the war ended, the figure rises to 65%.

"Still seen no one reach 30," wrote one airman in his diary in 1943. By that point in the war, the chance of a member of a bomber crew surviving a second tour was one in forty. In simple terms, the life expectancy of a Second World War airman was shorter than that of a junior officer on the Western Front in the First World War.

PRIVATE DOUGLAS HAIG BESWICK No. 7359030
ROYAL ARMY MEDICAL CORPS
DIED MARCH 30TH 1944 AGED 25

Douglas was born on November 14th 1918, just three days after the Armistice brought the Great War to an end. His parents gave him the middle name "Haig" from the Commander in Chief of British forces, Field Marshal Haig.

Douglas' father, Thomas Beswick, was a farmer's son from Summer Hill Farm, Flash, in Staffordshire, whilst his mother was Kate Haslam from New Street, Bakewell.

Thomas Beswick was both a blacksmith (shoeing horses etc.) and whitesmith (making objects from steel) and learned his trade with Tom Briddon on Bath Street, Bakewell. He lodged with Jim Frost on Haddon Road (Monyash Road).

When Thomas and Kate married they began married life at Yeld Street, before moving to North Church Street, where a daughter, Bessie, was born in 1916 and a son, Douglas, in 1918. Douglas went to the Church of England School on Bath Street and on leaving, joined the printing works of Joe Smith and Sons, in the Market Square (now a butchers), to learn his trade. He travelled by rail to Derby on certain nights to attend night classes in printing. As a boy he was a member of the Parish Church Choir and also a bell ringer and a member of the team of hand bell ringers.

Douglas was called up into the forces in the second wave of enlistment, in October 1939. In his leisure time at Bakewell he had been a member of the St. John's Ambulance Brigade and the Army therefore placed him in the Royal Army Medical Corps. In 1940 he married Doris Bates of Thornhill, near Bamford.

He trained in the south of England and at Leeds, where he was with the 28th Military Hospital Service. Douglas embarked for overseas service in November 1941 and for two years served with "Paiforce" (Persia and Iraq Command), as a first class nurse.

"Paiforce" had been created in April 1941 at about the time of the Iraq rebellion. Political disturbances, with attacks on British property, led to the occupation of the strategically important oil rich area of

Douglas Beswick, with his sister Bessie.
Bessie Whitworth

Mosul by British forces. The purpose of "Paiforce" was to check a possible move by the Nazis to conquer the Middle East. After Syria had been occupied by the Allies, "Paiforce" prepared to meet a German attack through either Turkey or via the Caucasus. When that threat had vanished, it became responsible for the delivery of war materials to the Soviet forces.

Douglas Haig Beswick, during his period in Iraq.
Bessie Whitworth

The flat, stony, dusty desert, combined with the tremendous heat and discomfort from sand flies, made conditions very uncomfortable. Occasional relief came when leave was granted to visit Basra or Baghdad.

By the end of 1943, Douglas and the 28th Military Hospital Service was brought back to the port of Alexandria, in Egypt, a complex of hospital and military bases. It was whilst he was riding on a military vehicle through the streets of Alexandria that Douglas fell off the vehicle and died from shock and haemorrhage following multiple injuries.

Douglas Haig Beswick was buried with full military honours in grave 6.B.21. Alexandria (Hadra) War

The burial ceremony of Douglas Beswick at Alexandria, Egypt.
Bessie Whitworth

Memorial Cemetery. His sister, Bessie, had married Jim Whitworth, a serving soldier, who was in Egypt at that time and Douglas' mother sent out a £5 note to Jim so that he could purchase flowers for the grave. He was also able to bring back photographs of the funeral and the grave.

PRIVATE JOHN WARING No. 14660794
6TH BATTALION WEST RIDING REGIMENT
DIED JUNE 18TH 1944 AGED 19

Born on March 27th 1925, John was the youngest child of Richard (Dick) and Lizzie Waring of Hassop. Two older sisters, Pat and Elsie, completed the family, although another son had been born, but died quite young.

Dick Waring had been born at Cauldon Lowe, a small hamlet in Staffordshire, to the west of Ashbourne, and had married Lizzie Booth, a girl from one of the cottages at Birchill's Farm, between Hassop Station and Baslow, on the Chatsworth Estate.

John Waring of Hassop.
Mary Glover

In 1934 they took over the running of Hassop Post Office, in a room in their home at the Dower House, with Lizzie in charge, whilst Dick continued working as forester and later gardener for the Stephenson family, on the Hassop Estate. He helped out at the post office by delivering letters on his bicycle and the shop also sold general provisions and newspapers.

Pat, Elsie and John Waring all attended Longstone School, walking there and back each day. They took sandwiches and at lunch time went to Hancock's shop (later the Co-op), opposite the White Lion Inn, where Bill Sales, the manager, made cups of tea for them. When John's sisters left school, Lizzie did not want John to walk to school by himself and so he was transferred to Bath Street School, Bakewell.

When he left school in 1938/1939, John was

Looking towards the old Dower House of Hassop Hall. The right-hand section
was Hassop Post Office, home to the Waring family from the 1930's.
Pat Lewis

employed at Needham's Garage, Bakewell, training as an electrician. However, when war started, he switched to munitions work and travelled to work in a Sheffield factory making piston rings for ships (on one occasion, he travelled with an older worker to Portsmouth, to replace piston rings in HMS "Sheffield"). John could have stayed at the factory during the war years, as it was a reserved occupation, but both sisters were serving in the forces, Pat in the WAAF and Elsie in the ATS and John therefore enlisted, joining eventually the 6th Battalion West Riding Regiment.

Having spent 1942 providing a defensive force in Iceland, based mostly around

John Waring's parents, Dick and Lizzie, together with
sisters Pat and Elsie, at Hassop Post Office. Their home was
part of the old Dower House for Hassop Hall.
Pat Lewis

John Waring at
Hassop Post Office as a boy.
Pat Lewis

Reykjavik, the 6th Battalion was replaced by American troops and returned to England to train and prepare for the invasion of Normandy. It was at this point that John joined the Battalion. A good deal of his training was in the Belfast area, and it was here that he met his sister Pat, serving in the WAAF.

Pat Waring on the left in WAAF uniform and Elsie Waring on the right in ATS uniform, during the Second World War. Their home was Hassop Post Office and their brother John was killed during the war.

Pat Lewis

On June 9th 1944 (D-Day plus 3) the 6th Battalion embarked on HMS "Cheshire", arriving off the Normandy coast on June 11th. By late evening of that day they were five miles inland. The Battalion first engaged the enemy on June 16th, when it was ordered to attack Parc de Boislande, a thickly wooded ridge overlooking Fontenay le Pesnil. The attack was supported by a squadron of tanks and artillery and was successful, but resulted in heavy losses to

British infantry prepare for the assault.

the Battalion.

The following day the German forces counter-attacked, forcing the 6th Battalion back, the bitter fighting seeing them lose 16 officers and 220 other ranks between the 16th and 18th June. John Waring was killed on June 18th during a rearguard action which saw the loss of most of his platoon. His body was buried in grave VIII.H.5. Hottot-les-Bagues War Cemetery, 14 kilometres SE of Bayeux.

Shortly after the war, Lizzie Waring saw an advert in the *Sheffield Telegraph* from a woman who had also lost her son in the Normandy campaign. They travelled together to visit the resting places of their sons and remained life-long friends.

Leading Aircraftman William McGregor
No. 1663665 RAFVR
died 24th July 1944 aged 25

The McGregor family lived in a small cottage on Water Street, Bakewell. John McGregor, a Bakewell man, had married Frances Mellor, a girl from Bakewell and their family consisted of Violet, Jack and William (Billy). Frances had already lost her younger brother, Joseph Mellor, during the Great War and now she was to lose her son in the present conflict.

The children's father worked at the DP Battery on Buxton Road, but Billy McGregor was employed at the Pretoria Chert Quarry. He had a fine singing voice and together with a number of friends and colleagues, they would gather on the pavement at Burgon's Grocery Store, near the Square, and entertain passers by with harmonised singing, accompanied by a person on the mouth organ.

Billy McGregor of Bakewell.
Barbara Wild

William (Billy) McGregor of Bakewell.

His brother Jack was one of the first Bakewell men to enlist and went into the Royal Artillery as a gunner, spending quite some time on the cliffs of Dover, operating the large guns that ran on rails, situated inside the chalk cliffs, and could send their lethal projectiles across the Straits of Dover.

Billy McGregor was in a reserved occupation, working at the Pretoria Chert Quarry. However, one day, an accident occurred at the Quarry, when a fall of rock seriously injured a colleague and Billy only just got out of the way in time. He decided he would enlist and joined the RAF in 1942, becoming a leading aircraftman on a local airfield, at Ashbourne. This situation pleased his mother because she believed that he would be a great deal safer there than fighting from the Kent coast line, as his brother Jack was doing.

Ashbourne Airfield was the base for an Operational Training Unit of the RAF. Airmen in training were brought together at Ashbourne and trained as crews on aircraft, gaining their skills, before being sent out to the RAF Squadrons operating against the enemy. Billy was a happy go lucky man and there was nothing he liked better than travelling home on leave to Bakewell to join his pals in the pub for a singsong.

On Saturday 23rd July 1944, the day before his 25th birthday, Billy was home on leave, but returned to base that evening. The following day, he and other ground crew and WAAF's were in a hangar on the airfield when a training aircraft overshot the runway and crashed into the building, killing Billy McGregor. When Frances received a telegram she believed it would be telling her of the death of her son Jack, never suspecting that it would be Billy who had died. Jack came home on leave and travelled to Ashbourne, hoping to see the body of his brother, but the authorities refused permission because the body was badly burned.

Billy McGregor's body was brought to Bakewell and the coffin, covered in the Union flag, rested in All Saints Church on the Thursday night, with the service on Friday conducted by the Reverend N. S. Kidson. Billy was a honorary member of the British Legion and the branch flag in the Bath Gardens was flown at half mast. Six RAF personnel from Ashbourne attended.

GUARDSMAN RONALD BUNTING NO. 2616656
2ND ARMOURED BATTALION GRENADIER GUARDS
DIED AUGUST 4TH 1944 AGED 24

Ron's father, Ernest James Bunting, was born at Matlock Green in 1884, the son of James Bunting, a grocer's warehouseman, and Henrietta. By 1901, Ernest James was employed as a bricklayer's apprentice and by the start of the First World War he had married Mary Ellen Jackson, and the couple were living in Matlock.

Ernest James Bunting fought during the Great War in a Siege Battery of the Royal Field Artillery and a son, Owen, was born during the war.

When the Armistice came and Ernest James Bunting was demobbed, the family moved to Butts Road, Bakewell, where Ronald was born on March 7th 1920. By this time, Ernest James was employed by R. Orme and Company, working in the warehouse, and eventually became their

Ronald Bunting and his elder brother Owen.
Mr. M. Bunting

master bottler. Both Owen and Ron joined the same firm as their father.

During the Second World War, Owen joined the Sherwood Foresters and saw service in North Africa.

Ron, who was a tall man, joined the Grenadier Guards and by 1944 was in the 2nd Armoured Battalion and in training for Normandy. Meanwhile, Ron had married Irene, a Lancashire girl from Moston, who was also serving in the forces.

Ernest James Bunting, father of Ronald, as a soldier during the Great War.
Mr. M. Bunting

Ronald and Irene Bunting at their wedding.
Mr. M. Bunting

After seeing action in June and July, during the Normandy landings and the extension of the bridgehead, the 2nd Armoured Battalion saw further action in Operation "Bluecoat", between July 30th and August 7th 1944.

The objective was to secure the key road junction of Vire and the high ground of Mont Pincon, in support of the American breakout on the western flank of the Normandy beachhead. The armour of the British Second Army under Lieutenant General Dempsey was switched westwards towards Villers-Bocage, adjacent

A British armoured column pushes forward in Normandy, August 1944.

to the American army.

A preliminary bombardment by over 1000 bombers was not as successful as intended due to the poor weather, and when the attack followed up, many units were held up by minefields and steep gullies in the difficult bocage landscape of Normandy. On July 31st, units of the British 11th Armoured Division captured a bridge and broke up the first German armoured counter-attack. British forces were now only 5 miles from the key road junction at Vire. However, when the British attack was diverted South-East, it gave the German Seventh Army time to regroup and SS Panzer Divisions reinforced their defences. The British advance was held up and brought to a temporary halt on August 4th, the date of Ronald Bunting's death. After renewed efforts, Vire fell to Allied forces two days later, on August 6th.

However, Ronald Bunting had been killed in action in the push on Vire, and his body was buried in grave V.A.7. St. Charles de Percy War Cemetery, 44 kilometres SW of Caen.

PRIVARE RICHARD HENRY HURST NO. 3968323
3RD BATTALION MONMOUTHSHIRE REGIMENT
DIED AUGUST 5TH 1944 AGED 28

Richard Henry Hurst, better known as Dick to family and friends, was the son of Harry and Mabel Agatha Hurst of Great Longstone.

Harry was born at Ashford in the Water in 1883, his father, William, being the head gardener at Ashford Hall. Harry worked for a time for the haulage firm of Daybells, whose horses and carts carried coal, plus chert and fluorspar from Longstone Edge to Hassop Station. On one journey Harry took a cart laden with Ashford marble to Buxton.

Eventually he worked with his brother William for Tom Smith, the Bakewell timber merchant, at the woodyard along Coombs Road. At times he spent the week away from home, felling timber on the Longshaw Estate.

Harry married Mabel Agatha Oxley, from Holymoorside, in 1905, when she was working as a cook at the Devonshire Arms, Ashford (nowadays the Ashford Arms). They eventually raised a family of 12 children (6 boys, 6 girls) and in the early days lived in Hall End Lane, Ashford.

As the family grew in size, they moved to live at The Mires, Great Longstone, and when war broke out in 1914 Harry volunteered for the Army in February 1915, joining the Royal Engineers as a mounted driver in charge of the horses in the 92nd Field Company.

In early January 1916 a shell burst killed two of his colleagues and caused serious injuries to Harry's head, stomach and thigh and resulted in him being blinded (they had been felling timber for dug-out supports and were only 50 yards away from the German lines).

Harry was discharged from the Army as medically unfit in February 1916. Within a short while he had been sent to St. Dunstan's in London to be taught braille,

Harry Hurst with the horses in France 1915.
Sheila and Frank Hurst

*Richard (Dick) Henry Hurst
of Great Longstone.*
Sheila and Frank Hurst

basket making and coconut mat making. He also took a course on poultry farming and pig keeping, as well as gardening.

In 1919 the family moved to "The Willows", The Mires, and in an outhouse, known as "The Shop", Harry expanded his small mat-making business, until he changed to the poultry business until 1936. Eggs and dressed table birds were supplied to George Furniss, MP, at "The Croft"; to Mr. Marples at Thornbridge Hall and Torrs Farm at Hassop, as well as to Ashford and Sheldon customers.

During the Second World War, four of Harry's children joined the forces. Phoebe, a mill worker at Cressbrook and later domestic servant at "The Grange", Longstone, and at Portsmouth, joined the WAAF as a cook. Gerald, a mineral extractor for Athertons on Longstone Moor and timber worker at Smith's sawmill, Bakewell, joined the army and began timber cutting in the Forest of Dean before working as a tunneller on the Rock of Gibraltar with the Royal Engineers. Frank was a gardener at Thornbridge Hall before joining up and serving with the King's Own Light Infantry in India, at Doollalie, the Kola Goldfields and Mysore Jungle and at the Chindit training camp in Central Provinces.

Sadly, the fourth member of the Hurst family to join

the forces, Richard Henry (Dick), would not survive the conflict.

Dick was a gardener apprentice at "The Grange" and then a gardener at Thornbridge Hall. When he enlisted, he eventually joined the 15th Battalion Welch Regiment and served in England, the Hebrides and Northern Ireland. By early 1944 he had been transferred to the 3rd Battalion Monmouthshire Regiment and they began training in earnest for the forthcoming invasion of Normandy in June.

Dick Hurst and the 3rd Battalion landed in Normandy on June 14th 1944, D-Day plus 8. The first battle was an unsuccessful attempt to break out of the Normandy bridgehead. They strayed into the village of Mouen and "C" Company was left to

Dick Hurst on embarkation leave 1944 with sisters Sheila (left) and Adeline (right).
Sheila and Frank Hurst

cover the withdrawal. It was attacked by superior German forces with tank support and after gallant resistance, only 14 men fought their way out.

In another attempt to break out east of Caen, the Battalion captured Cuverville and Demouville in quick succession. They advanced then across two miles of open country, littered with tanks knocked out in an armoured battle. The Battalion fought a fierce battle in the village of Bras, under a withering German artillery barrage. The village was taken but casualties were very heavy. In these three successive attacks the Battalion lost over 100 men. The breakthrough again failed and they moved into the Bocage country of ridges, high hedgerows and deep sunken roads,

The Battalion then penetrated behind the German defence and crossed the Souleuvre River undetected. Into this Salient the Battalion went mounted on tanks, fighting a running battle with the retreating enemy and took up positions with the Yeomanry tanks around Sourdevalle, on Bas Perier Ridge.

These units on the Ridge, near the village of Burcy, formed a small peninsula surrounded by the enemy on three sides, who now brought in more forces. Some parties of Germans even operated in their rear. On August 5th, the date of Dick's death, enemy shelling began and was followed by a fierce tank and infantry attack. The Battalion's tanks were driven back. "D" and "C" Companies were then attacked by enemy infantry and some of them managed to penetrate as far as Battalion HQ – but the Battalion held its ground and the enemy were beaten off. The Battalion's losses were so heavy that some platoons were down to half strength.

During the fighting on August 5th, Dick Hurst was killed. In a letter from his former CO of "C" Company 15th Battalion Welch Regiment, Captain Paul Kempson, written to his parents, he states that Dick was killed near Burcy. The enemy counter-attacked their position very heavily and was shelling and mortaring at the same time. Dick was killed outright by a mortar bomb. He was buried by a padre in the Brigade cemetery. The Captain told his mother that Dick was very well liked in the Company and was a "damn good soldier".

Richard Henry Hurst was buried in grave IX.E.4. Tilly-Sur-Seulles War Cemetery, 12 kilometres SE from Bayeux. His name is commemorated on the Great Longstone War Memorial and his name is to be found in a Book of Remembrance in Monmouth Cathedral.

Dick Hurst's grave in Normandy.

Sheila and Frank Hurst

MAJOR WILLIAM JOHN ROBERT CAVENDISH (MARQUIS OF HARTINGTON) COLDSTREAM GUARDS
DIED SEPTEMBER 9TH 1944 AGED 26

William Cavendish, eldest son of Edward William Spencer Cavendish K.G., 10th Duke of Devonshire and the Duchess of Devonshire, of Chatsworth House, was born at Arlington Street, London, on December 10th 1917, and as the eldest son, would receive the title of Marquis of Hartington.

He was educated at Eton and Trinity College, Cambridge, but shortly before the outbreak of war, he left Cambridge to join the Coldstream Guards. He served with the Guards in the British Expeditionary Force in France 1939/1940 and was evacuated from the Brittany port of St. Malo in June 1940, as the Germans completed their occupation of France. Meanwhile, the Duke and Duchess of Devonshire were to spend the war years living at Churchdale House, whilst Chatsworth House became the home to evacuee school girls from Penrhos College, North Wales.

William Cavendish was a popular young man on the Chatsworth Estate and his coming of age celebrations at Chatsworth in 1939 had been on an extensive scale, lasting two days. He had fallen in love with Kathleen Kennedy, daughter of Joseph Kennedy, the anti-British American Ambassador to London, just before the war began. However, the marriage was delayed because she was Catholic and the Cavendish family was Protestant, whilst her father was strongly opposed to the marriage. Despite this, the romance continued through the war years.

Kathleen Kennedy was in London, working for the American Red Cross, when, in February 1944, William Cavendish was recalled to Derbyshire to contest the West Derbyshire by-election, a political role his forebears had undertaken for nearly 300 years. As a serving officer (Captain) he was barred from fighting an election but the War Office transferred him to the Reserve and granted him leave for the period of the election.

It was bitterly contested. His Independent Socialist opponent, Alderman Charles White, turned the issue into an attack on what he deemed to be the "feudal"

The wedding of William Cavendish, 2nd Earl of Burlington and Kathleen Kennedy,
May 1944, at Chelsea Registry Office.
LEFT TO RIGHT: *Duchess of D evonshire, William Cavendish, Kathleen Kennedy,*
Joseph Kennedy (junior), 10th Duke of Devonshire.
In June 1944, Joseph Kennedy would be killed in action and on September 9th 1944,
William Cavendish would also be killed.

influence of families like the Cavendishes, on politics. When the vote was counted, Alderman Charles White defeated William Cavendish by a majority of 4561.

At the declaration of the poll from the Matlock Town Hall balcony, William declared, "It has been a fierce fight. Now I am going out to fight for you at the front." It was only a few days later that he and his colleagues in the Guards began their training for the D-Day landings in Normandy, due for June 1944.

However, before the fighting began on June 6th, William and Kathleen had married in a civil ceremony at Chelsea Register Office in May 1944. She had been prepared to change her religion in exchange for marrying the man she loved. The Duke and his family were there at the ceremony but the Kennedy parents were absent. One of those who signed the marriage register was the bride's brother, Lieutenant Joseph Kennedy, who shortly afterwards was involved in the fighting in Normandy. A few weeks into the desperate struggle, Joseph Kennedy was killed in action when an explosion took place in his aircraft.

Soon after William Cavendish arrived in Normandy he was promoted to Major, but sadly, some months later, on September 9th 1944, he was killed by a German sniper, a short distance across the French frontier, in Belgium. Many Guards officers, including William, favoured the wearing of pale corduroy trousers with their battledress, marking them out as possible targets. He was buried in grave IV.B.13. Leopoldsburg War Cemetery, 58 kilometres NE of Leuven, in Limburg Province, Belgium.

His sister, Elizabeth Cavendish, later said, "For my parents a light went out when Billy died." His younger brother, Andrew Cavendish, married to Deborah Mitford, inherited the title.

THE YEAR 1945

During the winter and spring months of 1945, British forces continued their advance towards the River Rhine and across the mighty river defences into the heart of Germany. Bomber Command aircrews maintained the pressure on German industry as they pounded what was left of the cities and towns, whilst Coastal Command continued to have the upper hand with regards to the U-boat threat. The German Reich would surrender at midnight on May 8th/9th 1945 and the following day the parishes in the Bakewell district were able to bring out the bunting, ring the church bells and light bonfires to celebrate VE Day. Out in the Far East, however, despite the celebrations in Britain for the end of the conflict in Europe, British forces, the so-called "Forgotten Army", would continue the desperate fight against the Japanese in Burma, Malaya and elsewhere in the Far East, until the surrender of Japan on September 2nd. Throughout these months of 1945, Bakewell and the villages would lose a further three servicemen.

FLIGHT SERGEANT WILLIAM VICTOR BIBBY NO. 1579109
576 SQUADRON ROYAL AIR FORCE VOLUNTEER RESERVE
DIED FEBRUARY 21ST 1945 AGED 25

There is little we have been able to find out about William Victor Bibby's background. His parents were William Victor Bibby senior and Catherine Jane Bibby and at the time of William's death, they were living at Narberth, a few miles inland from Tenby, Pembrokeshire.

It would appear to be that William was working in the Bakewell area before the war and this provides his connection with the town and its memorial.

Flight Sergeant Bibby was serving as a navigator/bomber with 576 Squadron, flying heavy Lancaster bombers out of RAF Fiskerton, just to the SW of Newark-on-Trent, Nottinghamshire. Lancaster NF975 took off at 2141 hours on February 20th 1945 for Dortmund. It was lost without trace.

The second half of February 1945 was extremely active, with raids on oil producing centres being maintained, while devastating area attacks were delivered on industrial targets in Dortmund, Duisburg, Worms, Essen and Mainz. The

The four-engined Avro Lancaster bomber. The first bombing raid by a Lancaster was on Essen in March 1942. By the end of the war 7,500 Lancasters had been built.

response from the enemy defences, both from night fighters and anti-aircraft fire, was particularly vicious. Fourteen Lancasters failed to return from Dortmund on the night of 20th / 21st February.

With William Victor Bibby's body never being recovered, his name is commemorated on Panel 270 of the RAF Memorial at Runnymede.

PRIVATE ALFRED JAMES TURNER NO. 6981665
2ND BATTALION KING'S OWN SCOTTISH BORDERERS
DIED FEBRUARY 23RD 1945 AGED 28

The Turner family lived at what is now called "The Channings" on Main Street, Wardlow, a two up, two down room cottage. Alfred, known as Alf to family and friends, had a brother Charlie and both children went to the village school.

The children's mother, Emma, had married their father, a local man, who worked as a fluor spar miner at the Cupola Mining Company's mine at Eyam, walking each day across the fields to his place of work. Charlie worked with his father at the mine but Alf worked for Derbyshire County Council on a road gang. Both Alf and his brother had a keen interest in bicycles and motor bikes. The family lived in one of the downstairs rooms and the two brothers made use of the other one as a motor bike workshop.

During the war years, Alf Turner joined up and was posted to the 2nd Battalion King's Own Scottish Borderers, training to join General Slim's Army in Burma, in the fight against the Japanese.

Alf had met Martha, a girl from the Rochdale area, and they were married, but not long afterwards Alf and his Battalion embarked for the Far East (eventually a child was born).

General Slim, leader of the 14th Army, planned three assaults across the Irrawaddy River in early 1945, with the 2nd Battalion involved in one of these. The Battalion left Kohima on December 28th 1944, marching southwards with 50 mules added to their transport, whilst being supplied on a regular basis from air drops by Dakota aircraft. The column steadily pushed on for 168 miles, fording streams and toiling up and down the switchback tracks over the hills, until they reached Yozayat on January 29th 1945, fifteen miles from the Irrawaddy.

On February 14th the assault across the river was made under extreme machine-gun fire and the whole Battalion was across by February 16th. The job of the 2nd Battalion was now to mop up Japanese positions along the banks of the Irrawaddy and on February 23rd they attacked the village of Nakyo-Aing, in an area of cactus hedges and small creeks.

The Japanese had made this a prickly hedgehog village, defended with numerous bunkers, manned by machine-gun teams. The Commanding Officer decided to probe from the east and he sent out a platoon, including Alf Turner, commanded by Sergeant Stockhill. This patrol, however, came into contact with strong enemy positions and the sergeant ordered his men to draw back, retiring to the vicinity of a pagoda, where other elements of "B" Company were in position.

Whilst this was happening, other platoons of "B" Company encountered trouble. Some Borderers were ambushed by Japanese hidden in cactus hedges, and others were picked off by snipers. The platoon commanded by Second Lieutenant Brazier was pinned down and the officer was killed. The CO ordered "B" Company to break off the battle and make their way back to Battalion headquarters in the darkness. Company Sergeant Major Broughton, who was awarded the MC for his actions, rallied the survivors of Second Lieutenant Brazier's platoon, along with his own party, got the men under cover and beat off a bayonet attack by the enemy.

In this fighting, Private Elder did deadly work with a Bren gun and gallantly went ahead as a lone scout while C.S.M. Broughton led the other men to the Irrawaddy. They made their way to Brigade headquarters, taking their wounded with them. Twenty six Borderers, including Alfred James Turner, were killed in this action, and ten were wounded.

After the war, Alf's body was buried in grave 21.E.8. at Taukkyan War Cemetery, 35 kilometres north of Rangoon.

SERGEANT MICHAEL JOHN GILLANE No. 1143836
14 SQUADRON RAFVR
DIED APRIL 19TH 1945 AGED 30

There is very little information we have discovered about Michael Gillane, whose name is inscribed on the Bakewell War Memorial. It is known that he was the son of Michael and Margaret Gillane of Ballinasloe, between Galway and Athlone, in County Galway, Republic of Ireland. It is quite unusual to find someone from the

Republic fighting with the British during the Second World War, for Anglo-Irish relations were strained during the inter-war years because of "The Troubles" and Eire remained "neutral" during the war. There is also a problem in finding a connection between Michael and the market town of Bakewell. It is likely, however, that he had come to work in Bakewell before the war started.

Whatever is the case, we know that he volunteered for the RAF and trained to become a wireless operator/ air-gunner, rising to the rank of sergeant. By 1945 he was flying with 14 Squadron.

The Squadron had been stationed in East Africa 1940-1941, flying Wellesley bombers at the start of the war and bombing the Italians in Eritrea, before re-equipping with Blenheims and being stationed in the Mediterranean between 1941 and 1943. In the summer of 1942 Marauder aircraft were taken on the strength and were used in an anti-shipping role.

In mid 1944 the Squadron and Sergeant Michael Gillane, moved to RAF Chivenor, four miles to the west of Barnstaple, Devon, where they flew Wellington bombers for Coastal Command in an anti-submarine role. Michael Gillane was on board Wellington bomber NB858 that was lost due to enemy action while on patrol over the South West approaches on April 19th 1945, just 19 days before the war ended in Europe at midnight, May 8th/9th.

Michael's body was not recovered from the sea and his name is commemorated on Panel 275 Runnymede Memorial.

VICTORY IN EUROPE (VE DAY) CELEBRATIONS

The sadness felt by Michael's family would be great, but happiness of a kind came to most people in Bakewell and district with the news that the German Reich would surrender at midnight on May 8th/May 9th. The following day, Wednesday, Victory in Europe Day, celebrations in all the parishes began.

All over the district on Tuesday there were scenes reflecting the spirit of the occasion. People gathered in the streets gaily decorated with flags of the Allies, linked arms and sang community songs, joining in organised celebrations and services of thanksgiving, while the church bells rang out their message of gladness over the hills. Unfortunately, the weather was not always in keeping with the occasion throughout the day.

Bakewell celebrated VE-Day quietly until the evening, when there were scenes of unbounded enthusiasm. Many houses and business premises were gaily decorated and the Royal Army Service Corps unit stationed near the town had a full day off. There were large congregations at a thanksgiving service held at the parish church, conducted by the vicar, Reverend N. S. Kidson and at the Wesleyan Methodist Church (Reverend E. L. Clift).

Later, Bakewell Band played in the Bath Gardens and the soldiers held a dance at the Town Hall which was packed to capacity. The war memorial in the Square was floodlit for the first time since the outbreak of war and from about 10 o' clock onwards crowds began to assemble in the Square.

Here, Bakewell "let herself go". Old, middle aged, young, soldiers, sailors and airmen and civilians cast dull care aside for a few hours. They packed the Square, they sang, they cheered, they danced, they made merry, they played games, without interference and with little to speak of in the way of disorder. There was no organised programme and it was not until the small hours of the morning that the crowd dispersed.

A Services Recreation Club, run voluntarily by a local committee throughout the war years, based in the Friends' Meeting House for the benefit of the troops stationed at Bakewell, had a very busy Tuesday night. All the troops were provided with refreshments free of charge.

The bells of the parish church rang out merry peals during the afternoon and evening, and there were constant loud reports and explosions. From somewhere, stocks of fireworks had been brought to light again and good use was made of them.

For the school girls of Penrhos College at Chatsworth House, VE-Day began with an extra hour in bed and continued with a short thanksgiving service. The rest of the morning was given off for free time until 12-30p.m. and some of the girls took the opportunity to bicycle to Pilsley and Baslow, even though it was raining heavily. Flags and bunting were hanging from the windows of Edensor village and Chatsworth House, whilst a large Union flag hung above Edensor Church.

At 3p.m. the girls and staff assembled in the Painted Hall to hear Winston Churchill broadcast to the nation, before trooping outside to play ping-pong and rounders. 5-30p.m. saw the college staff providing an entertainment: "Penrhos from 1939 to 1945", followed by supper of spam, crisps and school made cake with marzipan icing.

At 9-30p.m. a bonfire was lit in the grounds, with a dummy of Hitler being consumed by the flames, and the girls sang songs around the fire. Cocoa and biscuits were provided, the School Song was sung and the school retired to bed by 12p.m. Elsewhere on the Chatsworth Estate, there was poetic justice about a huge bonfire which was lighted at Bunker's Hill at 11p.m.. For some days the bonfire had been built from brushwood by German prisoners of war engaged in forestry work in the district.

Meanwhile, despite the relief that the war in Europe had come to an end, the fight against the Japanese continued in the Far East, with many of the district's servicemen involved. Thankfully, none of these men lost their lives in the last few weeks of the war. The official surrender of the Japanese on September 2nd 1945, resulting mainly from the dropping of atomic bombs on Hiroshima and Nagasaki in August, brought the Second World War to a conclusion. It was on August 14th, however, that Victory over Japan Day (VJ-Day) was celebrated.

The announcement on Tuesday 14th August took people by surprise so plans for celebrations were not made fully until late on Wednesday. Those who came to work on Wednesday morning were given the day off, except for those who manned the essential services.

For the most part, Wednesday passed off quietly in Bakewell. Flags were soon strewn from buildings in the town. Soldiers of the 5th Transport Battalion (D) Royal Army Service Corps, stationed at Burton Closes and Haddon House, who were given the day off duty, went around the town in lorries, singing loudly, and in one case accompanied by a hastily improvised band. They were provided with refreshments for four hours in the evening by the Services Recreation Club. Some people were busy building bonfires, whilst youngsters bought all the fireworks in the town.

The Bakewell Amateur Variety Entertainers made their first appearance in Bakewell since their successful pantomime in January, their revue being entitled: "Victory Parade" and performed at the Town Hall during the next three evenings. Bakewell Band paraded the town in the evening and afterwards played in Bath Gardens.

After dark there was dancing in the Square, the music being provided by Overton's Radio, under the direction of Mr. J. Hawkins, until the early hours of Thursday. At midnight, the Bakewell Amateur Variety Entertainers presented the tableau with which they had concluded their programme at the Town Hall earlier in the evening. In this, Britannia, America, Russia, China, France, Holland, the Army, Navy and Air Force, the Civil Defence Services, National Fire Service and Nursing Services were represented.

The rejoicings continued on Thursday. In some districts of the town tea parties were arranged for the children and in the evening another large crowd assembled in the Square for dancing, which was kept up until after midnight.

VJ-Day celebrations at Great Longstone included a social dance at the Social Institute during the evening, following a service at St. Giles Church. On the following day the infirm and elderly of the village had a little of the victory spirit taken to them when the Longstone Folk Dancers, together with some members of a Sheffield team who were camping in the district, danced national folk dances through Longstone, dressed in the costume of some of the Allies. Displays were presented at five points in the village and these were also enjoyed by various bus loads of visitors who passed through. In the evening there was a bonfire on the Recreation Ground. On Saturday the children living on Sunny Bank held a Victory Tea.

On Friday, a Victory drive and tea for all the children of Great and Little Longstone, Hassop and Rowland, up to the age of 14, took place. With Miss Walton, John Thornhill and Mr. Thompson in charge, the party of 80 left the village in two motor coaches for Hathersage, via Fox House and the Surprise View, where there was a halt for the children to pick heather. The return journey was made via Grindleford, Calver, and Baslow, where there was another short stay.

On their return, they were provided with a tea at Longstone School, the room being prettily decorated with flowers and flags by Mrs. Knight. At tea they were joined by some of the younger children with their mothers. The tea included an abundance of sandwiches and home made cakes given by friends in the village.

Japan's surrender brought to a conclusion the participation of Bakewell and district in the Second World War. For the families of 32 servicemen who had died in the war there was sadness. Yet even with an end to the conflict, it was not to be the end of the story of the men whose names are commemorated on the town and village war memorials. Sadly, four days after the official surrender of Japan, news arrived of the death of the final serviceman from this area, a native of the market town of Bakewell.

Private John Mansfield No. 7960085
103 Royal Pioneer Corps
Died September 6th 1945 aged 38

John, or Jack as he was known, was one of the six children of Joseph and Fanny Florence Mansfield of Mutton Row/Dagnell Terrace (nowadays called Chapel Row), near the Manners Public House, Bakewell. The other siblings were Fanny, Joe, Bill, Maggie and Alice. Fanny Florence Froggatt (known as Florence) was born in Stockport, before arriving to work in Bakewell and married Joseph Mansfield, who was a Bakewell cab driver by 1900. During the Great War and in the early 1920's Joseph travelled the Bakewell district on a horse and cart selling hardware items (in retirement in the late 1940's he sold newspapers from his house on Chapel Row).

By the time of Jack's death, at the age of 38 in 1945, he was married to Rosina (Rose) Mansfield of North Wingfield and they had a young son Raymond. When he enlisted, Jack joined the Pioneer Corps. In the previous war, 1914-1918, it had

John Mansfield's father, Joseph, was a general dealer in the Bakewell district.
J. Duncan

provided Labour Battalions on the Western Front that helped in the digging of trenches and the preparation of roads in the reserve areas behind the front line. During the Second World War they were also involved in manual work and organised civilian gangs to help. It was part of their job to look after prisoners of war in Europe, as the war came to a close.

Jack Mansfield's unit was involved in the invasion of Europe after the Battle for Normandy, fighting in France, Belgium and Holland. We have seen that the war in Europe ended on May 9th 1945 and that Japan surrendered on September 2nd. By that date, Jack was stationed in Holland, and he and his unit of the Pioneer Corps had been involved in clearance of wartime debris and munitions. Sadly, we find that four days after the end of the war and four months after cessation of hostilities in Europe, Jack Mansfield was involved in a motor accident on the roads of Holland and was killed on September 6th. He had survived the fighting, only to be killed in an accident.

Charles Henry Mansfield of Bakewell.

Sylvia Marsden

Jack Mansfield was buried in grave VI.H.1. Groesbeek Canadian War Cemetery, near Nijmegan, in the Netherlands.

It is interesting to note that Jack's elder brother, Joseph (Joe) Mansfield, had fought in the Great War and thankfully survived. Joe had been a member of the Derbyshire Yeomanry and fought in Salonika against the Bulgarians. In August 1917 he had been awarded the Military Medal for conspicuous gallantry and bravery in action. Whilst under heavy artillery fire he dashed out into the open and rescued a wounded comrade at the risk of his life and succeeded in bringing him back on the saddle of his own horse. He was just 21 years old at the time.

A more distant relative, Squadron Sergeant Major Charles Henry Mansfield of the Derbyshire Yeomanry also won the Military Medal, as well as the Distinguished Conduct Medal, for bravery in Salonika. He was married to Clara and in civilian life lived with his children, Hector, Edgar and Gladys on Rock Terrace, Bakewell. For 14 years he had been employed by the County Council as a steam roller driver on the roads in the Bakewell area, and had been in the High Peak Squadron of the Yeomanry for several years before the war. When war broke out in 1914 he mobilised at Bakewell with his troop and during the next three years had only been on leave once or twice, having served in the Dardanelles and Egypt, before travelling on to Salonika.

The stories of the lives and deaths of servicemen from the Bakewell area whose names are inscribed on the Second World War sections of the local parish war memorials is now completed, with the exception of two men, Reg Stimson of the

Royal Army Service Corps and Jack Morrison, who served in the Royal Navy. Their names are commemorated on the Bakewell War Memorial and on the town's Roll of Honour, but I cannot be 100% sure that I have found the correct information about these men.

I have found only one Reginald Stimson listed by the Commonwealth War Graves Commission who died during the war, but although it says he was in the Royal Pioneer Corps when he died, not the RASC, we are fairly confident that we have the correct man. However, there are eight John Morrison's listed as serving in the Royal Navy when they were killed and one man by the name of Jack Morrison. There are no clues provided connecting any of these men with Bakewell, but we have decided to put forward the possibility that the Jack Morrison from the CWGC website is our man. It is our belief that Reg Stimson and Jack Morrison's connection with Bakewell stems from their coming to work in the area prior to the start of the war.

PRIVATE REGINALD GEORGE STIMSON
NO. 13049679 PIONEERS CORPS
DIED MARCH 20TH 1942 AGED 29

Reg Stimson was born at Horbling, a small village seven miles south of Sleaford, Lincolnshire, on January 27th 1913, the son of William Stimson, an agricultural engine driver (operating a threshing machine) and Alice May Stimson (née Brothwell). We believe that Reg Stimson arrived in Bakewell to find work in the years just before the war began and when he enlisted he became a member of the Royal Pioneer Corps.

By March 1942 his Battalion was training in the Galashiels area of the Scottish Borders, when he was involved in a motor accident and received serious head injuries. Reg was taken to Peel Military Hospital, seven miles west of Galashiels (the same complex of wooden Nissen huts in which Sam Gratton from Ashford had died in 1941). He died on March 20th 1942. Reginald Stimson was not brought home to either Bakewell or Horbling, but instead was buried in Galashiels (Eastlands) Cemetery.

SEAMAN JACK KENNEDY MORRISON NO. P/X21519A
ROYAL NAVAL RESERVE HMS "FIDELITY"
DIED JANUARY 1ST 1943 AGED 23

Jack Morrison was born in Scotland in 1919, the son of Hugh and Georgina Morrison (by the time of Jack's death, his parents were living in the small, remote settlement of Balchrick, NW Scotland, ten miles south of Cape Wrath).

Once again, it is our belief that before the start of the war, Jack was working in the Bakewell district, but joined the Royal Naval Reserve as war began. Eventually he became a seaman and by 1942 became a member of HMS "Fidelity".

HMS "Fidelity" had originally been a French ship called "Le Rhin", based at Marseilles, but in 1940 its French captain sailed to Britain and it was taken over by the Royal Navy. Under its French captain it was used for taking spies to land on the southern French coast during 1941.

It returned to England late in 1941 to be re-equipped as a "Q" Ship, disguised as a Merchant Navy vessel (a Special Service Vessel (SSV), armed with four x 4 inch guns, four torpedo tubes, two sea planws and a motor torpedo boat).

The plan was to transport Royal Marine Commandos to Indo-China to fight the Japanese behind the lines. As the change was completed, extra crew members, including Jack Morrison, were taken on board.

Near the end of 1942 the ship sailed in Convoy ONS-154 for the Far East. Near the Azores, in the Atlantic Ocean, the convoy came under attack from a U-boat wolf pack. Fifteen ships were sunk, including HMS "Fidelity", the victim of U-435. Four hundred men were lost, including both Jack Morrison and people the "Fidelity" had only just rescued from other sunken ships.

Jack Morrison's name is commemorated on Panel 80 Column 1 Portsmouth Naval Memorial.

The Second World War had finally come to an end, and with it, the area's participation in five and a half years of dreadful conflict. The parishes had experienced the closeness of war with the activities of the local ARP, Fire Brigade, Home Guard and the arrival of the regular army, together with that of the evacuees from the threatened urban areas during the anxious days of 1940/1941.

Bringing the horrors of war even closer to many people in the area was the involvement of family members and friends in combat with the enemy in different theatres of war and the loss of 35 people whilst serving their country. For those who returned home safely there was relief and joy, but for 35 families and relatives, there was much sadness.

Despite this, the official celebration of victory in the Second World War, took place throughout the country on June 8th 1946. At Great Longstone there was a Victory Peal rung on the church bells at 10-30am, followed at 11am by a ten minute United Service at the War Memorial, led by the vicar, Reverend C.C.W. Trendall. At 2pm children's sports took place on the cricket field, followed at 4pm by a tea in Longstone Social Institute for children under 10 years, whilst children over the age of 10 were provided with a tea at 5pm. A Whist Drive was held in the school at 8pm, whilst between 8pm and 11-45pm, a dance occurred in the Institute.

However, for one Bakewell family, their sadness was yet to come, years after the celebration of victory. Inscribed on the memorial that was dedicated to the men of Bakewell who lost their lives during the Second World War, and erected in the Bath Gardens, is the addition of the lone name of Cecil Clark, who was killed in action in the Korean War, a post war conflict involving British forces.

At the end of the Second World War, Korea was occupied north and south of the

38th parallel of latitude by Russian and U.S. forces respectively. In 1948 the Republic of Korea was established in South Korea, with Seoul as its capital and the U.S. troops withdrew. The Russian-sponsored Korean People's Republic was established in the north, with Pyongyang as its capital. The Russians also left the country.

Without warning, North Korean troops invaded South Korea on June 25th 1950. Forces, mostly from the United States, representing the United Nations, went to the assistance of the South Koreans. After preliminary reverses, United Nations troops (including British) reached the 38th Parallel in October and advanced into North Korea. Chinese troops then came to the aid of the North Koreans and the United Nations force was driven south of the 38th Parallel. It was at this point that Cecil Clark, a regular army soldier from Bakewell, was killed attempting to stem the torrent of invading Chinese and North Korean forces.

SERGEANT CECIL CLARK No. 14453026
1ST BATTALION NORTHUMBERLAND FUSILIERS
DIED APRIL 25TH 1951 AGED 24

Cecil was born on January 27th 1927 at Fly Hill, Cunningham Place, in part of the building that now houses the Old House Museum, Bakewell. His father, Fred Clark, a quarryman employed at Holme Bank Chert Quarry, married a Chesterfield girl, Violet Duce. Younger siblings, John and Christine, completed the family.

Cecil attended Bath Street School and, being mad about joining the Army, became a keen member of the Army Cadets, attending the meetings in the Drill Hall on Bath Street.

*Cecil Clark of Bakewell,
killed in Korea.*
Harry Hutchinson

He spent two years at the quarry, after leaving school, but hated it and so joined the army when just over 17 years of age. He only just missed seeing active service at the end of the Second World War and this annoyed him greatly.

*Cecil Clark and his cousin
Marjorie.*
Harry Hutchinson

Cecil joined the Duke of Wellington's Regiment (West Ridings) and spent two years with them, some of that time being at Khartoum, in the Sudan. From there he spent time on Gibraltar with the 1st Battalion Northumberland Fusiliers and it was from there that he was sent out to Korea in 1950 (sadly he never got home on leave from Gibraltar, before embarking for Korea).

The departure was sudden and with little planning.

Clothed for the warm climate of Gibraltar, they were poorly equipped for the cold conditions in Korea and Cecil and his colleagues suffered from frostbite. By this time he was a Sergeant, and, although only 23 years of age, he was more mature than the 19 year old National Service men serving under him.

During the Chinese Spring Offensive of 1951 the Fusiliers became involved in the desperate fighting at the Battle of the Imjin River, as part of the 4000 strong British 29th Brigade.

On the southern bank were the 1st Battalion Gloucester Regiment on the left, !st Battalion Northumberland Fusiliers in the centre and on the right, the Ulster Rifles, with a Belgian Battalion in front of them. The battle opened on the night of April 22nd, after a fierce bombardment, when three Chinese divisions attacked along the front, concentrating on the Belgians and Gloucesters.

The Belgians were surrounded but escaped on the 23rd with the help of American tanks and artillery (the 4000 men of 29th Brigade were facing 27,000 men of the Chinese 63rd Army). Night attacks on the 23rd saw the Gloucesters surrounded on Hill 235 (Gloucester Hill) and the Chinese forced the Fusiliers to fight their way south. An attempt by U.S. and Filipino forces to break through on the 24th April to the Gloucesters was beaten back and on the 25th, all resistance on the hill was crushed. However, the three days of fighting had disrupted the Chinese offensive.

On the evening of April 22nd the enemy began crossing the only ford in front of the Northumberland Fusiliers and defensive fire was brought down on this crossing. The main attack was launched with fierce grenade and small arms battles. Number 4 Platoon was overrun and by 2-45a.m. on April 23rd (St. George's Day) the situation was critical. The outpost was withdrawn, bringing with them 15 wounded men.

"Z" Company was attacked at 3am as they defended a high hill and after first light it fell into their hands. A counter-attack was made in a fierce grenade battle but the Company was forced back. The enemy was still reinforcing and at 3-30am on April 24th "Y" Company was forced back.

On the night of the 24th, the enemy attempted to infiltrate, at 8pm. From then on he attacked the different platoon positions from every angle until at 2am on April 25th he obtained a footing on the hill on which No. 10 Platoon was defending, a position vital to the whole defence. A counter-attack was ordered which was successful and the fury of battle increased, as from 2-20am till dawn, the sound of mortaring and small arms fire was without break. Casualties were mounting. "Z" Company's casualties included five killed and 27 stretcher cases.

General withdrawal was ordered and enemy sniping became intense as ambulances and half-tracks carrying casualties were shot up all the way. The rear-guard found themselves heavily shot at from the front, behind, and at point blank range from the west side of the road.

The casualties for these days were 3 officers and 10 men killed, 7 officers and 76 men wounded, whilst 3 officers and 43 men were missing. One of the men killed on April 25th was Sergeant Cecil Clark. His body was recovered and he lies buried in grave Plot 24, Row 2 United Nations Memorial Cemetery, Korena.

Cecil Clark's death brings to an end my stories of the lives and deaths of the servicemen whose names are to be found on the Bakewell, Over Haddon, Ashford, Sheldon, Great and Little Longstone and Wardlow war memorials.

Born just after the conclusion of the Second World War, I have lived through 60 years of relative peace in these islands, without the necessity of being called to fight for "Queen and Country". It is my sincere belief that this is partly due to the sacrifice made by people such as those whose stories are told within the pages of this book, and to those who fought alongside them and thankfully survived. This book is dedicated in honour of the men from Bakewell and district who did not return.

THEY WILL BE REMEMBERED

INDEX

NOTE: *Names and places on photographs have not been indexed.*